Mike Meyers' CompTIA A+® Guide to Managing and Troubleshooting PCs Lab Manual

Second Edition

Mike Meyers
Dennis Haley

New York Chicago San Francisco Lisbon London Madrid
Mexico City Milan New Delhi San Juan Seoul
Singapore Sydney Toronto

The McGraw·Hill Companies

Cataloging-in-Publication Data is on file with the Library of Congress

Mike Meyers' CompTIA A+® Guide to Managing and Troubleshooting PCs Lab Manual, Second Edition

34567890 QPD QPD 0198

ISBN-13: 978-0-07-226362-6
ISBN-10: 0-07-226362-8

Sponsoring Editor Timothy Green	**Copy Editors** Robert Campbell, Bart Reed	**Illustration** International Typesetting and Composition
Editorial Supervisor Patty Mon	**Proofreader** Paul Tyler	**Art Director, Cover** Jeff Weeks
Project Editor Laura Stone	**Indexer** Jack Lewis	**Cover Designer** Pattie Lee
Acquisitions Coordinator Jennifer Housh	**Production Supervisor** James Kussow	**Cover Photograph** Ken Davies/Masterfile
Technical Editor Daniel Richardson	**Composition** International Typesetting and Composition	

This book is dedicated to all of you who want to become great techs.

—Mike Meyers

I dedicate this book to all of my students, past, present, and future. They inspire me to do my best. I also dedicate this book to Theresa, who is always there for me when that inspiration wanes.

—Dennis Haley

About the Authors

Mike Meyers, lovingly called the "AlphaGeek" by those who know him, is the industry's leading authority on CompTIA A+ certification. He is the president and co-founder of Total Seminars, LLC, a provider of PC and network repair seminars, books, videos, and courseware for thousands of organizations throughout the world. Mike has been involved in the computer and network repair industry since 1977 as a technician, instructor, author, consultant, and speaker. Author of numerous popular PC books and videos, Mike is also the series editor for the highly successful Mike Meyers' Certification Passport series, the Mike Meyers' Computer Skills series, and the Mike Meyers' Guide to series, all published by McGraw-Hill.

   Dennis Haley has worked in the Information Technology industry for over 20 years and has spent more than half of that time as a technical teacher. Dennis's responsibilities have included computer network training for the Oki Data Corporation and site director/instructor for Computer Networking Technologies. Presently he is the administrator and teacher for the E2C and Microsoft IT Academy programs at POLYTECH High School. Dennis holds a BSEET, CompTIA A+ and Network+ certifications, and Microsoft MCP, MCSA, MCSE, and MCT certifications. Dennis enjoys all aspects of technology; even his hobbies are technical, including electronic music and sound production.

About the Technical Editor

Daniel Richardson holds certifications in CompTIA A+, Network+, and Security+, as well as MCP, MCDST, and MCT certifications from Microsoft. Daniel is an experienced technical trainer with extensive firsthand knowledge of computer and printer repair, and is currently a consultant for a global software development company.

Contents

Acknowledgments

Many great people worked together to make this book happen.

As our sponsoring editor at McGraw-Hill, Tim Green set the entire book in motion and stayed at the helm as the guiding hand. Thanks, Tim!

We'd like to thank our in-house editor Cindy Clayton for her tireless wordsmithing. Her editing, revising, cat herding, and text massaging—all done wih humor—helped immensely throughout the process.

Also at Total Seminars, Dudley Lehmer was a great CEO, creating an environment for getting projects done. Scott Jernigan performed his usual magic as Editor in Chief. Michael Smyer provided excellent photographs and illustrations.

On the McGraw-Hill side, Laura Stone did it all—and did it well—as project editor. Our acquisitions coordinator, Jennifer Housh, helped us keep it all on track.

To the copy editors, page proofers, and layout folks—Robert Campbell, Bart Reed, Paul Tyler, and the folks at ITC—thank you!

Finally, Tanner Allen, Tim Basher, and John Fitzgerald provided excellent sounding boards for ideas and projects that work in the real world. You're the best, guys, thanks!

Chapter 1

The Path of the PC Tech

Lab Exercises

Well, now you've really done it. The fact that you hold this lab manual in your hands says one thing loud and clear—you're deadly serious about getting that CompTIA A+ certification! Good. Even though the CompTIA A+ certification exams are considered entry-level, you'll still need to take them seriously if you want to pass.

Because you're serious, I'm going to let you in on a secret: The key to passing these exams is preparation. When I say "preparation," I'm not talking about studying—although of course studying is important! I'm talking about *preparing to study*. You need to know exactly how to study for this exam, and you need to have the right tools to get that studying done. Sure, you've got a textbook and you've got a lab manual, but you're not yet ready to hit the books.

In this chapter, you'll go through the steps you need to start studying for the CompTIA A+ exams. First, you'll organize what you need to study. Second, you'll learn how the CompTIA A+ certification helps move you toward more advanced certifications. Finally, you'll get some ideas on how to gather equipment so that you can reinforce what you read with real hardware and software. So stay serious, roll up your sleeves, and start preparing to study for the CompTIA A+ exams!

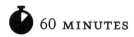 60 MINUTES

Lab Exercise 1.01: Study Preparation

If you're a child of the TV age—and who isn't these days?—then you might have heard of a TV show called *The A-Team* starring George Peppard and Mr. T. Okay, so maybe it wasn't the greatest television, but I always remember one line from this show: "I love it when a plan comes together!" That's how you should feel as you get ready to become CompTIA A+ certified. In fact, just for fun, let's call ourselves the "A+ Team" as we put a plan together to knock that test right into next week's episode!

Learning Objectives

This lab helps you lay out a logical path for your studies. To do this, you need to deal with three issues: determining your weak points, checking your study habits, and scheduling the exams.

At the end of this lab, you'll be able to

- Identify the CompTIA A+ topics you need to learn

- Develop a good study plan

- Understand how to schedule the CompTIA A+ exams

Lab Materials and Setup

The materials you need for this lab are

- A PC with Internet access

- A telephone

Getting Down to Business

Total Seminars has been teaching CompTIA A+ certification for years, and we've developed a handy template to help you determine what you need to study and how much time you need to devote to preparing for the CompTIA A+ exams. This is the same table shown in the Mike Meyers' *A+ Guide to Managing and Troubleshooting PCs* textbook, but with an extra step added to help you determine the topics you need to study.

Step 1 For each skill listed in the table that follows, circle the number that corresponds to the amount of experience you have: None, Once or Twice, Every Now and Then, or Quite a Bit. You'll use that number to calculate the total number of hours you have to study for the exams.

Technical Task	Amount of Experience			
	None	**Once or Twice**	**Every Now and Then**	**Quite a Bit**
Installing an adapter card	12	10	8	4
Installing hard drives	12	10	8	4
Installing modems and network interface cards (NICs)	8	6	4	2
Connecting a computer to the Internet	8	6	4	2
Installing printers and scanners	4	3	2	1
Installing random access memory (RAM)	8	6	4	2

Technical Task	Amount of Experience			
	None	Once or Twice	Every Now and Then	Quite a Bit
Installing central processing units (CPUs)	8	7	5	3
Fixing printers	6	5	4	3
Fixing boot problems	8	7	7	5
Fixing portable computers	8	6	4	2
Building complete systems	12	10	8	6
Using the command line	8	8	6	4
Installing/optimizing Windows	10	8	6	4
Using Windows 2000	6	6	4	2
Using Windows XP	6	6	4	2
Configuring NTFS permissions	6	4	3	2
Configuring a wireless network	6	5	3	2
Configuring a software firewall	6	4	2	1
Installing a sound card	2	2	1	0
Using operating system diagnostic tools	8	8	6	4
Using a volt-ohm meter (VOM)	4	3	2	1

Great! You now have a good feel for the topics you need to study. Now you need to determine the total study time. First, add up the numbers you've circled. Then add the result to the number from the following table that corresponds to your experience. The grand total is the number of hours you should study to be ready for the exams.

If you have this much direct, professional experience . . .	Add this number of hours to your study time
0	50
Up to 6 months	30
6 to 12 months	10
More than 12 months	0

A total neophyte usually needs around 200 hours of study time. An experienced technician shouldn't need more than 40 hours.

The total number of hours for you to study is _____.

Step 2   Go to the Computing Technology Industry Association (CompTIA) Web site and download a copy of the domains for both the CompTIA A+ Essentials and the CompTIA A+ 220-602 (IT Technician) exams. As of this writing, you can find them at http://certification.comptia.org/resources/objectives.aspx; you'll have to fill out a short form (requiring your name, e-mail address, country of residence, and how soon you'll be testing) before you can view the objectives. Bear in mind, however, that CompTIA changes its Web site more often than TV networks invent new reality shows, so be prepared to poke around if necessary! Compare the circled areas on the preceding form to the CompTIA A+ domains. Note that any single topic on the form will cover more than one domain on the CompTIA A+ exams. Circle the domains that you think parallel the weak areas you circled on the form, and don't be afraid to add or remove circles after you've seen the CompTIA A+ domains in detail.

✔ **Hint**

> If you are going to focus on one of the specialized paths for your CompTIA A+ certification—either the CompTIA A+ 220-603 exam (Help Desk Technician) or the CompTIA A+ 220-604 exam (Depot Technician)—you'll want to download the objectives for these domains.
>
> Follow the methodology outlined in Step 2 (circle the domains that you think parallel the weak areas you circled on the form) and concentrate on these domains as laid out in the objectives for the specialized exams.

Step 3   Now that you know what topics are most important to you and how much time they'll take, you need to develop your study plan. Take the amount of time you've set aside and determine how many days you have to prepare. Consider work, holidays, weekends, and anything else that will affect your study time. If you're in an instructor-led course, then this part is easy—just use the end of the course! Then break down your textbook into manageable chunks. Again, if you're in a course, then your instructor will already have done this for you. You now have your deadline—the day you'll say, "I'm ready to take the exams!"

Step 4   Go online and schedule your exams with either Thomson Prometric (www.prometric.com) or Pearson VUE (www.vue.com). You'll almost certainly need to make a phone call to do this. Make sure you have both a method of payment (credit cards are preferred) and some form of identification when you call. In the United States you need your Social Security number to schedule CompTIA exams. It's very important that you schedule your exams *now*—setting a test date early in the process will help motivate you to study, and keep you from procrastinating!

✔ **Cross-Reference**

> For details about taking the CompTIA A+ tests, go to the CompTIA Web site (www.comptia.org).

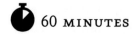 60 MINUTES

Lab Exercise 1.02: Other Certifications

CompTIA A+ certification may be your first certification, but it certainly should not be your last! The information technology (IT) industry considers obtaining certifications an ongoing process, one that continues as long as you're working in the IT field. You need to appreciate how the CompTIA A+ certification leads into other certifications.

Learning Objectives

This lab helps you learn about the various IT certifications that are available, and how they fit with both your skills and aptitude.

At the end of this lab, you'll be able to

- Understand some of the more common certifications that follow the CompTIA A+ certification
- Plan in what order you might attain those certifications

Lab Materials and Setup

The materials you need for this lab are

- A PC with Internet access

Getting Down to Business

It's time to jump onto the Internet and do a little research! You'll tour some of the more popular IT certifications and see how CompTIA A+ helps you gain these more advanced certifications. While you're at it, review how CompTIA has expanded the A+ certification. Additional exams have been added to further validate the specialized skills required of Help Desk Technicians and Depot Technicians.

✔ **Cross-Reference**

To review the domains of each of the four CompTIA A+ exams, refer to "The Basic Exam Structure" in Chapter 1 of *Mike Meyers' A+ Guide to Managing and Troubleshooting PCs*.

Step 1 Fire up a Web browser and go to the CompTIA Web site (www.comptia.org). Look at the three tracks offered to complete the CompTIA A+ certification. All three tracks require the CompTIA A+ Essentials exam. Many candidates choose the primary track, the CompTIA A+ 220-602 exam (IT Technician). The two secondary tracks will help the candidate to specialize their CompTIA A+ certification to the technical requirements of their job. You would take the Essentials exam and then follow with either the CompTIA

A+ 220-603 exam (Help Desk Technician) or the CompTIA A+ 220-604 exam (Depot Technician) to become certified. Examine the domains (objectives) for each path and develop a plan to meet your goals.

✔ **Hint**

The laboratory exercises contained within this lab manual cover all the domains of the four CompTIA A+ exams. You may want to allocate more time for review of the labs covering operating systems if you decide to take the CompTIA A+ 220-603 exam (Help Desk Technician). If you opt for the CompTIA A+ 220-604 exam (Depot Technician), you will want to maximize the time you spend working through the labs covering personal computer components. Either way, don't skimp on exploring the lab exercises for all the chapters.

CompTIA also offers additional certifications related to the IT field. Take some time to research the Network+, Server+, and Security+ certifications. Many schools strongly recommend Network+ as the next certification after CompTIA A+ certification. Why do you think they might do that?

Step 2 Head over to the Microsoft Certifications Overview site at www.microsoft.com/mcp/. What are some of the Microsoft certifications shown?

Research the Microsoft Certified Professional (MCP), Microsoft Certified Desktop Support Technician (MCDST), Microsoft Certified Systems Administrator (MCSA), and Microsoft Certified Systems Engineer (MCSE) certifications. What, in your opinion, would be the most natural order for you to achieve these certifications (that is, which one would you take first, second, third)? Does the CompTIA A+ certification come into play in here?

Step 3 Now go to the Cisco Web site (www.cisco.com), and research the Cisco Certified Network Associate (CCNA), Cisco Certified Network Professional (CCNP), and Cisco Certified Internetwork Expert (CCIE) certifications. Compare the CCNA to the Network+. How are they different?

Step 4 Now that you've seen the more common certifications that follow the CompTIA A+, chart out your next three certifications and explain why you chose them.

 TIMES WILL VARY

Lab Exercise 1.03: Gathering Equipment

Although it's theoretically possible to obtain your CompTIA A+ certification by doing nothing but reading books, you'll be far better prepared for the real world if you get your hands on some real equipment so that you can practice. You also need some tools so you can take things apart—and put them back together. Finally, you'll need some operating system software, in particular Windows 2000 and Windows

XP. If you're taking a course, all of this equipment should be provided to you. If not, you could find yourself facing some fairly serious cash outlay trying to buy everything you need!

Learning Objectives

In this lab, you'll discover some rather interesting ways to get inexpensive or free hardware and software. None of these ideas will work every time, but with a little patience you'll be amazed how much you can get for very little!

At the end of this lab, you'll be able to

- Acquire inexpensive or free hardware and software

- Acquire a standard PC technician toolkit

Lab Materials and Setup

The materials you need for this lab are

- A telephone

- Transportation

- A PC with Internet access

Getting Down to Business

Most of the objectives on the CompTIA A+ exams don't require state-of-the-art hardware. If you're willing to use systems that are a few years old, you can get plenty of good hands-on practice with the techniques you need to know to pass the CompTIA A+.

Step 1   Go on a scavenger hunt. Get a list of the smaller "mom and pop" PC repair companies and small PC parts suppliers in your town. Drive to these companies (don't call them) and ask them, "What do you guys do with your broken or obsolete parts?" The vast majority of these stores simply throw the parts away! Ask when they toss stuff and if you can have what they throw away. Most of these companies pay to get rid of equipment and will be glad to give it to you. Oh, and you can forget the big chain stores—they almost never let folks have equipment.

Step 2   Shop the sale bins at the local computer parts stores. You'll always find one or two pieces of equipment at outrageously low prices. Granted, you may end up using a bright pink Barbie keyboard, but if it only costs US$3, who cares? Don't forget about rebates—you can often get parts for free after rebate! Really!

Step 3   Tell everyone you know that you're looking for PC hardware. Almost every organization will have occasional in-house sales where they sell older (but still good) PCs, printers, and so on to employees. If you can get in on some of these, you'll have some amazing deals come your way!

✔ **Hint**

You'll often find that older machines still have the Windows 98 or Windows Me operating system software installed. If you come across one of these systems, see if you can work with the seller or donor to get the licensed disc. Working with an older operating system (even DOS) will introduce you to the installation and configuration process. Having an operating system installed will also enable you to verify that the hardware is working.

Step 4   Take one weekend to check out local garage sales. People often sell older PCs at a tiny fraction of their original cost. If you're not afraid to barter a bit, you'll get incredible deals—just watch out for equipment that's simply too old to be worthwhile.

✔ **Hint**

I avoid PC flea markets. The problem is that these folks know the value of their computer equipment, so it's often hard to find excellent deals.

Step 5   Locate the local PC user groups in your town—almost every town has at least one. Explain your situation to them; you'll usually find someone who's willing to give you a part or two, and you may also find others studying for the CompTIA A+ exams. You may even be able to start or join a study group!

Step 6   Speaking of study groups, try teaming up with as many fellow students as you can to pool cash for parts and to work as a study group. If you're in a course, this is easy—your fellow students are your study group! Have everyone go equipment hunting, using the different methods described to get equipment, and pool the items you find for everyone to use. You might even hold a drawing after you all get certified, to choose who gets to keep the equipment.

Chapter 2

The Visible PC

Laboratory Exercises

Every competent tech knows the PC inside and out. Nothing destroys your credibility in the eyes of a client as quickly as not knowing the basics, like the difference between a graceful shutdown and a forced power down. The word "Oops!" doesn't always go over well in the real world! This set of labs applies the information you learned in Chapter 2 of *Mike Meyers' A+ Guide to Managing and Troubleshooting PCs*, so you'll be poking and prodding a PC. You'll begin by exploring the functions of a PC, and then you'll examine the typical user-accessible components, as well as the external connectors found on most PCs. After taking a moment to protect both yourself and the PC components from electrical damage, you'll pop open the hood—that is, you'll open up the system unit's case—and take a tour inside. Finally, you'll finish up with a complete disassembly of the system.

 30 MINUTES

Lab Exercise 2.01: Exploring the Functions and Components of a PC

Everything a computer does falls into one of four categories: input, processing, output, and storage. You need a good understanding of these four processes, and the components that are involved with each one, to troubleshoot PC problems successfully.

At the end of this lab, you'll be able to

- Define the four functions of computer systems
- Detail common components involved in each of these four functions

Lab Materials and Setup

The materials you need for this lab are

- A notepad and pencil, to draw a four-column table
- Optional: Access to a working computer with a word processing or spreadsheet application installed, to aid in drawing the table
- The *Mike Meyers' A+ Guide to Managing and Troubleshooting PCs* textbook, for reference

✔ **Hint**

Get used to taking notes and drawing pictures. Even after many years of repairing computers from mainframes to PCs, I still use a notepad to keep track of what I see and what I change. I recommend that you save your drawings and notes, as you'll find them useful in subsequent labs.

Getting Down to Business

In this exercise, you'll review, list, and define the various components involved in the PC's vital functions.

Step 1   Re-read the "How the PC Works" section in Chapter 2 of *Mike Meyers' A+ Guide to Managing and Troubleshooting PCs*, paying particular attention to the sections on input, processing, output, and storage.

Step 2   For each of the following functions of a computer system, write a definition and give a brief example:

Input

_____

_____

Processing

_____

_____

Output.

_____

_____

Storage

_____

_____

Step 3 Using the following table, list the components that operate in each of the four functional categories. Try to include as many components as you can; you might take a peek at some of the later chapters in the textbook to see if you can add any other components. Think about how each of the components contributes to the overall workings of the PC, and include as much detail about the component as possible.

Input	Processing	Output	Storage

Step 4 If you completed the table right here in the lab book, you'll have it handy throughout the rest of the lessons. If you made a table in your notebook, or created an electronic version, make sure you can get to it easily. As you work on later chapters, you'll want to update the table with additional components and further detail on the components. The information on the table (and in your head) will expand as you develop a better understanding of how the components relate to the PC's "big picture."

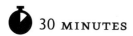 30 MINUTES

Lab Exercise 2.02: Examining User-Accessible Components

It's been one of those days. You walked into what should have been a simple job interview, only to meet a very frantic IT manager who was dealing with a crisis of epic proportions. She doesn't even bother to interview you—instead she shuttles you out of her office, points down the hall, and says, "Go check Jane's PC, fourth cubicle on the left. She says the PC has locked up on her, and she can't even turn it off! Don't change anything or open it up. Right now I simply need to know if it will shut down, boot properly, and access the drives." Then the IT manager is off to deal with her crisis, and you're on the spot.

This exercise looks at the many PC components that you can access without removing the case. You can use a quick scan to determine whether a PC is functioning properly at the most basic level. Take your time, and jot down notes where you feel the need. Practice each step until you're confident you can do it on the job as a PC tech.

Learning Objectives

In this lab exercise you will locate and describe the various cabinet parts, user controls, and built-in user-accessible devices of a PC system. You *will not* be opening the system case during this lab.

At the end of this lab, you'll be able to

- Recognize and manipulate user controls
- Describe the use of built-in user-accessible devices

Lab Materials and Setup

The materials you need for this lab are

- One fully functioning desktop computer system unit, with monitor
- A working optical drive (any drive that reads and/or records CD or DVD discs)
- One readable data CD with files
- One keyboard
- One mouse
- A notepad on which to take notes and make sketches of the computer and components
- Optionally, a digital camera to take photos of the computer and components

---

✔ **Hint**

In Lab Exercise 2.01, I recommended that you get used to taking notes and drawing pictures. Thanks to the wide popularity and availability of digital cameras (even most mobile phones now include a camera function), you have another excellent way to record the configuration of computer systems and the steps taken during disassembly, repair, and assembly. A digital camera can be a handy tool for supplementing your trusty pencil and paper.

Getting Down to Business

As a technician, you need to know how everything works on a PC. The best place to begin is with the externally accessible devices.

Step 1   Before you can do much work with a PC, you need a functioning output device, such as a monitor. Check the monitor to see if it has power. The small light emitting diode, or LED, on or near the monitor's power button should be lit: orange if the system is turned off or asleep, or green if the system is fully on. If you determine that the monitor is not plugged into a wall outlet, plug it in now.

Step 2   Look at the front of your system unit. Locate the power button. Compare your button to the one in Figure 2-1.

Once you have located the power button on your system, make a note of its appearance. Is it in plain sight, or hidden behind a door or lid? Is it round, square, or some odd shape? Pressing the power button to start a PC when the electricity is off is known as a *cold boot* or sometimes a *hard boot*.

Describe your power button here.

_____

Sometimes software will lock up your system and the only way to shut the system down is to force a *power down*. This requires that you press and hold the power button for four to six seconds.

FIGURE 2-1 Recognizing the power button on the front of a PC

Notice the two LEDs on the front panel near the power button. One will generally light up green to indicate that the power is on, and the other will flash when the internal hard drive is active.

✔ **Hint**

On older systems, the power button or switch may be located on the back of the system. Many newer systems have a power switch located on the back of the case that controls the flow of electricity to the power supply, and a power button on the front that boots and shuts down the PC. Most systems also have a reset button, which you can use to restart the PC if it becomes unstable or locked up because of some software glitch.

Step 3   Now locate the floppy drive. You can recognize it by the 3 1/2-inch horizontal slot. Do you see the eject button below the slot on the right side of the drive? Below the slot on the left side is an LED that lights up when the drive is actively reading or writing information on a floppy diskette.

✔ **Hint**

Because floppy diskettes can store only a relatively tiny amount of data, floppy drives are disappearing from PCs. In fact, many new computer systems ship without floppy drives. If your system doesn't have a floppy drive, you may want to explore an older machine to see one in action. As a computer tech, you will most likely still have to deal with floppy drives for at least a few years.

On the front of your system, you should also see the external face of your system's optical media drive. You'll see either the front edge of the tray that opens to accept a CD or DVD disc, or a small door that protects the tray when it's retracted. Once you've located this drive, notice that it too has a button in the lower right corner. When the system is on, you can press that button to open the tray door (if there is one) and slide the tray out to receive your disc (see Figure 2-2). Pressing the button while the tray is out retracts the tray so that the drive can read the disc.

Don't be tempted to force the disc tray to close. Always press the button on the front of the drive to close the tray or to eject a disc. Forcing the tray to close can cause the gears inside to become misaligned, so that the tray no longer closes properly.

✔ **Hint**

If you forget to remove a CD or DVD disc before turning off the system power, you can straighten a strong paper clip and insert one end into the tiny hole on the front of the drive. Pressing directly inward with the paper clip will cause the tray to open.

Figure 2-2 Can you locate the floppy drive and CD-ROM drive on this system unit?

Your system may have other devices installed, such as a USB flash drive (thumb drive), a Zip drive, a tape drive, or various media card readers, such as those for CompactFlash or Memory Stick cards. Each of these uses removable media; take care when inserting or removing the media.

Step 4   Now it's time to prepare your system for the scenario outlined in the opening text:

a) Turn your system on and log on in a normal fashion so that you are viewing the operating system desktop.

b) Now press the eject button on the front of the optical drive. When the tray opens, carefully insert a disc. Press the eject button again to close the tray. If you haven't done this a lot, practice inserting and removing a disc until you feel comfortable with the process. Does the LED on the front of the optical drive flash or stay on continuously at any point?

✖ Warning

Don't start any applications yet! Close any open applications or open windows before performing Step 5. You're going to force a "power down," and you do not want to damage any of the software applications.

Step 5   Now you're going to simulate a PC that has become non-responsive and "locked up." Perform a forced power down as follows:

a) Press *and hold* the power button.

b) While continuing to hold the power button in, count out loud (one–one thousand, two–one thousand, three–one thousand . . .) until the system powers down and the screen goes blank.

   According to your count, how many seconds did it take for the screen to go blank?

   _____

Step 6   After the system has been powered down for approximately one minute, do the following:

a) Press the power button and allow the system to boot.

   Did the system boot properly? _____

b) Log on in a normal fashion so that you are viewing the operating system desktop.

   Were you able to log on as normal? _____

c) Use the mouse to select Start | My Computer and double-click the icon that represents the optical-media drive. This should enable you to view the contents of the disc that was inserted prior to the forced power down.

   List some of the contents of the disc: _____

   _____

d) Use the mouse to select Start | Shut Down. In the Shut Down Windows box, select Shut down from the drop-down list. This performs a "graceful" shutdown of the system.

✔ Hint

If all of the actions in Step 6 were successful, you can probably be comfortable that the system is stable and can report to the IT manager that Jane's machine is back up and running. If any of the steps failed, you should use the mouse to select Start | Shut Down. In the Shut Down Windows box, select Restart from the drop-down list. After the system reboots, you may complete actions 2, 3, and 4 once more. Sometimes the forced power down leaves some of the files in a state of flux; restarting shuts the computer down "gracefully," properly closing all open files before powering down. This should clear everything up and enable the computer to function properly.

Step 7   While the computer is turned off, pretend you lost power and must remove the disc from the optical drive without power. Use a paper clip as noted in the accompanying Lab Hint to remove the disc.

Step 8   As a technician, you need to understand the keyboard, because it is still one of the most important human interfaces on a PC. Look at the way your keyboard is laid out: it basically has three main sections, with some extra keys thrown in for good measure (see Figure 2-3).

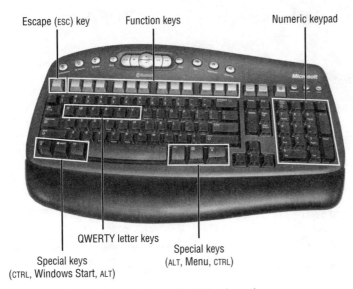

Escape (ESC) key   Function keys   Numeric keypad

QWERTY letter keys

Special keys
(CTRL, Windows Start, ALT)

Special keys
(ALT, Menu, CTRL)

FIGURE 2-3 Exploring the QWERTY keyboard

The largest area of the keyboard is the standard QWERTY (pronounced "kwerty") letter key layout, which is familiar to touch typists everywhere. If you never took a typing or keyboarding class, you may be wondering what I mean by QWERTY; it's simply the standard keyboard used in the U.S. and most English-speaking countries, so named for the first six letters in the top row of letter keys.

To the right of the letter keys you'll usually see a square numeric keypad similar to those found on old adding machines. This feature is popular with people like accountants and merchants, because it makes entering numbers quicker and easier.

Above the letter keys, you'll find a special row of keys called function keys, normally labeled FI through FI2. What these keys do depends on the software you're using when you press them; pressing the FI key, for example, generally calls up a program's help feature. Function keys are used for various tasks, including accessing basic system settings at startup. You'll use the function keys a lot when troubleshooting a downed system.

In the keyboard's upper left corner, next to the function keys, you'll see the Escape key, labeled ESC. In many programs, particularly older ones, pressing this key backs you out of what you're doing, sometimes even causing your current program to close down. In more modern software, pressing ESC is a way to make a program "let go of" some text or graphic you've selected, or to close the current dialog box without implementing any changes.

To the right of the function keys are the PRINT SCREEN, SCROLL LOCK, and PAUSE/BREAK keys; depending on your keyboard, any or all of these key names may be abbreviated. These specialized keys aren't heavily used these days, although some programs (such as the Windows Clipboard) use the PRINT SCREEN key to capture snapshots of the monitor display (known as a *screen shot*). Screen shots can come in handy when you're troubleshooting program or application problems and need to show someone else what you're seeing (see Figure 2-4).

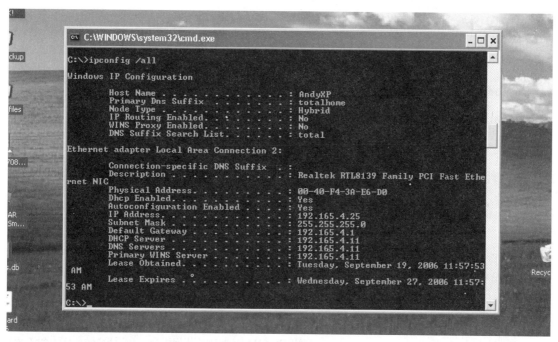

FIGURE 2-4 A screen shot showing important information for a networked PC

Along the bottom row of the keyboard, on either side of the spacebar, you'll find the special keys labeled CTRL (for Control) and ALT (for Alternate). On keyboards designed for use with Windows operating systems, you'll also find a key with the Windows logo (which opens the Windows Start menu), and possibly one with a menu symbol as well (which opens a context menu without using the mouse). For the most part, the CTRL and ALT keys don't do anything by themselves, but they are incredibly useful when combined with other keys. In many word processing programs, for example, holding down the CTRL key while pressing the s key has the same effect as selecting File | Save using the mouse—only faster and easier. Techs use these types of key combinations a lot; in this manual you'll see them represented with a hyphen between the keys, for example CTRL-S.

 30 MINUTES

Lab Exercise 2.03: Recognizing External Connections

Just as you finish working with Jane's PC, her intercom buzzes. It's the head of IT, and she has a new assignment for you: The new satellite office in Albuquerque has received a delivery of new PCs, but the machines are all in boxes and not one of the salespeople there knows a mouse from a monkey wrench. Your job is to call them up and walk them through the process of connecting a PC, describing each cable and connector, and explaining how they connect to the PC.

Learning Objectives

In this lab, you will identify, describe, and explain the function of the external connections on a standard PC.

At the end of this lab, you will be able to

- Identify the external connectors on a PC and the related cables
- Explain the function of each external connection

Lab Materials and Setup

The materials you need for this lab are

- A study partner, if possible (or this lab can be done alone)
- At least one fully functioning PC that's less than two years old (two or more systems is ideal, with one older and one newer than two years old)
- A notepad on which to take notes and make sketches of the computer, connections, and connectors
- Optionally, a digital camera to record the connections and connectors instead of sketching

✔ Cross-Reference

Before you begin this lab, read the section "External Connections" and also the section "Devices and Their Connectors" in Chapter 2 of *Mike Meyers' A+ Guide to Managing and Troubleshooting PCs.*

Getting Down to Business

Now it's time to learn about all the external things that can be attached to a PC. This lab exercise will step you through identifying and understanding the functions of the various connectors. If you have access to the same computer that you used in the previous lab, consult your drawings, notes, and any photos you may have taken to assist you in the completion of the exercise.

✖ Warning

Shut off the power to your system and *unplug your PC* from the wall socket before starting the following exercise.

Step 1   Look at all those wires coming from the back of your PC! There's a power cable, a telephone or network cable, probably a printer cable, a keyboard cable, a mouse cable, and maybe a few others, depending on your system. Looking at the back of my current system (the one I'm using to write this manual), I count 15 cables directly connected to it. Yowza!

The great thing about PCs is that it's difficult to connect the cables incorrectly. Each one has a unique connector; some are male (connectors with pins), and some are female (connectors with holes). Each connector has a particular shape and a specific number of pins or holes that match those of a specific device connected to the system unit.

Get your notepad ready to take notes and draw pictures.

✔ Hint

Cables have conductors. A conductor is a wire that can carry electrical signals. You may see a cable described by the number of conductors it has; for example, a telephone cable can be a two- or four-conductor cable. A power cable is a three-conductor cable. A network cable is an eight-conductor cable.

Step 2   Unplug each of your PC's cables one at a time and practice plugging it back in until you get a feel for how it fits. You should not have to force any of the cables, though they may be firm. How is each cable held in place and prevented from coming loose? Is there a screw, clip, or some other fastener that holds the cable connector tight to the system? Is the connector keyed? What does it connect to? What is the shape of the connector on each end? Is it round, rectangular, D-shaped? How many pins or holes does it have? How many rows of pins or holes?

Step 3   Is it possible to plug any cable into the wrong connector? If so, which one(s)? What do you think would happen if you plugged something into the wrong connector?

_____

_____

Step 4   Remove or disconnect any of the following cables from your system and describe its connector. Follow this example:

- Data cable from the monitor to the PC

    Type of connector: End 1 (PC) _____D-sub_____ End 2 _____D-sub_____

    Male or Female: End 1 (PC) _____F_____ End 2 _____M_____

    Number of pins/holes/conductors _____15_____

✔ Hint

Your PC may not have all of these cables; just document the ones you do have.

Now it's your turn!

- Data cable from the printer to the PC (both ends)

     Type of connector: End 1 (PC) _____ End 2 _____

     Male or Female: End 1 (PC) _____ End 2 _____

     Number of pins/holes/conductors _____

- Data cable from the keyboard to the PC

     Type of connector: End 1 (PC) _____ End 2 _____

     Male or Female: End 1 (PC) _____ End 2 _____

     Number of pins/holes/conductors _____

- Data cable from the mouse to the PC

     Type of connector: End 1 (PC) _____ End 2 _____

     Male or Female: End 1 (PC) _____ End 2 _____

     Number of pins/holes/conductors _____

- Data cable from the network (cable modem / DSL modem) to the PC

     Type of connector: End 1 (PC) _____ End 2 _____

     Male or Female: End 1 (PC) _____ End 2 _____

     Number of pins/holes/conductors _____

- Data cable (telephone wire) from the internal modem to the telephone jack

     Type of connector: End 1 (PC) _____ End 2 _____

     Male or Female: End 1 (PC) _____ End 2 _____

     Number of pins/holes/conductors _____

Step 5   If you're working with someone else, play "Flash Cords." Have your partner hold up various cables, and try to guess what they connect to by the connectors on the ends. Then switch roles and quiz your partner.

Step 6   Properly reconnect all of the cables that you removed and prepare to turn on the system. If you have an On/Off button on the back of the system, be sure it is set to the on position. Make sure the monitor is turned on as well.

Step 7   Examine other computers to see if they have different connectors than the ones you've already documented. See if you can identify the peripherals that connect to those sockets and plugs.

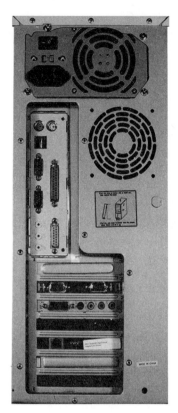 

FIGURE 2-5 Can you match the connectors on these two system units?

Step 8 The two system units in Figure 2-5 look different, but they have many connectors in common. Try to find the following connectors on each system unit:

- Power
- Keyboard
- Monitor
- Printer
- Mouse
- Network

Step 9 Describe the connector that matches each type of cable in the list. Use Chapter 2 of *Mike Meyers' A+ Guide to Managing and Troubleshooting PCs* or your notes (photos) for reference.

Cable Type	Connector Type(s)
Keyboard cable	_____
Mouse cable	_____
Speaker cable	_____

Monitor data cable   _____

Printer data cable (printer end)   _____

Printer data cable (PC end)   _____

Network data cable   _____

Modem/telephone wire   _____

Step 10   Identify the connectors pictured next. What is the name of each connector and what does it connect to?

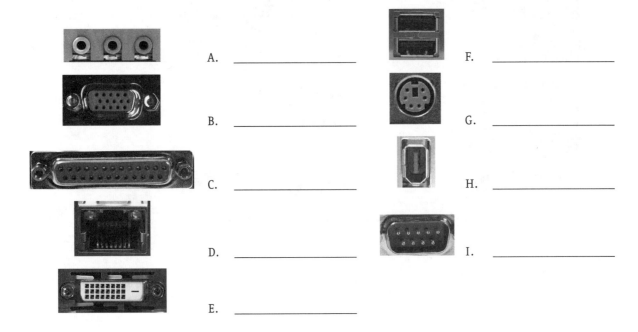

A. _____

B. _____

C. _____

D. _____

E. _____

F. _____

G. _____

H. _____

I. _____

 30 MINUTES

Lab Exercise 2.04: Safeguarding Against Damage from Electrostatic Discharge (ESD)

So far, everything that you've explored has been accessible without removing the cover of the PC. In the next few labs, you'll be opening up the case to explore the components inside. As discussed in *Mike Meyers' A+ Guide to Managing and Troubleshooting PCs*, good techs always protect themselves and the systems they work on from electrical damage. Protecting yourself is fairly easy at this point: unplug the power cord from the electrical outlet and from the power supply on the PC (see Figure 2-6).

FIGURE 2-6 Unplugging the power to protect yourself

To protect the system unit's sensitive components, you can use the following tools:

- Anti-static wrist strap

- Anti-static mat or anti-static wrist strap and mat combination

- Anti-static bag

Proper use of these tools will help safeguard the components of the system unit against electrostatic discharge damage—just as removing the power cord from the PC and the wall will help ensure that you are around to work on PCs for many years to come!

Learning Objectives

In this lab you will learn the techniques to protect both yourself and the sensitive components of the computer system from damage caused by electricity and electrostatic discharge.

After completing this lab, you'll be able to

- Disconnect the power cord from the PC and the wall outlet, protecting yourself from electrocution

- Properly connect an anti-static wrist strap or anti-static wrist strap/mat combination

- Properly store unused components in an anti-static bag

Lab Materials and Setup

The materials you need for this lab are

- A lab partner, if possible

- At least one PC that isn't vital to your (or anyone else's) home or business, not necessarily in working order but preferably less than a few years old

- An anti-static wrist strap

- Optional: anti-static mat

- Twelve anti-static bags of various sizes
- A clean, well-lighted workspace of about 3'×4' (a kitchen table with some newspaper spread about usually makes a fairly decent ad hoc lab bench)

Getting Down to Business

The key to working on PCs without damaging their delicate components is caution. In this exercise, you'll prepare for a cautious (and if done properly, harmless) exploration of the system's internal organs.

✖ Warning

Shut off the power to your system and *unplug* the power cord from your PC and from the wall socket before doing the following exercise.

Step 1   Disconnect all the external cables (monitor, keyboard, mouse, printer, etc.) from the PC you are going to use and place it on a flat, stable surface (preferably on an anti-static mat) where you can sit or stand comfortably to inspect the insides.

Step 2   Using whichever method applies to your case (thumbscrews, Phillips-head screws, locking tabs), remove the cover of your system unit. Don't get frustrated if the opening method isn't obvious at first—even seasoned techs can have a hard time figuring out how an unfamiliar case opens.

Step 3   Locate a place on the chassis (the metal frame inside the case) where you can attach the alligator clip of the anti-static wrist strap or anti-static mat (whichever one you decided to purchase). Be prepared to wear the anti-static wrist strap in later labs (see Figure 2-7).

FIGURE 2-7 Proper use of an anti-static wrist strap

Step 4   Locate and place the anti-static bags on your workspace. These will be used in later labs to store components safely after removal. This machine may be disassembled for a few days, so you'll need to protect the components from any ESD exposure during that time. Anti-static bags do a great job of preventing ESD.

 60 MINUTES

Lab Exercise 2.05: Disassembling the System Unit and Identifying Internal Components and Connections

As promised, it's finally time to go under the hood!

You're now going to walk through the complete disassembly of the system unit. Try to do this in an orderly sequence, but depending on the configuration of the machine you are disassembling, you may have to perform one or two of the steps out of sequence. For example, you may have to remove an optical-media drive before you can gain access to remove the power supply.

When you're on the job, you'll encounter different models of personal computers manufactured by different companies. Along with learning the slightly different methods of component removal and installation, you should be able to identify the major internal parts of the PC system, regardless of the manufacturer. This lab exercise will help you practice doing that.

Ready, Set, GO!

Learning Objectives

In this lab exercise you will locate, remove, and describe the various internal components and connectors of a standard PC system.

At the end of this lab, you'll be able to

- Remove all major components of a PC

- Recognize all major components inside a PC

- Name the function of each component

- Define the relationship of internal components to external connections

Lab Materials and Setup

The materials you need for this lab are

- A lab partner, if possible

- At least one PC that isn't vital to your (or anyone else's) home or business, not necessarily in working order but preferably less than a few years old

- An anti-static wrist strap

- Optional: an anti-static mat

- 12 anti-static bags of various sizes

- A simple technician's toolkit

- A plastic cup or box to organize the various screws, nuts, and bolts that you'll remove

- A clean, well-lighted workspace of about 3'×4' (a kitchen table with some newspaper spread about usually makes a fairly decent ad hoc lab bench)

- A notepad on which to take notes and make sketches of the computer and components

- Optionally, a digital camera to record the placement, configuration, connections, and connectors associated with the components you'll be removing from the system unit

Getting Down to Business

This lab exercise might remind you of the dissection labs that biology students perform on animal specimens. You'll be going inside to examine and remove various parts—but unlike in those labs, your specimen has a good chance of leading a perfectly normal life afterward!

✖ Warning

Shut off the power to your system and *unplug* the power cord from your PC and from the wall socket before doing the following exercise.

Step 1   Disconnect all the external cables (monitor, keyboard, mouse, printer, etc.) from the PC you are going to use and place it on a flat, stable surface (preferably on an anti-static mat) where you can sit or stand comfortably to inspect the insides.

Step 2   Use proper anti-static procedures while opening the case and during this entire exercise (see Lab Exercise 2.04). Using whichever method applies to your case (thumbscrews, Phillips-head screws, locking tabs), remove the cover of your system unit and then lay the system down so that the open side faces the ceiling.

✔ Cross-Reference

Review Chapter 2 of *Mike Meyers' A+ Guide to Managing and Troubleshooting PCs* to confirm your understanding of proper ESD procedures, and how to open a PC system case.

Look inside your system case. What do you see? To begin with, you'll see lots of cables and wires. Some appear to be single-colored wires, while others seem to be multiple gray-colored wires in the shape of wide ribbons. Most colored wires originate at the power supply and end at the various devices to supply the needed direct current (DC) power to run the PC. The wide *ribbon cables* attach at various points and are used to transfer data. These are sometimes referred to as *logic cables* or *data cables*.

See if you can locate in your system case the major components labeled in Figure 2-8. You may have to move some of the fan shrouds, wires, and cables in order to find them, especially components on the motherboard—but remember your anti-static procedures and be gentle. Sometimes the slightest bump is enough to unseat a connection.

Step 3   Now it's time to take some notes, draw some sketches, or take a few pictures. Before you start disassembling this machine, document where the components belong and what wires and cables are connected to the different components. Be prepared to take a few notes on how you actually removed the component (this will really help when you go to reinstall the components). Include as much detail as possible; it will only help in getting the system unit back together.

Step 4   To start, you'll need to clear the way—a bit like peeling an onion, layer by layer—by removing the easily accessible components and cables first.

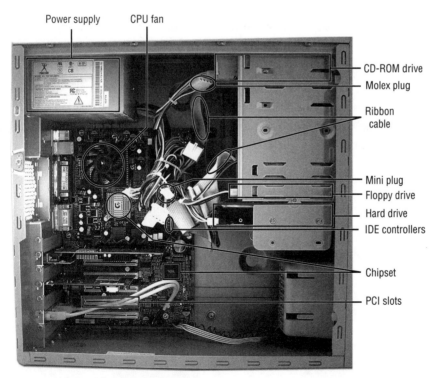

FIGURE 2-8 Inside a typical PC

Look inside the PC and find the expansion slots. How many total expansion cards can be plugged into your system? _____

Some of the expansion slots may have cards in them. These may be modem cards, sound cards, network cards, or video cards. Since expansion cards are designed to "expand" the capability of the computer system, they are designed to be installed after the system unit is assembled. For this reason, the expansion cards are a great place to begin your disassembly.

Look at the expansion cards installed in your PC, and then look at the external connectors on each. Can you match the cable to the expansion card?

Remove all installed expansion cards from your system unit. Place each card into an anti-static bag to protect it from ESD damage.

Step 5   If the machine you are disassembling is only a few years old, it will probably have multiple fan shrouds to make sure the airflow is getting to the main components to keep them cool.

Remove any fan shrouds from your system unit and place them out of the way on your workspace.

✔ **Hint**

After removing each item, especially the bulky items such as fan shrouds, wiring, and cables, it would be good to take a few more notes or pictures. Now that you have a better view of the components underneath, you will be able to consult these notes or pictures during reassembly.

You can complete the next three steps in the order written, or out of order if that works best for your system unit. You'll be removing the power supply wires, the power supply, and the data cables from the components and motherboard. If one of the data cables is in the way of one of the wires, it's okay to remove the data cable first. Please remember to keep good records (notes or photos) of your configuration.

Step 6   Locate the power supply, which is a large silver box in one corner of the system unit case. Trace the colored wires leading out of it. Remember to be gentle!

Find the power plug(s) for the motherboard. If you have a newer PC, it will probably look like the one in Figure 2-9. If you have an older PC, you might see two power connectors installed side by side.

Find the power connectors for the floppy, optical-media drive, and hard drives. Do they look like one of the connectors in Figure 2-10? They should!

Remove all of the power connectors from the motherboard and all data drives. Place them to the side as best as you can until you remove the power supply itself.

Step 7   If possible, remove the power supply at this point. If there are still many cables and components in the way, you can perform this step later in the lab.

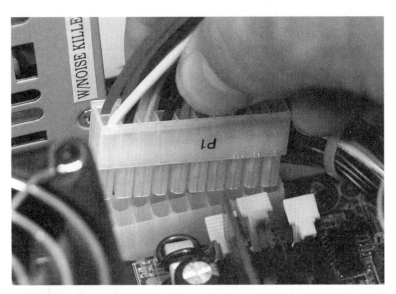

Figure 2-9 Power plug for the motherboard

Step 8 Now look at the floppy drive, which should be attached to a flat ribbon cable. (Don't worry if your system doesn't have a floppy drive—just move on and explore your other data drives.) Trace the ribbon cable to the motherboard. Do the same for all your other data drives, both hard drives and optical-media drives.

These ribbon cables are about 1.5 inches wide, and they are normally gray with a colored stripe on one side. The stripe—usually red—orients the cable properly to the connections on the motherboard and the drive.

The cable to the floppy drive has 34 wires (conductors) and in most cases has a twist in the center. Its position relative to this seven-wire twist determines whether a floppy drive is the primary or A: drive for the system (attached to the connector at the end of the cable past the twist), or the secondary B: drive on the system (attached to the center connector).

Figure 2-10 Power connectors

> ✔ **Hint**
>
> It's rare to find two floppy drives in a newer system; in fact, floppy drives are going away completely on most brand-new systems. On systems that don't have floppy drives, you will not find a floppy cable at all, though you may still have a 34-pin connector on the motherboard. On systems with only one floppy drive, manufacturers may use a shorter floppy cable with no twist and no second drive connector.

The type of ribbon cable that connects the hard drive(s) and optical drives to the motherboard has 40 wires and no twist. You may even have the newest cable type, which has 80 conductors to allow for faster transmission speed of the data to and from the hard drives. Both of these cable types still have a colored edge on one side for orientation. Many current systems use much smaller, seven-wire cables for Serial ATA, or SATA, hard drives; these cables have connectors keyed like the letter L.

Step 9   After noting the current state of the ribbon cables, disconnect and reconnect each device's cable in turn. Practice this a few times. Can you plug a cable in backwards? Try it. Put the cable on the device the wrong way if you can. Older types of cables can be put on incorrectly, but newer cables and connectors have built-in keying to prevent this from happening. Make sure that the cables are properly connected when you've finished.

Now look at where the ribbon cables connect to the motherboard. Make note of the proper cable orientation. Practice disconnecting and reconnecting the cables at the motherboard. Do you have any problems if you try to plug these cables in backwards?

When you feel you have practiced enough, remove the cables and place them safely away from the computer on your work surface. Now would be a great time to make a drawing or take a photograph of the de-cluttered system unit interior.

Step 10   Most modern systems have a set of small wire and cable runs connecting front panel indicator lights (primarily the power-on and hard drive activity LEDs) and front panel Universal Serial Bus (USB) ports to the motherboard (see Figure 2-11). Look for these individual wire connections (often collectively called *case wires*), which are usually grouped together near one corner of the motherboard. Make careful note of where each tiny connector plugs in—a photo would be incredibly helpful here—and then disconnect them all and tuck the wires out of the way.

Step 11   Now that all of the wires and cables are removed, you should have plenty of room to finish up the disassembly. You're now going to remove all the drives. Drives are usually the most cumbersome to remove because of the drive cages or frames where they're mounted (see Figure 2-12). Depending on the mounting the manufacturer has used, removing a drive may be as simple as pulling out a sliding mechanism, or as complicated as opening up the other side of the system case, removing all the decorative plastic facing, and removing a handful of screws.

Figure 2-11 Various case wires connected to a motherboard

Remove the floppy drive, all optical-media drives that are present, and the hard drive(s), and set them on your work surface.

Step 12   Look in your PC and find the random access memory (RAM) modules. RAM comes in thin wafer-like modules, about three to five inches long by one inch wide. A row of metal contacts running along one of the long edges plugs into a matching socket, three to five inches in length, located on the motherboard. Look for a long wafer standing on its edge; often you'll find two or more RAM modules lined up in a row.

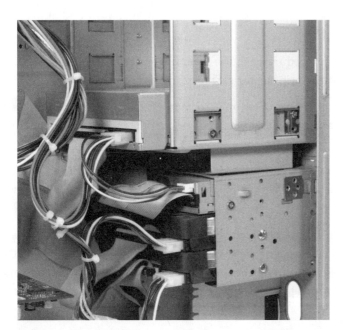

Figure 2-12 Typical drive configuration in a PC tower system case; note the cages or frames used for mounting the various drives

How many RAM modules do you have? _____

Do you have Dual Inline Memory Modules (DIMMs) or Single Inline Memory Modules (SIMMs)? _____

Making sure to follow proper anti-static procedures, remove the SIMMs or DIMMs from their slots and place them in an anti-static bag for safekeeping.

Step 13   Look in your PC and see if you can locate the central processing unit (CPU). Running CPUs generate a fair amount of heat, so they need their own dedicated cooling mechanisms. Because of this, when you search the motherboard trying to find the CPU, you'll generally find it hidden under a fan/heat sink unit.

Carefully remove the fan/heat sink unit from the CPU.

✖ Warning

Make sure you fully understand how to remove your particular model of CPU fan before you try it!

If you were able to remove the fan, make a note of the type of CPU chip you have:

_____

If you're in a computer lab with multiple systems, examine a number of different CPU chips. Note where each CPU is located on the motherboard.

Making sure to follow proper anti-static procedures, lift the lever of the zero insertion force (ZIF) socket, remove the CPU, and place it in an anti-static bag for safekeeping.

Step 14   See if you can locate any jumpers or DIP switches on your motherboard. Resist the temptation to play with them at this point—just make a note of what you find. In particular, look for the identifying labels on the motherboard.

Step 15   Making sure to follow proper anti-static procedures, remove the screws that secure the motherboard to the chassis or frame of the system case. Place the motherboard in a properly sized anti-static bag and put it aside.

Congratulations! You have just successfully disassembled your first PC! If you have used an area where you can leave the components, wires, cabling, and hardware for a while, you can leave the PC disassembled for later labs. If you really need to clean up the area for now, you can either follow your notes (and lab steps) in reverse order to reassemble the system, or find a large box to store the disassembled machine until your next lab session.

Don't worry about the ESD-sensitive components; as long as they are in their anti-static bags, they should be fine.

FIGURE 2-13 Do you recognize these components inside your PC?

Step 16 You have explored and removed nearly all the components of a typical PC system unit. To finish this lab exercise, see if you can correctly match the components in the following list to the items indicated in Figure 2-13.

Hard drive	_____	PCIe ×16 card	_____
Chipset	_____	Power connector	_____
CPU and fan assembly	_____	Optical drive	_____
PCI slot	_____	PCIe ×1 card	_____
Power supply	_____	RAM	_____

Lab Analysis Test

1. Joe has just moved his PC to his new office. After hooking up all the cables, he turns on the system, and when it asks for his password, the keyboard will not respond. What could possibly be wrong?

_____

_____

2. Theresa has just finished the production of a PowerPoint presentation detailing the design of a new office building. She has included some cool 3-D animations in the presentation to really show

off the design. When she attempts to save the presentation to a floppy disk, an error occurs. What might have caused the error? Do you have any suggestions that may solve the problem?

_____

_____

3. Cal has purchased a new set of speakers for his PC. The old ones worked just fine, but he wanted more power and a subwoofer. When he plugged in the new speakers, they would not work. Power is on to the speakers. What is the first thing you would check?

_____

_____

4. John had a new modem installed in his computer at a local mom and pop shop, where he watched as the system successfully connected to his AOL account. When he got home and tried, however, he couldn't get a dial tone. He calls you to ask for help. What should you suggest that he check first?

_____

_____

5. Audrey removed the case of her PC to check the type of RAM she has installed. When she put the case back on and tried to start the PC, she got a message that there's a problem with her hard drive. What is a good reason this might have happened?

_____

_____

Key Term Quiz

Use the following vocabulary terms to complete the following sentences. Not all terms will be used.

ALT key

CTRL key

data cable

electrostatic discharge (ESD)

female connector

function key

LED

male connector

power cable

ribbon cable

1. The modern hard drive may utilize technology that requires a flat, 80-wire _____.

2. When a floppy or optical drive is being accessed, a(n) _____ on the face of the drive lights up.

3. A keyboard shortcut for saving a document is to press the _____ in combination with the s key.

4. Anti-static wrist straps and anti-static bags are used to protect devices from _____ damage.

5. Pressing the FI _____ often calls up a program's Help feature.

Chapter 3
Microprocessors

Lab Exercises

Many PC users are comfortable performing simple installation and upgrade tasks, such as adding RAM or installing a modem or sound card. When it comes to the more complicated tasks, however, such as installing or replacing a central processing unit (CPU), wise users turn to the experts—this means you!

Installing a CPU is one of the many tasks that you'll find yourself performing as a PC tech. Whether you're building a new system from scratch or replacing the CPU on an existing computer, it's your job to know the important characteristics of the CPU, match the CPU to compatible motherboards, and configure the CPU on the PC.

In this set of lab exercises, you'll identify current CPU types, form factors, sockets, and slots, and you'll practice installing a CPU/fan assembly on a motherboard. You'll then explore the specifications of the microprocessor with a freeware program known as CPU-Z.

It's time to find your anti-static wrist strap and get started with your exploration of CPUs!

 30 MINUTES

Lab Exercise 3.01: CPU Characteristics

There you are, innocently strolling down the hall at work, following the smell of freshly brewed coffee, when you're ambushed by Joe the accountant, brandishing a CPU/fan unit. He wants to replace the CPU in his machine with this new one he bought on eBay, and he wants you to help him. When you're the resident computer tech geek, your coworkers will expect you to be able to deal competently with a situation like Joe's.

Staying on top of the many developments in CPU technology can be challenging, but it's also a necessary part of your job as a PC technician. By this point, you know that you can't just plug any CPU into any motherboard and expect it to work—you have to match the right CPU to the right motherboard. To accomplish this, you need to identify important CPU characteristics such as form factor, clock speed, and bus speed, as well as things like voltage settings, clock multiplier configurations, and cooling requirements.

Learning Objectives

In this lab, you'll practice identifying CPUs and CPU fan components.

At the end of this lab, you'll be able to

- Recognize the different kinds of CPUs

- Recognize different CPU fan attachments

- Identify the basic specifications of different classes of CPUs

Lab Materials and Setup

The materials you need for this lab are

- A notepad and pencil to document the specifications

- Optional: Access to a working computer with a word processing or spreadsheet application installed and access to the Internet, to facilitate research and documentation of the CPU specifications

- The *Mike Meyers' A+ Guide to Managing and Troubleshooting PCs* textbook for reference

- The disassembled, non-production PC computer system used in the lab exercises in Chapter 2

Getting Down to Business

In the following steps, you'll review your knowledge of CPU specifications, and then examine the CPU and fan attachment on a PC.

✔ **Cross-Reference**

Use Chapter 3 of *Mike Meyers' A+ Guide to Managing and Troubleshooting PCs* to help fill in the specifications for each CPU in the following charts.

Step 1   A good tech will not only learn the specifications of different CPU chips but will also master the use of reference tools such as the Internet, manufacturers' Web sites, product documentation, and reference books. A quick search of the Web or your motherboard book will generally yield a full list of specifications for a given CPU.

See how many CPU chip features you can fill in given the maker and CPU type:

Maker	CPU Type	Package	Clock Speed	FSB Speed (MHz)	L2 Cache (KB)	Clock Speed Multiplier
Intel	Pentium III 750	_____	_____	_____	_____	_____
AMD	Athlon XP 1500+	_____	_____	_____	_____	_____
AMD	Sempron 3100+	_____	_____	_____	_____	_____
Intel	Celeron 2200	_____	_____	_____	_____	_____
AMD	Athlon 64 X2 3800+	_____	_____	_____	_____	_____
Intel	Pentium D 2800	_____	_____	_____	_____	_____
Intel	Pentium 4 2540	_____	_____	_____	_____	_____
Intel	Core DUO T2300	_____	_____	_____	_____	_____
Intel	Itanium	_____	_____	_____	_____	_____

Step 2   Look at the CPUs pictured in Figure 3-1, making note of the differences you see. In particular, look for the following:

- Differing pin grid array (PGA) or Single Edge Contact (SEC) packages

- Orientation guide notches

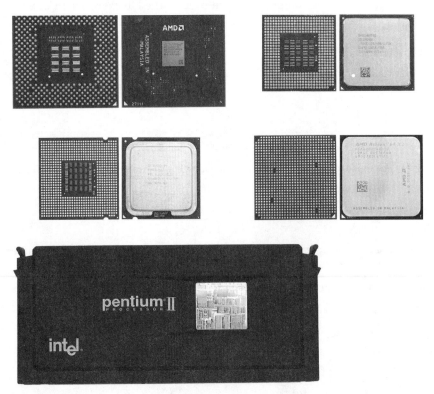

Figure 3-1 Exploring different CPUs

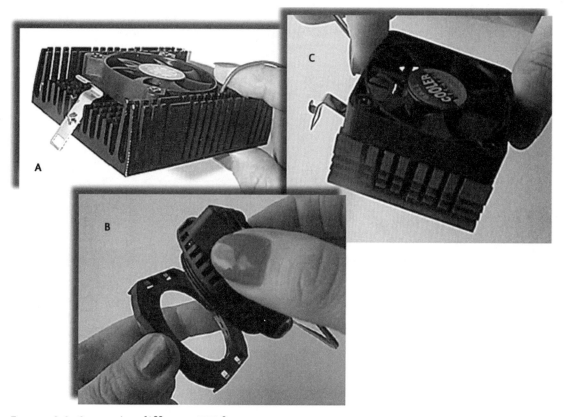

FIGURE 3-2 Comparing different CPU fans

Step 3   Many different types of fans can be attached to CPUs in many different ways. Describe the characteristics of the types of fans shown in Figure 3-2.

A. _____

B. _____

C. _____

Step 4   On your disassembled PC, locate the CPU and fan assembly. Make note of the type of CPU package and fan assembly. Also note the type of power connector used for the fan: Molex, three-prong motherboard plug, or none. Then replace the CPU into the anti-static bag and return the fan assembly to your work surface.

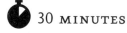 30 MINUTES

Lab Exercise 3.02: CPU Sockets

Because you know your CPUs, you have identified Joe's purchase, but you explain to him that until you look at his motherboard, you can't say whether he'll be able to use it. CPU compatibility is determined largely by the motherboard's support capabilities. Some motherboards enable you to upgrade the PC by replacing the existing CPU with a faster model of the same type. In many cases, however, you must replace the entire motherboard if you want to move up to a faster microprocessor.

Learning Objectives

In this lab, you'll identify various CPU sockets.

At the end of this lab, you'll be able to

- Recognize different kinds of CPU sockets

- Know which CPUs require which sockets

Lab Materials and Setup

The materials you need for this lab are

- A notepad and pencil to document the specifications

- Optional: Access to a working computer with a word processing or spreadsheet application installed and access to the Internet, to facilitate research and documentation of the CPU socket specifications

- The *Mike Meyers' A+ Guide to Managing and Troubleshooting PCs* textbook for reference

This lab is more effective if you have access to different types of motherboards with different types of CPU sockets.

Getting Down to Business

In the following steps, you'll review your knowledge of CPU socket types.

Step 1   Draw a line connecting each CPU to its corresponding socket type:

CPU	Socket Type
Pentium D 820	Socket 939
AMD Opteron 248	Socket AM2
Athlon 64 X2 4200+	Socket A (PGA-462)
Pentium 4	Socket 478
Athlon XP 1500+	Socket 940
AMD Sempron 3500+	Socket LGA-775

Step 2   Identify and describe the different socket types in Figure 3-3. Include the socket number/letter and the make and model of CPU that would fit that socket.

Example: <u>Socket A (PGA-462), AMD Athlon XP CPUs</u>

A   B

C   D

FIGURE 3-3 Identifying sockets

A. _____

B. _____

C. _____

D. _____

 30 MINUTES

Lab Exercise 3.03: CPU Removal and Installation

Luckily for Joe, his motherboard is compatible with his new CPU. Now he expects you to play your "computer expert" role and install the new CPU in his PC. As a PC tech, you must be comfortable with such basic tasks. In this exercise, you'll familiarize yourself with the procedure; using your disassembled PC, you'll practice removing and reinstalling the CPU and fan assembly.

Learning Objectives

In this lab, you'll practice removing and installing a CPU and CPU fan assembly.

At the end of this lab, you'll be able to

- Remove and install a CPU safely and correctly

- Remove and install a CPU fan assembly safely and correctly

Lab Materials and Setup

The materials you need for this lab are

- The disassembled, non-production PC you used in the lab exercises in Chapter 2
- Anti-static mat, or other static-safe material on which to place the CPU following removal
- Anti-static wrist strap
- Thermal compound
- A small flat-head (slotted) screwdriver

Getting Down to Business

Time to get your hands dirty! Removing and installing CPUs is one of the most nerve-wracking tasks that new PC techs undertake, but there's no need to panic. You'll be fine as long as you take the proper precautions to prevent ESD damage, and handle the CPU and fan assembly with care.

✖ Warning

Be careful not to touch any of the exposed metal contacts on either the CPU or the CPU socket.

Step 1   Using the disassembled PC, determine whether the process of reinstalling and removing the CPU and fan assembly will be easier with the motherboard on an anti-static mat or installed in its case; if you prefer, reinstall the motherboard into the case before proceeding. You may find that it is easier to work with the stubborn fan assembly clamp if the motherboard is secured in the case.

Step 2   In most cases you'll have to remove the fan assembly before you can remove the CPU. Screw-down fans are easier to remove than clip fans. Screw-down fans require only that you unscrew the securing hardware. Clip fans, found on many types of CPUs, require you to apply pressure on the clip to release it from the fan mount. Use a small flat-head screwdriver to do this, as shown in Figure 3-4. Use caution when prying the clip open, and don't forget to unplug the CPU fan!

✔ Hint

You'll discover that releasing a fan clip takes way more force than you want to apply to anything so near a delicate CPU chip. Realizing this in advance, you can be sure to brace yourself and position the screwdriver carefully, to minimize the possibility of it slipping off and gouging something.

The CPU and fan assembly will have thermal compound residue on the surfaces that were previously touching. You cannot reuse thermal compound, so you'll need to apply a fresh layer when you reinstall the CPU fan. Using a clean, lint-free cloth, carefully wipe the thermal compound residue from the CPU and fan assembly, and then place the fan assembly on an anti-static surface.

Figure 3-4 Using a screwdriver to remove a clip-type
CPU fan from its mount

Step 3   Before proceeding, notice the orientation of the CPU's notched corner. Almost all CPUs have
such a notch.

Now remove the CPU. Start by moving the end of the zero insertion force (ZIF) lever a little outward to clear the safety notch; then raise the lever to a vertical position. Next, grasp the chip carefully
by its edges and lift it straight up out of the socket. Be careful not to lift the CPU at an angle, or you'll
bend its tiny pins. As you lift out the CPU, make sure that the ZIF lever stays in an upright position.

Step 4   Now that you have the CPU chip out, examine it closely. The manufacturer usually prints the
chip's brand and type directly on the chip, providing you with some important facts about the chip's
design and performance capabilities. If your chip is an AMD Duron 1300, for example, you know that its
PGA packaging fits in a Socket A (462 pins), its bus speed is 100 MHz (double-pumped), and it runs at
1.3 GHz. Make a note of the relevant specs for your chip.

What is the CPU information printed on the chip package?

The recommendation to use an older, non-production PC for the disassembly and reassembly exercises may present you with the task of working with some older technology. PGA-style packages,
even the early designs, are fairly similar from processor to processor. If your CPU is an Intel Pentium II or III, or an early AMD Athlon, you may have to work with a Single Edge Cartridge (SEC)
package inserted in a Slot 1 or Slot A socket.

Removing an SEC CPU that uses a slot interface normally does not require removing the fan, which
is usually attached to the chip cartridge itself. To remove a slot CPU, first check for and release
any retaining clips that may be securing it to the slot, and then grasp the cartridge firmly on
both ends and pull straight up from the motherboard.

✖ Warning

Always handle a CPU chip like a fragile old photograph: very gently, holding it only by the edges. Make sure you take *complete* ESD precautions because even a tiny amount of static electricity can harm a CPU!

Step 5   Reinsert the CPU with the correct orientation, lock down the ZIF lever, and reattach the fan. Now remove the fan assembly and the CPU again. Practice this a few times to become comfortable with the process. When you're finished practicing, reinsert the CPU for the last time. Be sure to apply a thin film of fresh thermal compound onto the square in the center of the top of the CPU before you place the fan. Now reattach the fan assembly. Don't forget to plug the fan back in!

✔ Hint

If this were a production system with RAM and other components installed, this would be an ideal time to turn the system back on and make sure you had the CPU seated properly. In real life, you should always test your hardware before you put the case back on!

Step 6   You may leave your CPU/fan assembly installed on the motherboard and place the motherboard on your anti-static mat. Optionally, if you reinstalled the motherboard in the case, you may leave it assembled.

 30 MINUTES

Lab Exercise 3.04: Exploring CPU Specifications with CPU-Z

Joe is very impressed with your knowledge and expertise—and he's relieved that the CPU he purchased on eBay happened to work out. You explain that not only did it work out, but he has really improved the performance of his system with the upgraded CPU. In fact, to further display the characteristics of the CPU Joe has just purchased, you download a utility known as CPU-Z from www.cpuid.com. This utility reads the specifications of different PC components from information embedded in those components. You launch the utility to display the parameters of the new CPU for Joe.

Learning Objectives

In this lab, you'll identify various CPU specifications.

At the end of this lab, you'll be able to

- Run the CPU-Z utility
- Recognize key characteristics of CPUs

Lab Materials and Setup

The materials you need for this lab are

- Access to a working computer with Internet access, to facilitate downloading and running the CPU-Z utility

- A notepad and pencil to document the specifications

- Optional: A word processor or spreadsheet application to facilitate the documentation

This lab is more informative if you have access to different types of systems with different classifications of CPUs.

Getting Down to Business

In the following steps, you'll download a reference utility known as CPU-Z and use it to further explore the characteristics of the CPU.

Step 1   Log on to a computer with Internet access and point your browser to the following Web site: www.cpuid.com. Follow the directions to download the current version of CPU-Z (the current version at this writing is 1.37). Unzip the file and launch CPU-Z.

Step 2   The CPU-Z utility displays a number of tabs across the top of the window (Figure 3-5). At this time you are only concerned with the CPU and Cache tabs.

Using the data gathered by CPU-Z, record some of the pertinent information here:

Name _____

Code Name _____

Package _____

Core Speed _____

Multiplier _____

Bus Speed _____

L2 Cache _____

✔ **Hint**

Because of variations in CPUs, chipsets, BIOS, and motherboards, CPU-Z may not be able to display all of the information about your CPU. In some cases, the information may actually be erroneous. The CPUID Web site has good documentation on some of the common incompatibilities.

Step 3   If possible, launch CPU-Z on various machines to compare the characteristics of different CPUs. Save the utility for use in future lab exercises.

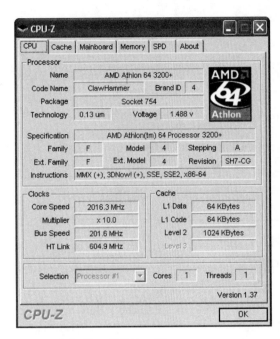

FIGURE 3-5 The CPU-Z utility

Lab Analysis Test

1. James has an AMD Duron CPU motherboard and has bought a faster Intel Pentium D 820 from an eBay auction. He asks you to install the new CPU. What is your first reaction?

2. Joanna called you to say that ever since you installed her new CPU, the PC gives intermittent problems when it runs. Sometimes it just quits and freezes up. What could possibly be wrong?

3. Theresa has a Socket 462 motherboard with an AMD Duron 800-MHz processor and would like to put in a faster CPU. Can she install an AMD Athlon Thunderbird 1.4-GHz processor? Why or why not?

4. Lindsey runs CPU-Z on her system and notices that the processor's core speed is 2191.2 and the displayed multiplier is x22. What is the speed of the system clock in Debbie's machine? How would the industry display this system clock speed?

5. David has been reading the trade magazines and keeps seeing all the hype over the "dual-core" processors. David decides, since he is a power gamer, that he will upgrade to a dual-core CPU to improve the performance of his system when playing his favorite game. Will a dual-core processor improve the performance in this scenario? Explain.

Key Term Quiz

Use the following vocabulary terms to complete the following sentences. Not all terms will be used.

clip connector

code name

CPU

fan assembly

land grid array (LGA)

microprocessor

package

pin grid array (PGA)

screw-down connector

1. The Intel Pentium D CPU uses a package known as a _____.

2. Both Intel and AMD have adopted the use of a _____ to distinguish among revisions of their CPUs.

3. You often need to remove the _____ to get to a system's CPU.

4. Another name for a CPU is _____.

5. A common type of CPU fan connector, which requires a flat-head screwdriver to remove, is the _____.

Chapter 4
RAM

Lab Exercises

One of the easiest and most cost-effective upgrades you can make to a PC is to add more memory. As such, RAM installation is probably the most common type of upgrade you'll perform as a PC tech.

RAM installation tasks include determining how much RAM the PC has installed, how much RAM the PC can support, and what type of RAM it uses, as well as physically installing the RAM on the motherboard. The following labs are designed to give you practice working with RAM by using visual recognition of the different types and packages and by walking you through the steps of installing RAM.

 15 MINUTES

Lab Exercise 4.01: Determining the Amount of RAM in Your PC

So there you are, a week after upgrading Joe's CPU (see Chapter 3), using your lunch hour to pummel your fellow PC techs in Half-Life 2, when who should show up again but Joe, this time clutching a stick of RAM he got from a guy on the fourth floor. He wants you to install it in his system. You tell him you have to check on some things first, including how much RAM his system can handle and how much it already has, before you can help him.

✔ **Hint**

High-end PCs usually come straight from the factory equipped with hefty amounts of RAM. One of the areas where makers of lower-cost PCs cut corners is by skimping on RAM.

Your first task in performing a RAM upgrade is determining how much RAM you need. Start by finding out how much RAM is currently installed on the system, and then consult with the motherboard book to determine how much RAM the system supports.

Learning Objectives

In this lab exercise, you'll use various methods to determine how much memory is currently installed in your system, and how much it is capable of holding.

At the end of this lab, you'll be able to

- Find RAM measurements

- Identify how much RAM is installed in a system

- Determine how much RAM a particular motherboard supports

Lab Materials and Setup

The materials you need for this lab are

- A working Windows PC

- A notepad

✔ **Hint**

If you're in a computer lab or you have access to multiple PCs, you should practice on as many different PCs as possible.

Getting Down to Business

There are several ways to determine how much RAM is installed on a PC. First, you can check the RAM count during the boot process (some of the newer machines hide the RAM count, even if it's enabled in BIOS). This tells you how much RAM the system BIOS recognizes during its check of the system. Second, you can check the amount of RAM that Windows recognizes from within the OS. And third, you can remove the PC case cover and physically examine the RAM sticks installed on the motherboard.

✔ **Cross-Reference**

To review the ways you can check the amount of RAM installed in a PC, refer to the "Determining Current RAM Capacity" section in Chapter 4 of *Mike Meyers' A+ Guide to Managing and Troubleshooting PCs.*

Step 1 Turn on your PC, and watch the display as the system goes through its startup routine. Typically, the RAM count runs near the top-left side of the screen. Figure 4-1 shows an example of a typical RAM count.

Most BIOS programs display the RAM count in kilobytes (KB). To convert this figure to megabytes (MB), divide it by 1024.

Many systems run through the startup routine quickly, so the RAM count may only appear on the screen for a few seconds. Press the PAUSE/BREAK key to pause the boot process so you have time to write down the number accurately. When you want the count to restart, press the ENTER key.

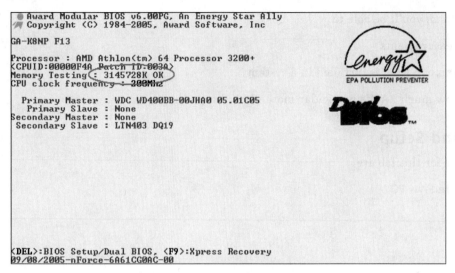

```
● Award Modular BIOS v6.00PG, An Energy Star Ally
🏃 Copyright (C) 1984-2005, Award Software, Inc

GA-K8NP F13

Processor : AMD Athlon(tm) 64 Processor 3200+
<CPUID:00000F4A  Patch ID:003A>
Memory Testing : 3145728K OK
CPU clock frequency : 300Mhz

   Primary Master : WDC WD400BB-00JHA0 05.01C05
    Primary Slave : None
Secondary Master : None
 Secondary Slave : LTN403 DQ19




<DEL>:BIOS Setup/Dual BIOS, <F9>:Xpress Recovery
09/08/2005-nForce-6A61CG0AC-00
```

FIGURE 4-1: Viewing a typical RAM count during boot-up

What is the RAM count number displayed on your monitor?

_____

✔ Hint

If you're starting the PC for the first time of the day, the startup routine may run through the RAM count before the monitor has a chance to warm up. If this happens, just reboot the PC and try again.

Depending on your system's BIOS, you may also see a RAM count in the system configuration summary. This is a screen that lists the PC's CPU type and clock speed, mass storage devices, port addresses, and so on. Typically, you'll also see an entry for the system's base memory (640 KB) and extended memory (the total amount of RAM installed).

Step 2   Use the following methods to determine the amount of RAM on your system from within any version of Windows.

a)   Right-click the My Computer icon and select Properties to see the amount of RAM in your system (see Figure 4-2).

b)   You'll notice that Windows shows RAM as megabytes instead of kilobytes, but the numbers add up to the same total amount.

Another way to see the amount of memory installed is to follow this procedure:

a)   Click Start | Programs (or All Programs in Windows XP) | Accessories | System Tools | System Information. In the System Summary, look for a value called Total Physical Memory (see Figure 4-3).

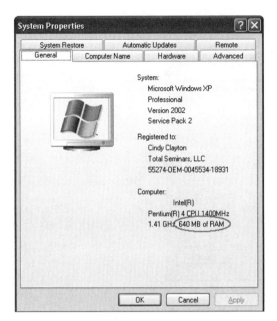

FIGURE 4-2 Viewing the RAM count in
Windows XP via My Computer

b) The amount of RAM will be listed in the displayed information.

How much memory is in your system?

_____

Does this number agree with what you found in Step 1?

_____

We'll save the last method for determining how much RAM is installed for the next exercise in this lab. For the moment, let's talk about how to determine the maximum amount of RAM your system is capable of supporting.

Are all the amounts of RAM correlating? If you have 512 MB or 1 GB of memory installed, are the displayed figures correct, or are they off by 32 MB or 64 MB?

Entry-level PCs and laptops often have onboard display adapters (the display adapter is built into the motherboard). Manufacturers will include little to no video RAM on the motherboard, so the display adapter must "steal" some portion of the system RAM to be able to handle today's intense graphic applications.

If the amounts are not adding up, and you're seeing a number such as 448 MB or 992 MB, then your system has probably allocated some of the system memory to handle your display adapter's needs.

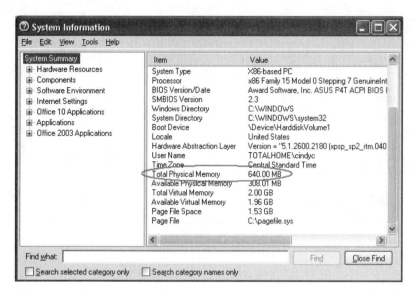

FIGURE 4-3 The System Information dialog box showing Total
Physical Memory

Step 3   Because modern versions of the Windows OS are able to address 4 GB or more of physical RAM,
the amount of RAM you can install on a modern system depends on the limitations of the motherboard
hardware.

Neither the CMOS nor the OS can help you determine how much RAM a PC is capable of handling.
The best source for this information is the system's motherboard book, if you have it, or the PC maker's
or motherboard manufacturer's Web site.

Examine the documentation that came with your PC, or visit the manufacturer's Web site, to determine how much RAM you can install on the system.

What is the maximum amount of RAM that your system can support?

_____

 30 MINUTES

Lab Exercise 4.02: Identifying Types of RAM

Once you determine how much RAM Joe has installed on his PC, and how much his motherboard can
handle, you conclude that there's room for more. But, you explain to Joe, this doesn't mean you can add
his RAM stick, because not all RAM is the same. Having looked at the specs for his system, you know it
takes 184-pin DDR SDRAM. Joe thinks the stick he got is the right size to fit, but you know it's 240-pin
DDR2 RAM, so it won't. This is why they pay you the big bucks—and why you get to take the RAM stick
Joe can't use and add it to your own machine! (Just kidding. Of course you'd return it to inventory.)

RAM comes in several standardized form factors, each compatible with specific types of systems. Modern desktop systems use full-sized dual inline memory modules (DIMMs) of various pin configurations (168, 184, and 240). Older desktop models may still support banks of single inline memory modules (SIMMs). Laptop computers use scaled-down DIMM versions called Small Outline DIMMs, or SO-DIMMs.

✔ **Cross-Reference**

For details on the various types of RAM found in modern systems, refer to the "DDR SDRAM" and "DDR2" sections in Chapter 4 of *Mike Meyers' A+ Guide to Managing and Troubleshooting PCs*.

Steps for identifying the different types of RAM are listed below.

Learning Objectives

In this lab, you'll examine and compare different RAM packages.

At the end of this lab, you'll be able to

- Recognize and differentiate between different kinds of RAM packages

Lab Materials and Setup

The materials you need for this lab are

- The disassembled, non-production PC used in the lab exercises in Chapters 2 and 3

- Demonstration units of various RAM packages (optional)

✔ **Hint**

It is helpful to examine the RAM configurations in multiple PCs, if you have them available. Having a laptop with removable RAM is a plus.

Getting Down to Business

Let's do a quick review of the types of RAM packages you'll see on modern PCs. Then you'll check your PC or motherboard documentation to determine the type of RAM it uses. Finally, you'll examine the RAM from the disassembled PC to determine what type of RAM it is.

Step 1 Typically, as older machines become obsolete and fall into disuse, they are easier to acquire for little or no cost. Many times, this is exactly the type of PC you have available to disassemble, so there is a good chance that it will use older memory (RAM) as well. If you are using an older, non-production

Figure 4-4 A 168-pin DIMM

machine for your exploration, there's a good chance the motherboard supports one of these older types of RAM packages (included here for your information):

72-pin SIMMs   Single Inline Memory Modules (SIMMs) are about four inches long and have 72 physical pins (edge connectors) on each side, but only one side is actually used for operation. The board has a notch in the bottom center that is offset slightly. You'll only find SIMM RAM on very old PCs.

168-pin DIMMs   These are about five inches long and have 84 physical pins (edge connectors) on each side, and all 168 connectors are used. The board has two notches on the bottom: one near the center, and the other near an end (see Figure 4-4).

184-pin RIMMs   Rambus Dynamic RAM (RDRAM) is the type of RAM you might find if you are working with an old Intel Pentium III or Pentium 4 motherboard. You call a stick of RDRAM a RIMM. RIMM is actually trademarked as a word; it's not an acronym like DIMM, despite what many people assume (see Figure 4-5).

If you are using a typical desktop system and it is relatively new (less than two years old), the motherboard will most likely support one of the following two types of RAM packages:

184-pin DDR DIMMs   DDR RAM sticks are about five inches long and look a lot like 168-pin DIMMs, but with only one notch and more connectors. These are known as double data rate (DDR) memory. The notches are different from 168-pin DIMMs, so these RAM types are not interchangeable (see Figure 4-6).

240-pin DDR2 DIMMs   DDR2 RAM sticks are physically the same size as the 184-pin DDR DIMMs, but the guide notch is in a different location and there are obviously more connectors. DDR2 uses a

Figure 4-5 A 184-pin RIMM

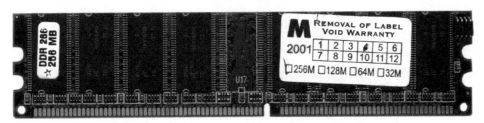

FIGURE 4-6 A 184-pin DDR DIMM

240-pin DIMM that's not compatible with DDR RAM slots (see Figure 4-7). DDR2 is expected to perform better than DDR due to lower voltage requirements, clock doubling on the chips' input/output
circuits, and special prefetch buffers.

✔ **Hint**

Both DDR and DDR2 SDRAM can be used in motherboards that support dual-channel architecture
to increase throughput. These motherboards typically have one or two pairs of brightly colored
RAM slots; you'll need to install a matched pair of either DDR or DDR2 RAM sticks into slots of the
same color. Most often, this will mean that the matched pair of RAM sticks will *not* be installed
next to one another. If you have access to any systems using dual-channel architecture, check
out their innards to see these RAM slots in action.

Step 2   In your PC or motherboard documentation, or on the manufacturer's Web site, locate the section listing the type of RAM your system uses.

What speed of RAM does your system need? _____

Step 3   Using the disassembled PC at your workspace, locate the motherboard and the anti-static bag
containing the RAM sticks, and make note of the following:

FIGURE 4-7: A 240-pin DDR2 DIMM

How many RAM slots does your motherboard have? _____

How many RAM slots are filled with RAM sticks? _____

Can you tell at a glance whether your system has SIMMs, DIMMs, RIMMs, DDR DIMMs, or DDR2 DIMMs? _____

 30 MINUTES

Lab Exercise 4.03: Removing and Installing RAM

Taking pity on Joe, you've found a stick of RAM for him that works with his system, and now you have to install it. Meanwhile, you can "re-inventory" that stick of DDR2 RAM into another computer!

Although RAM installation is one of the simpler PC hardware upgrades, it's still important that you follow the correct steps and take all appropriate safety precautions. You will once again practice using the disassembled, non-production system. This time, you will be removing and installing RAM sticks.

Learning Objectives

In this lab, you'll practice removing and installing RAM.

At the end of this lab, you'll be able to

- Remove RAM safely and correctly

- Install RAM safely and correctly

Lab Materials and Setup

The materials you need for this lab are

- The disassembled, non-production PC used in the lab exercises in Chapter 2

- An anti-static mat or other static-safe material on which to place the RAM

- An anti-static wrist strap

- A notepad

✔ Hint

If you're in a computer lab or you have access to multiple PCs, you should practice on a variety of systems.

Getting Down to Business

Removal and installation procedures vary depending on the type of RAM your system uses. DIMMs and RIMMs snap into the RAM slots vertically, whereas SIMM installation is a bit more involved; these modules insert at an angle and then pivot into their final locked position. The following steps describe the removal and installation procedures for DIMMs.

✖ Warning

Regardless of the type of RAM on your system, be certain to take measures to prevent ESD damage. Shut down and unplug your PC and place it on your anti-static mat. Strap on your anti-static bracelet and ground yourself. If necessary, remove any cables or components that block access to your system RAM before you begin.

You should have already removed the RAM from your tear-down machine and have it safely stored in an anti-static bag. You may either install the RAM in the sockets on the motherboard with the motherboard on the anti-static mat, or reinstall the motherboard into the case first. The following removal steps are listed for reference, especially if you have access to additional machines for exploration.

Follow these steps to remove DIMM or RIMM RAM from your PC:

Step 1 Locate the retention clips on either end of the RAM module.

Step 2 Press outward on the clips to disengage them from the retention slots on the sides of the RAM sticks (see Figure 4-8).

Step 3 Press down on the clips firmly and evenly. The retention clips act as levers to lift the DIMM sticks up and slightly out of the RAM slots.

Step 4 Remove the DIMM sticks and place them on your anti-static mat, or in an anti-static bag.

Step 5 Make note of the following:

FIGURE 4-8 Removing a 184-pin DIMM (DDR SDRAM)

How many pins does your RAM have? _____

Where are the guide notches located? _____

What information is on the RAM's label? _____

Step 6   While you've got your system RAM out, this is a good time to check the condition of the metal contacts on both the RAM sticks and the motherboard RAM sockets.

Are the contacts free of dirt and corrosion? _____

After you've examined your system RAM and inspected the motherboard RAM sockets, reinstall the RAM as described below.

To install a DIMM or RIMM:

Step 1   Orient the DIMM or RIMM so that the guide notches on the RAM module match up to the guide ridges on the RAM socket.

Step 2   Press the RAM stick firmly and evenly straight down into the socket until the retention clips engage the retention notches on the ends of the RAM stick.

→ **Try This: SIMMs**

If the machine you are using as a tear-down machine is fairly old, there's a chance that it will be populated with 72-pin SIMM RAM sticks. For reference, I've included a few tips for working with this type of memory.

Follow these steps to remove SIMMs (remember that it takes two of them to complete a memory bank) from your PC:

Step 1   Locate the retention clips on either end of the SIMMs.

Step 2   Press outward on the clips to disengage them from the retention slots on the sides of the RAM sticks. Some motherboards don't leave you with much room to operate, so you may need a small screwdriver or needle nose pliers to undo the retention clips. Be very careful not to touch any of the circuitry with metal tools!

Step 3   Once the SIMMs are loose, pivot their slots to a 45-degree angle and then slide the SIMM sticks out.

To reinstall SIMM RAM:

Step 1   Orient the SIMM RAM stick so that the guide notch on the end matches the guide ridge on the socket.

Step 2   Slide the RAM stick into the socket at a 45-degree angle until it seats firmly.

Step 3   Pivot the RAM upright until it snaps into place, making sure that both retention clips are secured.

Step 3   Snap the retention clips firmly into place.

Step 4   Repeat these steps to install other RAM modules as appropriate. If you're using RIMM RAM, don't forget to install the continuity RIMM (CRIMM) sticks into any empty RAM slots.

To professionally finish a RAM installation, specifically if you are on a production-level machine, follow these steps:

Step 1   Once your system RAM is in place, reattach any cables that you may have had to move, and plug the system power cable in. Do not reinstall the PC case cover until after you've confirmed that RAM installation was successful.

Step 2   Boot the system up and watch the RAM count to confirm that you correctly installed the RAM.

✔ **Hint**

If your system has any problems when you reboot, remember that you must turn off the power and unplug the computer again before reseating the RAM.

 30 MINUTES

Lab Exercise 4.04: Exploring RAM Specifications with CPU-Z

Now that you have Joe's system up and running with double the memory it had before, you can take a moment to analyze the re-inventoried memory on your machine. You've already downloaded the utility CPU-Z from the Internet; now you'll need to launch CPU-Z and examine the information on the Memory and SPD tabs.

Learning Objectives

In this lab, you'll identify various RAM specifications.

At the end of this lab, you'll be able to

- Recognize key characteristics of RAM

Lab Materials and Setup

The materials you need for this lab are

- Access to a working computer with the utility CPU-Z installed

- A notepad and pencil to document the specifications

- Optional: A word processor or spreadsheet application to facilitate the documentation

This lab is more informative if you have access to different types of systems with different types of RAM.

Getting Down to Business

In the following steps, you'll explore the different characteristics of RAM.

Step 1   Launch the CPU-Z application.

Step 2   Navigate to the Memory tab. The CPU-Z utility displays the current statistics of the RAM installed, as shown in Figure 4-9.

Using the data gathered by CPU-Z, record the following information:

Type _____

Size _____

CAS# Latency (CL) _____

RAS# to CAS# Delay (tRCD) _____

RAS# Precharge (tRP) _____

✔ **Cross-Reference**

To learn about the meanings of RAS and CAS with regard to RAM and its timing, look up the definition for DRAM on Wikipedia (go to http://en.wikipedia.org for the English version) and check out the information about asynchronous RAM.

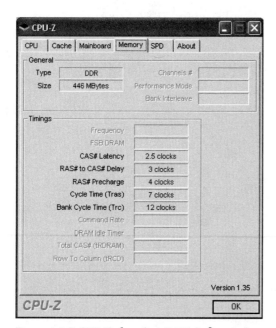

FIGURE 4-9 CPU-Z showing RAM information

FIGURE 4-10 CPU-Z showing SPD information

Step 3   Click the SPD tab in CPU-Z.

Step 4   The SPD tab, shown in Figure 4-10, lists a number of technical bits of information about a particular stick of RAM. This information is contained on an additional chip on every SDRAM stick called the serial presence detect (SPD) chip.

Using the data gathered by CPU-Z, record the following information for each of the system's RAM modules:

	Module 1	Module 2	Module 3	Module 4
Slot #	_____	_____	_____	_____
Module size	_____	_____	_____	_____
Maximum bandwidth	_____	_____	_____	_____
Manufacturer	_____	_____	_____	_____

✔ Cross-Reference

To review how the SPD chip works with the system, refer to the "SPD" section in Chapter 4 of *Mike Meyers' A+ Guide to Managing and Troubleshooting PCs*.

Step 5   If possible, launch CPU-Z on various machines to compare the characteristics of different types of RAM. Save the utility for use in future lab exercises.

→ **Try This: PC Wizard**

On a computer with Internet access, point your browser to the following Web site: www.cpuid.com. Follow the onscreen directions and download a copy of PC Wizard.

Extract the files into a folder and launch the PC Wizard application. Once PC Wizard is running, find and click the Mainboard icon in the Hardware area. This brings up a list of components in the right pane of the application window. Click the Physical Memory item and then browse through the information displayed in the lower portion of the window.

Using this information, can you determine the maximum size for individual RAM modules allowed on this system, and the maximum amount of total memory that it supports? Does this correspond to the information you found earlier in the PC or motherboard documentation?

Note that because of variations in chipsets, BIOS, and motherboards, PC Wizard may or may not provide detailed information on the RAM. In some cases, the information may actually be erroneous. The CPUID Web site has good documentation on some of the common incompatibilities.

Lab Analysis Test

1. Jarel wants to upgrade his memory and calls you for help. He knows that he's using DDR RAM and that his system clock is 133 MHz, but he isn't sure what type of DDR SDRAM sticks he should purchase. What DDR RAM would you recommend that he use?

2. Theresa's Windows 2000 Professional system has 512 MB of RAM. She adds another stick with 512 MB of RAM, but the RAM count still only shows 512 MB. What could be causing this?

3. John's system has 512 MB of PC4200 DDR2 SDRAM. He recently installed an additional 512 MB of DDR2 SDRAM that a co-worker gave him. He tells you that his system now boots up correctly and shows the correct amount of RAM, but then it freezes after several minutes. He notes that if he removes the new RAM, the system runs fine. What could be a possible reason for this?

4. Kyle has a system that supports dual-channel architecture (there are two blue DIMM slots on the motherboard). The motherboard has space for three sticks of RAM, so Kyle installs three 512-MB RAM sticks. What will be the result?

5. Joe reads that in some instances DDR SDRAM is faster than the DDR2 SDRAM he has installed on his system, and he wants to know if he can simply swap out his current RAM for DDR SDRAM DIMMs. What do you tell him?

Key Term Quiz

Use the following vocabulary terms to complete the following sentences. Not all terms will be used.

168-pin DIMM

184-pin DIMM

240-pin DIMM

CRIMM

DIMM

DDR RAM

DDR2 RAM

dual-channel

EDO

megabytes (MB)

RIMM

SDRAM

SO-DIMM

SPD

1. Today's PCs use DDR2 RAM, which comes in a(n) _____ package.

2. A RAM module used in a laptop is called a(n) _____.

3. A component known as a(n) _____ chip provides additional information about an SDRAM module.

4. A stick of _____ looks a lot like a 168-pin DIMM, but it has 184 pins.

5. The technology that uses two sticks of RAM together to increase throughput is known as _____ architecture.

Chapter 5
BIOS and CMOS

Lab Exercises

Basic input/output services (BIOS) provide the primary interface between the operating system's device drivers and most of its hardware. Although modern BIOS is automated and tolerant of misconfiguration, a good PC technician must be comfortable with those occasional situations in which the BIOS may need some maintenance or repair.

The PC needs the BIOS to tell it how each different basic component is to communicate with the system. At the beginning of the PC revolution, many different manufacturers developed BIOS for PCs, but over the years the BIOS business has consolidated to only three brands: AMI, Award Software, and Phoenix Technologies. Each of these manufacturers provides a utility called the CMOS setup program (CMOS stands for *complementary metal-oxide semiconductor*, which is why everyone says "CMOS") that enables you to reconfigure BIOS settings for boot device order, amount of memory, hard disk drive configuration, and so on. Most of these configurations are automated, but as a PC tech, you'll find yourself doing this more often than you might think!

As an example, let's say that your company is planning a mass upgrade from your current OS—Windows 2000 Professional—to Windows XP Professional. You've tested the upgrade process on a few lab machines, and found that systems with an out-of-date BIOS have had problems upgrading successfully. In preparation for Windows XP installation, besides upgrading any older BIOS versions you find, you'll disable any BIOS-level antivirus checking functions. You're also aware that the prior IT manager did not use consistent CMOS passwords, so you may need to reset the passwords on a few machines.

The lab exercises in this chapter will teach you to identify, access, and configure system BIOS.

 10 MINUTES

Lab Exercise 5.01: Identifying BIOS ROM

Having received your orders to do the big OS upgrade, your first task is to check the BIOS types and versions on all the machines in your office, and then visit each BIOS maker's Web site to determine whether more recent versions are available.

The system BIOS is stored on non-volatile memory called BIOS ROM. BIOS makers label their BIOS ROM chips prominently on the motherboard. In this exercise, you'll look at two different ways to identify your BIOS ROM chip.

✔ **Cross-Reference**

For details on the three big companies that manufacture BIOS on modern systems, refer to the "Updating CMOS: The Setup Program" section in Chapter 5 of *Mike Meyers' A+ Guide to Managing and Troubleshooting PCs*.

Learning Objectives

In this lab, you'll learn two ways to identify your BIOS.

At the end of this lab, you'll be able to

- Locate the BIOS ROM chip on the motherboard
- Identify the BIOS manufacturer
- Determine the BIOS creation date and version

Lab Materials and Setup

The materials you need for this lab are

- A working PC
- An anti-static mat
- A notepad

Getting Down to Business

The first thing you'll do is remove your PC case cover and locate the BIOS ROM chip. Next, you'll make note of the BIOS information displayed during system startup.

Figure 5-1 A typical system BIOS ROM chip

✖ Warning

Any time you take the cover off of your PC, remember to follow all proper safety and ESD precautions.

Step 1   Remove the case from the PC and locate the system BIOS ROM chip. Look for a chip with a shiny printed label on it. Compare your system BIOS ROM chip to the one in Figure 5-1.

Read the manufacturer's label if you can, and answer the following questions:

Who made the BIOS? _____

What year was the BIOS written? _____

Are there any other numbers on the label? Record them. _____

Does it look like you could easily remove the system BIOS chip, or does it look soldered to the motherboard? _____

Step 2   Replace the PC case cover and start the system. Be sure the monitor is turned on. When the first POST data appears on the screen, press the PAUSE/BREAK key on the keyboard. This suspends further operation until you press ENTER.

Figure 5-2 shows an example of what you may see. At the top of the screen is the BIOS manufacturer's name and version number. At the bottom of the screen is the date of manufacture and the product identification number.

Make note of the following information:

Who made the BIOS? _____

```
  Award Modular BIOS v6.00PG, An Energy Star Ally
  Copyright (C) 1984-2000, Award Software, Inc.

GREEN AGP/PCI/ISA SYSTEM

Main Processor : Pentium III 850MHz(100x8.5)
Memory Testing : 114688K

Award Plug and Play BIOS Extension v1.0A
Copyright (C) 2000 Award Software, Inc.

   Primary Master  : WDC WD1020AA, 80.10A80
   Primary Slave   : None
 Secondary Master : ATAPI CD-ROM DRIVE 40X
 Secondary Slave  : None




Press DEL to enter SETUP
06/02/2000-694X-686A-XXXXXXXX-QW
```

FIGURE 5-2 A typical boot screen

What version is the BIOS? _____

What year was the BIOS written? _____

✔ **Hint**

Not all BIOS display the same type of information. Some BIOS makers modify the BIOS to show nothing more than their logos during the boot process.

Step 3   Press ENTER on the keyboard to continue booting. Once the system is up and running, go online and find out whether a more recent version of your BIOS is available. Your first stop should be your PC maker's Web site. If they do not have this information available, try your motherboard manufacturer or the BIOS maker.

✖ **Warning**

Do not "flash" your system BIOS at this time!

15 MINUTES

Lab Exercise 5.02: Accessing BIOS via the CMOS Setup Program

Once you've assessed and, where necessary, upgraded the BIOS on each machine, before you proceed with the Windows XP installation, you should check to be sure the BIOS is properly configured using the special program for this purpose.

You don't access the hundreds of individual programs contained in the system BIOS directly, or from anywhere within the Windows OS. Instead, you use a utility that interfaces with the BIOS programs to enable you to reconfigure settings. This utility is the CMOS setup program.

Learning Objectives

In this lab, you'll go into CMOS and explore your BIOS configuration settings.

At the end of this lab, you'll be able to

- Enter the CMOS setup program
- Navigate the display screens of the setup utility

Lab Materials and Setup

The materials you need for this lab are

- A working PC whose BIOS settings you have permission to change

Getting Down to Business

In the following steps, you'll reboot your PC and access the CMOS setup program. Each BIOS maker has its own special way to do this, so how you go about it depends on which BIOS your system has installed. Common methods include the following:

- Press DELETE during the boot process.
- Press F2 during the boot process.
- Press F10 during the boot process.
- Press CTRL-ALT-INSERT during the boot process.
- Press CTRL-A during the boot process.
- Press CTRL-FI during the boot process.

There are four ways for you to determine which method works for your BIOS:

- Check your motherboard or PC documentation.
- Visit your motherboard or PC maker's Web site.
- Watch the screen display after booting your PC. Most direct you to press a specific key to enter CMOS.
- Use the trial-and-error method! Boot your system and go down the preceding list, trying each key or key combination until one works. You won't hurt anything if you get it wrong, but if you hold the wrong key down for too long you may get a keyboard error message. If this happens, just reboot and try again.

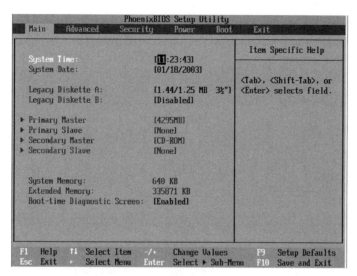

FIGURE 5-3 Phoenix CMOS Main screen

Step 1   Determine which method you need to use to enter the CMOS setup program. Then reboot your system and use that method to enter CMOS.

Step 2   Once you've entered the CMOS setup program, look at the screen and compare it to Figures 5-3 and 5-4. The Phoenix BIOS shown in Figure 5-3 opens immediately into the Main screen, whereas the Award BIOS in Figure 5-4 presents an initial menu. Although the screens for different CMOS setup programs may look different, they all contain basically the same functions.

✖ Warning

Do not make any changes in BIOS settings during this lab exercise. You'll make changes in the next two lab exercises.

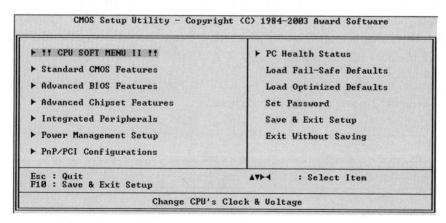

FIGURE 5-4 Award BIOS opening screen

The CMOS setup program controls the "changeable" BIOS settings. Many settings depend on what you add to the system. The following are some sample entries on your system you can change or update (there are more depending on your BIOS):

- Date

- Time

- Hard drive configuration

- Boot sequence

- RAM

- IRQ reservations

- Serial and parallel port assignments

- Enable/disable onboard controllers

- Enable/disable supervisor and user passwords

Step 3 Explore each screen and make notes about what each one does. Navigation, like the method to enter the CMOS setup program, varies from maker to maker. Most are navigable by keyboard only, but some (AMI, for instance) support a mouse. Look at the bottom of the CMOS setup program screen to see how to navigate in your particular CMOS utility.

✔ **Hint**

Usually the arrow keys and the PAGE UP and PAGE DOWN keys will select and change settings. Sometimes the + and – keys or the space bar will toggle settings. There is usually a key to the navigation and selection keys displayed on the screen; refer to it as well.

While navigating through the different setup screens, pay particular attention to any password or security menu, which enable you to configure administrator/supervisor passwords and user passwords. Do not make any changes at this time; just make a note of where you configure these passwords. You will configure a password in the next lab exercise.

Step 4 Record some of the more common settings here for a review reference. View every screen of your CMOS setup utility to locate these settings and record them:

Primary Master (Type) _____

Drive A _____

Video _____

Halt On _____

Boot Sequence _____

Resources Controlled By _____

FDC Controller _____

Serial Port I _____

Parallel Port Mode _____

Once you're done exploring, press ESC a couple of times until you get the message "Quit Without Saving (Y/N)?" Press Y, and then press ENTER. The system will boot into your operating system.

 30 MINUTES

Lab Exercise 5.03: Configuring and Clearing CMOS Setup Program Passwords

In many professional environments, the IT department doesn't want users to fool with any of the PC's settings, especially detailed items such as the BIOS settings. The IT manager may even devise a password to prevent entry to the CMOS setup utility by unauthorized users. Unfortunately, in your organization, the IT manager has resigned and was not very thorough about documenting these passwords.

When a CMOS setup utility has been password protected and its password has been subsequently lost, the typical way to clear the password is to shunt a jumper on the motherboard that clears either the password or the entire contents of CMOS.

✔ Cross-Reference

For further information, refer to the "Clearing CMOS" section in Chapter 5 of *Mike Meyers' A+ Guide to Managing and Troubleshooting PCs.*

Learning Objectives

In this lab, you'll learn how to configure CMOS setup utility passwords and how to clear the contents of the password and CMOS using the onboard clear CMOS jumper.

At the end of this lab, you'll be able to

- Set a password using the CMOS setup utility

- Locate the clear CMOS jumper on the motherboard

- Clear passwords and CMOS settings using the clear CMOS jumper

Lab Materials and Setup

The materials you need for this lab are

- A working PC whose BIOS settings you have permission to change, with access to the clear CMOS jumper on the motherboard

- An anti-static mat/wrist strap

- A notepad

Getting Down to Business

In the following steps, you'll reboot your PC and access the CMOS setup program using the key combination you verified in Lab Exercise 5.02. You will then navigate to the password or security menu and configure a CMOS setup utility password. Then you'll verify the password by rebooting the machine and entering CMOS setup. Finally, you'll open up the case and reset the CMOS settings by physically shunting the clear CMOS jumper.

> ✖ **Warning**
>
> Any time you remove the cover from your PC, remember to follow all proper safety and ESD precautions.

Step 1   Reboot your system and use the appropriate key or key combination to enter the CMOS setup program.

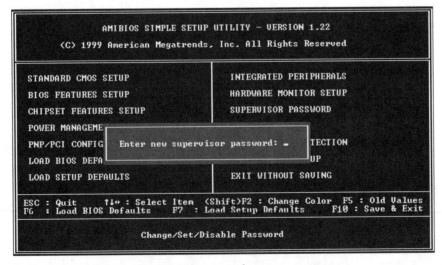

FIGURE 5-5 AMIBIOS supervisor password setup

Step 2 Once you've entered the CMOS setup program, navigate to the security or password menu (see Figure 5-5). Select the supervisor password and enter a four- to eight-character password. Save changes and exit CMOS setup.

Record your password here: _____

✔ **Hint**

Typically two types of passwords can be set in CMOS:

The *supervisor* password restricts access to the CMOS setup program so that only authorized personnel can change or modify BIOS settings. Organizations, especially schools, will usually configure a supervisor password to keep curious users from causing system errors.

The *user* or *system* password restricts access to the PC itself, and is required every time the system boots (before an operating system is even loaded). This type of password is often used when an individual's PC is located in a public area.

Step 3 Reboot the PC and press the key or key combination required to enter the CMOS setup program. If you completed Step 2 correctly, you should be prompted to enter a password. Enter the password you configured in Step 2 and press ENTER. The main menu of the CMOS setup program will appear.

Discard changes and exit the CMOS setup program.

✖ **Warning**

The next step will erase all CMOS settings! While you are in the CMOS setup program, take the time to write down important settings such as the CPU Soft menu settings, boot order, which integrated peripherals are enabled/disabled, and the Power Management Setup. While the system should run fine using the default settings, taking notes now will help you get back to any custom settings that may have been configured.

Step 4 Shut down the PC and unplug the power cord from the PC and the wall outlet. Remove the case from the PC and, referring to the PC or motherboard documentation, locate the clear CMOS jumper. Follow the instructions included with the documentation and move the jumper (see Figure 5-6) to clear the CMOS.

Step 5 Replace the PC case cover, plug the system back in, and start the system. Press the appropriate key(s) to enter the CMOS setup program.

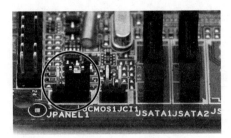

Figure 5-6 The clear CMOS jumper on a motherboard

Were you prompted for a password? _____

Do you need to configure any of the other settings? _____

 30 MINUTES

Lab Exercise 5.04: Configuring BIOS Settings

If you find any issues when you examine the BIOS settings using the CMOS setup program, you'll need to reconfigure the settings. Remember also that you're preparing the PC for an upgrade to Windows XP Professional. BIOS-level virus checking is known to cause problems with the Windows 2000/XP installation process, so Microsoft advises that you disable it.

Many BIOS functions are unchangeable—such as keyboard and floppy drive recognition—and are therefore inaccessible via the CMOS setup program. Other functions are under your control. These include the boot sequence order and the date/time setting, as mentioned previously, but also some potentially hazardous settings such as BIOS shadowing and memory timing.

✔ **Hint**

If you're not absolutely certain what a particular setting does, the best course of action is to leave it alone! If you have any doubts, you can always exit the CMOS setup program without saving.

Learning Objectives

In this exercise, you'll access the CMOS setup utility and navigate through to find the various BIOS settings you would commonly need to modify, and practice disabling BIOS-level virus checking.

At the end of this lab, you'll be able to

- Modify the settings in BIOS

Lab Materials and Setup

The materials you need for this lab are

- A working PC whose BIOS settings you have permission to change

- If possible, a BIOS that includes virus checking

Getting Down to Business

In the following steps, you'll learn to navigate to the CMOS setup program configuration screen that includes the virus-checking option. This example uses the Award BIOS CMOS setup program. Your CMOS setup program may vary, but all BIOS makers and versions should offer the same option.

✔ Cross-Reference

For more details about the features of CMOS setup programs, refer to the section called "A Quick Tour Through a Typical CMOS Setup Program" in Chapter 5 of *Mike Meyers' A+ Guide to Managing and Troubleshooting PCs.*

Step 1   Enter your CMOS setup program using the steps you learned in Lab Exercise 5.02.

Step 2   Check your notes and navigate to the configuration screen that has the BIOS-level virus-checking option. It's not always obvious where to find this option. For example, the Award BIOS CMOS setup program screen shown in Figure 5-4 doesn't give any hints about where to find the correct screen. As Figure 5-7

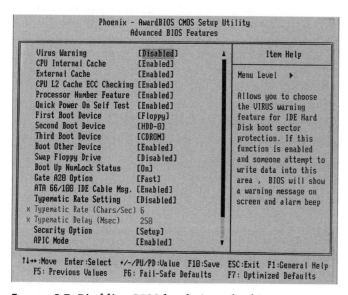

FIGURE 5-7 Disabling BIOS-level virus checking

shows, virus checking can be disabled in this BIOS from the Advanced BIOS Features screen. Don't hesitate to explore.

Step 3   Follow the screen prompts to navigate to the correct configuration screen and find the virus-checking setting option. Highlight the option (either using the arrow keys or mouse), and change it from Enabled to Disabled. Once again, your CMOS setup program's wording or appearance may be different, but the option to control BIOS-level virus checking should be common to all modern types of BIOS.

Step 4   Save and exit the CMOS setup program. After you exit, the system will reboot automatically. You have just made a change to BIOS.

The process you just followed is the same process you'll use for any changes you make to BIOS. Be sure to save the settings before exiting the setup utility.

Lab Analysis Test

1.   Katherine has noticed recently that when she boots her system, it displays a CMOS Mismatch message. What could be the problem?

2.   After running Windows XP for a few years, Chris has decided to perform a clean install of Windows 2000. After backing up his important files, he places the Windows 2000 CD in the CD-ROM drive and reboots his machine—but it just boots into Windows XP like normal. What setting will he most likely need to configure in the BIOS to correct this situation?

3.   Arnold has just installed a new sound card. He boots his system to install the drivers, but his system does not recognize the new card. What BIOS settings might he change using CMOS setup?

4.   Alex has just finished making changes to the BIOS-level virus checking and would now like to save these changes. Name two ways to save BIOS settings after making changes in the CMOS setup program.

5.   Ryan is working on an older Pentium II system. What key or keys should he press to enter the CMOS setup program?

Key Term Quiz

Use the following vocabulary terms to complete the following sentences. Not all terms will be used.

AMI

Award Software

BIOS (basic input/output services)

BIOS ROM

CMOS (complementary metal-oxide semiconductor)

CMOS setup program

DELETE key

PAUSE/BREAK key

Phoenix Technologies

1. The system BIOS is stored on non-volatile memory called _____.

2. Technicians configure the BIOS using the _____.

3. Press the _____ to suspend operation of the POST.

4. _____ provides the primary interface between the operating system's device drivers and most of the system's hardware.

5. A common way to enter CMOS setup is to press the _____ during startup.

Chapter 6

Expansion Bus

Lab Exercises

One of the many reasons that PCs are so useful is their amazing versatility. Modern PCs support a wide array of peripheral devices and attachments that expand their capabilities and boost performance. Peripherals attach to the PC via the expansion bus.

The expansion bus is the pathway that enables you to plug new devices and device controllers into the motherboard. This pathway can be split up into two groups: the internal expansion bus and the external expansion bus.

The internal expansion bus includes the Peripheral Component Interconnect (PCI) bus, Accelerated Graphics Port (AGP) bus, the PCI Express (PCIe) bus, and on older systems, the Industry Standard Architecture (ISA) bus. Other, specialized internal buses, such as Audio/Modem Riser (AMR) and Communication Network Riser (CNR), also pop up on some systems. The external expansion bus includes the Universal Serial Bus (USB) and the IEEE 1394 (FireWire) bus. You'll explore the external expansion bus in great detail when you work through the lab exercises for Chapter 16.

In these lab exercises, you'll learn how to determine which expansion slots are available in a system, and how to install and remove expansion cards properly. This will help you gain confidence in handling expansion card issues in the real world.

For the purposes of this chapter, suppose that you've befriended the owner of a small Internet café. Currently, the café has 12 PCs of various makes and models, all running Windows XP Professional. Paul, the owner, wanted the systems to perform well, so he ensured that each system had at least a 2.8-GHz processor and 512 MB of memory. In an attempt to keep the initial cost under budget, however, he purchased the systems without upgraded graphics or sound, so they are using the on-board graphics and sound.

Paul has noticed that many of the patrons seem to be using the systems to play games against each other in addition to the normal Internet surfing. Some of them have asked if there's any way to improve the performance of the systems so that they can play more advanced games. Paul has been thinking of branching off into hosting LAN parties anyway, so he asks you to look into what it will take to upgrade the machines.

You would enjoy recommending that Paul buy new PCs with the latest high-performance components—what tech wouldn't want to play with the latest and greatest tech toys?—but since the machines are fairly new and well appointed, you decide to experiment with some upgrades. Because PC games are graphics- and sound-intensive, you believe that installing individual cards, such as an AGP or PCIe graphics card and a PCI sound card, will improve the overall performance. You begin by assessing what expansion slots (PCI, AGP, and/or PCIe) are available on the current machines. You ask Paul for some cash up front, and choose two of the machines to test your theory.

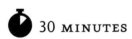 30 MINUTES

Lab Exercise 6.01: Identifying Internal Expansion Slots

Unless you've got X-ray vision, the best way to examine the expansion slots is to remove the PC case cover. In this exercise, you'll identify the type of expansion slots on your disassembled system, your working system, and as many systems (or motherboards) as you're authorized to examine. Does your system use a PCI Express (PCIe), AGP, or PCI graphics card, or does it use on-board video as in our lab scenario? Check to see how many other expansion slots are available for adding a sound card and (if required) upgrading the graphics adapter.

✖ Warning

Remember to use proper safety and electrostatic discharge (ESD) procedures when working inside the PC case.

Learning Objectives

In this exercise, you'll properly identify expansion slots and the basic features of each type of expansion technology.

At the end of this lab, you'll be able to

- Identify legacy ISA expansion bus slots and component cards
- Identify PCI expansion bus slots and component cards
- Identify the AGP expansion bus slot and video card
- Identify PCIe ×1 and PCIe ×16 expansion bus slots and component cards

Lab Materials and Setup

The non-production, disassembled PC and the working PC are adequate for this exercise, but it's more beneficial to be able to see motherboards inside different systems.

The materials you need for this lab are

- Your non-production, disassembled PC
- A working PC (or more than one if possible)
- An anti-static mat
- A notepad
- Some sample motherboards (optional)

Getting Down to Business

Start with the disassembled PC. Since the only components you have reinserted are the CPU and RAM, you should have a very clear view of the expansion bus slots and connections. You should also locate any expansion cards you removed during disassembly to identify what functions they serve. If the motherboard is still removed from the case, place it on the anti-static mat for exploration. If you have installed the motherboard into the case, lay the case down on the anti-static mat and follow all ESD precautions.

After completing the steps using the tear-down machine, switch over to your working PC. Shut down your PC and unplug it from the wall. Place it on your anti-static mat, remove the PC case cover, and take a good look inside. Your aim is to determine what type of expansion slots your motherboard has, and what peripheral card components are currently installed.

Step 1 If you acquired an older system to disassemble, you may find some old expansion bus slot types on the motherboard. Check to see if you have any ISA expansion slots; a few legacy systems with 16-bit ISA expansion slots are still in use today. Here are the physical characteristics of ISA expansion slots:

- About five inches long

- Usually black in color

- Offset from the edge of the motherboard by about 1/2 inch

- Large metal contacts easily visible inside the slot

- Divided by a small gap into two parts: the 8-bit portion (about three inches long) and the 16-bit portion (one and a half inches long)

Figure 6-1 shows ISA slots alongside other types of slots on a motherboard.

Record the following information, as applicable:

How many ISA slots are on your motherboard? _____

What ISA devices are installed on your system? _____

How many ISA slots are empty? _____

Step 2 The next type of expansion slot you'll explore is the 32-bit PCI bus. This technology has had a long run as the most common type of expansion slot on modern PCs, though it is expected to be eclipsed by PCIe on desktop systems. Here are the physical characteristics of PCI expansion slots:

- About three inches long

- Usually white in color (modern motherboards may use bright colors like yellow or green to enhance the visual appeal of the motherboard)

- Offset from the edge of the motherboard by about one inch

FIGURE 6-1 A group of three ISA slots, at the lower right

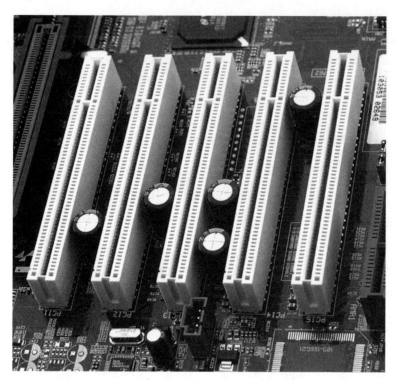

Figure 6-2 A group of PCI slots

Figure 6-2 shows PCI slots on a modern motherboard.

Record the following information:

How many PCI slots are on your motherboard? _____

What PCI devices are installed on your system? _____

How many PCI slots are empty? _____

Step 3   Now locate the 32-bit AGP slot. As the name suggests, the AGP slot is used for one component only—the graphics adapter. Here are the physical characteristics of the AGP slot:

- One slot per motherboard

- A little less than three inches long

- Usually brown in color

- Offset from the edge of the motherboard by about two inches

Figure 6-3 shows an AGP slot in its natural habitat.

Record the following information:

Is there an AGP video card slot on your motherboard? _____

What can you tell about the type and brand of video card without removing it? _____

FIGURE 6-3 An AGP slot

Step 4   Take a look at your motherboard and see if there are any PCIe ×1 or PCIe ×16 slot connectors. These are fairly new (circa 2004), so you may not see them on all of the motherboards you are exploring. PCI Express is very interesting, offering a theoretical throughput of 2.5 Gbps per lane and supporting from 1 to 32 lanes. The first devices to really take advantage of PCIe are graphics cards using the 16-lane configuration. The physical characteristics of the PCIe expansion slots depend on the number of lanes.

PCIe ×1 slots have the following characteristics:

- About one inch long

- Often brightly colored (blue and white being fairly common)

- Offset from the edge of the motherboard by about 1.25 inches

PCIe ×16 slots have the following characteristics:

- About 3.5 inches long

- Often brightly colored (blue and white being fairly common)

- Offset from the edge of the motherboard by about 1.25 inches

Figure 6-4 shows PCIe slots on a modern motherboard.

Record the following information:

Are there any PCIe slots on your motherboard? _____

If yes, how many PCIe ×1 slots are there? _____

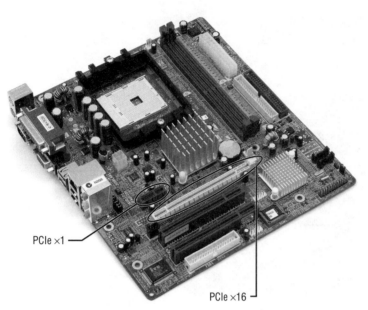

PCIe ×1

PCIe ×16

FIGURE 6-4 A motherboard with both PCIe ×1 and PCIe ×16 expansion slots

How many PCIe ×16 slots are there? _____

Are there any PCIe cards installed in the system? _____

✔ **Cross-Reference**

For more detail about the PCI, AGP, and PCIe buses, refer to the "PCI" section in Chapter 6 of *Mike Meyers' A+ Guide to Managing and Troubleshooting PCs*.

After you've completed your inventory of installed expansion bus devices, put the case cover back on your PC, plug it back in, and restart the system.

 30 MINUTES

Lab Exercise 6.02: Understanding System Resources

The typical modern PC has many component devices installed: video cards, sound cards, modems, NICs, and controller cards (such as SCSI controllers, SATA controllers, and so on), not to mention the built-in devices such as IDE and floppy disk drive controllers. As amazing as it seems, a PC's CPU only talks to one device at a time. This means that at any given time, one device has exclusive access to the CPU. Of course, this happens so quickly that it seems like the CPU is addressing multiple components all at once. The PC keeps track of which device is which through *system resources*, the collective term for device settings such as input/output (I/O) addresses, interrupt requests (IRQs), direct memory access (DMA) channels, and memory address settings.

On modern PCs, Plug and Play (PnP) handles all of the details about assigning system resources to devices, but this doesn't mean that you can always leave it up to the system! Even as sophisticated as PnP is, things don't always work as they're supposed to—especially if you're mixing old, non-PnP devices with newer PnP devices. Therefore, it's important for techs to know how to identify a device's system resources and, when necessary, manually configure them.

In the old days, configuring device resources meant setting jumpers and DIP switches on the device and running a setup program supplied by the device maker. If you're using very old, non-PnP devices, this is still the case—but on modern PnP devices, all resource configuration is handled from within the Windows OS. Let's look now at how to determine and configure your component devices' system resource settings.

✔ **Cross-Reference**

If you need a refresher on system resources, refer to the "System Resources" section in Chapter 6 of *Mike Meyers' A+ Guide to Managing and Troubleshooting PCs*.

Learning Objectives

In this lab, you'll reinforce your knowledge of system resources.

At the end of this lab, you'll be able to

- Use the Device Manager to examine devices and determine what IRQs and I/O addresses are allocated to a given device

- Define the rules of assigning IRQs and I/O addresses

- State the default IRQ and I/O assignments for some common devices

Lab Materials and Setup

The materials you need for this lab are

- A working computer running Windows

✔ **Hint**

As usual, if you have access to more than one system, take advantage of it.

FIGURE 6-5 Device Manager in Windows XP

Getting Down to Business

In this exercise, you'll use the Windows Device Manager to view the system resource settings on your PC.

Step 1   Open the Windows Control Panel and double-click the icon for the System applet. Note that you can also access this applet by pressing the Windows key and the PAUSE/BREAK key at the same time.

On Windows 2000/XP systems, select the Hardware tab and then click the Device Manager button; this brings up the Device Manager in a separate window (see Figure 6-5).

Step 2   The Device Manager shows you at a glance all of your system's IRQ, I/O, DMA, and memory address settings for each device. In Windows 2000/XP, select View | Resources by type, and then expand the node for the resource type that you want to investigate (see Figure 6-6).

Step 3   Select the option to view the input/output (I/O) settings on your system. Scroll down the list to review and locate the addresses to answer these questions:

What is the address for the keyboard?

_____

What is the address for the printer port (LPT1)?

_____

FIGURE 6-6 Viewing system resources

What is the address for the real time clock?

_____

What is the address for the communications port (COM1)?

_____

What is the address for the system timer?

_____

✔ **Hint**

On many new systems, the COM ports, LPT ports, and floppy drive are optional. The resources that were traditionally assigned to these devices may not be displayed in the Device Manager.

Step 4 Repeat Steps 1–3, this time looking at the IRQ settings.

Does your system use IRQ 14? _____

What device uses IRQ 14? _____

Step 5 Most seasoned techs (also known simply as *old folks*) know what the default system resource settings are for COM and LPT ports. Compare the COM and LPT settings in the following table to the settings on your system. Does your system list entries for all four devices? _____

Port	I/O Address	IRQ
COM1	3F8	4
COM2	2F8	3
LPT1	378	7
LPT2	278	5

 30 MINUTES

Lab Exercise 6.03: Installing Expansion Cards

There are five steps to installing any expansion card device properly:

1. Arm yourself with knowledge of the device before you install it. Is the device certified to run on the Windows OS that you're running? Is it compatible with your motherboard and other hardware? Be sure to check the Windows Marketplace, formerly known as the Hardware Compatibility List (HCL), before you do anything. The Windows Marketplace (found at http://testedproducts.windowsmarketplace.com) is the definitive authority on which devices are guaranteed to work on modern Windows operating systems.

2. Remove the cover from your PC case and install the device. As always, follow all ESD and safety precautions, and handle the card with care.

3. Assign system resources to the device. In approximately 99.73 percent of cases (a rough estimate), you'll never have to do this because PnP takes care of it for you, but if you're mixing old components with new, then you may have to assign resources manually to accommodate the old, non-PnP device.

4. Install device drivers for the component. Windows comes with many device drivers preinstalled, so it may try to help you by installing the driver that it thinks the device needs. In most cases, you should visit the card manufacturer's Web site, download the latest drivers for the card and your operating system, and then install the updated drivers.

5. Verify that the device is functional and that it's not creating any conflicts with other devices on your system.

The following exercise is a somewhat abridged version of this procedure; instead of installing a new device, you'll remove and reinstall devices that are already on your system.

✔ **Cross-Reference**

To review the details of device installation, refer to the "Installing Expansion Cards" section in Chapter 6 of *Mike Meyers' A+ Guide to Managing and Troubleshooting PCs*.

Learning Objectives

In this lab, you'll practice removing and installing internal expansion cards.

At the end of this lab, you'll be able to

- Safely remove and install expansion cards in a system

Lab Materials and Setup

The materials you need for this lab are

- At least one working Windows computer with expansion cards installed

- Phillips-head screwdriver

- Anti-static mat and wrist strap

- Anti-static storage bags

- Notepad

✔ **Hint**

As usual, if you have access to more than one system, take advantage of it—with one exception. You may be asking yourself, "Hey, how come I'm not reinstalling the cards into this disassembled PC I have sitting here?" That's a very good question!

In the next chapter, you'll be practicing removing the motherboard from the case and reinstalling it. This process would be complicated by having a card or two sticking out of the motherboard. After you complete your practice on the motherboard, you can check back with this chapter and reinstall the expansion cards in the disassembled PC.

Getting Down to Business

In this exercise, you'll physically remove expansion card devices from your PC. You'll then make note of any important information you can find on the device's label: device maker, version, and so on. You will then visit the manufacturer's Web site to check for any updated drivers for the device in your version of Windows. Finally, you'll reassemble and restart the system and install the updated drivers.

Shut down the system and unplug the power cable, and then place it on your anti-static mat. Remove the PC case cover and strap on your anti-static wrist strap, and you're ready to start.

Step 1   Check your notes from Lab Exercise 6.01 and draw a sketch showing which device is installed in which slot on the motherboard (assuming that you are using the same working machine from Lab Exercise 6.01).

Step 2   Remove the cards one at a time from your system. For each card, follow these procedures:

a) Remove the retaining screw and store it safely.

✔ **Hint**

You'll see two main types of screws used in PCs. At first glance, they may look all the same, but while these screws are the same overall size, they have different sizes of threads. Screws with the larger threads, commonly called *coarse-threaded* screws, are generally used to secure expansion cards, power supplies, and case covers. Screws with the smaller threads, commonly called *fine-threaded* screws, are typically used to secure storage devices such as hard drives, floppy disk drives, and CD media drives into their respective bays.

b) Taking hold of the card by its edges, carefully and firmly pull it straight up and out of its slot.

✔ **Hint**

These cards can be difficult to remove. If a card seems stuck, try rocking it back and forth (from front to back in the direction of the slot, not side to side).

c) Holding the card only by the edges and the metal flange, place it in an anti-static bag for safe-keeping.

Step 3   Examine each of the cards you removed from your system and record the pertinent information.

- Do any of the cards have writing or labels on them? If so, what information do these labels provide?

- Can you identify the manufacturers of the cards? List each card with its manufacturer.

- Are there any version numbers or codes on the cards? List this information for each card.

- If there are any jumpers or DIP switches on any of the cards, how are they set? You might want to make a quick drawing of the switches and their current positions.

- Can you locate a key or legend that shows you how to set the jumpers or DIP switches? If so, make a note about where you found this information—was it in the instruction manual, or perhaps printed directly on the expansion card circuit board?

Step 4 Reinstall the expansion cards you removed into your system. For each card, follow these procedures:

a) Check your notes to confirm where to reinstall the card.

b) Align the card over its motherboard slot, making sure that the metal flange is aligned properly with the case slot. Holding the flange with one hand, place the heel of your hand on the top edge of the card and push the card firmly into the expansion slot.

c) Once the card is in the slot and the flange is flush with the case, replace the screw that holds the card in place. Don't be tempted to skip the screw! It keeps the card properly grounded and prevents it from working loose over time.

✖ Warning

After all of the expansion cards have been reinstalled, take a look at the back of your system (where you can see input/output connections for the cards). Are there any holes where no cards are installed and a slot cover has not been used? It's very important to install slot covers wherever an expansion card is not installed. This ensures that air will flow properly through the computer case, keeping your critical components cool.

Step 5 Restart your PC and use Device Manager to confirm that each device is working properly. If there is a missing driver, you'll see a yellow circle with a black exclamation point next to the device listing. If there is a resource conflict, the problem device will be disabled and a red X will appear next to its listing.

Step 6 Now download and install the latest device drivers for each of your expansion cards. There are many methods you can use to accomplish this task, but the two that follow are the most common.

- If your working PC is connected to the Internet, you can use the Update Driver Wizard from the device's Driver tab in Device Manager to connect to the Windows Update Web site. Open Device Manager and select *View device by type*. Locate the device that matches the expansion card you have installed, and open its properties. Select the Driver tab, and then click Update Driver as shown in Figure 6-7. This brings up the Hardware Update Wizard, as shown in Figure 6-8; from here you can follow the directions to download the signed driver from the Windows Update site.

- If your working PC is not connected to the Internet, or the device does not have a signed driver available on the Windows Update site, you will have to follow these instructions before clicking Update Driver. Using a computer with Internet access, find and connect to the manufacturer's Web site. Using the model number of the device, locate and download the correct driver for the operating system on the PC where the device is installed. Save the driver to a floppy disk or USB thumb drive, remove the floppy or thumb drive from that system, and

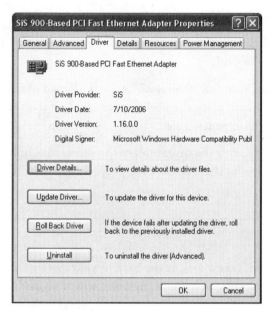

FIGURE 6-7 The Driver tab from the device properties in Windows

insert it into your working PC. Open Device Manager and select *View device by type*. Locate the device that matches the expansion card you have installed, and open its properties. Select the Driver tab, and then click Update Driver. When prompted to connect to the Internet, choose "No, Not this time," and follow the directions to locate and load the new device driver (see Figure 6-9).

FIGURE 6-8 Accessing the Windows Update site

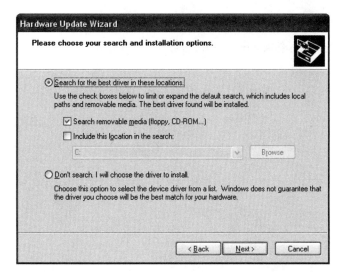

Figure 6-9 The Hardware Update Wizard finding device drivers on removable media

---

✔ **Hint**

Many manufacturers include installation wizards for their devices, so this is yet another method that you can use to update device drivers. Many times, the manufacturer will include related applications along with the drivers to enhance the performance of the device. A good example of this is an inkjet printer that includes the driver and utilities for adjusting print quality, performing printer maintenance, and so on.

Lab Analysis Test

1. When you examined the two machines from the Internet café, you were very pleased to find that one of them had a PCIe ×16 expansion slot. What is the advantage of the PCIe expansion bus, and how will it contribute to providing a solution at the Internet café?

2. John has a system that runs at 3.2 GHz and uses a 128-MB AGP video card. He uses Windows XP Professional and wants to try its multiple-monitor support feature. Can he add another AGP video card?

3. You've installed a NIC and a PCI FireWire controller card on Susan's Windows XP Professional system. The system starts up fine, but when you check Device Manager, you see a yellow circle with a black exclamation mark beside the NIC icon. What is the problem?

4. Given the scenario in the preceding question, what steps should you take to rectify the problem?

5. Tim has installed a PCIe 10-GB NIC. He boots the machine and navigates to Device Manager, only to find a red X icon next to this device. What should Tim do next?

Key Term Quiz

Use the following vocabulary terms to complete the following sentences. Not all terms will be used.

AGP

device drivers

DMA

expansion card

I/O address

IRQ

ISA

PCI

PCIe

system resources

memory address

1. Most current motherboards continue to provide several _____ slots.

2. Many video cards use the dedicated _____ slot.

3. The settings for I/O addresses and IRQs have pretty much become automated with the introduction of PnP. These, along with DMA and memory addresses, are collectively known as _____.

4. The _____ bus provides for ×1, ×2, ×4, ×8, ×16, and ×32 lanes of bidirectional communication.

5. The Hardware Update Wizard makes it easy to update the _____ for a device.

Chapter 7
Motherboards

Lab Exercises

With all due respect to the CPU, system RAM, power supply, hard drive, and all the other sundry pieces of a typical PC, the motherboard is the real workhorse of the system. Every component on the PC plugs into the motherboard either directly or indirectly. Every bit and byte of data that moves between devices passes through the motherboard's sockets and traces. The motherboard is what brings all of the individual parts of the PC into a working whole. As such, replacing a motherboard is one of the most challenging tasks a PC tech will face. Luckily, only a couple of circumstances require you to undertake this chore. The first, of course, is when the motherboard malfunctions or is damaged; modern motherboards aren't made to be repaired, so when they go bad, they must be replaced as a whole unit. The other is when you want to upgrade the PC to a more powerful CPU than its current motherboard supports.

In either of these cases, you've got a bit of work ahead of you! Installing a motherboard requires more effort than any other type of installation—more preparation, more time performing the installation, and more cleanup afterward. Still, you shouldn't be intimidated by the prospect of replacing a motherboard—it's a common and necessary part of PC repair. In this chapter, you'll go through the process from end to end.

In the following lab exercises, you'll make preparations for a motherboard installation, including identifying the proper motherboard form factor, labeling cables and connectors, and removing the motherboard from a working PC. You'll then write down notes about key motherboard features, and finally you'll reinstall the motherboard.

 30 MINUTES

Lab Exercise 7.01: Identifying Motherboard Form Factors

You're consulting for a small graphics firm that's upgrading its PCs to accommodate a major software upgrade and network restructuring. While assessing the company's PC stock, you discover that a number of their systems lack sufficient CPU power to run an important new CAD program. To remedy this, you must replace the motherboards of these systems with models that support newer and faster CPUs.

To determine which of your client's systems need upgrading for the new CAD software, you have to be comfortable identifying motherboard types. If your client has any of the old AT-style motherboards, these were phased out around the time of the Intel Pentium II and the early AMD Athlon processors. Not only should the motherboards in these systems be retired, the systems themselves should be retired! These systems will not have the same form factor needed by the ATX-style motherboard, so you would need to replace the case, power supply, CPU, and system RAM. You most likely will need newer hard drives, keyboard, and mouse—pretty much the whole system.

Current PC motherboards come in a few different styles, or *form factors*: ATX, microATX and Flex-ATX, BTX (Balanced Technology eXtended), and proprietary form factors from companies such as Dell and Sony. ATX motherboards are what you find in most PCs on the market.

Your first task when replacing motherboards is to determine which form factor each PC requires. ATX, microATX, and FlexATX are all in the same family, so the main consideration is which PC case you're using. The FlexATX is physically the smallest in size, the microATX is in the middle, and the ATX is the largest. Typically, all three will work in the large ATX case because all three variations retain the same form factor for the external connections.

You may see some BTX motherboards on newer machines. These are essentially the same components rearranged for better cooling, but this form factor requires a BTX case, so it is not interchangeable with ATX. As of this writing, it remains to be seen whether BTX will become the new popular design or fade into obscurity.

Proprietary motherboards tend to be difficult to upgrade. The components usually need to be purchased directly from the manufacturer, so those components are less readily available and often more expensive.

Learning Objectives

In this lab, you'll become familiar with different motherboard layouts.

At the end of this lab, you'll be able to

- Recognize different motherboard form factors
- Understand considerations for upgrading a system with a newer motherboard

Lab Materials and Setup

The materials you need for this lab are

- The disassembled, non-production PC computer system used in the lab exercises in Chapter 2

- If possible, various systems with ATX, microATX, and FlexATX motherboards

- Anti-static mat

- Anti-static wrist strap

✔ **Hint**

As usual, if you have access to multiple systems, take advantage of it. It's most useful to have a variety of motherboards to study.

Getting Down to Business

To start, you will review the main features and characteristics of the ATX family of motherboards. Though the overall size of the ATX family of motherboards varies, the features and characteristics remain relatively standard. You will then examine the motherboard from your disassembled machine to determine what type of motherboard is installed.

✔ **Hint**

If you determine that the disassembled machine is using an AT form factor motherboard, you will still be able to use it for assembly/disassembly lab exercises. Be careful when working with the AT form factor P8/P9 power connectors—make sure you install them correctly (with the black wires closest to the center when connected to the motherboard) or you will fry the motherboard. The AT form factor motherboard is not the best choice for reviewing current motherboard features and characteristics. If possible, locate a system with an ATX motherboard that you are authorized to explore. No matter which machine you explore, disconnect the power cable from the wall and the case, place the machine or the motherboard on your anti-static mat, and then perform the following steps.

✔ **Cross-Reference**

To refresh your recognition of motherboard types, refer to the "ATX Form Factor," "BTX Form Factor," and "Proprietary Form Factors" sections in Chapter 7 of *Mike Meyers' A+ Guide to Managing and Troubleshooting PCs*.

FIGURE 7-1 Connections on a current PC with an ATX motherboard

Step 1 Answer the following questions, referring back to the textbook chapter as needed:

- What are some of the characteristics that define the ATX motherboard?

- What is the physical size difference between the ATX motherboard, a microATX motherboard, and a FlexATX motherboard?

- Can you replace a full ATX motherboard with a FlexATX motherboard?

Step 2 Look on the back of your PC to find the panel of external motherboard connectors (see Figure 7-1) to answer the following questions.

- What external connections are available?

- Does your PC use a mini-DIN (PS/2) connector for the keyboard and mouse, or does it make the assumption that you'll use a USB keyboard and mouse?

- Based on the answers to the preceding questions, what can you tell about the type of motherboard your PC uses?

Step 3 Remove the case cover from your PC and view the motherboard (see Figure 7-2) to answer the following questions:

- What power connections are present?

- What expansion slots are supported?

- What CPU socket and chipset are used on this motherboard?

- Based on the answers to the preceding questions, what can you tell about the type of motherboard your PC uses?

If you have used a PC other than the disassembled machine, replace the PC case cover, but since the next lab exercise requires you to access the inside of your PC case, leave it unplugged and turned off.

FIGURE 7-2 High-end motherboard

 15 MINUTES

Lab Exercise 7.02: Removing and Labeling Components and Cables

Once you've selected those of your client's systems that will need new motherboards, you can't just rip the old ones out. To get to the motherboard, you have to first remove the installed expansion cards and cables. Many of us have had the experience of taking something apart only to wind up with leftover parts after we put it back together. To avoid this result when you disassemble a PC, you should get into the habit of properly storing and labeling any parts that you remove from the system. This includes everything from the major components to the screws that hold them in place and the cables that connect them to the motherboard.

✔ **Hint**

If you are using the disassembled non-production machine for this lab, you have already removed and organized the components and cables from the machine. Use this step to review the labeling and storage of components and cables in preparation for removal and installation of the motherboard. If you are using a second machine for this exercise, make use of this lab to build the "good habit" of organization. Of course, you don't need to attach a label to each individual screw, but do keep them organized in labeled containers to avoid confusion!

Learning Objectives

In this lab, you'll remove and label expansion card components, cables, and connectors in preparation for removing the motherboard.

At the end of this lab, you'll be able to

- Remove and label expansion cards

- Remove and label data cables and connectors

- Remove and label power cables

Lab Materials and Setup

The materials you need for this lab are

- A working computer

- The motherboard book or online documentation for the motherboard

- Sticky notes and a pen

- Screwdriver

- Anti-static mat

- Anti-static wrist strap

- Anti-static bags

Getting Down to Business

Starting with your system shut down (and as always, the power cable unplugged from the wall and the case), set your system on the anti-static mat, remove the PC case cover, and strap on your anti-static wrist strap. Have your labeling materials handy and perform the following steps.

Step 1   Following the procedure laid out in Lab Exercise 6.03 in the previous chapter, remove any expansion cards from the PC. Label each one with a sticky note that identifies the card, and store it in an anti-static bag.

Step 2 Disconnect and label the following data cables:

- Hard drive cables
- CD- or DVD-media drive cables
- Floppy drive cable
- Sound cable (runs from the CD- or DVD-media drive to the sound card)
- USB front panel connector dongle (if applicable)

Step 3 Disconnect and label the following power cables:

- Hard drive cables
- CD- or DVD-media drive cables
- Floppy drive cable
- Power plugs for CPU fan, power supply fan (if present), and case fan (if present)
- Motherboard power (P1 or P4 on ATX motherboards)

Step 4 Disconnect and label the front panel control wires (also called the *harness wires*) from the motherboard. Be certain to use the motherboard book to properly label these wires! Front panel control wires typically include the power button (on ATX motherboards), reset button, front panel LEDs (power, hard disk activity, and so on), and system speaker.

✔ Hint

To label wires, use small sticky notes, or cut the square ones into strips. Fold the sticky part of the sticky note over the wire and stick it to the back to make a tag you can write on.

Step 5 Depending on your system, you may have to remove other devices to ensure that you have sufficient clearance to lift the motherboard out of the PC case in the next exercise. Visually confirm that there aren't any components blocking a path for easy removal. Are any hard drives or CD- or DVD-media drives in the way? Is the power supply in the way? Remove anything that could block the motherboard's exit or bump into important attached components (namely the RAM or CPU fan) during removal.

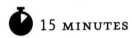 15 MINUTES

Lab Exercise 7.03: Removing a Motherboard

With all of your PC components and cables safely tucked away, the next step in your upgrade job is to remove the old motherboards so that you can replace them. Techs will tell you that motherboard removal is the exercise that separates the geek from the meek and the true PC tech from the wannabe, but don't let that intimidate you! Motherboard removal is completely straightforward and simple.

Once again, if you're using the disassembled non-production machine, you have already removed the motherboard from the case, but you should use this exercise to review. If you're using a different machine for this exercise, follow the instructions.

Learning Objectives

In this lab, you'll remove your PC's motherboard.

At the end of this lab, you'll be able to

- Remove a motherboard safely and correctly

Lab Materials and Setup

The materials you need for this lab are

- The working computer on which you performed Lab Exercise 7.02
- Phillips-head screwdriver
- Anti-static mat and anti-static wrist strap
- Large anti-static bag

Getting Down to Business

Following the same ESD procedures listed in the previous exercises, you'll now remove the mounting screws for the motherboard and lift it out of the PC case.

Step 1 Locate and remove the screws holding the motherboard to the frame of the case. There are most likely six to nine screws, which may also have small washers. Be sure not to lose these washers because they help prevent over-tightening the screws during installation. Some systems may use small plastic or metal supports called *standoffs* between the motherboard and the frame. Remove these and store them in a labeled container.

✖ **Warning**

Remember to handle the motherboard as you would any printed circuit board: gently, by the edges, as if you were holding a delicate old photograph.

Step 2 Carefully remove the motherboard from the PC case and place it on your anti-static mat. You should place the motherboard in a large anti-static bag for the best protection.

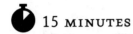 15 MINUTES

Lab Exercise 7.04: Identifying Motherboard Features

At a glance, one motherboard pretty much looks like another. Of course, as a PC tech, you know that this isn't true: Two identical-looking motherboards can easily have completely different feature sets. Chipsets, bus speed, CPU socket type, and clock speed are just some of the important features that separate one motherboard from another. These differences don't always make themselves obvious, but you can turn to your motherboard book to identify your motherboard's features, as described in the following steps.

Learning Objectives

In this lab, you'll become familiar with different motherboard features.

At the end of this lab, you'll be able to

- Recognize different motherboard features
- Identify the location of motherboard features

Lab Materials and Setup

The materials you need for this lab are

- A motherboard, such as the one you removed in Lab Exercise 7.03
- The motherboard book or online documentation for that motherboard

Getting Down to Business

In the following steps, you'll identify the location of key features on your motherboard.

> ✔ **Hint**
>
> If you're using the motherboard you removed in the previous lab, take this opportunity to clean any dust off of it using canned air before you begin.

Step 1 Note the location of the make and model information on the motherboards in Figure 7-3. Compare this to your motherboard and locate the manufacturer name and model number.

> ✔ **Cross-Reference**
>
> For details on chipsets, refer to the "Chipset" section in Chapter 7 of *Mike Meyers' A+ Guide to Managing and Troubleshooting PCs.*

FIGURE 7-3 Two examples of model number information printed on motherboards

What is the name of your motherboard manufacturer?

_____

What is the model number of your motherboard?

_____

What CPU socket do you have on your motherboard?

_____

What type of chipset do you have on your motherboard?

_____

Keep this information handy! Having the make and model of your motherboard readily available makes it easy to search the Web for drivers and updated BIOS.

Step 2   Look for any charts or numbers printed on the surface of the motherboard.

Are there any jumper blocks? _____

What are some of the settings that can be configured using jumpers?

_____

_____

_____

Step 3   Locate the following on your motherboard:

- System clock battery
- BIOS
- RAM slots (What type? Dual-channel support?)
- SATA or RAID (if present)
- Graphics adapter support (onboard, PCI, AGP, PCIe?)

 30 MINUTES

Lab Exercise 7.05: Installing a Motherboard

Now that you've removed the old inadequate motherboards from your client's systems, you get to the real test of your tech skills: installing the new motherboards and reconnecting everything so that the computers work! Once again, however, there's no need to be intimidated. Everything you need to install a motherboard (in your case, probably the motherboard you just removed in Lab Exercise 7.03) is right in front of you.

Learning Objectives

In this lab, you'll install a motherboard. You can use the motherboard and system you disassembled in Lab Exercise 7.03.

At the end of this lab, you'll be able to

- Install a PC motherboard and connect all of its associated components

Lab Materials and Setup

The materials you need for this lab are

- The disassembled, non-production PC computer system used in the lab exercises in Chapter 2
- A working system from which the motherboard has been removed
- Components and cables previously connected to the removed motherboard
- Motherboard book or online documentation for the motherboard
- Anti-static mat
- Anti-static wrist strap
- Notepad and pen

✔ **Hint**

When installing a motherboard, it's handy to use your notepad to check off assembly steps as you go along.

Getting Down to Business

Physically installing the motherboard itself is mostly a matter of being careful and methodical. The more complex part of the task is reattaching all the cables and cards in their proper places.

Over the last few labs, you have concentrated on hardware removal and installation, using either the disassembled non-production system or a working non-production system—or in some cases both. It is very easy to become casual or even careless about technique and organization since these machines are non-critical.

One of the really important concepts to remember is that all of these efforts—the studying, the labs, and the CompTIA A+ Certification itself—are designed to help you become the highest quality tech that you can be! It's very important that you develop and practice patience, attention to detail, and finesse while working through the lab exercises.

To this end, when you remove and replace a motherboard in a system, you interact with almost every component of the computer system. In the field, you must not only successfully disassemble/assemble the hardware, but also verify that the system powers up and operates properly afterward. Many competent techs, when installing a new motherboard, will check for proper operation along the way. Here's a good checkpoint: After you've installed the CPU and RAM, configured any jumpers or switches, and installed the motherboard in the case, insert the power connections and test the system. A POST card is a real timesaver here, but you can also connect the PC speaker, a graphics card, monitor, and a keyboard to verify that the system is booting properly.

✖ Warning

Motherboards are full of delicate electronics! Remember to follow the proper ESD and safety procedures.

Step 1 Carefully line up the motherboard inside the PC case and secure it in place with the mounting screws. Be sure to use the washers and plastic/metal standoffs, if supplied.

Step 2 Insert the front panel control wires in their appropriate places. These should include your power button (on ATX motherboards), reset button, front panel LEDs (power, hard disk activity, and so on), system speaker, and so on. Refer to the labels and your motherboard documentation for the proper connections.

✔ Hint

At this point, if you're working on the disassembled, non-production system, skip to Step 5, install the expansion cards, and then set the system aside. You will continue to build the disassembled system in future lab exercises where you will explore the power supply, hard drives, removable storage, and audio/video components.

Step 3   Connect all power cables to the hard drive, CD- or DVD-media drive, floppy drive, CPU fan, main motherboard, and so on.

Step 4   Connect data cables to the hard drive, CD- or DVD-media drive, and floppy drive, as well as the sound cable and USB connector dongles, if applicable.

Step 5   Following the procedure laid out in Lab Exercise 6.03 in the previous chapter, install the expansion card components.

Step 6   Now comes perhaps the most important step: Double-check all of your connections and cards to make sure that they're properly seated and connected where they're supposed to be! If something is wrong, it's definitely better to discover it now than to smell smoke after you've hit the power switch.

Step 7   Finally, if you're using the working PC you previously disassembled, you can now replace the case cover on your PC. Then plug the keyboard, mouse, and monitor back in, plug the power cable back in, and finally turn on the PC. Assuming you've done everything correctly, your system will boot up normally.

 15 MINUTES

Lab Exercise 7.06: Exploring Motherboard Features with CPU-Z

Now that you've completed the analysis and upgrade of your client's systems with new motherboards and CPUs where needed, you can verify some of the characteristics and features the motherboard manufacturer has promoted. You already downloaded the CPU-Z utility from the Internet, so you can launch that to examine the information on the Mainboard tab.

✔ **Hint**

Over the years, motherboards have been called many names—and not just the bad names you might use when one doesn't work properly! Early motherboards were sometimes called the *planar board*. A motherboard can be referred to as the *system board*, *mainboard*, and sometimes just *board* or *mobo*. Regardless of the name, these terms refer to the large printed circuit board (PCB) used to connect all of the components in a computer system.

Learning Objectives

In this lab, you'll identify various motherboard features.

At the end of this lab, you'll be able to

- Verify motherboard features

Lab Materials and Setup

The materials you need for this lab are

- Access to a working computer with the CPU-Z utility installed

- A notepad and pencil to document the specifications

- Optional: A word processor or spreadsheet application to facilitate the documentation

This lab is more informative if you have access to different systems using various motherboards.

Getting Down to Business

In the following steps, you'll verify the features of your motherboard.

Step 1   Launch CPU-Z and navigate to the Mainboard tab.

Step 2   The CPU-Z utility displays some of the key features of your motherboard as shown in Figure 7-4.

Using the data gathered by CPU-Z, record as much pertinent information as possible:

Manufacturer _____

Model _____

Chipset _____

Southbridge _____

Figure 7-4 CPU-Z displaying motherboard information

Sensor _____

BIOS brand _____

Graphic interface version _____

Step 3 If possible, launch CPU-Z on various machines to compare the features of different motherboards.

→ **Try This: PC Wizard**

Using the system from Chapter 4, "RAM," launch the PC Wizard application. Once PC Wizard is running, click the Mainboard icon. This brings up a number of items (components) in the top-right pane of the window. Click the Mainboard item to display detailed information in the lower-right pane of the window, as shown here.

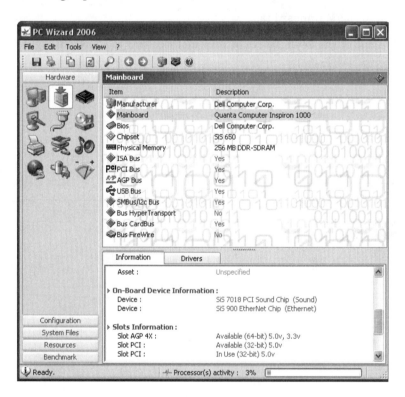

Using this information, can you determine the integrated devices supported by your motherboard? Does this correspond to the information in the PC or motherboard documentation?

Lab Analysis Test

1. Jonathan is building a system using an Intel Core 2 Duo processor, and he's purchased a new motherboard from ASUS. He would like to use an old (but working!) ATX power supply he has lying around to power the system. Why might this not be a good idea?

2. Keith bought a fancy new case for his system. He removed the motherboard from his old case, but discovered it wouldn't fit in the new one. What did Keith forget to check?

3. Dianne is trying to install an ATX motherboard in a new, empty ATX case. She tries to set it down in the bottom of the case, but it won't fit—the ports on the side are too low to poke out the back of the case, and she can't make the screws work at all. What has she forgotten?

4. After Erik reassembled his PC and turned it on, he noticed that the green LED and the disk active LED never light up, but everything seems to work okay. What is the problem?

5. Jeremy wants to upgrade his system by replacing the CPU. His friend works at a local computer shop and has offered him a Pentium D processor for a great price! Jeremy's current system uses a Pentium 4 2.54-GHz CPU. Will this work? Why or why not?

Key Term Quiz

Use the following vocabulary terms to complete the following sentences. Not all terms will be used.

AT

ATX

BTX

chipset

FlexATX

microATX

motherboard book

P1 power connector

P4 power connector

P8/P9 power connector

1. The power supplies for modern ATX motherboards connect using the

   _____.

2. To check the technical specifications of a motherboard, consult its

   _____.

3. The _____ motherboard was the first motherboard to offer soft power.

4. The Northbridge and Southbridge are components of a motherboard's

   _____.

5. One motherboard design has reconfigured the components and layout to maximize the cooling

   properties of the system; this is known as the _____ motherboard.

Chapter 8
Power Supplies

Lab Exercises

The term "power supply" is somewhat misleading. After all, the power supply in a PC does not actually *supply* power; it just takes the alternating current (AC) supplied by the power company and converts it to the direct current (DC) used by the computer system. Local power companies supply AC to the outlet in your home or office, and some conversion must take place to supply the lower operating voltages and DC power required for the PC to function.

As a PC technician, you need to understand the difference between AC and DC power. You should be able to measure the AC power at the wall outlet and determine whether the hot, neutral, and ground wires are properly connected. You must also measure the DC output of the power supply inside the PC case to determine whether the power supply is providing the correct DC voltage.

The power supply in a PC is an electronic device that converts the higher voltage—120 volts of alternating current (VAC) in the United States or 240 VAC outside the United States—into the three power levels of 12, 5, and 3.3 volts of direct current (VDC) used in today's PC systems. The 12-volt level is traditionally used for devices that have motors to spin, such as hard drives, floppy drives, CD-ROM drives, and cooling fans. The 5-volt and 3.3-volt power usually supports all of the onboard electronics. Modern CPUs often use less than 3.3 volts, so there are further step-down regulators and filters to provide core voltages as low as 1.4 volts.

The various versions of the ATX power supplies are, by far, the most common power supplies you will see on desktop computer systems. These include ATX (with a 20-pin P1 power connector), ATX 12V 1.3 (which added the AUX 4-pin connector commonly referred to as P4), and the ATX 12V 2.0 (which added the 24-pin P1 connector and dropped the P4 connector).

Server motherboards often require much more current, so you may start to see the Server System Infrastructure (SSI)–developed, non-ATX-standard motherboard with a power supply named EPS 12V; it uses a 24-pin P1 connector, a 4-pin P4 connector, and a unique 8-pin connector.

Suppose a client calls you saying that her PC keeps locking up. After walking her through a few simple troubleshooting steps, you rule out a virus or a misbehaving application. This leaves hardware as the likely culprit, and in all likelihood, it's the power supply. In these lab exercises, you'll practice the procedures for measuring power going to the PC, testing the PC's power supply, and replacing a PC power supply.

✔ **Hint**

The CompTIA A+ Essentials and 220-602 (IT Technician) exams really show their American roots in the area of electrical power. Watch for power questions that discuss American power standards—especially ones related to household voltage and outlet plug design.

The exams will also typically refer to the power supply using the abbreviation PSU (power supply unit) or the acronym FRU (field replaceable unit). FRU can describe any component that would be replaced in the field by a technician.

 30 MINUTES

Lab Exercise 8.01: Electricity

Troubleshooting power-related problems is one of the trickier tasks you'll undertake as a PC tech. Your first step is to go right to the source, so to speak, and make certain that the power being supplied to the PC from the electrical outlet is good.

✔ **Cross-Reference**

For details on AC power from the power company, refer to the "Supplying AC" section in Chapter 8 of *Mike Meyers' A+ Guide to Managing and Troubleshooting PCs.*

Learning Objectives

At the end of this lab, you'll be able to

- Determine if the AC wiring is correct at a wall outlet
- Determine if the AC voltages are correct at a wall outlet

Lab Materials and Setup

The materials you need for this lab are

- An AC electrical outlet tester
- A multimeter

Getting Down to Business

Measuring the voltage coming from an AC outlet is a nerve-wracking task even for experienced techs! Sticking objects into a live power outlet goes against everything you've been taught since infancy, but when done properly it really is completely safe.

Be sure to use common sense and appropriate safety procedures. If you're not familiar with using a multimeter, please review the "Supplying AC" section in Chapter 8 of *Mike Meyers' A+ Guide to Managing and Troubleshooting PCs*, or ask your instructor for a demonstration.

✔ Hint

If a PC is having unexplained errors and you suspect the power supply, don't be too hasty in replacing it. First check the wall outlet. In some buildings, especially older ones, the wiring can be improperly connected or otherwise provide poor power.

Step 1 Look at Figure 8-1, and compare it to your electrical outlet.

FIGURE 8-1 A typical AC electrical outlet

A typical electrical socket has three openings: hot, neutral, and ground. The hot wire delivers the juice. The neutral wire acts as a drain and returns electricity to the local source (the breaker panel). The semi-rounded ground socket returns excess electricity to the ground. If your outlet doesn't have a ground socket—and many older buildings don't—then don't use it! Ungrounded outlets aren't appropriate for PCs.

> ✖ **Warning**
>
> Take all appropriate safety precautions before measuring live electrical outlets. In a classroom, you have the benefit of an instructor to show you how to do these exercises the first time. If you're doing these on your own with no experience, seek the advice of a trained technician or instructor.

Step 2   Determine whether or not your electrical socket is "live." Do this with your electrical outlet tester. Plug your outlet tester (see Figure 8-2) into the electrical outlet or power strip where you plug in the PC. Look at the LED indicators. Are they showing good power?

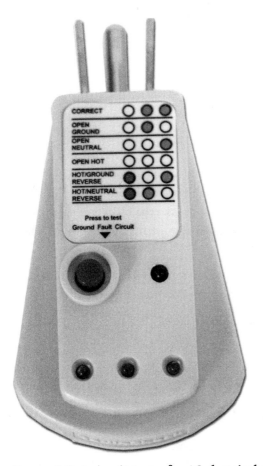

Figure 8-2 A circuit tester for AC electrical outlets

Figure 8-3 Multimeter probe locations when testing an AC outlet's hot-to-neutral circuit

Step 3   Now measure the voltage between the hot and neutral openings of the outlet. Start by setting your multimeter to AC voltage; do not proceed until you're sure you have done this correctly! If you aren't sure, ask your instructor for guidance. Referring to Figure 8-3, take the black probe and place it in the neutral opening of the wall socket. Make sure you have good contact inside the outlet. The metal probe tip must contact the metal connector inside the outlet.

Next, place the red probe inside the hot opening. Again, you must make good metal-to-metal contact. You may have to reposition the probes to get a good connection and proper reading for the AC circuit. Your reading should be somewhere between 110 and 120 V.

What is your reading? _____

Step 4   Measure the voltage in the hot-to-ground circuit. Place the black probe into the ground opening of the outlet, as shown in Figure 8-4. Make sure you have good contact. Then place the red probe into the hot opening. Move the probes around until you get a good reading for the AC voltage. Again, your reading should be in the 110- to 120-V range.

What is your reading? _____

Figure 8-4 Multimeter probe locations when testing an AC outlet's hot-to-ground circuit

Step 5   The last measurement you need to take is the voltage in the neutral-to-ground safety circuit. When the neutral wire is broken or missing, the ground wire is the only way for wayward electrons to depart safely. Any electricity on both the neutral and ground wires should have a direct path back to earth, so there should be no voltage between these wires.

Place the black probe into the ground opening of the outlet. Make sure you have good contact. Place the red probe into the neutral opening (refer to Figure 8-5). Move the probes around until you get a good reading for the AC voltage. You should get a reading of 0 V.

What is your reading? _____

Step 6   Measure another outlet in the same building, and repeat the previous steps. Are the readings similar? If the readings from your electrical outlets are outside of the ranges described, it's time to call an electrician. Assuming your reading is showing good power, go to the next exercise.

FIGURE 8-5 Multimeter probe locations when testing an AC outlet's neutral-to-ground circuit

 30 MINUTES

Lab Exercise 8.02: Power Supply Output

Once you've determined that the AC power going to your client's PC is good, the next troubleshooting step is to test whether the DC power traveling from the power supply to the rest of her system is good.

✔ **Hint**

Since this lab exercise takes you through the steps you would perform on an actual trouble ticket, the scenario has you working on a machine that is completely assembled. If, however, you are working on the disassembled, non-production machine, you should proceed to Lab Exercise 8.03 ("Replacing a Power Supply") and reinstall the power supply in the tear-down machine. You may then return here and perform the power supply output exercises.

Learning Objectives

At the end of this lab, you'll be able to

- Identify the connectors of a PC power supply

- Measure the output of a PC power supply

Lab Materials and Setup

The materials you need for this lab are

- The disassembled, non-production PC computer system used in the lab exercises in Chapter 2 (with the power supply reinstalled)

- Optionally, a working PC with an ATX power supply

- A multimeter

- A PC power supply tester

Getting Down to Business

There are two ways to determine whether a power supply is providing the proper voltages to the components of the computer. One is the traditional method, using a multimeter to measure the actual voltages. Another method growing in popularity is the use of a PC power supply tester.

✔ **Cross-Reference**

For details on DC power from the power supply, refer to the "Supplying DC" section in Chapter 8 of *Mike Meyers' A+ Guide to Managing and Troubleshooting PCs*.

In the following steps, you'll measure DC voltage coming from the PC power supply. The two places to measure power supply output are at the Molex power connectors and at the motherboard power connector. Molex power connectors plug into devices that need 5 or 12 volts of power. These include hard drives and CD- or DVD-media drives. Mini connectors also carry 5 or 12 volts, but on modern systems these are used only for floppy drives. On most recent systems, the power supply will provide two motherboard power connectors: the 20- or 24-pin P1 and the smaller P4 (see Figure 8-6). Both of these power connectors are used on motherboards requiring an additional 12 V power supply.

You'll then plug the P1 power connector into a PC power supply tester and verify that the readings you measured with the multimeter are within tolerance. The power supply tester has LEDs that will glow green for each of the voltages that it passes.

Figure 8-6 Motherboard power connectors: P1 (left) and P4 (right)

> ✖ **Warning**
>
> Although the power coming out of the PC power supply is considerably less lethal than that coming directly out of the electrical outlet, you should still take all appropriate safety precautions before taking measurements.

Step 1   Set the multimeter to read DC voltage. Find a Molex connector that's not being used for a device. If no Molex connectors are unused, turn the system off and disconnect the one from the CD- or DVD-media drive, and then turn the PC back on.

Step 2   Referring to Figure 8-7, place the black probe into either one of the holes on the Molex connector that is aligned with a black wire. Now place the red probe into each of the other three holes of the Molex connector in turn, first the other black wire, then the red, then yellow, and record your findings.

Black wire to black wire   _____ V

Black wire to red wire   _____ V

Black wire to yellow wire   _____ V

Step 3   Measuring the voltage from the motherboard connector is a little trickier. Leave the power connector plugged into the motherboard and push the probes into the end of the connector that the wires run into. You must push the probe deep enough to touch the metal contact pins, but be careful not to push too deeply or you might push the pin out of the connector.

Push the black probe into the motherboard connector alongside any black wire, and leave it there. Insert the red probe into each of the other wires, and record your findings. Depending on your motherboard connector, you may not have all of these wires.

Figure 8-7 Measuring the voltage in a Molex connector

Black wire to red wire   _____ V

Black wire to yellow wire   _____ V

Black wire to purple wire   _____ V

Black wire to white wire   _____ V

Black wire to black wire   _____ V

Black wire to blue wire   _____ V

Black wire to green wire   _____ V

The voltages generated by the power supply must be within a tolerance (range) level; readings outside these ranges mean the power supply should be replaced. The 5 V connections have a tolerance of ±2 percent (4.9 to 5.1 V is okay), and 12 V connections have a tolerance of ±6 percent (11.25 to 12.75 V is okay).

✔ **Hint**

A single reading from your power supply may not be enough to pinpoint a power-related problem. Sometimes a power problem becomes evident only when the power supply is placed under a heavier-than-normal load, such as burning a CD. Also, some RAM-related errors mimic a failing power supply.

The other method to verify that the power supply is operating properly and supplying all the voltages within tolerance is to use a power supply tester. There are many styles of PSU testers on the market, so make sure you follow the specific directions included with your tester as you complete the steps.

Step 1 Starting with the P1 connector, follow the directions to connect the P1 connector for your specific PSU tester. Verify that all of the voltages provided through the P1 connector are acceptable (usually an LED will light to verify voltage present and within tolerance).

✔ **Hint**

When connecting and disconnecting the power supply connectors, always take care to insert the connector with the proper orientation. Most power connectors are keyed to make it difficult to install the connector backwards, but if you use excessive force, you may be able to insert the connector improperly. This applies to powering the motherboard, plugging in devices, and even using the PSU tester.

Step 2 Now, depending on your tester and power supply, plug either the 4-pin, 6-pin, or 8-pin auxiliary connector into the appropriate socket on the PSU tester and verify the voltages provided through this connector. Once they are verified, remove the connector from the socket.

Step 3 Next, plug the Molex connector into the PSU tester and verify the voltages provided through this connector. Once they are verified, remove the connector from the socket.

Step 4 Plug the SATA HDD power connector into the appropriate socket and verify the voltages provided through this connector. Once they are verified, remove the connector from the socket.

Step 5 Finally, plug the mini floppy drive power connector into the PSU tester and verify the voltages provided through this connector. Once they are verified, remove the connector from the socket and remove the P1 from the socket.

 30 MINUTES

Lab Exercise 8.03: Replacing a Power Supply

Let's assume that you've found a variance in the 12 V range that explains your client's system lockups. You know that power supplies aren't user-serviceable components—you don't fix them, you replace them as a unit—so it's time to replace her power supply. Next to the motherboard, the power supply is the most time-consuming component to replace, simply because of all those wires! Nonetheless, replacing the power supply is a simple operation, as described in this exercise.

Learning Objectives

At the end of this lab, you'll be able to

- Determine the total wattage requirements of the system and select the proper power supply

- Replace a power supply

Lab Materials and Setup

The materials you need for this lab are

- The disassembled, non-production PC computer system used in the lab exercises in Chapter 2

- Optionally, a working PC with an ATX power supply

- A Phillips-head screwdriver

- A labeled container for holding screws

Getting Down to Business

One of the areas where PC manufacturers cut corners on lower-end systems is power supplies. High-end systems typically come with higher-wattage power supplies, whereas entry-level PCs typically have lower-wattage power supplies. This might not be evident until you add power-hungry components to the system, placing a heavier load on the power supply and causing an early failure.

In the following steps you'll determine the wattage of the power supply on your system, calculate the power usage of your PC, and then remove and reinstall the power supply.

Step 1   To find out what the wattage rating of your power supply is, look at the label on the power supply (see Figure 8-8).

Find the similar label on your power supply, and locate the watts rating. If you don't see a clear wattage rating as shown in Figure 8-8, or if you see something less evident, like the smaller "430 W"

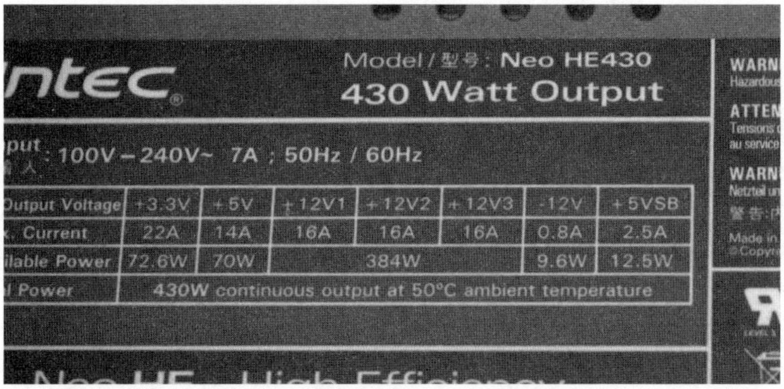

Figure 8-8 Typical ATX power supply ratings label

marking on the label, the power supply rating may be hidden in the model number, which in this example is "Neo HE430."

✔ Hint

All power supplies have a wattage rating. If it is not apparent on the power supply itself, search the Internet using the model number for reference.

What is the wattage of your power supply? _____

Step 2   When it comes time to replace a power supply, don't skimp on the wattage! Modern power supplies typically range from 300 watts to 1000 watts or more; 300-watt power supplies are the bare minimum you would use on a system that has only a few installed components (such as a single hard drive and CD- or DVD-media drive), while the 1000-watt models are usually found on server systems that have multiple hard drives (such as a RAID array), multiple processors, or other power-hungry components. Many gaming systems with high-performance graphics, dual-core processors, and SATA RAID configurations will use PSUs that provide 550–650 watts to meet these systems' power requirements. As a general rule, get the highest-wattage replacement you can afford while maintaining compatibility with your system. Remember, the system will draw only the current it requires, so you will never damage a system by installing a higher-wattage power supply.

✖ Warning

Never replace a PC's power supply with one of lower wattage!

Use the following table to calculate the overall wattage needed for your system. Add the numbers for each component and determine the lowest and highest wattage requirements.

Component	Requirement	Voltage(s) Used
PCIe video card	45–75 W	3.3 V
AGP video card	30–50 W	3.3 V
PCI card	5–10 W	5 V
10/100 NIC	4 W	3.3 V
SCSI controller PCI	20 W	3.3 V and 5 V
Floppy drive	5 W	5 V
7200 rpm IDE hard drive	5–20 W	5 V and 12 V
7200 rpm SATA hard drive	5–20 W	5 V and 12 V

Component	Requirement	Voltage(s) Used
10,000 rpm SCSI drive	10–40 W	5 V and 12 V
CD/DVD media drive	10–25 W	5 V and 12 V
Case/CPU fans	3 W (each)	12 V
Motherboard (without CPU or RAM)	25–40 W	3.3 V and 5 V
RAM	10 W per 128 MB	3.3 V
Pentium 4 processor	70 W	12 V
Pentium D processor	65–104 W	12 V
AMD Athlon 64 X2 processor	92 W	12 V

If the highest total exceeds the power supply wattage rating, you may run into problems. When selecting a new power supply, you should multiply the load by a factor of 1.5. The multiplier provides a safety factor and allows the power supply to run more efficiently. A power supply is more efficient at 30 to 70 percent of its full capacity rating. Thus, a 450-watt PSU works best when only 135 to 315 watts are being used.

What wattage is appropriate for your system? _____

✔ **Hint**

Depending on the design of your PC case, you may have to remove data cables or components before you can get to the power supply. Make certain that you have plenty of room to work inside the case!

Step 3 Shut down the system and remove the power cable from the back of the power supply. Then remove the power supply.

1. Disconnect the Molex, SATA, and mini connectors from your drive devices, then unplug the main power connector from the motherboard.

2. If your power supply uses a P4 connector, disconnect it from the motherboard.

3. Unscrew the four screws holding the power supply onto the PC case (remembering to support it while you remove the last one!), and remove the power supply from the case. Store the screws in the labeled container.

Step 4 Take this opportunity to inspect and clean the power supply. Check for any rust or corrosion on the power supply casing or on any of the contacts. Inspect the wires for damage or frayed insulation. Use canned air to blow dust and dirt out of the intake and exhaust vents.

Step 5 Reinstall the power supply by performing the preceding steps in reverse order. If you had to remove data cables or other components to get at the power supply, be sure to reattach them.

 30 MINUTES

Lab Exercise 8.04: Power Protection

You've successfully fixed your client's power-problem-plagued PC (say that five times fast!), but now you've noted that she has nothing in the way of power protection for her system, nor do any of her coworkers. None!

When you mention this to her, she tells you that her boss never really saw the point of spending money on surge protectors, uninterruptible power supplies, or any of "that stuff." With a straight face, she asks, "Do those things really do any good?"

Now it's your task to sell the boss on the idea of power protection. To do this, you must explain the types of power problems that lurk in the bushes just waiting to pounce on unwary users without power protection, and suggest precautions that they can take to prevent power-related damage.

Learning Objectives

At the end of this lab, you'll be able to

- Explain the need for power protection

- Explain the types of power protection available for a PC

✔ **Cross-Reference**

For details on power protection, refer to the "Surge Suppressors" and "UPS" sections in Chapter 8 of *Mike Meyers' A+ Guide to Managing and Troubleshooting PCs*.

Lab Materials and Setup

The materials you need for this lab are

- A working PC

Getting Down to Business

Too often, PC users take the electricity that powers their system for granted. After all, there's not much you can do about the electricity, is there? Not so! Armed with the knowledge of the types of power conditions that can affect your PC, you can best determine what precautions to take.

Step 1 Describe the following types of power conditions and the types of damage they can cause.

Power spike _____

Brownout _____

Blackout _____

Step 2 Describe the following types of power protection equipment.

Surge suppressor _____

Online uninterruptible power supply (UPS) _____

Standby UPS _____

Lab Analysis Test

1. Your client calls you and says that her PC is unusually quiet and keeps rebooting for no apparent reason. What should you ask her to check?

2. Athena lives in an area where the power is often interrupted. She bought a good surge protector strip, but that does not seem to help. What does she need to prevent her system from shutting down unexpectedly?

3. Your assistant technician calls you and says he suspects a bad power supply in one of your client's systems. He said the multimeter readings are 12.65 volts and 4.15 volts. What should he do?

4. One of your clients has an older Pentium 4 system with a single IDE hard drive and 512 MB of RAM. He had been using this PC as his main workstation, but he's recently purchased a newer system and now wants to redeploy the older system as a file server on his network. He has ordered a PCI SCSI controller board and three SCSI hard drives, so that he can configure a RAID array, and an additional 2 GB of RAM. He also ordered two Y adapters for the power supply connectors. He asks for your advice about any additional hardware he should order. What do you tell him?

5. What are the power requirements of the following system? _____

    *   AMD Athlon 64 X2 CPU and 512 MB RAM
    *   Two Serial Advanced Technology Attached (SATA) hard drives and one floppy drive
    *   One CD-RW drive and one DVD-ROM drive
    *   PCIe video
    *   PCI sound card
    *   NIC

Key Term Quiz

Use the following vocabulary terms to complete the following sentences. Not all terms will be used.

3.3 V

5 V

12 V

20-pin P1

24-pin P1

Molex connector

P4

P8/P9

power sags

power spikes

power supply

UPS

1. The ATX 12V 2.0 power supply plugs into the motherboard using the _____ connector(s).

2. PC devices with motors, such as hard drives and CD-ROM drives, usually require _____ of DC electricity from the power supply.

3. Hard drives and CD-ROM drives connect to the power supply with a _____.

4. A surge protector prevents damage from _____ in the voltage.

5. Pentium 4 motherboards have both _____ and _____ power connectors.

Chapter 9

Hard Drive Technologies

Lab Exercises

As the primary storage area for the operating system, applications, and vital data, the hard drive takes on a level of importance to PC users that borders on reverence. Considering the fact that the death of a drive can mean many hours or days of tediously rebuilding, reloading applications, and re-creating data, such strong feelings make sense. And that reverence can turn quickly to agony if the user hasn't backed up his or her data in a while when the hard drive dies!

Every tech must know how to connect, configure, maintain, and troubleshoot hard drives of all types. A fully operational drive requires proper hardware setup and installation, CMOS configuration, and software setup usually performed by tools that come with the operating system. The first few labs in this chapter cover physical installation and CMOS configuration of the mainstream hard drive technology, namely Integrated Drive Electronics (IDE), in both parallel and serial flavors. You will then conduct research on the developments of the rapidly changing Small Computer Systems Interface (SCSI), primarily used for large, fault-tolerant data storage. The next exercise will have you troubleshoot installations, and finally you'll install additional hard drives in preparation for an exercise in the next chapter. You'll work with the software aspects of all hard drives—partitioning, formatting, and running drive utilities—in Chapter 10, "Implementing Hard Drives."

 1 HOUR

Lab Exercise 9.01: Installing Parallel ATA Hard Drives

The local nonprofit organization where you volunteer has received a donation of ten used PCs. Most of them have tiny hard drives, so they need an upgrade before you can distribute them to the various workers at the agency. All of the motherboards have built-in parallel ATA (PATA) controllers; some even have the better ATA/100 controllers. Your boss breaks out a stack of donated hard drives and tells you to get to work!

Installing a PATA hard drive successfully requires little more than connecting data and power cables to the drive and plugging the other end of the data cable into the motherboard. Sounds simple enough on the surface, but because all PATA drives give you options to install two on each motherboard controller, unwary techs get tripped up here. This lab walks you through the first major step in drive installation: the physical part.

✔ **Hint**

As you know from Chapter 9 of your textbook, IDE drives have several names that techs use pretty much interchangeably: IDE, EIDE, and ATA. You'll see all three terms in this lab manual and on the CompTIA A+ Certification exams. Except for discussions of very old technology, the terms describe the same type of hard drive today.

Learning Objectives

In this lab exercise, you'll identify the different components of PATA hard drives and cables and learn installation procedures.

At the end of this lab, you'll be able to

- Remove a hard drive safely and correctly

- Describe PATA cables and connectors

- Describe the geometry of a hard drive

- Calculate the capacity of a hard drive

- Describe jumper settings

- Identify the major parts of a hard drive

- Install a hard drive safely and correctly

Lab Materials and Setup

The materials you need for this lab are

- The disassembled, non-production computer system from the lab exercises in Chapter 2, with at least one PATA hard drive

- A working PC with a PATA hard drive installed

- The Windows operating system installed on the PC

- Optionally, access to one or more broken hard drives that have the covers removed for observation of the internal parts

Getting Down to Business

Grab your handy screwdriver and anti-static wrist strap; it's time to remove a hard drive! As in previous labs, if you are using the disassembled, non-production PC for this lab, you have already removed all of the hard drives, CD-media drive, and floppy drive (if present). You should gather together the drives you removed from the system, along with all associated cables and mounting hardware, to facilitate their reinstallation at the end of this exercise. The following removal instructions are included for clarification; however, you will use the drives and cables to work through the identification steps that follow.

Step 1   Shut down your system and remove the system cover, following proper electrostatic discharge (ESD) procedures.

Step 2   Disconnect all the ribbon cables from the hard drives and CD-ROM drives, but first note which device is connected to which cable and where the orientation stripe is located on each device. Be careful but firm. Grasp the cable as closely as possible to the connector on the drive and pull, rocking the connector gently from side to side.

Examine the connector on the end of the ribbon cable. Use Figure 9-1 to help you.

How many holes does it have for pins? _____

Are any of the holes in the connector filled in? Does the connector have a raised portion on one side so that it only fits one way? In other words, is it keyed? _____

Take a close look at the top connector in Figure 9-1.

How many connectors are on your ribbon cable? _____

80-wire ribbon cable

40-wire ribbon cable

FIGURE 9-1: ATA cables: Comparing 80-wire and 40-wire ribbon cable connectors

Do you have a 40-wire or 80-wire ribbon cable?_____

Disconnect the power supply from all of the PATA devices by unplugging the Molex connector from each one.

✖ Warning

Molex plugs can be difficult to remove and brutal on the fingers. Little "bumps" on each side of the plug enable you to rock the plug back and forth to remove it.

✔ Hint

You will explore removable storage devices (CD-ROM, DVD-ROM, tape drives, USB thumb drives, floppy drives) and associated media in Chapter 11, "Removable Media."

Step 3 Now look at the motherboard connections, and note the orientation of the cable connectors. Disconnect the ribbon cables from the motherboard. Be careful but firm. Grasp the cable as closely as possible to the connector on the motherboard and pull, rocking the connector gently from side to side.

Lay the cables aside for later reinstallation.

Step 4 Look at the PATA connections on your motherboard (see Figure 9-2).

How many PATA controllers do you see on your motherboard?

_____

Look closely at your motherboard, and see if you can find writing on the board next to the IDE connections. Are the interfaces grouped into pairs? Are any of them dedicated to special configurations such as RAID? _____

What color are the IDE connections on the motherboard?

_____

Step 5 Remove a hard drive from the system. Be careful to note the type of screws you removed and store them for safekeeping. Also be sure to use proper ESD procedures when removing the drive from your system.

Because of the variety of cases, caddies, bays, slots, and so on, it's not possible to give detailed instructions on how to remove the drive from your particular system. Look closely for caddy releases or retaining screws. Close inspection and a little logic will usually make it clear how to remove the drive. Make notes of how the drive comes out, as you'll have to reinstall it later.

Step 6 With the hard drive out of the system and on a static-free surface, ground yourself, pick up the drive, and examine it carefully.

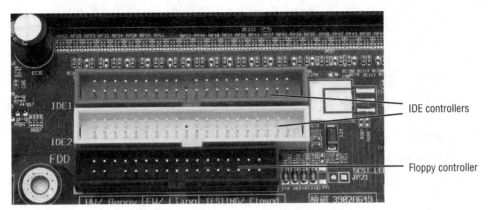

FIGURE 9-2: Viewing the PATA connectors on a motherboard

Note its dimensions. It should measure about 6″ × 3.5″ × 1″. Some drives may be larger than this, measuring 6″ × 5.25″ × 1″—these are known as *bigfoot drives*. Some drives are smaller, but those are used mostly in laptops.

Look at the largest surfaces of the drive (the top and bottom). The bottom is where the printed circuit board with a ROM chip is located. This circuitry is the hard drive controller. The top side of the drive normally has a label or another means of listing the specifications for the drive, but this is not always the case.

Write down all the information on the label. Be sure to include the manufacturer and the model number for future reference.

Usually the label lists the total capacity of the hard drive and the power requirements of the drive (voltage and current). On older drives, the label lists the three main measurements of hard drive geometry: the number of cylinders, the number of heads, and the number of sectors per track. Together these measurements may be listed simply as CHS.

✔ Cross-Reference

For more information about CHS, refer to the "Geometry" section in Chapter 9 of *Mike Meyers' A+ Guide to Managing and Troubleshooting PCs*.

Using these three measurements, you can calculate the capacity of the hard drive. The formula is cylinders × heads × sectors per track × 512 = bytes of data. (The number of bytes in one sector is 512.)

For example, an older drive has the following information on the label. What is the total capacity of this drive?

- C = 859
- H = 16

- S = 63

859 × 16 × 63 × 512 = 443,326,464 bytes

To convert this to megabytes, divide the answer by 1,048,576, as shown here:

443,326,464 / 1,048,576 = 422.8 MB

A Seagate ST310211A PATA hard drive has CHS values of 16383, 16, and 63. What is its total capacity in bytes? In megabytes? In gigabytes? (To convert from megabytes to gigabytes, divide the number of megabytes by 1024.)

Step 7   Look at the end of the drive where the ribbon cable connects. Find the markings for where pin 1 of the ribbon cable should go.

Is it closer to the center of the drive (near the power connector) or to the side of the drive?

Does your hard drive have jumpers like the ones in Figure 9-3? _____

Notice that the drive in Figure 9-3 has the jumper set to CS (which stands for *cable select*).

Each PC system that boots from a PATA hard drive should have the hard drive located on the first PATA interface (IDE1). Normally the jumper must be set to Master so that the system can recognize it as the boot drive. A second drive (hard drive or CD/DVD-media drive) can be on the same cable, but must be set to Slave.

How are the jumpers set on your hard drive? _____

How are the jumpers set on your CD or DVD drive? _____

Can you have two master drives in the system? _____

FIGURE 9-3: Locating the PATA hard drive jumper setting

For the purposes of this exercise, make sure you leave your hard drive jumpered as it was when you removed it.

Step 8 Locate a broken hard drive (if you're in a class, ask your instructor for one) and remove its cover.

✖ Warning

Never remove the cover from a functioning hard drive! Hard drives are extremely sensitive, so merely exposing the inside to the air will cause *irreparable* damage.

Notice the round polished platters that spin in the middle of the drive. This is where the data is stored magnetically.

The actuator arms that move across the platters have tiny coils of wire attached to their ends. These coils hold the read/write heads.

How many surfaces does your sample drive have (one platter = two surfaces)? _____

How many physical heads does your sample drive have? _____

Both answers are most likely the same because usually there is a read/write head for each surface.

Look at Figure 9-4 and identify the following parts by number.

Read/write heads _____

Platters _____

Voice coil motor _____

FIGURE 9-4: The internal parts of a hard drive

FIGURE 9-5: The external parts of a hard
drive

Now look at Figure 9-5 and match the numbered components.

Enhanced Integrated Drive Electronics (EIDE) controller _____

Molex connector _____

PATA connector _____

Master/slave jumper _____

Step 9   Insert the drive back into your system, and secure it with the proper screws. Connect all the ribbon cables to all the drives, and pay attention to the proper alignment of the connectors. Connect the Molex power connectors. Leave the system case off until you verify that everything works properly.

If you used a working machine for the prior steps, you can verify that you've reinstalled the drives correctly by going to the next major step in the process of hard drive installation: CMOS configuration. Lab Exercise 9.03 in this chapter covers the CMOS details, but if you just can't wait, try Step 10. This bonus step should work on newer motherboard models.

Step 10   Turn on the system and wait for it to boot to the desktop. Double-click the My Computer icon, and confirm that the icons for the reinstalled drives are displayed. The fact that you were able to get to the desktop confirms that you've reinstalled the boot drive correctly, but do the other drives (if you have them) and your CD-ROM drive work?

✔ **Hint**

If you cannot boot the system or the CD-ROM drive does not work, the first and obvious place to start is to verify all the cable connections. Any kind of disk errors at this time were most likely caused by the technician; after all, it worked before you touched it!

 45 MINUTES

Lab Exercise 9.02: Installing Serial ATA Hard Drives

A wealthy donor has just given your nonprofit organization a dozen brand-new desktop machines. Since these are new machines, their motherboards have built-in serial ATA (SATA) controllers, but the SATA hard drives have yet to be installed or configured. You're tasked to do the job!

Installing SATA hard drives is a simple matter of plugging in the data and power cables to the drive and attaching the other end of the data cable to the SATA controller card or motherboard connection. You don't have to pull the power from the PC. You don't even have to shut down Windows. No, really—it's that simple! Let's go through the steps.

Learning Objectives

This lab is designed to introduce you to the two current flavors of SATA and walk you through the straightforward installation. At the end of this lab, you'll be able to

- Explain key features of SATA I and SATA II

- Install a SATA hard drive

Lab Materials and Setup

The materials you need for this lab are

- A newer PC system with an onboard SATA I or SATA II controller and either Windows 2000 Professional or Windows XP Professional installed

- At least one additional SATA hard drive

- Optionally, a PCI SATA controller may be installed into an older PC system

Getting Down to Business

To start, you'll review the features and specifications of SATA, and then you'll compare and contrast the technology with PATA. Keep that screwdriver handy, because you'll finish with the installation and hot-swap of a SATA drive.

✔ Cross-Reference

To help in answering the following questions, reference the "ATA-7" section in Chapter 9 of *Mike Meyers' A+ Guide to Managing and Troubleshooting PCs*.

Step 1 Using your reference materials, review the features and specifications of SATA hard drive technology. Then answer these questions:

What is the speed of data transfer with ATA/133 drives? _____

What is the speed of data transfer with SATA I (SATA 1.5-Gb) drives? _____

What is the speed of data transfer with SATA II (SATA 3-Gb) drives? _____

What is the maximum length of a SATA cable? _____

How many wires are in a SATA cable? _____

What is the maximum length of an 80-wire PATA cable? _____

How many drives can a single SATA cable support? _____

SATA RAID has waltzed into the mainstream today. Motherboards are now being sold with a SATA RAID controller from Promise or another company built in, or you can readily buy a PCI SATA RAID controller at your local computer parts store. You'll install additional hard drives in Lab Exercise 9.06, and you'll explore the implementation of a software RAID solution in Chapter 10.

Step 2 It's time to get working with some SATA drives. Shut down your system and remove the system cover, following proper electrostatic discharge (ESD) procedures.

Step 3 Disconnect the data cable(s) from the SATA hard drive(s), as shown in Figure 9-6. Grasp the cable as closely as possible to the connector on the drive and pull, rocking the connector gently from side to side.

FIGURE 9-6: Removing the SATA data cable

FIGURE 9-7: Molex-to-SATA power adapter

Disconnect the power supply from the SATA drive(s) by unplugging the SATA connector from each one. Is the power supply a newer model with SATA connectors directly attached, or is there a Molex-to-SATA power adapter like the one shown in Figure 9-7?

Step 4 Now look at the motherboard connections and note the orientation of the connectors. Disconnect the data cables from the motherboard, being careful but firm. Grasp the cable as closely as possible to the connector on the motherboard and pull, rocking the connector gently from side to side.

Lay the cables aside for later reinstallation.

Step 5 Look at the SATA connections on your motherboard (see Figure 9-8).

How many SATA connectors do you see on your motherboard? _____

Look closely at your motherboard, and see if you can find writing on the board next to the SATA connectors. Are the interfaces grouped into pairs? Are any of them dedicated to special configurations such as RAID? _____

Step 6 As in the previous exercise, remove the hard drive from the system, note the type of screws you removed, and store the screws for safekeeping. Be sure to use proper ESD procedures when removing the drive from your system.

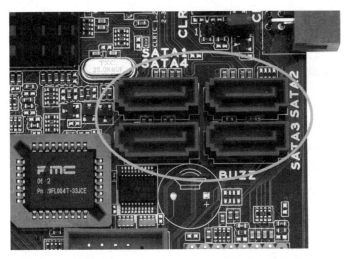

Figure 9-8: The SATA connectors on a motherboard

Because of the variety of cases, caddies, bays, slots, and so on, it's not possible to give detailed instructions on how to remove the drive from your particular system. Look closely for caddy releases or retaining screws. Close inspection and a little logic will usually make it clear how to remove the drive. Make notes of how the drive comes out; you'll have to reinstall it later.

Step 7 With the hard drive out of the system and on a static-free surface, ground yourself, pick up the drive, and examine it carefully.

Note its dimensions; it should measure about 6″ × 3.5″ × 1″, the same as a PATA drive. Here, too, the bottom of the drive boasts the hard drive controller, and the top of the drive is normally labeled with the drive's specifications.

Write down all the information on the label. Be sure to include the manufacturer and the model number for future reference.

Step 8 To demonstrate one of the benefits of SATA—hot-swapping—you will now reinstall all the drives you removed and, if necessary, install an additional SATA drive to be hot-swapped. With the PC still powered down, insert all of the original drives back into your system, and at least one additional SATA drive with no critical data. Secure the drives with the proper screws, connect all the data cables, and connect the SATA power connectors using Molex-to-SATA adapters if required.

Leave the system case off, to verify that everything is working properly and to facilitate the last steps.

✔ **Hint**

If you are performing this lab using a PCI SATA controller card, you'll have to install the expansion card and load the drivers for the card. If you haven't loaded drivers for the SATA controller, you should do so now. Otherwise, this is going to be a very frustrating lab for you!

Power up the PC and boot into Windows. Windows should pick up the drive(s) with no problems at all. Check My Computer to verify that the drive is installed and functional. If the drive has no partition, then of course it won't show up in My Computer; if this is the case, you can use the Computer Management console to verify that the drive works.

Step 9   With Windows still running, disconnect the SATA data cable from the additional drive. What happened? _____

Step 10   Plug the data cable back in. Does Windows see the drive? _____

Step 11   Try the same hot-swap test with the SATA power cable—unplug it and then plug it back in. Does this produce the same effect as the hot-swap with the data cable?

 30 MINUTES

Lab Exercise 9.03: Configuring CMOS Settings

After installing either PATA or SATA devices, the second step you'll want to perform is the configuration of the BIOS to support these devices. On most motherboards, the BIOS automatically detects devices, so you will primarily be confirming the detection of all of the devices and configuring advanced features such as RAID, S.M.A.R.T., and boot options. Autodetection does not render CMOS irrelevant, though; you can do or undo all kinds of problems relating to hard drives using CMOS setup. This lab walks you through the important configuration options.

Learning Objectives

At the end of this lab, you'll be able to

- Configure the CMOS settings for the hard drive
- Confirm that the hard drive is indeed installed properly

Lab Materials and Setup

The materials you need for this lab are

- A fully functioning PC with PATA and/or SATA devices installed
- A second drive with no important data (optional)

Getting Down to Business

There are many possible CMOS settings for the hard drive, depending on the BIOS installed on the motherboard. For example, every motherboard gives you the option to disable the built-in hard drive controllers. Why is this relevant? You can install a drive into a perfectly good system, but it won't work if the controllers are disabled!

Step 1   Turn on your system, and enter the CMOS setup utility by pressing the appropriate key(s) while your system is booting.

Select the Integrated Peripherals option from the main menu, or the Drive Configuration option from the Advanced menu (you may have to hunt around for where you enable the PATA/SATA devices in your CMOS setup program), and look for the various controllers. You can enable or disable the controllers here.

✔ Hint

This option may look somewhat different depending on the version of CMOS you are using. Look for a menu option such as one of these:

- Onboard Primary PCI IDE

- Onboard Secondary PCI IDE

- PCI Primary and Secondary IDE

- Onboard IDE

- Use Automatic Mode

- SATA Port 0

When the controllers are disabled in CMOS, no device attached to them can be used—not even the CD-ROM or Zip drives. This is why some systems will not let you disable the controllers at all.

If you are performing the labs in sequence, and have arrived at this lab directly from Lab Exercise 9.01 or Lab Exercise 9.02, here's where you find out whether or not you installed and jumpered the drive correctly.

Make sure all controllers are enabled, and then look for the Autodetection option in the CMOS settings. Older systems have a separate category in CMOS, appropriately named Autodetect or something similar; newer systems have it integrated into the main settings screen. Run this utility now. If your hard drive shows up in Autodetect as the drive you thought it would be—primary master, secondary master, SATA Port 0, or what have you—then you installed and (if necessary) jumpered it properly (see Figure 9-9).

Step 2   Save your settings, exit CMOS, and reboot your PC. You should boot into Windows normally. Check My Computer to verify that you can see and access all drives.

Step 3   Reboot your PC and go into CMOS. Access the settings to enable or disable the various controllers, and disable them all. (This won't affect your data; it will just prevent drive access for the next couple of steps in this lab.)

Step 4   Save your settings, then exit CMOS to reboot the system. Making sure there is no floppy disk in the floppy drive, reboot normally and watch the monitor display for messages.

What message is displayed last? _____

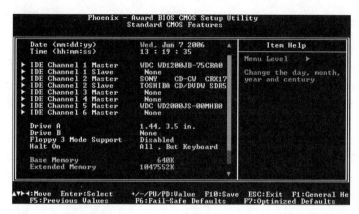

```
        Phoenix - Award BIOS CMOS Setup Utility
                 Standard CMOS Features

   Date (mm:dd:yy)       Wed, Jun 7 2006      ▲       Item Help
   Time (hh:mm:ss)       13 : 19 : 35
                                                   Menu Level    ▶
 ▶ IDE Channel 1 Master  WDC WD1200JB-75CRA0
 ▶ IDE Channel 1 Slave   None                      Change the day, month,
 ▶ IDE Channel 2 Master  SONY    CD-CW  CRX17       year and century
 ▶ IDE Channel 2 Slave   TOSHIBA CD/DVDW SDR5
 ▶ IDE Channel 3 Master  None
 ▶ IDE Channel 4 Master  None
 ▶ IDE Channel 5 Master  WDC WD2000JS-00MHB0
 ▶ IDE Channel 6 Master  None

   Drive A               1.44, 3.5 in.
   Drive B               None
   Floppy 3 Mode Support Disabled
   Halt On               All , But Keyboard

   Base Memory              640K
   Extended Memory       1047552K             ▼

▲▼◀:Move  Enter:Select   +/-/PU/PD:Value  F10:Save  ESC:Exit  F1:General He
       F5:Previous Values     F6:Fail-Safe Defaults   F7:Optimized Defaults
```

FIGURE 9-9: Various drives and their roles as listed in CMOS setup

With most systems, the PC searches its various storage devices for a way to boot. It looks for a bootable drive (connected to an EIDE, SATA, or SCSI controller), a bootable CD or floppy disk, or a network connection—not necessarily in that order—and then stops if it cannot find the operating system. It then displays a message indicating "no bootable device" and waits for your instructions to continue.

✖ Warning

If your system is connected to a network and uses the network boot option, disconnect the network cable for this exercise to get the desired results. Be sure to plug the network cable back in when finished.

When the system is not able to find a disk (because you disabled the controller), it will probably hang for a long period of time and then return a Primary Hard Drive Failure code or error message. Some systems try to recognize that you have a hard drive regardless of the disabling of features, but this is rare.

Okay, so the system can't find your hard drive. You obviously know why—you turned off the controller!

Step 5   Reboot your system, entering the CMOS setup utility by pressing the appropriate keystroke combination while your system is booting. Navigate to the menu where you disabled all of the controllers and reenable them.

Step 6   Now that the controllers are enabled, go back to the Autodetection utility and look for any drives connected.

If Autodetection still does not see a hard drive, save your settings, reboot your system, and reenter the CMOS setup utility. Then try it again.

Do you now see all of the storage devices that are installed in the system?

Step 7   While you're still in CMOS, navigate to the menu where all of the storage devices can be configured. Use this screen (sometimes there are multiple screens) to examine the device settings and answer the following questions:

Are there any devices listed as ATA/IDE devices (Primary Master, Primary Slave, Secondary Master, or Secondary Slave)? _____

Are there any SATA controllers present? If yes, are there any SATA devices installed on the system (SATA Port 0, SATA Port 1, and so on)? _____

Is the motherboard capable of implementing RAID? If yes, how is it currently configured?

_____

Exit CMOS without saving changes and let the PC reboot.

Step 8   At this point, if you did everything as described and if you started with a known good hard drive containing a working operating system, the system will boot back into the operating system. Otherwise, you'll have to wait until you partition and format the drive to see if everything's working as it should (for example, if your instructor gave you a demo hard drive to use with nothing on it).

✔ **Cross-Reference**

For details about partitioning and formatting drives, refer to Chapter 10, "Implementing Hard Drives," in *Mike Meyers' A+ Guide to Managing and Troubleshooting PCs*.

 1 HOUR

Lab Exercise 9.04: Exploring SCSI, SAS, and SATA

As you inventory the machines that were just donated to your nonprofit organization, you discover two additional machines, both dual-CPU, Serial Attached Small Computer Systems Interface (SAS/SCSI) file servers. Yippee! Your company can really put these to use. You've been hearing about the new SAS/SCSI technology, but haven't yet had the opportunity to work with it.

With the rapid changes taking place in the world of SCSI (not the least of which is SAS), you should take the time to research this technology and the best way to incorporate it into your organization.

Learning Objectives

This lab touches on important tech skills, teaching you how to research hardware so you can provide good information to clients. With the introduction of the SATA interface, the need for Small Computer Systems Interface (SCSI) implementation on desktop machines is quickly fading. However, SCSI—which is 20 years old as of this writing—still rules the hot-swappable, large-capacity, data server environment. With the introduction of Serial Attached SCSI (SAS), which enables you to use both SAS and SATA drives simultaneously on a serial SCSI controller, it looks like SCSI could be around for another 20 years.

At the end of this lab, you'll be able to

- Explain key features of SCSI

- Explain key features of SAS

- Discuss the uses of SAS/SATA technology

- Define the levels of RAID

Lab Materials and Setup

The materials you need for this lab are

- Access to a PC system and the Internet

- A trip to the local computer store for research

Getting Down to Business

Limber up your surfing fingers, as you'll start your search on the Internet. Then you might want to make a visit to the local computer store to explore further how the technologies of SCSI and SAS are being used in today's computing environments.

Step 1   Access the Internet and search for information on parallel SCSI devices, primarily hard drives. Use keywords such as *Ultra320*, *white paper*, *controllers*, and *storage solutions*. Then answer the following questions:

What speed of data transfer can be achieved with parallel SCSI? _____

How many drives can be attached to a single controller?

_____

What is the price range of parallel SCSI drives? _____

What is a SCSI chain? _____

✔ Cross-Reference

For more information on SCSI, refer to the "SCSI: Still Around" section in Chapter 9 of *Mike Meyers' A+ Guide to Managing and Troubleshooting PCs.*

Step 2   Access the Internet and search for information on Serial Attached SCSI (SAS) devices, primarily hard drives. Use keywords such as *SAS hard drives*, *white paper*, *controllers*, and *storage solutions*. Then answer the following questions:

What speed of data transfer can be achieved with SAS-specific hard drives? _____

How many drives can be attached to a single controller? How many total drives can one system support? _____

What is the price range of SAS-specific hard drives?

_____

What are typical revolutions-per-minute (RPM) speeds of SAS-specific hard drives?

_____

What are some of the reported mean-time-between-failure (MTBF) figures for SAS-specific drives?

_____

✖ Warning

The system you're using should have Adobe Reader installed to view many of the data sheets on the different technologies. If it's not already installed and you're in a classroom setting, ask for permission from your instructor before downloading this or any other program, just to be sure you're complying with school policy. You may download the current Adobe Reader from the Adobe Web site (www.adobe.com).

Step 3 One of the benefits of SAS is the ability to use either SAS-specific hard drives, SATA hard drives, or both. Access the Internet and search for information on SAS implementing SATA drives. Use keywords such as *SAS/SATA hard drives*, *white paper*, *controllers*, and *storage solutions*. Then answer the following questions:

What speed of data transfer can be achieved with SAS/SATA?_____

How many drives can be attached to a single controller? How many total drives can one system support? _____

What is the price range of SATA hard drives? _____

What are typical RPM speeds of SATA hard drives?

_____

What are some of the reported MTBF figures for SATA hard drives?

_____

Step 4 As you surfed around to the different sites on SCSI, SAS, and SATA drives, you probably noticed that many of these drives are implemented in different RAID configurations. With the overall cost of hard drives dropping, many desktop motherboard manufacturers (ASUS, Gigabyte, Intel, and so on) are incorporating RAID controllers into their motherboards. Visit a few of the motherboard manufacturers' Web sites and research their implementation of RAID. Use the following questions to refine your focus.

✔ Cross-Reference

For more information on RAID, refer to the "Protecting Data with RAID," "RAID," and "Implementing RAID" sections in Chapter 9 of *Mike Meyers' A+ Guide to Managing and Troubleshooting PCs*.

What are the most popular implementations of RAID used on desktop machines?

_____

How many drives are required to support the various RAID levels?

_____

Can you configure desktop RAID using both PATA and SATA drives?

_____

What are the two goals when implementing a RAID solution?

_____

Step 5   Gather the information you've found in your Internet research and head to your local computer store. Explore the current trends, based on the systems and components your local supplier is promoting. Write a brief summary of your findings and share it with your instructor and classmates.

 45 MINUTES

Lab Exercise 9.05: Troubleshooting Hard Drive Installations

The newest tech in your office has had trouble installing hard drives properly. In fact, he's tried it on four different machines with eight different drives and succeeded only once! You've been tasked to troubleshoot his failed installations and patiently explain the proper installation process to him. What fun!

Learning Objectives

This lab walks you through the errors new techs typically make on hard drive installation, particularly with PATA drives. The lab also addresses the main problems with SATA drives—usually faulty hardware—and how to address this in the field.

At the end of this lab, you'll be able to

- Troubleshoot hard drive installation problems effectively

- Explain the proper installation techniques for PATA and SATA drives

Lab Materials and Setup

The materials you need for this lab are

- Access to a PC system with PATA and SATA interfaces

- At least one PATA or SATA hard drive (preferably two or more)

Getting Down to Business

It might seem odd to mess up a hard drive installation deliberately, but you can't hurt anything, so give it a whirl. Seeing how the PC responds to mistakes when you know specifically what's wrong can help you when you run into similar situations later in the field.

Step 1   You have to have a properly functioning PC for this lab to be effective, so verify first that you have a system up and running with one or more hard drives installed.

Step 2   Power down the system. Disconnect the data cable for the hard drive used to boot the system, then power up the system. What happens? Will the PC autodetect the drive?

It is difficult to imagine not connecting the data cables to hard drives, but many times to add RAM or new devices, we have to disconnect the cables to gain access to the component. It is easy to miss reconnecting one of the cables after installing the new device.

Disconnecting the cable also simulates a broken IDE or SATA cable. These cables are somewhat delicate, and can fail after a sharp crease or a crimp from the system case. If you're having unexplained problems with your drive, check the cables prior to replacing the drive.

Step 3   Power down the PC and put the cable back on properly.

Step 4   On a PATA drive, change the jumper for the primary master hard drive to slave, and then power on the PC. What happens? Will the PC autodetect the drive? How should the jumper be installed?

Step 5   Power down the PC and put the jumper back on properly.

Step 6   Install a second PATA drive onto the primary controller, and set the jumpers on both drives incorrectly. Try variations: both as master; both as standalone; both as slave; both as cable select. Power on the PC and test each variation. What happens? Will the PC autodetect the drive? How should the jumpers be set for two PATA drives to work properly on the same controller?

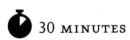 30 MINUTES

Lab Exercise 9.06: Installing Multiple Hard Drives in Preparation for RAID

Remember those two server machines you discovered—the ones with the dual CPUs and the SAS/SCSI controllers? Well, each of them has eight 150-GB SATA hard drives ready to be installed. You haven't had the opportunity to configure a RAID system before, so you ask a colleague for advice. She recommends that you install some additional drives in one of the workstations and then practice configuring RAID o using the software solution that comes with Microsoft Windows XP. This should help build your confidence before tackling the hardware RAID controllers on the servers.

Learning Objectives

In this lab, you will install additional hard drives—PATA, SATA, or both—in an existing system. You will access CMOS to verify that all of the drives have been recognized by the system. You will then set the system aside to be used in Lab Exercise 10.05, "Implementing Software RAID," in Chapter 10.

At the end of this lab, you'll be able to

- Install multiple hard drives in computer systems

- Verify multiple drives in CMOS

Lab Materials and Setup

The materials you need for this lab are

- A working PC with PATA or SATA interfaces and Microsoft Windows 2000 or Windows XP installed

- At least two additional, system-compatible hard drives—PATA or SATA as appropriate

Getting Down to Business

Even though you haven't been reminded during the last few exercises, you know that you should always take the proper anti-static precautions when opening the system case and working with the delicate components inside. Take those precautions now, and get ready to install a few extra hard drives into your system. In this exercise, you'll make sure these drives are recognized by the system; in the next chapter's labs, you'll configure them.

✔ **Hint**

For many of the exercises in the next chapter, it is very important that you have a working system with either Windows 2000 Professional or Windows XP Professional installed. Obviously, you will need to keep the system partition and boot partition intact (usually these are the same partition, and are the first partition on the first hard drive of the system) with the operating system running.

Even if you have available space on the first hard drive, it is much cleaner if you can install at least two additional hard drives. That way, you can partition, format, and convert to dynamic disks to your heart's content, without the worry of losing data (or the operating system).

Follow these steps to install an additional PATA drive:

Step 1 Determine on which controller, and in which order, you will be installing the drives.

Step 2 Set the jumpers properly for both the master and slave drives. (Usually, the boot device is the master drive on the primary controller, whereas the optical media drive is the master drive on the secondary controller, so the new drive is likely to be a slave to one of those drives.)

Step 3 Physically install the second drive, connecting the power and data cables properly.

Follow these steps to install additional SATA drives:

Step 1 Determine which controller you will use for the first additional drive and connect the SATA data cable to the controller on the motherboard.

Step 2 Physically install the first additional drive and connect the SATA power and data cables to the new drive.

Step 3 Determine which controller you will use for the second additional drive and connect the SATA data cable to the controller on the motherboard.

Step 4 Physically install the second additional drive and connect the SATA power and data cables to the new drive.

Follow these steps to verify the drives in CMOS:

Step 1 After installing all of the hard drives, plug the power back in and boot the machine.

Step 2 Press the appropriate key(s) to enter CMOS setup, and navigate to the configuration screen for installed devices.

Step 3 Perform autodetection if required, and confirm that all of the installed devices are present. If any of the devices are missing (and you remembered to reboot the machine if your system requires it), power the machine down, disconnect the power, and double-check all of the cables and drive settings.

Lab Analysis Test

1. Matthew has decided to use the RAID integrated into the SATA controller on his new system. He uses the system for high-end video editing, and would like to improve the performance of the system for this task. What implementation of RAID would you recommend to improve performance?

2. In what situation(s) might it be appropriate to disable the motherboard's hard drive controllers?

3. Brock, a new tech in your firm, informs you that the PC he's working on can't autodetect a hard drive he installed. He thinks the motherboard is broken. What's the more likely problem here?

4. The second SATA hard drive on your company's server has just died. You have a replacement drive, but it's critical that the server remain up and functioning. What, if anything, can you do to resolve this problem and get the second drive replaced?

5. Sean would like to install four additional hard drives in his system. His motherboard has two IDE controllers and two SATA controllers. There is one SATA drive installed, and the CD-RW drive is an IDE device. How would you configure Sean's system?

Key Term Quiz

Use the following vocabulary terms to complete the following sentences. Not all terms will be used.

autodetect

cable select

CHS

master

PATA

platters

RAID

SAS

SATA

slave

1. A new implementation of SCSI, typically used in servers, can use SCSI devices, SATA devices, or both. This new implementation is termed _____.

2. The data in a hard drive is actually stored magnetically on disks called _____.

3. One type of IDE drive transfers data in a parallel fashion. The other type of IDE drive transfers data in a serial fashion. These two types are known as _____ and _____, respectively.

4. To secure data in servers and high-end PCs, use a(n) _____ controller.

5. A great way to determine whether a new drive is installed and configured correctly is to run _____.

Chapter 10
Implementing Hard Drives

Lab Exercises

Once you've installed a new drive on a PC and it has been recognized by the system, you've got two more steps to complete before you can start storing data: partitioning and formatting.

✔ **Hint**

The tasks of partitioning and formatting have really become automated into the installation of the operating system (and the tools included in the operating system). Many of the steps are now completed in sequence, blurring the line between partitioning and formatting. Make sure you're clear on the distinction between partitioning and formatting, because you must do them in the proper order. Partitioning the disk simply means defining physical sections that are used to store data. Formatting the disk means *configuring the partition* with a file system.

In the early days of DOS, Windows 3.*x*, and Windows 9*x*, your hard drive had to be partitioned and formatted before you could run the installation setup routine. Windows NT, 2000, and XP incorporate these disk-preparation steps into the installation routine itself. However, it's still important for you to be able to perform these tasks from scratch as part of your basic PC tech repertoire.

You have a number of tools at your disposal for performing partitioning and formatting tasks. If you are working with a fresh hard drive, you need to get to these tools without necessarily having an operating system installed (this may be the first disk in the system, and you are preparing it for the OS installation). The first of these tools is the Windows 2000 Professional or Windows XP Professional installation CD itself. Also, a number of third-party utilities are available for partitioning and formatting, such as Symantec's PartitionMagic, VCOM's Partition Commander Professional, and the open-source Linux tool Gnome Partition Editor, affectionately known as GParted. These specific tools are beyond the scope of the CompTIA A+ exams; however, a good tech should develop skills in the use of these tools. The second tool you'll explore in this chapter is a LiveCD of GParted.

Once you have an operating system up and running, you should have some type of partitioning and formatting tool that you can run from the GUI. Windows 2000 and XP use a tool known as the Disk Management utility. Disk Management enables you to create, modify, and format partitions. You can also format partitions from within My Computer on the Windows desktop.

After looking at how to create and format partitions using the Windows 2000/XP installation CD and the LiveCD of GParted, you'll start up Windows to look at how to accomplish these tasks using the built-in tools. Next, you'll use the Disk Management utility to convert basic disks to dynamic disks and implement a RAID 0 stripe set. Then you'll look at the procedures for performing regular hard drive maintenance and troubleshooting tasks.

✔ **Hint**

The following exercises walk you through the basic management of hard drive storage available on your system. If you have only one drive installed, you will need to install the operating system after the first few exercises to perform the later exercises. In Lab Exercise 9.06, you installed two additional hard drives into a machine with either Windows 2000 Professional or Windows XP Professional installed. I recommend that you use this machine for all of the implementation labs (being careful not to partition or format the first drive, which should contain the operating system). Not only will this enable you to practice creating and deleting partitions and formatting and reformatting those partitions, it will also enable you to verify the partitions and file systems with the Disk Management tool in Windows 2000 or XP.

 30 MINUTES

Lab Exercise 10.01: Creating and Formatting Partitions with the Windows 2000/XP Installation CD-ROM

As you'll recall from the labs in Chapter 9, you have just worked with a number of donated machines, physically installing and configuring multiple hard drive technologies, primarily PATA and SATA hard drives. Once these drives have been recognized in CMOS, you are only halfway to your goal of using the drives for data storage. You must now partition each drive into usable space (even if only one partition uses all of the available drive space) and then format each partition with a file system.

In this lab, you will use the Windows install CD to partition and format hard drives in your system. If this were the only drive in your system, once you partition and format it with a file system, you have a blank partition in need of an operating system to boot the machine from the hard drive. In the labs for Chapter 12, "Installing and Upgrading Windows," you will complete the process of installing the operating system.

✔ **Cross-Reference**

For details about partitioning and formatting drives with the Windows install CD, refer to the "Partitioning and Formatting with Windows Install CD" section in Chapter 10 of *Mike Meyers' A+ Guide to Managing and Troubleshooting PCs*.

Learning Objectives

In this exercise, you'll use the Windows install CD to partition a hard drive and format the partition for use.

At the end of this lab, you'll be able to

- Set up a primary partition on a hard drive
- Format the partition with the NTFS file system

Lab Materials and Setup

The materials you need for this lab are

- The PC from Lab Exercise 9.06 with a primary hard drive that holds your Windows OS, and the two blank hard drives that you can partition and format to your heart's content
- A Windows 2000 or Windows XP install CD

✖ **Warning**

Partitioning and formatting a hard drive destroys any data on it! Practice this lab using only drives that don't store any data you need.

Getting Down to Business

In this exercise, you'll start the system by booting from the Windows XP install CD (you will have to configure your system CMOS to boot from the CD). You'll partition a portion of one of the hard drives and format it with the NTFS file system, as if you're preparing to install the operating system.

Step 1 Enter the CMOS setup program and configure the boot order, selecting the CD-ROM drive as the first boot device. Also make sure that the setting called "Boot Other Device" (or something similar) is enabled; otherwise, your system may not recognize the CD-ROM drive as a bootable drive.

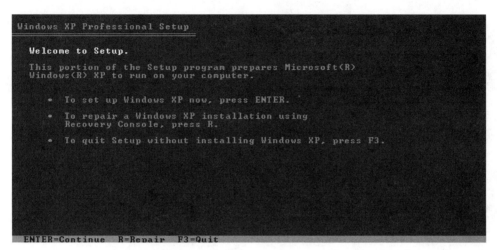

FIGURE 10-1 The first Windows Setup screen

Step 2   Place the Windows XP install CD in the CD-ROM drive tray and boot the machine. Windows Setup copies a number of files and then presents you with the screen shown in Figure 10-1. Press ENTER to set up Windows XP now.

Step 3   Press F8 to accept the license agreement and enter the main partitioning screen.

✔ **Hint**

If you are using the machine configured in Lab Exercise 9.06, Windows XP has been installed on one of the drives in the system. Setup asks if you would like to repair this installation, and advises you to press ESC if you want to install a fresh copy. Press ESC to progress to the next step—partitioning the drive.

The screen displays the installed drives and any partitions and/or file systems that have been configured on the drives prior to this session (see Figure 10-2).

Step 4   If any partitions exist on the drives you have installed to practice this lab (and the data on these drives is expendable), delete them at this time.

To delete a partition, simply select the partition, press D to delete, and then press L to commit the delete process. The partition will be returned to unpartitioned space.

Step 5   To create a partition, follow these steps:

a)   Press C.

b)   Select the size of the partition you want to create (10 GB is a good size for a system partition or a boot partition, but you should try multiple sizes).

c)   Press ENTER.

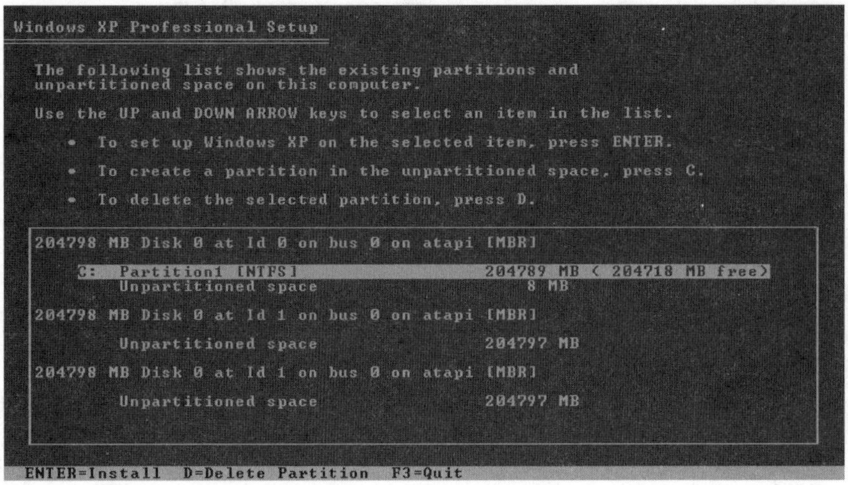

FIGURE 10-2 Partitioning screen

d) The new partition should appear in the partitioning screen.

Congratulations! You have created a partition.

Step 6 Press ENTER to see a list of file system options, as shown in Figure 10-3. Choose a file system (NTFS is the default) and indicate whether you will perform an exhaustive formatting process or the "Quick" formatting process.

Press ENTER. Windows formats the partition and proceeds with the operating system installation. You can shut down the PC once this step is completed.

Step 7 Reboot the machine and allow your Windows OS to boot. Then use the Disk Management tool to verify the partition(s) you have created with the install CD. Alternatively, you can verify the partitions you created and the file systems you configured when you try using the GParted tool in the next lab.

Step 8 Practice deleting, creating, and formatting different combinations of partitions and file systems to become comfortable with the tools used in this exercise. Have fun!

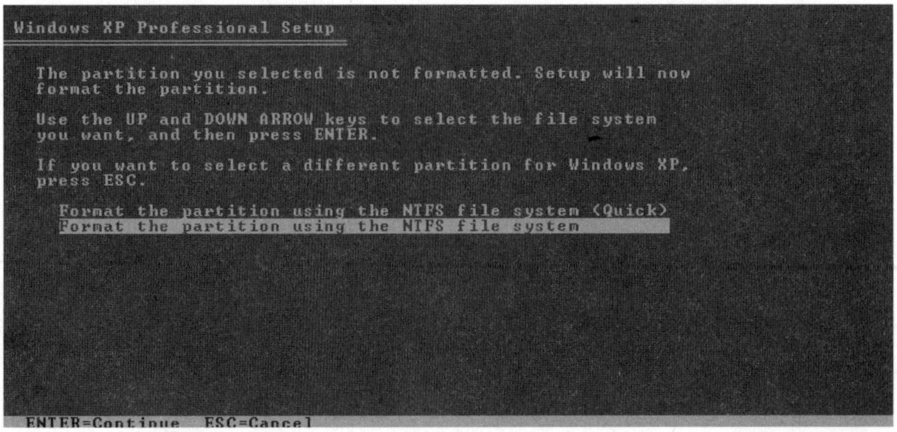

FIGURE 10-3 Format screen

 30 MINUTES

Lab Exercise 10.02: Creating and Formatting Partitions with Gnome Partition Editor (GParted)

As a competent tech, you want to keep up with the newest methods for accomplishing old tasks. Using the donated computers as an example, you might want to partition and format all of the machines before installing an operating system and deploying the machines to users. To accomplish this task, it might be easier to use a standalone partitioning/formatting tool such as the open-source Gnome Partition Editor (GParted). Gnome is one of the many versions of the Linux operating system. GParted uses a basic, bootable version of Gnome with disk management tools built in. This method is somewhat beyond the scope of the CompTIA A+ exams, but the skills and techniques you will practice in this lab are valuable to a real-world tech, and can help you gain a deeper understanding of partitioning and formatting hard drives.

In this exercise, you will use the LiveCD of GParted to partition and format the two additional hard drives installed in your lab system. If you are working in a classroom setting, the instructor should be able to provide copies of the GParted LiveCD to you for this exercise. Alternatively, you could jump ahead to Lab Exercise 11.05, where you will create a LiveCD by burning a CD with an ISO image.

✔ Cross-Reference

For additional details about the GParted LiveCD, refer to the "Third-Party Partition Tools" section in Chapter 10 of *Mike Meyers' A+ Guide to Managing and Troubleshooting PCs*.

Learning Objectives

In this exercise, you'll use the GParted LiveCD to partition a hard drive and format the partition for use.

At the end of this lab, you'll be able to

- Set up primary and extended partitions on hard drives

- Format the partitions with various file systems

→ Try This: Drive Imaging

Many techs, and specifically techs employed by the IT departments of small to large businesses, often use one of the popular drive-imaging tools such as Symantec's Ghost. Drive imaging is used to roll out the operating system and applications on multiple machines expediently. This method creates the partition, and copies the OS, applications, and user profiles onto the file system that was used to make the image, all in one step. This method is also beyond the scope of the CompTIA A+ exams, but you should explore drive imaging for completeness.

Lab Materials and Setup

The materials you need for this lab are

- The PC from Lab Exercise 9.06 with a primary hard drive that holds your Windows OS, and the two blank hard drives that you can partition and format to your heart's content

- Optionally, a system with one hard drive that you can safely erase

- A GParted LiveCD

✖ **Warning**

Partitioning and formatting a hard drive destroys any data on the drive! Practice this lab only on drives that don't store any data you need.

Getting Down to Business

In this exercise, you'll start the system by booting from the GParted LiveCD. (You will have to configure your system CMOS to boot from the CD.) You'll then partition a portion of one of the hard drives and format it with the file system of your choice.

Step 1   Enter the CMOS setup program and configure the boot order, selecting the CD-ROM drive as the first boot device. Also make sure that the setting called "Boot Other Device" (or something similar) is enabled; otherwise, your system may not recognize the CD-ROM drive as a bootable drive.

Step 2   Place the GParted LiveCD in the CD-ROM drive tray and boot the machine. GParted displays an introduction screen, as shown in Figure 10-4. Press ENTER to boot; Gnome Linux should begin to load. As the system loads, you will be queried a number of times for settings related to boot options, language, keyboard, and screen depth and resolution. Unless told to do otherwise by your instructor, select the defaults for these settings by highlighting OK and pressing ENTER.

GParted should finish booting and arrive at a screen displaying various menu items, icons, and the current drive focus with strange Linux names such as /dev/hda1, /dev/hda3, and so forth. Notice the

Figure 10-4 The Gnome Partition Editor initial screen

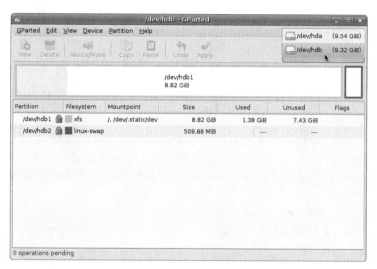

FIGURE 10-5 Selecting a drive on the main GParted partitioning/formatting screen

item at the far right of the menu bar; here, you can click the drop-down arrow to select which physical drive the GParted screen is focused on (see Figure 10-5).

Step 3 Now change the focus to the second or third drive installed on your system. This will probably be labeled /dev/hdb or /dev/hdc in the drop-down list of hard drives.

✔ **Hint**

If you are using the machine that you configured in Lab Exercise 9.06, Windows XP has been installed on one of the drives in the system (most likely the first drive). When GParted first launches, the screen focus will be on this drive and the label will probably read /dev/hda1. Make sure that you use the menu drop-down list to select one of the drives that has been set up to be partitioned and formatted, or you'll find yourself reinstalling Windows XP.

The screen now focuses on the drive you've selected, and shows any partitions and/or file systems that have been configured on that drive prior to this session. If any partitions are displayed, highlight the partition, right-click to bring up the menu, and select Delete.

Step 4 GParted requires that you commit any changes that you make to the partitions on the disk, so after deleting the partition, you must click the Apply button to apply the settings and actually delete the partition.

When you click Apply, GParted applies the pending operations. You should now have a drive visible with all of the available space denoted as unallocated space.

Step 5 Select the unallocated space, right-click, and select New from the drop-down menu. Then follow these steps:

a) Enter the size of the partition in megabytes; either type a number or use the up and down arrows to select a size. For the purposes of practice, 4000 MB (4 GB) to 10,000 MB (10 GB) is a good size for the partition.

b) Select Primary Partition or Extended Partition; primary is a good choice for the initial partition on the drive.

c) Select a file system; FAT32 and NTFS are good choices for Windows machines.

d) Click the Add button. The new partition with the formatted file system should appear on the screen.

e) Click Apply to create the formatted partition. A message box will pop up, asking you to confirm that you want to apply the pending operations. Click Apply again, then watch as the "Applying pending operations" dialog appears, shows you the status of the operation, and then disappears.

f) Click Close.

Congratulations! You should now have a drive with a formatted partition visible in the main screen (see Figure 10-6).

Step 6   There is one last step, which depends on whether you plan to use this partition to boot the machine with an OS (active partition) and which file system you have selected.

With the partition highlighted, right-click on the partition and select Manage Flags from the drop-down menu. A small window appears where you'll see a number of flags that you can set (see Figure 10-7). Many of these apply to operating systems other than Windows, but two of them must be set if you are to use the partition in Windows:

- **boot**   This flag must be set if the partition is to be the active partition in the system (this is usually the first partition on the first hard drive in the system).

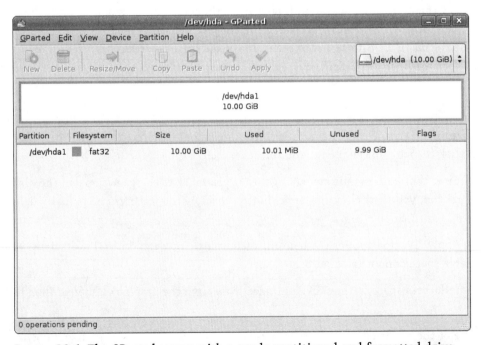

Figure 10-6 The GParted screen with a newly partitioned and formatted drive

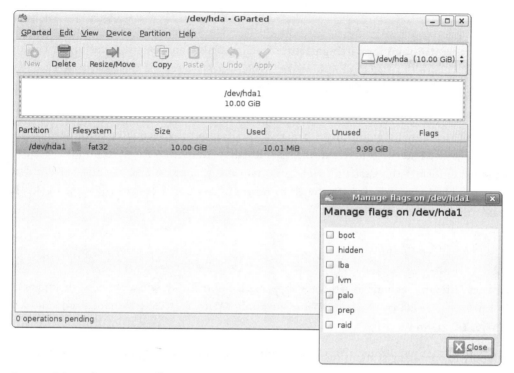

FIGURE 10-7 The Manage flags window in GParted

- **lba**   If you have selected the FAT32 file system, the flag to indicate Large Block Addressing (LBA) must be selected for Windows to see the partition after it has been created.

Set the appropriate flags for your partition and file system and close the Manage flags window. Notice that you will not have to apply changes, as the settings take effect immediately.

Step 7   Reboot the machine and allow your Windows OS to boot. You can then use Disk Management to verify the partition(s) you have created with GParted.

Step 8   Practice deleting, creating, and formatting different combinations of partitions and file systems to become comfortable with the GParted program.

 30 MINUTES

Lab Exercise 10.03: Using Windows Tools to Create and Format Partitions

Once you have all of the donated machines' drives configured, partitioned, formatted, and the Windows XP Professional operating system installed, working with hard drive storage becomes much more intuitive. Windows 2000 and XP include tools that let you create, modify, and format partitions "on the fly" from within Windows. One of these utilities is called Disk Management.

✔ **Cross-Reference**

For details about creating and formatting partitions using Disk Management, refer to the "Disk Management" section in Chapter 10 of *Mike Meyers' A+ Guide to Managing and Troubleshooting PCs*.

This lab exercise assumes that you want to create a partition on the second or third hard drive installed on the Windows XP lab system, then format that partition with a file system. Disk Management will enable you to format the partition right away; however, you can also use another Windows utility that you should be intimately familiar with by now: My Computer. Follow the steps in this lab exercise to create and format a new partition.

✔ **Hint**

Remember that different versions of Windows support different file systems: Windows 9x supports only FAT, either FAT16 or FAT32; Windows NT supports only FAT16 and NTFS4; Windows 2000 and XP support FAT16, FAT32, and NTFS5.

Note that if you format partitions with NTFS, you're not given a choice of an NTFS version—Windows 2000 and XP automatically format with NTFS5.

NTFS5 is completely backward compatible with NTFS4, but Windows NT systems must have Service Pack 4 installed to read NTFS5-formatted partitions.

Learning Objectives

In this exercise, you'll use the Disk Management program to partition a hard drive for use and format the partition with a file system.

At the end of this lab, you'll be able to

- Set up a primary, active partition on a hard drive
- Set up an extended partition and logical drives in that partition
- Format partitions with various file systems

Lab Materials and Setup

The materials you need for this lab are

- The PC from Lab Exercise 9.06, with a primary hard drive that holds your Windows XP Professional installation and the two blank hard drives that you can partition and format

✖ **Warning**

Partitioning a hard drive destroys any data on it! Practice this lab only on drives that don't contain any data you need.

Getting Down to Business

The steps for partitioning drives and formatting partitions in Windows 2000 and XP are very similar. Follow these steps for Windows XP Professional:

Step 1   Right-click the My Computer icon and select Manage to open a Computer Management window. Under the Storage node, click on Disk Management.

Step 2   As in prior lab exercises, if there are any existing partitions on the second or third drive, highlight the partitions and either right-click and delete the partitions or simply press DELETE.

Step 3   Start the process of creating a partition by right-clicking an unpartitioned section of drive space and telling the utility what type of partition you want to create: primary or extended.

In Disk Management, highlight your second or third hard drive and select a section of unpartitioned space labeled Unallocated, and then select New Partition from the pop-up menu to start the New Partition Wizard (see Figure 10-8).

Step 4   Click Next, and then select Primary Partition from the partition type pull-down menu. At the next screen, enter the size of your new partition in megabytes.

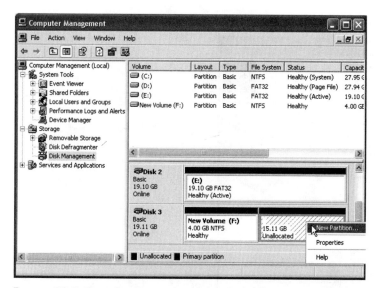

FIGURE 10-8   Creating a new partition in Disk Management

As you've no doubt noticed, I keep warning you to protect your data because you'll lose it when you create or format a partition. While the partitioning and formatting utilities you've practiced with thus far are destructive to data, it is possible to resize a partition without losing data; programs such as PartitionMagic (http://partitionmagic.com) can do this.

There's also a way to convert earlier file systems to NTFS without the loss of data. Windows has a built-in command called CONVERT that you can use to change a partition from FAT32 to NTFS. You will perform this conversion in the lab exercises for Chapter 14, "Working with the Command-Line Interface."

Step 5   You can now assign a drive letter or mount the partition to an empty folder. For now, go with the default drive letter assignment and click Next again.

Step 6   The next screen offers you the option to format the new partition with a file system. Select a file system: FAT, FAT32, or NTFS. Then enter a volume label if you want and click OK. Figure 10-9 shows this selection screen in the Disk Management utility.

Step 7   The utility warns you that formatting will erase all data on the drive. Click OK to begin formatting.

Step 8   My Computer also enables you to format partitions, but generally speaking you'll use this method only to format removable media such as floppy disks, Zip disks, USB thumb drives, and so on.

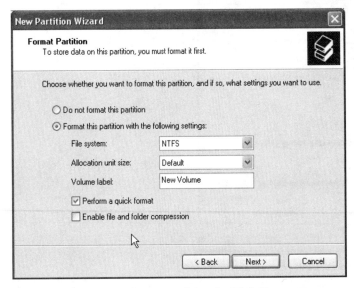

FIGURE 10-9 Formatting a partition in Disk Management

FIGURE 10-10 Formatting a
partition in My Computer

Right-click a drive icon in My Computer and select Format from the pop-up menu to open the Formatting dialog box (see Figure 10-10). Now proceed as in Step 6.

Step 9   Practice deleting, creating, and formatting different combinations of partitions and file systems to become comfortable with the Disk Management utility.

 30 MINUTES

Lab Exercise 10.04: Converting Basic Disks to Dynamic Disks with Disk Management

In Lab Exercise 9.06, you configured two additional hard drives in a system to facilitate a software implementation of RAID. Starting with the introduction of Windows 2000 and continuing with Windows XP
Professional and Windows Server 2003, Microsoft requires that a disk be converted to a dynamic disk to
allow the implementation of RAID. In this lab, you will prepare the two additional drives to be used in
the next lab exercise using Disk Management to perform the simple, nondestructive conversion from
basic disks to dynamic disks.

✔ Cross-Reference

To learn more about dynamic disks, refer to the "Dynamic Disks" section in Chapter 10 of *Mike
Meyers' A+ Guide to Managing and Troubleshooting PCs.*

Learning Objectives

In this exercise, you'll use the Disk Management utility to convert basic disks to dynamic disks.

At the end of this lab, you'll be able to

- Convert basic disks to dynamic disks

Lab Materials and Setup

The materials you need for this lab are

- The PC from Lab Exercise 9.06 with a primary hard drive that holds your Windows XP Professional installation and the two blank hard drives that you will convert to dynamic disks

Getting Down to Business

The steps to convert a basic disk to a dynamic disk are really quite simple. Follow these steps for Windows XP Professional:

Step 1 Open the Disk Management utility as in the previous exercise.

Step 2 Select the first drive to be converted, and positioning the mouse pointer over the left-hand drive icon, right-click and select Convert to Dynamic Disk (see Figure 10-11).

Step 3 Follow the wizard instructions to complete the dynamic disk conversion. Reboot the PC (if necessary) and then open Disk Management again. The disk should now be labeled as a dynamic disk instead of a basic disk (see Figure 10-12).

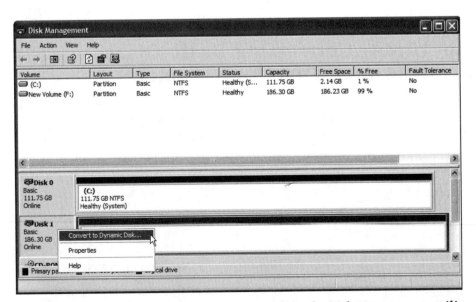

FIGURE 10-11 Selecting Convert to Dynamic Disk in the Disk Management utility

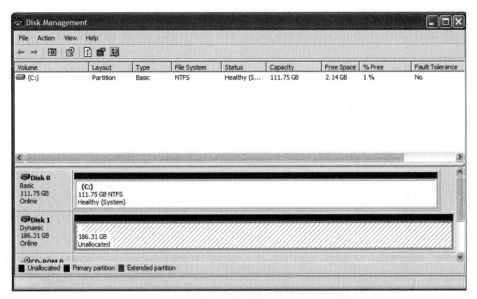

FIGURE 10-12 Disk Management showing basic and dynamic storage

Step 4 Repeat Steps 2 and 3 on the third drive in the system (you will need two dynamic disks to implement a RAID 0 stripe set), then proceed to Lab Exercise 10.05.

 30 MINUTES

Lab Exercise 10.05: Implementing Software RAID 0 with Disk Management

It's finally time to flex your RAID muscles in preparation to deploy the two server machines—remember, these are the systems with dual CPUs and SAS/SCSI controllers. Windows 2000, XP Professional, and Server 2003 allow you to configure software RAID implementations using Disk Management and multiple hard drives. Windows XP Professional offers only RAID 0, a stripe set, which offers improved disk access time but no fault tolerance. At the end of this lab, you will have configured a stripe set using two disks.

✔ Cross-Reference

Additional information on RAID 0, 1, and 5 may be found in the "Dynamic Disks" section in Chapter 10 of *Mike Meyers' A+ Guide to Managing and Troubleshooting PCs.*

This lab exercise guides you through the creation of a RAID 0 stripe set using free, unpartitioned space on the second and third hard drives installed on the Windows XP lab system. These are the same disks that you converted from basic disks to dynamic disks in the prior exercise. Disk Management allows you to configure simple volumes, spanned volumes, and striped volumes on dynamic disks.

✔ **Hint**

Microsoft's dynamic storage provides five types of volumes: simple volumes, spanned volumes, striped volumes, mirrored volumes, and RAID 5 volumes. The first three—simple, spanned, and striped—are the only volumes currently available on Windows 2000 Professional or Windows XP Professional.

- Simple volumes on dynamic disks are equivalent to primary partitions on basic disks. Simple volumes use a contiguous area of a single drive and are represented by one drive letter or mount point.

- Spanned volumes enable you to extend the size of a simple volume to include any unallocated space (contiguous or noncontiguous) on one or more dynamic disks. Spanned volumes are represented by one drive letter or mount point and fill the volume sequentially.

- Striped volumes use two or more dynamic disks, and spread data across all of them. Striped volumes are represented by one drive letter or mount point and will speed up disk access times due to concurrent disk write and read operations. The more disks in the stripe set, the faster the throughput.

Learning Objectives

In this exercise, you'll use the Disk Management program to configure a RAID 0 striped volume.

At the end of this lab, you'll be able to

- Create and configure a RAID 0 striped volume

Lab Materials and Setup

The materials you need for this lab are

- The PC from Lab Exercise 9.06 with a primary hard drive that holds your Windows XP Professional installation and the two blank hard drives that have been converted to dynamic disks

---

✖ **Warning**

Partitioning a hard drive destroys any data on the drive! Practice this lab only on drives that don't contain any data you need.

Getting Down to Business

You're in the home stretch now! Once you've worked with the Disk Management tool and converted basic disks to dynamic disks, it's just a matter of using the Disk Management New Volume Wizard, choosing the size allocated to the striped volume, and formatting the striped volume.

Step 1 Launch the Disk Management utility and right-click on the unallocated space on the first disk of the planned striped volume. Select New Volume and then select Striped (see Figure 10-13).

Step 2 The wizard asks you to select at least one additional dynamic disk for the striped volume. You will then select the size of the volume you want to create and decide what file system to use to format the striped volume.

Are there any restrictions on the size of the volume?

_____

Step 3 Disk Management now allocates the space on the drives and formats them with the file system you've selected. You should now have a healthy, formatted, striped volume.

Step 4 Practice deleting and creating various sizes of striped volumes using various file systems. Can you format a striped volume with FAT? Why or why not?

_____

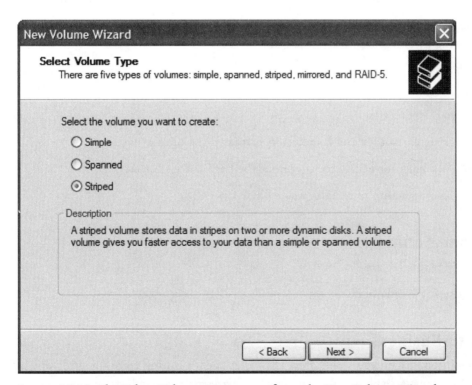

FIGURE 10-13 The Select Volume Type screen from the New Volume Wizard

1 HOUR

Lab Exercise 10.06: Maintaining and Troubleshooting Hard Drives

Of all the devices installed in a PC, hard drives tend to need the most attention. Maintaining and troubleshooting hard drives is one of the most common tasks you'll undertake as a PC tech, but also one of the most important.

After all, the loss of other components such as video cards or NICs is inconvenient, but hardly disastrous. The loss of a hard drive, on the other hand, means the loss of data. This data might be as trivial as your favorite bookmarked Web pages or a saved Half-Life 2 game, or as important as your business records, family photos, or the 1200-page novel that you've spent the last two years writing! Unless you want to spend valuable time and money trying to retrieve data from a damaged or corrupted hard drive, you should familiarize yourself with the built-in Windows drive maintenance tools. These tools include:

- **Error-checking** This GUI tool enables you to examine the physical structure of the drive and retrieve data from bad clusters. Command-line utilities that perform the same duties are called CHKDSK and SCANDISK.

- **Disk Defragmenter** This tool reorganizes disorganized file structures into contiguous clusters.

- **Disk Cleanup** This tool reclaims wasted space on the hard drive by deleting unneeded files and compressing files that are rarely accessed.

Learning Objectives

At the end of this lab, you'll be able to

- Use error-checking to scan for and fix physical errors on the hard drive

- Use the Disk Defragmenter utility to reorganize the hard drive's file structure

- Use the Disk Cleanup utility to reclaim wasted disk space

Lab Materials and Setup

The materials you need for this lab are

- A fully functioning Windows PC

Getting Down to Business

Performing regular maintenance on your hard drives can keep them running more smoothly and efficiently. If you're getting obvious disk-related errors (such as error messages indicating that your disk has bad clusters or cannot be read), or if files are missing or corrupt, a tune-up is in order. Another sign that your drive needs maintenance is excessive disk activity, or disk "thrashing." It's also a good idea to do some maintenance after a serious system crash or virus infection by scanning your drive for damage or fragmentation.

✔ Hint

In a computer system, the hard drive wins the prize as the most critical storage device and for having the most moving parts of any of the components. For this reason, it is extremely important that you not only perform routine preventive maintenance (error-checking, defragmentation, and disk cleanup), but also regularly back up critical data.

✔ Cross-Reference

You will work with some backup techniques and tools in the lab exercises for Chapter 15.

Step 1   To scan a hard drive for physical problems, open My Computer and right-click the drive's icon. Select Properties from the pop-up menu, and then select the Tools tab, shown in Figure 10-14. Click Check Now to start the error-checking utility.

In the Check Disk dialog box, you can opt to fix file system errors automatically, scan for and attempt to recover bad sectors, or both. When you've made your selections, click Start.

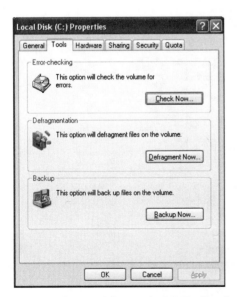

Figure 10-14 Disk Properties Tools tab

✔ **Hint**

The error-checking utility must have *exclusive* access to the drive to finish scanning it. If you have services or applications running in the background, the utility will halt. In some cases, the utility will schedule itself to run the next time you restart your PC.

The error-checking utility has two command-line equivalents: CHKDSK (used on Windows NT, 2000, and XP) and SCANDISK (used on Windows 9x). There's no inherent advantage to running these utilities as opposed to the GUI version, except that you can launch the utilities as part of a scripted batch file.

Step 2   To launch the Disk Defragmenter, click Defragment Now. The Windows 2000/XP version of the Disk Defragmenter is shown in Figure 10-15.

Disk Defragmenter offers you a choice: You can click Analyze to examine the disk to see if a defragmenting operation is needed, or simply click Defragment to start the process without first analyzing the drive.

Step 3   Select properties for a drive and click Disk Cleanup on the General tab. Disk Cleanup calculates the space you'll be able to free up, and then displays the Disk Cleanup dialog box, shown in Figure 10-16.

Near the top of the dialog box you can see how much disk space (maximum) you could free up using Disk Cleanup. But look carefully! Depending on which categories in the list of Files To Delete are checked, the actual amount of disk space you'll gain could be much smaller than the estimate at the top. As you select and deselect choices, watch this value change.

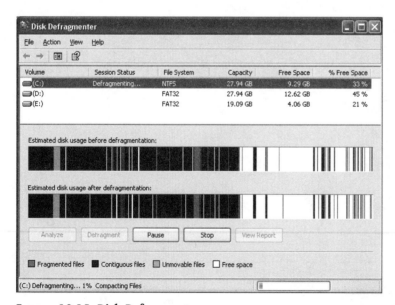

FIGURE 10-15 Disk Defragmenter

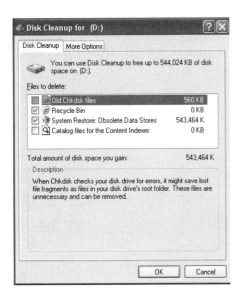

FIGURE 10-16 Disk Cleanup

Pretty cool, but wait, there's more—Disk Cleanup does more than just delete files! If you scroll down through the list, you'll see an option to compress old files. In fact, this file compression trick is where Disk Cleanup really, uh, cleans up. File compression is where you'll gain the most space. The other big heavyweight category is temporary Internet files, which you should usually have Disk Cleanup delete for you.

Lab Analysis Test

1. Name at least two indicators that you should perform maintenance on your hard drive.

2. What are the two command-line versions of the Windows error-checking utility?

3. Amanda argues that a hard drive must be formatted before you can set up the partitions. Samantha says the drive must be partitioned first. Who is correct, and why?

4. Kyle is running out of disk space on his hard drive on a Windows XP Professional system. He has installed and configured a third hard drive in the system to increase the total storage. He is planning on converting his current drive to dynamic storage and extending the storage space to the newly installed drive (also dynamic storage). Pablo argues that the conversion is destructive and that Kyle would not be able to extend the volume anyway. Is Kyle going to be able to make this work?

5. Sean has created a RAID 0 stripe set using three drives on a Windows 2000 Professional system. After running the system for a few years, he arrived at work one day to find one of the three drives had failed. He thought that if only one drive failed, he would still be able to access his data. What facts about RAID did Sean misunderstand?

Key Term Quiz

Use the following vocabulary terms to complete the following sentences. Not all terms will be used.

basic disk

CHKDSK

defragmentation

Disk Cleanup

Disk Management

dynamic disk

error-checking

FDISK

format

GParted

partition

SCANDISK

volumes

Windows XP install CD

1. To partition and format a hard drive when no operating system has been installed, you may use either _____ or _____ to boot the system and run disk setup utilities.

2. Use a(n) _____ tool to fix noncontiguous file clusters on a hard drive.

3. The _____ tool enables you to partition and format drives in Windows XP.

4. Microsoft supports two types of storage configurations now; the _____ uses partitions, whereas the _____ uses _____.

5. If your hard drive is running out of free space, you should use the _____ utility.

Chapter 11

Removable Media

Lab Exercises

Removable media storage is one of the fastest-changing components of the PC, and these days it's also very much in the public eye. With the advent of USB thumb drives, MP3 players with large-capacity hard drives, and digital cameras using CompactFlash and Secure Digital memory cards, all kinds of people—from children to great-grandmothers, from artists to zookeepers—are using removable storage. With the high resolution of today's audio and video files, photographs, and games, the need for portable large-capacity storage is greater than ever.

The lowly floppy drive has the distinction of being the only component of a modern PC to employ basically the same technology as the original IBM PC. It's hard to believe, but when the first PCs came out, the entire data storage system consisted of a single floppy drive and multiple floppy disks holding a little more than 300,000 bytes of data each! Floppies have been around ever since, but with the recent advances in storage technology, the floppy is finally entering its twilight, due mostly to its tiny capacity.

Technicians were the last holdout in keeping floppy drives around. While hard drives can contain trillions of bytes of data, they can also fail; until recently, techs could still depend on the floppy drive, and a disk that can hold less than 2 MB of data, to boot a failed system and provide troubleshooting utilities that might breathe life back into the PC. While techs still need these tools, they now come in the form of bootable CDs, DVDs, and even U3 bootable USB thumb drives.

As a budding tech, you'll work with all types of removable media. The labs in this chapter will introduce you to the installation, configuration, and use of optical (that is, CD- and DVD-based) drives, burners, and media. You'll work with thumb drives and even learn to install the venerable floppy drive—this is important, as many corporations still order floppy drives with new machines. The final lab in the chapter looks at some troubleshooting techniques for removable media.

✔ **Hint**

Do you still have that non-production, disassembled PC from the lab exercises back in Chapter 2? Well, if you haven't done so already, you should have it completely assembled and running again after the floppy and optical-media drive installation lab exercises in this chapter. You can still use it to explore the hardware of video and sound cards in future chapters, and if you can install an OS on it, so much the better!

 30 MINUTES

Lab Exercise 11.01: Installing Floppy Drives

Your boss recently approved the purchase of a number of new workstations, all without floppy disk drives. "Times are changing," he explained, "and floppies just hold too little data. Plus they're slow and cumbersome!" Now, however, the employees assigned to the new machines have complained so much that the boss has decided to retrofit all the new workstations with 3.5-inch floppy drives. Many manufacturers offer USB 3.5-inch floppy disk drives, but you found a supply house close-out on the old original FDD. You've been assigned the task of adding floppy drives to these PCs.

✔ **Cross-Reference**

To review the details of floppy drive installation, refer to the "Installing Floppy Drives" section in Chapter 11 of *Mike Meyers' A+ Guide to Managing and Troubleshooting PCs.*

Learning Objectives

In this lab, you'll practice removing and installing a floppy drive.

At the end of this lab, you'll be able to

- Remove a floppy drive safely and correctly
- Install a floppy drive safely and correctly

Lab Materials and Setup

The materials you need for this lab are

- A working computer system with a floppy drive installed

- A known good floppy disk with data

Getting Down to Business

Although this lab starts with a working floppy drive installed in a PC—a likely scenario in a classroom setting—when building a system, you'd obviously need to install one from scratch. On a new system (or if you are reassembling the disassembled, non-production machine from Chapter 2), you'd start this lab at Step 5.

Step 1   Begin with the PC turned on and the standard Windows desktop displayed. To verify that the floppy drive works, insert a known good floppy disk containing files into the drive, and then view the files on it by following these steps:

a) Double-click the My Computer icon on the Desktop.

b) Double-click the 3 1/2 Floppy (A:) icon in the window (see Figure 11-1).

c) Observe the files and folders displayed.

Do you see files displayed? _____

 Hint

If no files are displayed, try another floppy disk. Also, be sure to insert the disk properly. You should hear a ratcheting sound when you double-click the floppy drive icon. This is the sound of the read mechanism opening the metal cover so that it can read the data on the disk.

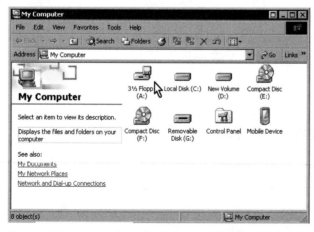

FIGURE 11-1 Accessing the contents of a floppy disk

Step 2 Properly shut down the system, unplug the main power cable, and open the case following good ESD procedures.

Step 3 Carefully disconnect the two cables from the back of the floppy drive. One is the four-wire cable from the power supply (with its mini connector), and the other is the flat ribbon cable that carries the data to and from the drive.

✖ Warning

Be sure to notice the seven-wire twist in the ribbon cable before you disconnect it. Is the twist closer to the drive or to the motherboard? If you put this cable back on incorrectly, the floppy drive will not work. The end with the twist (see the illustration) always goes closest to the floppy drive.

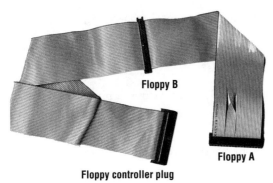

✔ Hint

If your lab has gone sleekly high-tech and uses rounded data cables rather than the traditional flat ribbon cables, you can safely assume that the connector on the end will have a marking for the A: drive.

Now disconnect the other end of the ribbon cable from the motherboard. These cables can be quite firmly attached to the motherboard, so use caution! Grab the connector, or grab as close to the connector as you can, and pull straight up firmly but gently. Sometimes a connector will seem to stick on one side—make sure that you don't pull unevenly, or you may bend the pins on the motherboard.

How many wires make up the ribbon cable? (Go ahead, count 'em!)

_____

Is one of the wires a different color from the rest, and if so, what does that mean?

_____

Look at the motherboard where the cable was attached, and examine the pins.

How many pins do you count? _____

Look at the shape of the connection.

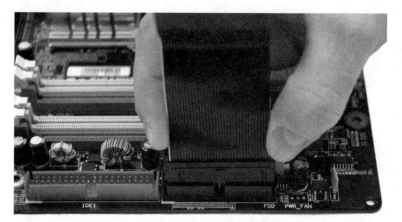

Figure 11-2 The orientation of the floppy drive connector on the motherboard

Is it symmetrical, meaning you can plug the connector in either direction, or is one side of the connector keyed to prevent you from inserting it backwards? _____

Locate pin 1 (where the colored wire attaches) and pin 34. The thirty-fourth pin is the drive change signal/disk change signal. It indicates when a disk has been physically changed. If this wire is broken or not connected, the system will read the initial disk placed in the floppy drive after power is applied and remember the contents for that disk, no matter how many times you change disks during a session, until you reboot the system.

Compare your motherboard connection for the floppy drive with the one shown in Figure 11-2.

Step 4   Remove the floppy drive from the case. There are so many different ways that floppy drives are held into system cases that it would be impossible to list all of the various carriers, caddies, bays, and so on that might be used to hold your floppy drive.

Almost all floppy drives are secured to these carriers, caddies, and bays with fine-threaded screws. The threads on these screws are narrower than those on the screws commonly used to secure expansion cards and the case cover. There should be two screws in each side of the floppy drive for support.

✔ Hint

Get in the habit of storing screws safely while you're changing out or inspecting hardware. You can use a small plastic bowl, a coffee cup, or an empty baby food jar or breath mint tin—but if you let those screws roll around loose, you may not have enough of them the next time you need to install a device!

Step 5   Now that you've removed the floppy drive, give it a thorough inspection. Look at the area where the cables connect (see Figure 11-3).

Is this ribbon cable area keyed or notched? _____

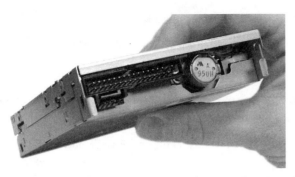

FIGURE 11-3 Examining the connections for the ribbon cable (top) and power cable (bottom) on the back of a floppy drive

Find the indicator for the location of pin 1 on the floppy drive.

What and where is it? _____

On which side of the connector does the red (or other colored) orientation stripe of the cable go— toward the center or toward the outside?

_____

How many physical pins are on your floppy drive? _____

Look at the area where the power is attached.

How many pins are there? _____

Take a moment to experiment to see if you can insert the power connector into the floppy drive incorrectly. Be gentle!

Can you connect it upside down? _____

Can you connect it without covering every pin? _____

On which side of the Mini connector does the orientation stripe go: toward the center or toward the outside?

_____

✖ Warning

It is possible to force the power connector on incorrectly, which will cause damage to the drive. Practice how it feels to make this connection properly and improperly, so that when you do it from an odd angle (for example, lying on your back under a desk), you know how it should feel.

Step 6   Reinstall the floppy drive by placing it back where you found it in the case. Be sure to use the proper fine-threaded screws to secure the drive.

Now attach a mini power connector to the floppy drive to provide power, and attach the 34-pin ribbon cable securely to the drive.

Attach the ribbon cable to the motherboard. Make sure it is secure and all the pins are covered.

Did you make sure that pin 1 was connected properly at both ends of the ribbon cable?

Are the connectors properly aligned so that pin 34 is connected on both ends of the cable?

Step 7   Once everything is back in place, leave the system cover off so that you can make adjustments if needed. Start the system, and watch the green LED on the front of the floppy drive.

If the green LED does not turn on at all during the boot process, then check your power connection.

If the green LED comes on and stays on all the time, then the ribbon cable is not connected properly (it is probably reversed either on the motherboard or on the floppy drive).

Is everything working properly? _____

After you confirm that everything is working, place the cover back onto your system. Start Windows and test your floppy drive as you did in Step 1 of this lab.

 30 MINUTES

Lab Exercise 11.02: Installing Optical Drives

Your supervisor calls you in one day and announces that he wants to simplify the daily database backup procedures for your company. You will still use tape backups for archival backups, but he wants all the CD-R/RW drives on your company's servers replaced with the latest DVD-R/RW drives. The increased storage capacity of this type of drive will enable you to back up most of the critical files that change during the day onto a single disc. To accomplish this task, you must physically uninstall all the existing CD-R/RW drives and replace them with DVD-R/RW equivalents.

As a PC tech, you'll need to be comfortable removing and installing optical drives. Fortunately, the vast majority of these drives still use the popular PATA interface to connect to your system, making the installation process fairly simple. If you are lucky enough to be working with a newer system, you will probably uninstall and install SATA optical drives.

Learning Objectives

In this lab, you'll remove and inspect an optical drive, and then reinstall the drive.

At the end of this lab, you'll be able to

- Understand how to remove and install an optical drive safely and properly

- Know the physical features of an optical drive

Lab Materials and Setup

The materials you need for this lab are

- A working computer with Windows 2000 or Windows XP and a CD-ROM or DVD-ROM drive of some type installed

Getting Down to Business

Removing an optical-media drive is almost too easy. The only real secret here is to remember which cable you removed and how the cable ends were oriented to make sure you can put it back! Also, PATA optical drives use the standard master/slave jumpers—these also need to be inspected to make sure that the drive runs properly on the PATA connection!

Step 1   Properly shut down your system. As I've mentioned before, there are so many different ways that drives are held into system cases that it would be impossible to list all of the various carriers, caddies, bays, and so on that might be used to hold your optical-media drive. Using whichever method is appropriate, remove the cover from the PC case so that you can access the screws on both sides of the drive. Using proper ESD procedures, perform the following steps to remove the optical drive from your system:

a) Unplug the connections: First unplug the Molex connector from the back of the optical drive, and then remove the PATA ribbon cable from the drive's connector. Unplug the audio cable coming from the sound card (if present) that plugs into the back of the drive.

b) Using a Phillips-head screwdriver, remove the screws holding the optical drive in place. Notice that the screws are small-threaded screws—the same type you encountered when you removed and installed your floppy drive.

✔ **Hint**

Some optical-media drives are held in their bays by rails. Simply squeeze the rail toggles (sticking out of the front), and remove the drive by pulling it forward.

Step 2   Inspect the optical drive. Look at the front of the drive where you insert a disc. Do you see a tiny hole near the edge of the tray door? Most optical drives have such a hole. You can take a straightened-out paper clip and push it into this hole to release the disc tray. This is handy in case you accidentally leave a disc in the drive when you remove it from the system. Go ahead and push a straightened-out paper clip into the hole to eject the tray.

Look at the back of the drive. You should see several areas for connections:

- The Molex power connection
- The connection for the flat ribbon cable (usually a 40-pin EIDE connection)

- An audio connection for a cable to the sound card (there may be more than one connector because of different styles of cables, but only one cable should be connected)

- Jumper settings: master, slave, and cable select

✔ **Hint**

Look for the orientation of pin 1. It is usually closest to the power connection. This also applies to the SCSI connection on some systems.

Step 3 Reinstall the optical drive into your system. It can be a master drive or a slave drive, depending on what other PATA devices are installed. Figure 11-4 shows a properly installed CD-ROM drive.

Now answer these questions:

Did you fasten the drive using the correct screws? _____

Is the master/slave jumper set correctly? _____

Is the PATA cable connected properly? _____

Is the Molex plug fully inserted? _____

Is the audio cable connected to the drive? _____

Step 4 Leave the covers off the system and boot the PC to the Windows Desktop.

FIGURE 11-4 Viewing a properly installed CD-ROM drive

Step 5   Select My Computer, and notice if the drive's icon is present. If so, all is well. If not, repeat Steps 2 and 3. The most common problem when installing hardware is a loose connection, so re-check your cable ends and try again. Replace the PC cover once the drive is recognized in Windows.

 30 MINUTES

Lab Exercise 11.03: Working with USB Thumb Drives

Your company is finally being forced to provide larger-capacity removable storage for all of the sales organization staff. In the not-so-distant past, PowerPoint presentations were moved from machine to machine via floppy disks, and then CD-Rs. With the ease of use and convenient size of USB thumb drives, all sales personnel will now be issued 2-GB thumb drives. Your mission (should you choose to accept it) is to walk all of the field sales personnel through the procedures to use their new thumb drives.

✔ **Cross-Reference**

For a primer on USB flash memory drives (often called thumb drives), see the "USB Thumb Drives" section in Chapter 11 of *Mike Meyers' A+ Guide to Managing and Troubleshooting PCs*.

Learning Objectives

In this lab, you'll learn to insert, use, and safely remove USB thumb drives.

At the end of this lab, you'll be able to

- Insert and remove USB thumb drives

- Save and transfer data using USB thumb drives

Lab Materials and Setup

The materials you need for this lab are

- A Windows XP system with USB 1.0 or 2.0 support

- A USB thumb drive

Getting Down to Business

In Lab Exercise 11.01, you physically removed and reinstalled a floppy drive, but as you are aware, this technology is slowly being retired. This lab exercise uses the newest technology to replace the function and ease of the floppy disk, the USB flash drive (thumb drive). You will simulate using a USB thumb drive to transfer a large file by inserting the drive into a Windows XP system, copying some data onto it, removing it, and re-inserting it into a new system (or the same lab machine) and transferring the data to the new machine.

Step 1 USB thumb drives come in many shapes and colors, as well as many data capacities: 256 MB, 512 MB, 1 GB, 2 GB, and so on. They are typically a few inches long, and most provide protection for the USB connector, either a cover of some type or a retractable mechanism as shown in Figure 11-5.

Boot your lab system and allow it to finish displaying the Windows desktop. Insert the USB drive and note any activity on the screen.

Did a window appear asking what you want Windows to do? _____

If yes, what were some of the options you could choose? _____

_____

Close the options window.

✔ **Hint**

Current USB thumb drives support the USB 2.0 specification, allowing a faster transfer of data (480 Mbps). Some systems (motherboards) offer both USB 1.0 and USB 2.0 ports, so when you insert the USB thumb drive into a USB 1.0 port, you may see a pop-up message in the system tray (notification area) pointing out that this device can perform faster if inserted into a USB 2.0 port.

Step 2 Open an application on your PC, such as Word or PowerPoint, and select and open a file. If you can find a file larger than 1.44 MB, you can experience firsthand the benefit of USB thumb drives over floppies.

Figure 11-5 A USB thumb drive with a retractable connector

Step 3 In the application window, select File | Save As. In the Save As dialog box, click the drop-down arrow for the Save in field. You will see a number of folders and drives where you could choose to save the file. One of these should be the thumb drive, as shown in Figure 11-6. Select the thumb drive and save the file. Close all open windows.

Step 4 In the system tray, find and click the Safely Remove Hardware icon, which shows a green arrow and a gray rectangle. A tiny pop-up message appears adjacent to the icon, listing all removable devices; click the name of the thumb drive. An information balloon with a *Safe to Remove Hardware* message should notify you that you can now remove the USB mass storage device.

Remove the thumb drive from the USB port.

✔ **Hint**

If you forget to close one or more windows with a focus on the thumb drive, you will receive an error message: *The device 'Generic Volume' cannot be stopped right now. Try stopping it later.* If you receive this message, just click OK, close all open files and folders on the thumb drive, and try again.

If you have some open files or folders on the thumb drive and you just pull it out of the machine, you may receive an error message such as "Fail Write Delay." Most of the time the files and folders will remain intact, but this is not the recommended removal method.

Step 5 At this point, if you have a second machine where you can plug in the thumb drive, it will make the lab exercise more realistic. If you don't, you can just use the same system again for this step. Insert the thumb drive into a USB port and again note any activity on the screen. This time, double-click *Open folder to view files using Windows Explorer*.

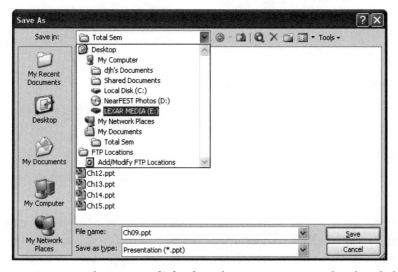

FIGURE 11-6 The Save As dialog box showing a Lexar Media thumb drive

Step 6 Double-click the file you saved previously; if the file has an associated application, this should launch that application and open the file.

You have now successfully used a USB thumb drive—also referred to as a *jump drive*—to "jump" files from one machine to another.

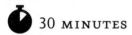 30 MINUTES

Lab Exercise 11.04: Configuring Removable Media Drives

A new client has very specific needs for the boot order and access to removable media in his computer center's seven computers. For the two servers, the floppy drive and USB ports will be installed, but disabled in CMOS. Three of the five workstations need the CD-ROM drive set as the first drive in the boot sequence, but the other two need the USB drive to be first in the boot sequence, with the CD-ROM drive second. It's your job to set up these PCs properly, so get to work!

Learning Objectives

In this lab, you'll use the CMOS setup program to configure the settings for the floppy drive, USB devices, and boot order.

At the end of this lab, you'll be able to

- Locate the CMOS setup screens for configuring the floppy drives, USB devices, and boot order

- Configure various scenarios for the floppy drive, USB devices, and boot order

Lab Materials and Setup

The materials you need for this lab are

- A working computer system with a floppy drive, a CD-ROM drive, and USB device support

Getting Down to Business

This lab exercise involves the floppy drive controller, CD-ROM drive, and USB controller, and shows you how to configure these devices and the boot order of these devices in CMOS.

Depending on your BIOS manufacturer and version, you may or may not be able to perform all of the following steps. Explore the different screens to discover whether you can enable/disable the floppy drive controller (FDC) and the USB controller, and which devices you can put in the boot order (floppy drive, CD-ROM, hard drive, and possibly USB devices).

Step 1   You will start by disabling the floppy drive and USB ports on the two servers. Enter the CMOS setup program by pressing the appropriate key or key combination (which you should remember from Lab Exercise 5.02) while your system is booting.

✖ Warning

If you were to disable the USB controller on a production machine, you would disable not only USB thumb drives, but also USB keyboards and mice, as well as any cameras, external hard drives, or other USB devices in use. Disabling the controller is overkill for keeping users from removing important information through the use of USB thumb drives. The USB controller is disabled in this lab exercise for demonstration purposes only.

Having previously browsed through your version of CMOS, you should be able to locate the screen that contains settings for the FDC and the USB controller (often called Integrated Peripherals or I/O Device Configuration). If you can't remember which screen deals with the FDC and USB controller, browse through the CMOS screens until you find it.

Do you have an option in CMOS to disable the FDC and/or USB controller? _____

Under what title heading did you find these options?

_____

How do you disable these settings?

_____

Do it! Disable them!

✔ Hint

Disabling the FDC is a good way for a network administrator to prevent users from either taking information off the network or introducing viruses into the network using floppy disks. Restricting the use of USB ports, on the other hand, can be handled more effectively in the security settings of the operating system.

Step 2   Restart your system and see if you can access the floppy drive. Did the LED on the front of the floppy drive turn on as the system booted up?

Launch Device Manager—my favorite way is to right-click My Computer and select Manage, then select Device Manager from the Computer Management MMC—and find the listing for Universal Serial Bus Controllers. Are they even listed as being disabled?

Step 3 Re-enter the CMOS setup utility and turn both controllers back on. Reboot the system, and test the floppy drive and USB ports. Do they function properly?

Step 4 One of the most important aspects of removable media is that you can boot a non-functioning system from a device other than the hard drive with diagnostic and troubleshooting tools included. The next CMOS setting to play with is the boot sequence.

When you boot up a PC, the system needs to know where to get the operating system software to load into memory. The three standard places to store this software are the floppy drive, the hard drive, and the CD-ROM drive. USB thumb drives are emerging as the next big bootable media. In some cases the needed software is stored in another location, such as a network server.

Using the CMOS setup utility, you can designate the order in which your system will check the devices for the operating system software. Specifying the proper boot sequence—that is, the search order—saves time by telling the system where to look first. After all, why should your system waste time looking on the CD-ROM or USB thumb drive every time you boot, if your operating system is on the hard drive?

Enter the CMOS setup utility, and look for a screen that includes a Boot Sequence setting.

How many different boot sequences can you configure in CMOS? _____

How many different devices can be in the search sequence? _____

Set your system to boot from the CD-ROM drive first (Figure 11-7).

Step 5 Restart your system. Typically, the boot screen will prompt you with the message *Press any key to boot from the CD*. If there is a bootable CD in the drive, the system will boot from that disc. Leave this boot order in place for the next lab exercise, in which you'll learn to create bootable CDs.

Step 6 Re-enter the CMOS setup utility, and note whether your system will allow you to boot from a USB device, such as a USB thumb drive.

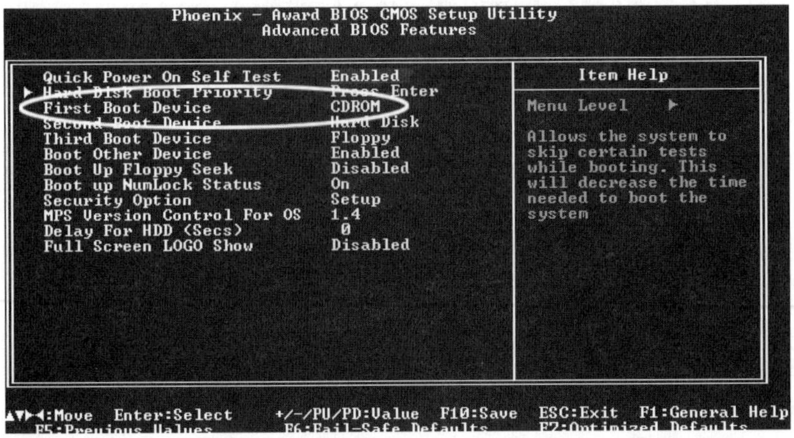

FIGURE 11-7 Boot Sequence screen from CMOS with CD-ROM as first boot device

If your machine is capable, you can substitute a USB thumb drive for the CD-ROM drive in the next lab exercise and create a LiveUSB of the GParted partition editor. For now, leave the CD-ROM as the first device in the boot order and shut down the machine.

 1 HOUR

Lab Exercise 11.05: Burning CDs

PCs today are used more than ever for storage of digital photographs, music, and video, in addition to more traditional types of data. Even a modest collection of MP3 files, family photos, and home video clips requires many gigabytes of space! Hard drives do have space limits, and at some point they tend to fail, so wise PC users turn to recordable CDs and DVDs. These discs provide an affordable large-capacity portable storage option; you can put your important data onto a disc, or make multiple copies of that disc to store in two or more secure locations.

This lab will introduce you to the process by which we record, or *burn*, CDs and DVDs. Rather than burning a disc full of your favorite tunes or photos, you'll be making the type of disc that a technician would have in his toolkit when troubleshooting a machine that won't boot.

✔ Cross-Reference

For additional information on burning CDs and DVDs, refer to the "Applications" section in Chapter 11 of *Mike Meyers' A+ Guide to Managing and Troubleshooting PCs*.

Learning Objectives

In this lab, you'll use a third-party burning program to create bootable ISO images on CD-R discs.

At the end of this lab, you'll be able to

- Work with writable optical media and burning tools
- Create a bootable CD-R

Lab Materials and Setup

The materials you need for this lab are

- A working computer system with a CD-RW or DVD-RW drive installed
- Internet access (preferably a high-speed connection) for downloading
- A CD burning application such as Nero Burning ROM or freeware CDBurnerXP
- Blank CD-R or CD-RW discs (more than one if possible)

Getting Down to Business

In Lab Exercise 10.02, you were asked to prep a number of newly donated PCs by preparing their hard drives for the installation of an operating system; you already partitioned and formatted the drives. To do that, you used an open source utility called GParted. GParted is a Gnome Linux LiveCD with the Gnome Partition Editor application installed. Your instructor may have provided you the bootable CD, or you may have jumped ahead to this lab to make it yourself. In this lab you will burn the ISO image of the open-source, bootable LiveCD of Gnome Linux and the utility GParted.

Step 1   Ensure that you have CD/DVD burning software that will allow you to burn ISO images. An ISO image is a complete copy of a CD, including all of the boot information in the boot record. Windows XP's built-in burning software is unable to write ISO images (at the time of this writing), so you'll need a third-party product such as Nero Burning ROM software.

You can also try CDBurnerXP, an excellent freeware burning tool that supports the burning of ISO images; it's available at www.cdburnerxp.se. Just go to the CDBurnerXP Web site, follow the instructions, and run the installation. After you've successfully installed the program, you should have all the tools necessary to burn ISO images (see Figure 11-8).

✔ **Hint**

Microsoft is constantly updating operating systems and applications such as Internet Explorer and Windows Media Player, so don't forget to check occasionally to see if they have updated the built-in burning application with the ability to handle ISO images.

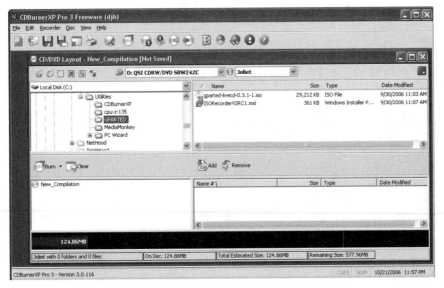

FIGURE 11-8 CDBurnerXP

→ **Try This: Ultimate Boot CD**

Now that you have an understanding of why you might want to boot a machine from removable media—to perform low-level diagnostics, troubleshoot, or just prep the disk before installing an operating system—take a cruise over to www.ultimatebootcd.com.

You can download the ISO image of "The Ultimate Boot CD, UBCD" which has over 100 different freeware tools, all placed on a LiveCD. Use the method you learned in this exercise to burn the ISO image to a CD, boot a machine with the UBCD, and explore some of the tools. You might find that using some of the drive manufacturer's low-level formatting tools will bring a dead drive back to life.

Step 2 Now visit the GParted Web site at gparted.sourceforge.net. Select Download and follow the instructions. You can download the full ISO, or download the .zip file to improve transfer times (remember you will have to expand the .zip file after it's on your system).

Step 3 Once you have the ISO image, open the tray on your CD/DVD drive and insert a blank writable disc. Close the tray and launch your CD/DVD burning software. Navigate to the GParted ISO file and follow the instructions to burn the ISO image on the disc. Most programs will eject the tray with the disc once the writing process is complete.

Step 4 With the newly created disc in the drive and the tray closed, reboot the computer. If all has gone well, GParted will boot, detect your hard drives, and give you the option to partition and format these drives.

✖ **Warning**

Remember, any time you partition or format a hard disk, you will delete the data currently on that drive. Do not run GParted on the disk containing your operating system unless you have been instructed to delete this system's OS.

Lab Analysis Test

1. Jovan installed a CD-ROM drive on the same cable as his primary hard drive, and now the system will not boot. What could be causing this?

2. While looking around in the BIOS settings, Kaitlin set the PIO and DMA settings to Auto. Will this affect the system in any way? Explain.

3. Cecelia is a freelance web designer who is delivering some files to a client. She sits down at a Windows XP system in the client's office and plugs in her trusty USB thumb drive, but nothing happens—Windows doesn't acknowledge the device at all. The thumb drive has been working perfectly well, as recently as this morning. What is most likely the reason that the USB drive won't connect with the client PC?

4. When Philip puts his CD-RW disc in the drive and copies files to and from it, he notices that the drive speeds up and slows down. Is this normal? What should he do to fix it?

5. After removing a CD-ROM drive for replacement, you remember that you left a CD in the drive. You look for a hole to insert the paper clip into, but there is none. How do you remove the CD?

Key Term Quiz

Use the following vocabulary terms to complete the following sentences. Not all terms will be used.

CD-ROM drive

CMOS

disc

DMA

DVD+R

label

scratches

spiral

surface

USB 1.0

USB 2.0

1. An optical-media drive must be identified in the _____ settings.

2. The recording of data on a CD is done in a _____ fashion.

3. With capacities in the range of 4.37–8.74 GB, _____ drives are being used more and more for easy data backups.

4. The _____ version of thumb drives supports a throughput of 480 Mbps.

5. The reflective aluminum layer of an optical disc can be damaged by _____.

Chapter 12

Installing and Upgrading Windows

Lab Exercises

As a PC technician, you'll spend a lot of time installing and upgrading operating systems. For this reason, it's important that you become familiar with the tasks involved; otherwise, you might find yourself in a tight spot when Windows XP Professional won't install on the laptop that your boss needs to have working for a presentation this afternoon.

A number of different operating systems are in use today, including Apple Macintosh OS X, several different flavors of Linux, and of course the Microsoft Windows family. Because CompTIA's A+ Certification focuses primarily on Microsoft products—and because Microsoft products represent the majority of the market—these lab exercises are dedicated to the installation of Windows.

Just about anyone can install software if everything goes right and no problems come up during the process; plenty of people with minimal software knowledge have upgraded Windows without the slightest incident. Even an experienced technician may have problems, though, if the system has incompatible expansion cards, broken devices, or bad drivers. As a PC technician, you have to be prepared to handle both the simple installations—the ones with only new, compatible components—and the more complex installations on older and more problematic systems.

Installing and upgrading Windows is more than popping in the installation CD and running the install program. You need to plan the installation thoughtfully, check for component compatibility, and thoroughly understand the installation options and how to configure them. Good planning up front will give you the best chances for a successful installation or upgrade.

Be sure to have everything you need before you start, from the installation CD to the discs containing your device drivers. If you should start to feel a bit over-prepared, remember the old adage "Measure twice, cut once."

Believe me, it's no fun to start over on an installation or upgrade if you mess it up! Do it right the first time—you'll be glad you did.

 30 MINUTES

Lab Exercise 12.01: Pre-installation Planning

Your client has asked you to upgrade his system to Windows XP Professional. He's currently running Windows 2000 Professional, and everything works fine. He has the documentation that came with his system, which states that it has an ASUS P4G8X Deluxe motherboard. He isn't sure how fast the processor is, but he does know that he's already using 512 MB of memory. Where do you start the planning process?

✔ **Cross-Reference**

To review the details of pre-installation planning, refer to the "Preparing for Installation or Upgrade" section in Chapter 12 of *Mike Meyers' A+ Guide to Managing and Troubleshooting PCs*.

Learning Objectives

In this lab exercise, you'll become more familiar with using the Internet to help answer pre-installation questions.

At the end of this lab, you'll be able to

- Access the Microsoft support Web site
- Determine the minimal requirements for a system installation

Lab Materials and Setup

The materials you need for this lab are

- A working PC
- Internet access
- Pencil and notebook

Getting Down to Business

The first step in a successful Windows installation or upgrade is to determine whether the hardware meets the requirements of the new operating system. Your first stop in this process is the Microsoft support Web site.

Microsoft has invested massive amounts of energy and time in building its support Web site. Sometimes digging through all of the articles on the huge number of Web pages can be overwhelming, but I'm a firm believer in this site's usefulness. When I have a question that directly concerns a Windows operating system (or any Microsoft product, for that matter), I check this site first, and I'm rarely disappointed. In fact, while searching for the answer to a problem or question, I usually learn two or three new, sometimes unrelated, things just by reading through the search results. Also, my search techniques improve with each visit. I consider the Microsoft support Web site an invaluable tool and resource.

Step 1   Start by looking up the requirements for Windows XP Professional. Go to www.microsoft.com/windowsxp/pro/howtobuy/upgrading, and view the four choices that will help you determine whether your client's machine is actually capable of running Windows XP (see Figure 12-1).

✔ Hint

Web sites are infamous for losing information that was once relevant to a particular subject—or sometimes disappearing altogether. If the Microsoft Web site should change significantly from the time this book was printed to the time you're reading this, and you find that a link listed here is no longer valid, a quick search of the site should get you where you need to be.

Select the first option, Check Your System Requirements, and then answer these questions:

What's the recommended/minimum CPU speed? _____

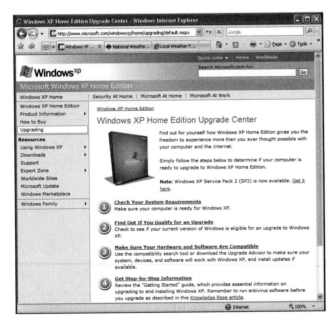

FIGURE 12-1 Using the Windows XP Professional Edition Upgrade Center

What's the recommended/minimum amount of RAM? _____

How much hard drive space is required? _____

What video resolution is required? _____

At a minimum, what other devices are required? _____

Click your browser's Back button, select Find Out If You Qualify for an Upgrade, and then answer these questions:

Can Windows XP Home Edition be used to upgrade Windows 98 SE? _____

Can Windows XP Home Edition be used to upgrade Windows 2000 Professional? _____

Can Windows XP Professional be used to upgrade Windows 98 SE? _____

Can Windows XP Professional be used to upgrade Windows 2000 Professional? _____

Click your browser's Back button, and this time select Make Sure Your Hardware and Software Are Compatible.

Select Search Windows Marketplace. On the resulting screen, enter the following components to see if they're compatible with the recommended settings for Windows XP (see Figure 12-2), and record the results here.

ASUS P5VDC-X motherboard _____

ASUS P4G8X Deluxe motherboard _____

Close all open windows.

FIGURE 12-2 Searching Windows Marketplace

Step 2   Because the ASUS P4G8X Deluxe motherboard isn't listed, you'll now try to find out why.

Open an Internet browser window, and perform a search on *ASUS P4G8X Deluxe*. You might find references to other versions, such as ASUS P4G8X Deluxe Gold, but it's important that you look for the specifications of the basic P4G8X Deluxe model.

Would this motherboard support upgrading to Windows XP Professional? _____

Why do you think this motherboard is not on the Windows XP compatibility list?

_____

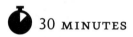 30 MINUTES

Lab Exercise 12.02: Installing/Upgrading Considerations

You get a call from a client who wants to standardize the Windows operating systems that her employees use. She explains that as her company grew over the past few years, she bought new PCs and kept whatever version of Windows came pre-loaded on them. Now, some employees are using Windows 2000 Professional, while others with newer systems have Windows XP Professional; team members on the same project are using different operating systems, and your client feels that this is a drain on productivity. She wants you to come in and upgrade all the Windows 2000 machines to XP.

✔ Cross-Reference

For a refresher on the considerations that come into play when you install or upgrade to Windows 2000/XP, refer to the "Upgrade Advisor" section in Chapter 12 of *Mike Meyers' A+ Guide to Managing and Troubleshooting PCs*.

Learning Objectives

You'll review the steps for upgrading from Windows 2000 to Windows XP Professional. The basic concepts are the same whether you upgrade to Windows XP from Windows 98 SE or from Windows Me.

At the end of this lab, you'll be able to

- Use the Microsoft Upgrade Center to check hardware compatibility for upgrading Windows
- Use the Upgrade Advisor

Lab Materials and Setup

The materials you need for this lab are

- A PC running Windows 2000 Professional

- Access to the Internet

Getting Down to Business

You need to upgrade a Windows 2000 system to Windows XP; this exercise assumes that you've done the preliminary research and collected all of the Windows XP drivers for your components. After looking at all of the issues, you've decided to do an upgrade rather than a clean install. You've visited the Microsoft Upgrade Center, and it appears that all of your hardware is compatible. Everything seems ready, but there's one final step you should take. Microsoft offers a tool to help check your software compatibility and provide a final check of the hardware compatibility. This tool is called the Upgrade Advisor, and it's a good idea to use it.

Step 1   To begin verifying that your system is ready for an upgrade, make sure that the system's existing devices are getting along with one another under the current operating system:

a) Go to Device Manager (see Figure 12-3), and check for the symbols that indicate problems.

b) If you find any conflicts, you should resolve these before you perform the upgrade. Consult with your teacher if necessary to make sure that this happens correctly.

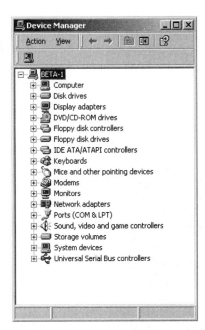

Figure 12-3 Checking Device Manager in Windows 2000 Professional for possible device conflicts

Step 2 Insert the Windows XP CD-ROM into the CD drive, close the tray, and wait for the Welcome to Microsoft Windows XP screen to appear.

✔ **Hint**

If the CD doesn't auto-start, try this alternate method to get started: Open My Computer and right-click the CD-ROM icon. Select Explore, and then double-click the SETUP.EXE icon.

Microsoft has built the Upgrade Advisor into the installation routine, so you can look once more at the compatibility of your system from the operating system's point of view. It's always best to run the Upgrade Advisor before upgrading to XP, to make sure that you've addressed any issues before the upgrade begins.

a) Click Check System Compatibility to start the Upgrade Advisor (see Figure 12-4).

b) On the *What do you want to do?* screen, click Check My System Automatically.

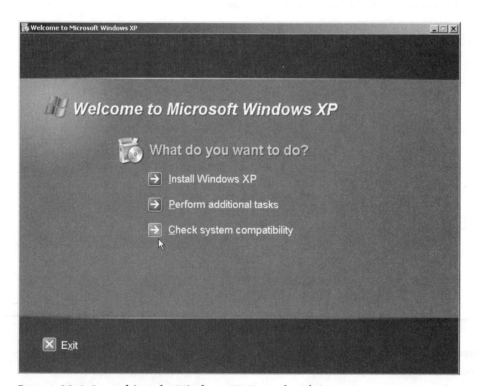

FIGURE 12-4 Launching the Windows XP Upgrade Advisor

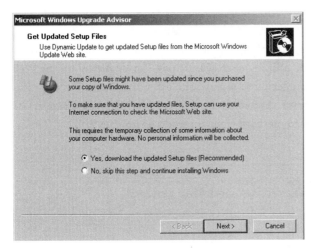

FIGURE 12-5 Getting updated setup files

✔ **Hint**

Clicking Visit the Compatibility Web Site links you to a page that resembles an online retail store. You have to search around a little to make any progress on this Web site, but you'll eventually find where the compatibility lists are stored.

If you're connected to the Internet and your teacher gives you permission, select *Yes, download the updated Setup files (Recommended)*, as shown in Figure 12-5. If you have no Internet connection, select *No, skip this step and continue installing Windows*.

When the Upgrade Advisor completes the check, it will display a report. If there are no errors, as shown in Figure 12-6, then the system is ready to upgrade from Windows 2000 Professional to Windows XP Professional.

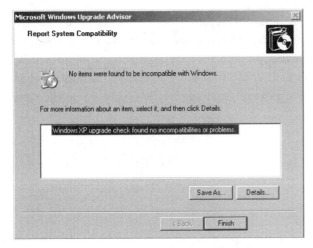

FIGURE 12-6 No incompatible items found!

✔ **Hint**

If the Upgrade Advisor informs you that an application or piece of hardware you have loaded is incompatible with Windows XP, you should do a little more searching—for example, on the Web site for that device's manufacturer—before you decide to remove the offending item. The Upgrade Advisor isn't always correct! If you do determine that something should be removed, then by all means remove it; if you don't, you may be in for some serious upgrade headaches.

c) Click Finish, then Back, and finish the lab exercise by clicking Exit.

✔ **Hint**

Microsoft also provides the Upgrade Advisor as a free download. I recommend using a high-speed connection to download it because it's a very large file—about 50 MB. I have a copy of this file stored on a separate CD so that I can test systems before giving my clients the bottom line on upgrading. If you do this, be sure to update the file periodically, as new hardware and software are continually added to the list. The download site is www.microsoft.com/windowsxp/pro/howtobuy/upgrading/advisor.asp.

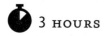 3 HOURS

Lab Exercise 12.03: Upgrading a Windows Operating System

A client of yours, who has a high-end system but still uses Windows 98 SE, decides to modernize by moving to a more recent OS. He asks you to upgrade his system to Windows 2000 Professional. You agree, and make the upgrade for him, only to find the next day that after reading up on the Web about Windows XP, he would really prefer to use that OS instead. Without missing a beat, you determine that his system meets the requirements for Windows XP Professional, and upgrade his system a second time.

Learning Objectives

You need to finish at least one complete upgrade, both for practice and to prepare for questions asked on the A+ exams.

At the end of this lab, you'll be able to

- Upgrade an operating system

✔ **Cross-Reference**

To refresh your memory about the ins and outs of performing a Windows upgrade, read the "Performing the Installation or Upgrade," "Installing or Upgrading to Windows 2000 Professional," and "Installing or Upgrading to Windows XP Professional" sections in Chapter 12 of *Mike Meyers' A+ Guide to Managing and Troubleshooting PCs*.

Lab Materials and Setup

The materials you need for this lab are

- A working PC with a hard drive that you can write to without negative consequences

✔ **Hint**

To complete the exercise as described, you should begin with a system that has a copy of Windows 98 SE installed. For the full effect of this lab, you should have copies of both Windows 2000 Professional and Windows XP Professional. If you're unable to start with Windows 98 SE and upgrade in two steps—first to Windows 2000 and then to Windows XP—you can modify the lab to complete at least one upgrade from an earlier version of Windows to a newer version.

Getting Down to Business

You'll need quite a bit of time to complete this lab; most of that time will be spent waiting for Windows to install files. The exercise will walk you through upgrading a Windows 98 SE system to Windows 2000; you'll then upgrade the system to Windows XP. Depending on the systems and software licenses you have available, you may not be able to do this lab exactly as it's laid out here. The important thing is that you actually perform a Windows upgrade, to see the questions that are asked during the installation and to become familiar with the process so that you're prepared for the CompTIA A+ Certification exams. If time constraints make it necessary, you can complete this lab in two separate sessions: first the upgrade from Windows 98 SE to Windows 2000, and then the upgrade from Windows 2000 to Windows XP.

When you start the installation process, you'll be asked what type of file system you want to install—FAT16, FAT32, or NTFS—and where you want the files installed. The program will set the default location as the C: drive. You should think about this before you begin, referring to the textbook for guidance on this issue. The next step is the big file-copy process. Finally, you'll be asked a series of questions about naming your system and what networking configuration is applicable to your situation.

✖ Warning

While I would normally encourage you to answer the installation questions on network configuration yourself after consulting the information on networking settings covered in Chapter 21 of *Mike Meyers' A+ Guide to Managing and Troubleshooting PCs*, if you're in a classroom environment, you should ask your instructor about these settings before you begin the upgrade process.

Step 1 You've completed the compatibility exercise in the earlier labs, and you know that your system can handle Windows XP. With few exceptions, any system that can successfully load Windows XP can also load Windows 2000. For this lab, you'll do an upgrade rather than a clean installation; note that you'll also be migrating to NTFS during the upgrade to Windows 2000.

If you're starting with Windows 98 SE, the first step is to upgrade to Windows 2000. Ask the instructor (or decide for yourself, if you aren't in a classroom environment) what naming conventions you'll use, and gather the information for any network you'll be connecting to, if applicable. Be sure that you have the Windows 2000 Professional CD handy, and then follow these steps:

a) Insert the Windows 2000 CD. The Setup Wizard will start automatically. If it doesn't, go to My Computer, locate your CD drive, and browse to and double-click SETUP.EXE.

b) From the Setup Wizard screen, select Upgrade to Windows 2000 (see Figure 12-7).

c) Follow the instructions on the screen, which you'll find are pretty straightforward. When asked what file system you want to use, choose NTFS and continue.

d) When prompted, enter your user information and the information about your network, if applicable.

e) When the installation is complete, start Windows and navigate to Device Manger to confirm that there are no conflicts.

f) Ask the instructor whether you should continue with the next step at this time.

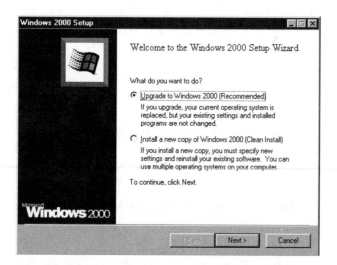

FIGURE 12-7 Selecting Upgrade to Windows 2000

Step 2   Be sure that you have the Windows XP Professional CD handy, along with the appropriate network and user data (again, in a classroom environment, check with your instructor for this information). Then follow these steps:

a) Insert the Windows XP CD. The Setup Wizard will start automatically. If it doesn't, you can go to My Computer, locate your CD-ROM drive, and then browse to and double-click SETUP.EXE.

b) From the Setup Wizard screen, select Install Windows XP.

c) Follow the instructions on the screen; again, they're pretty straightforward.

d) When prompted, enter your user information and the information about your network, if applicable.

e) When the installation is complete, start Windows XP and navigate to Device Manger to confirm that there are no conflicts.

 1 HOUR

Lab Exercise 12.04: Performing a Clean Installation

Your boss has traditionally ordered new workstations already assembled and loaded with the desired Windows OS. She recently decided that with her great in-house techs, she should be buying PC parts from a wholesaler instead, and having you and your team build the systems. You've enjoyed choosing the various hardware components and building these custom machines, but now it's time to bring your creations to life! You need to load Windows XP Professional onto these new machines that have never seen the light of day.

Learning Objectives

You should complete at least one clean Windows installation, both for the experience and to prepare for questions asked on the CompTIA A+ exams.

At the end of this lab, you'll be able to

- Install a Windows operating system on a blank drive

Lab Materials and Setup

The materials you need for this lab are

- A working PC with a blank hard drive, or with a hard drive that you can write to without negative consequences

- A Windows XP Professional CD-ROM with a valid product key

Getting Down to Business

In this exercise, you'll be putting an operating system onto a drive that doesn't currently have one. If the hard drive that you plan to use currently has data on it (even data that no one needs), then you must wipe that drive clean before you begin the exercise. Once you have a clean hard drive, you can proceed as directed.

✔ Cross-Reference

If you need to refresh your memory on how to format a hard drive, review Lab Exercise 10.01: Creating and Formatting Partitions with the Windows 2000/XP Installation CD-ROM.

Step 1   Insert the Windows XP CD-ROM into the CD drive, close the tray, and wait for the Welcome to Setup text screen to appear.

Step 2   Follow the directions to install the OS. Read the End User License Agreement thoroughly and agree to it to proceed. When the setup program prompts you to partition your drive, set up a single NTFS partition that uses all the available drive space. Then you'll simply need to wait and watch while the setup program does its magic and reboots the computer.

Step 3   When the computer has rebooted, work through the graphical portion of the installation process by carefully reading each screen and filling in the appropriate information. Be sure to enter the product key correctly, as you won't get past that screen with an invalid key.

Step 4   When you come to the Networking Settings screen, ask your instructor (if you're in a classroom setting) whether to use Typical or Custom settings, and what specific information to use.

Step 5   On the Let's Activate Windows screen, do *not* activate at this time. Instead, select *No, log me off* and click Next. You should see a blank Windows desktop, signifying that you've completed a successful installation of Windows XP.

 30 MINUTES

Lab Exercise 12.05: Pre-installation Planning for Windows Vista

At the time that CompTIA formulated its exam objectives for the 2007 version of the A+ exams, the Vista operating system—Microsoft's follow-up to the XP family—was not yet released to the general public. This does *not* mean that you can ignore it for the purposes of your A+ exams! CompTIA reserves the right to add in questions about emerging technologies, and few things make a bigger splash in the PC world than a new version of Windows.

Imagine, then, that you have a friend who has been happily using Windows XP Professional for a few years, but now wants to upgrade to Vista. His PC isn't the very latest and greatest, but it's still pretty respectable. Before you agree to upgrade the OS, you want to make sure that his system meets the Vista requirements. You also have been thinking about finally upgrading your own XP system, so you head to Microsoft's Web site to do some research.

✔ **Cross-Reference**

To review the operating systems offered by Microsoft, including Vista, refer to the "Microsoft Windows" section in Chapter 12 of *Mike Meyers' A+ Guide to Managing and Troubleshooting PCs.*

Learning Objectives

In this lab exercise, you'll explore the features and system requirements of Windows Vista.

At the end of this lab, you'll be able to

- Access the Microsoft Web site for the Windows Vista OS
- Determine the requirements for installing Windows Vista

Lab Materials and Setup

The materials you need for this lab are

- A working PC
- Internet access
- Pencil and notebook

Getting Down to Business

As you learned in Lab Exercise 12.01, the first step in a successful Windows installation or upgrade is to determine whether your hardware meets the requirements of the new operating system. Your first stop in this process for any of the Microsoft offerings, including Windows Vista, should be the Microsoft support Web site.

Step 1   Start by visiting the home page for Windows Vista (www.microsoft.com/windowsvista), shown in Figure 12-8. This page will evolve over time, so the exact options on the main screen may no longer be the ones I've listed here; if this should be the case, you should be able to find the information you need with a little searching.

Navigate through the screens and see if you can answer the following questions.

First, select the tab labeled The Experience and then answer these questions:

How does Windows Vista enhance digital photography organization? _____

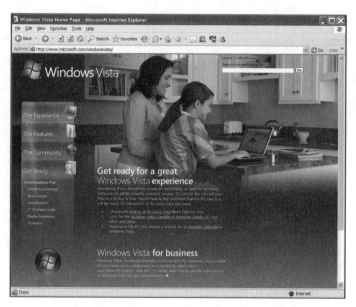

FIGURE 12-8 Windows Vista home page as of this printing

List some of the external devices supported by Windows Backup Center in Windows Vista Business.

_____

Next, select the tab labeled The Features and then answer these questions:

What is the function of the power state called Sleep? _____

What is Windows Vista ReadyBoost? _____

Finally, select the tab labeled Get Ready and then select the Windows Vista Capable and Premium Ready PCs option. Answer these questions:

What's the minimum/recommended CPU speed? _____

What's the minimum/recommended amount of RAM? _____

How much hard drive space is required? _____

What video resolution is required? _____

At a minimum, what other devices are required? _____

Lab Analysis Test

1. Betsy is preparing an installation of Windows XP Professional. She has used a partitioning tool to prep the hard drive, but when she initiates the installation she receives a blue screen with the following error message: *Windows XP requires a hard drive volume with at least 318 megabytes (333926400 bytes) of free disk space.* What's the problem?

2. What's the recommended CPU speed and amount of RAM needed to install Windows XP Professional?

3. Dwight wants to upgrade his old Windows 98 system to Windows XP Professional, but he isn't sure about his hardware. What Microsoft tools would you recommend that he use to check his system?

4. Joe is just starting to study PC repair and has been reading about file systems. He asks you, the veteran tech, to explain why it's best to use NTFS for a new installation. What do you tell him?

5. What happens if you don't complete the Microsoft Product Activation (MPA) for Windows XP Home Edition within 30 days of installation?

Key Term Quiz

Use the following vocabulary terms to complete the following sentences. Not all terms will be used.

133 MHz

233 MHz

800 MHz

1 GHz

CD-ROM drive

floppy disks

installation

network drive

upgrade

Upgrade Advisor

Windows 2000 Professional

Windows XP Home Edition

Windows XP Professional

1. If you plan to install Windows XP onto a system, it must have a(n) _____.

2. You can start with a blank hard drive to perform a clean _____ of Windows 2000.

3. If you are planning on installing Windows Vista Home Premium, you must have a processor that runs at a minimum speed of _____.

4. Installing Windows XP on a system currently running Windows 98 is known as a(n) _____.

5. You cannot upgrade directly from _____ to Windows XP Home Edition.

Chapter 13

Understanding Windows

Lab Exercises

Every good PC technician should know the Windows environment inside and out. This is vital to any troubleshooting scenario, and it won't happen automatically—it takes some practice and discovery on the technician's part. You need to be fluent in navigating the PC from a user's perspective. If there's anything magical about Windows, it's that there's almost always more than one way to get a desired result, and your preferred way might not be the same as your client's. As a good customer-oriented tech, you need to be flexible in your thinking, and this only comes through practice and more practice. As you study and work through these labs, always look for more than one way to access the files or programs you need. Many of the shortcuts and hot keys you'll discover can be invaluable aids for a busy tech!

✔ **Hint**

Windows XP enables right-click menus for most of its buttons, icons, and other screen elements. Be sure to right-click everything you see in Windows XP to explore the many shortcut menus and options.

In the field, the PC tech is perceived as the Master (or Mistress) of All Things Technical. This might not be a fair assessment—for example, why should a PC hardware technician need to know how to open and close the user's programs?—but that's the way it is. You need to be comfortable and confident with the Windows interface, or you'll lose credibility as a PC technician. If you show up to service a PC and have trouble moving or resizing a window or locating the information you seek, this won't instill a lot of confidence in your client! There's nothing more embarrassing to a tech than having to ask the user how to find or use a Windows feature!

The creators of the CompTIA A+ Certification exams understand this, so they test you on Windows user-level information, such as using power saving settings, changing the appearance of the interface, manipulating files and folders, locating information stored on drives, and using Windows' built-in OS tools. You must also know how to navigate to the basic Windows features—the CompTIA A+ exams are big on identifying paths to features. Although you may already know much of the information about to be covered, the labs in this chapter will help you review and perhaps catch a few bits and pieces you might have missed along the way.

 30 MINUTES

Lab Exercise 13.01: Windows XP Interface

Most new PC systems sold as of this writing have Windows XP installed, so that's where you'll start. This operating system comes in several versions, the most common being XP Professional, XP Home Edition, and XP Media Center Edition. Microsoft targets XP Home Edition and Media Center Edition at consumers, while business and power users tend to use XP Professional. At its most basic level, XP Home Edition is a subset or truncated version of XP Professional. "Everything you can do in Home Edition, you can do in Pro," Microsoft says. Media Center Edition is essentially Home Edition with some added functionality to simplify access to music, video, and photos. The major advantages of XP Professional include remote access, tighter security, and the ability to network in domains. For the purposes of these lab exercises, you'll use Windows XP Professional.

✔ **Hint**

You can learn more about the different versions of Windows XP on Microsoft's Web site. Find the page called "Five editions of Windows XP compared" at www.microsoft.com/windowsxp/evaluation/compare.mspx.

Learning Objectives

The main objective of this exercise is to familiarize you with the different "looks" of Windows XP. Because the Windows XP default theme looks different from Windows 9x and Windows 2000 Professional, the paths to the old familiar ways of finding or configuring things such as the Desktop, Control Panel, and other options have changed.

At the end of this lab, you'll be able to

- Switch the system appearance between the Windows XP–style (default) interface and the Windows Classic style, which looks more like Windows 98/2000

- Switch between the XP Start menu mode (default) and the Classic Start menu mode

- Switch the view of the Control Panel between the Category view (default) and Classic view

Lab Materials and Setup

The materials you need for this lab are

- A fully functioning PC with Windows XP Professional installed

- Ideally, access to another system with Windows 2000 installed for comparison

Getting Down to Business

Windows XP has a look that's aligned with a task-oriented Web view. You'll notice this right away when you open a window and look at the title bar and window contents. It's filled with bright colors, round edges, and big icons. Some feel that this look is a great improvement over previous versions of Windows, while others don't really like it. Happily, though, if you don't like XP's native look, you can choose to use the Windows 98/2000 *Classic* look instead.

✔ **Hint**

As a technician, you'll probably be working with all the flavors of Windows. Because many systems installed still have the Classic look, it'll benefit you to learn Windows XP in the Classic modes and views first. Once you're comfortable with locating the configuration screens, continue your practice with the newer Windows XP style.

Step 1   To set the system theme to Classic mode, follow these steps:

a) Right-click the Desktop.

b) Select Properties.

c) Select the Themes tab.

d) Under Theme, use the drop-down menu to select Windows Classic (see Figure 13-1).

e) Click Apply and then OK.

Switch back and forth between the two interfaces. Each time, open other windows to observe the different looks.

✔ **Hint**

To give your windows and buttons the Windows Classic look without changing personalized settings such as your wallpaper, you can select the Appearance tab instead of Themes; click the *Windows and buttons* drop-down list and select *Windows Classic style*.

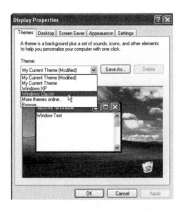

FIGURE 13-1 Changing the
theme to Windows Classic

Step 2 Changing the theme of your Windows XP interface doesn't change the way the Start menu works,
which is significantly different from earlier versions of Windows. The Start menu has the same functionality as in previous Windows versions, but it was restyled for XP. As it does for the overall screen look,
Windows XP enables you to change the Start menu to Classic mode, if you prefer it that way. Before you
can explore the XP style of Start menu, though, you need to know which style you're working with. The
following steps will ensure that your system is using the Windows XP Start menu style:

a) Right-click the Start button and select Properties to display the Taskbar and Start Menu Properties dialog box.

b) Select the Start Menu tab.

c) Select the Start Menu radio button.

d) Click OK.

Click Start to open the Start menu. Notice that the left side of the Start menu shows your recently
used applications. You can adjust the number of applications that Windows displays there. The top two
applications are the default Web browser and e-mail client, which you can also modify. Follow these steps:

a) Right-click the Start button, and select Properties.

b) Select the Start Menu tab.

c) Be sure the Start Menu radio button is selected, and click Customize.

d) Under the General tab (Figure 13-2), change any of the following settings if you like:

- The number of programs on the Start menu

- Whether to show the icons for the Internet and e-mail

- Which browser and e-mail client to use

The Start menu's All Programs command shows a list of all programs installed on the system; it
works like the Programs list in Windows 9x or 2000.

FIGURE 13-2 The General tab on the Customize Start Menu dialog box

Step 3 Unlike earlier versions of Windows, which included icons for My Computer and My Documents on the desktop by default, in Windows XP the only icon present on the desktop after installation is the Recycle Bin. These icons are now in the Start menu, but you can add them to the desktop:

a) Click the Start button.

b) Right-click My Computer in the menu.

c) Select Show on Desktop.

d) Repeat Steps a) through c) for My Documents.

Step 4 For greatest compatibility with the lab exercises in upcoming chapters, you should now put your Start menu in the Classic Start menu mode.

To set the Start menu to Classic mode, follow these steps:

a) Right-click the Start button.

b) Select Properties.

c) Choose *Classic Start menu*.

d) Click OK.

✖ Warning

Most of the following lab exercises will assume you have the XP system in the Classic mode or are using Windows 2000 Professional.

Step 5 Another change that came with the advent of Windows XP is the way you view the Control Panel. The Control Panel icon now opens by default in Category mode (see Figure 13-3).

FIGURE 13-3 Viewing the Control Panel in Category mode

Follow these steps:

a) On the Classic Start menu, Select Start | Settings | Control Panel.

b) Depending how it was configured when you turned on the system, you'll see either the Category (default) or Classic view of the Control Panel.

c) An option on the top left sidebar in the Control Panel enables you to switch between the two modes.

d) Set your Control Panel to Classic View for the rest of the exercises.

 30 MINUTES

Lab Exercise 13.02: Windows Desktop

The Windows Desktop is the starting point for all operations. It doesn't matter whether you have a new XP installation or an existing installation of Windows 98 from years ago; there's a desktop graphical user interface (GUI) that you can use as a home base. The purpose of this lab exercise is to ensure that you're familiar with the desktop.

Learning Objectives

In this lab, you'll work with certain features of the Windows Desktop.

At the end of this lab, you'll be able to

• Use the Windows taskbar

• Run a program from the Start menu

- Change settings for the Recycle Bin
- Change the appearance of the desktop

Lab Materials and Setup

The materials you need for this lab are

- A working computer running Windows 2000 or Windows XP

✔ **Hint**

Though outlining every step for each Windows operating system is beyond the scope of this book, these labs are designed to be as Windows-generic as possible. You should develop and practice the ability to navigate through the interface, achieving the end result, even if you are working with a legacy version of Windows 98 SE, or the latest version of Windows Vista Ultimate. If the lab exercise doesn't produce the expected results, it may be because you're using a different operating system than the one used to write and illustrate the exercise. I've tried to show you a variety of examples. Be flexible and look on your system for the same results via a different method.

Getting Down to Business

For most users, the Windows Desktop is the interface to computer applications and folders that are used every day. Even though you may already be comfortable with the desktop, you should walk through the steps to validate and refresh your skills. Everything you see has a purpose, with the possible exception of the background wallpaper—but even that has amusement value! You most likely have icons that start a variety of programs, such as My Computer, Internet Explorer, and Outlook Express, and you have the taskbar with all of its built-in features. Make sure you know where everything is, and what everything does!

✔ **Cross-Reference**

To refresh your memory on the various parts of the Windows interface, refer to the "User Interface" section in Chapter 13 of *Mike Meyers' A+ Guide to Managing and Troubleshooting PCs*.

Step 1 The taskbar, by default, runs along the bottom of the Windows Desktop (although you can move it to any side: top, bottom, left, or right). The taskbar handles a number of critical jobs. Most important, it displays the Start button, probably the most frequently clicked button on all Windows systems. To find the Start button, look at the far left end of the taskbar (see Figure 13-4). Next to it is the Quick Launch area,

Figure 13-4 The Windows XP taskbar

if it's currently turned on (see the accompanying Hint). At the right end of the taskbar is the notification area—often referred to as the *system tray*—which displays the time and any number of small icons for system programs currently stored in RAM. In the middle of the taskbar are buttons representing the user-started programs that are currently running.

✔ **Hint**

If you don't see the Quick Launch area, point to an unused area of the taskbar, right-click, and select Properties. Check the Show Quick Launch box and click OK. You can now drag program icons or even folder shortcuts from the desktop onto the Quick Launch toolbar for quick access any time.

Step 2 Microsoft says, "Everything starts with Start." Clicking the Start button opens the Start menu, where you'll find the programs available on the system, the system settings via the Control Panel, and various system tools such as Search and Help. Another useful feature is the ability to review your recent documents. The Start button is also where you'll find the Shut Down command, as odd as that may seem.

Click the Start button. Move your mouse pointer slowly up to the Programs menu (remember, XP should be in Classic Start menu mode), and hesitate at each icon along the way. As the mouse moves upward through the Programs menu, notice how other submenus appear.

Look closely at the icons on the Start menu. Some icons have a small arrow pointing to the right on the edge of the menu bar. When you see an arrow, it means there's another menu beyond the one you're observing. To access the next menu, slide your mouse pointer across the highlighted Start menu icon area toward the arrow and into the next menu. This concept applies throughout Windows (see Figure 13-5). If you don't choose to click an option, you'll need to click somewhere else on the desktop to tell Windows, "Never mind—close the Start menu." Work through the following navigation steps using Notepad to explore many of the methods, menus, settings, and options that are provided to you through the Windows Desktop.

FIGURE 13-5 Exploring cascading menus

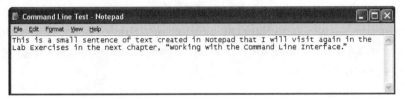

FIGURE 13-6 Using Notepad

a) Open Notepad by clicking Start | Programs | Accessories | Notepad.

- Type the following sentence and save the file in the My Documents folder as Command Line Test.txt (see Figure 13-6):

  This is a small sentence of text created in Notepad that I will visit again in the Lab Exercises in the next chapter, "Working with the Command-Line Interface."

- Close Notepad.

b) Now open Notepad by clicking Start | Run, typing **notepad** in the dialog box, and clicking OK.

- Open Command Line Test.txt by clicking File | Open, navigating to the My Documents folder, and selecting the appropriate file.

- Close Notepad.

c) Finally, open Notepad from the Start menu's recent documents list.

- Click Start | Documents | Command Line Test.txt.

- Close Notepad.

✔ Hint

Each time you open Notepad, you should be able to open and edit the text file Command Line Test.txt. You should also see a corresponding button appear in the taskbar. The button, space permitting, includes an icon for the application, the filename, and the application name. Folders also appear in the taskbar with an icon and folder name, but no associated application.

Step 3 Now look all the way on the right side of the taskbar. This is officially called the *notification area*, but as I noted earlier, it's often called the *system tray*. In spite of Microsoft's official terminology, most techs call it the system tray, so I'll call it that for the sake of this exercise as well.

At the far right end of the system tray, you should see a display of the current time; on most Windows systems, you'll also see a number of small icons in this area of the taskbar. These icons represent programs running in the background.

You often see icons in the system tray for network status, volume controls, and virus programs, and laptops may have additional icons for battery state and PC Card status. What you see in the system tray depends on your version of Windows, what hardware you use, and what programs you have loaded.

Click the various icons in your system tray to see what they do. Depending on the icon, you may need to click, double-click, or right-click and select from a menu.

Step 4 Now you'll look at customizing your environment. (Once again, if you're using XP, the Start menu should be in the Classic mode.)

Click the Start button and select Settings | Taskbar and Start Menu. This opens the Taskbar and Start Menu Properties dialog box, which you brought up before by right-clicking the Start button and selecting Properties.

Windows 2000 and XP each have a slightly different look, but you'll find the following three items listed in some manner on the leftmost tab of the Taskbar and Start Menu Properties (or equivalent) dialog box in all Windows versions:

- **Show the clock** controls the time display in the right side of the taskbar.

Turn off the *Show the clock* option and click Apply. What happens in the taskbar?

_____

Select the *Show the clock* option again and click Apply. Does the time display reappear in the taskbar?

_____

- **Auto-hide the taskbar** makes the taskbar disappear until you point the mouse at the edge of the screen where the taskbar resides (generally the bottom edge), or press the Windows Start key on the keyboard. Why would you want to hide the taskbar? For certain programs, you need all the display area you can get. The auto-hide feature minimizes the taskbar to allow more room on the screen.

Select *Auto-hide the taskbar* and click Apply. What happens?

_____

Move your mouse pointer toward the bottom of the screen. What happens when you reach the bottom?

_____

Turn the auto-hide feature off again. How does the taskbar behave now?

_____

- **Keep the taskbar on top of other windows** prevents programs from covering up the taskbar. If you observe a program using the entire screen, you know this feature is turned off, and you can't access the taskbar until you resize the program window or press the Windows Start button on your keyboard.

Step 5 As you know, a file isn't actually erased from your hard drive when you delete it. When you delete a file in Windows, a shortcut to the deleted file is saved in the Recycle Bin. It stays there until you empty the Recycle Bin, until you restore the folder or file, or until the Recycle Bin grows larger than a preset size. Once you empty it, the files are permanently deleted, so make sure you're certain before you do this.

Figure 13-7 Setting properties
for the Recycle Bin

✔ **Hint**

Remember that most everything in Windows has Properties settings, which you can generally
access by right-clicking the object and selecting Properties. You can also access Properties by
highlighting the object and pressing ALT-ENTER.

To change the Recycle Bin's properties, access the Recycle Bin settings by right-clicking the
Recycle Bin icon on the Desktop and selecting Properties. Your Recycle Bin Properties dialog box
may look different because of the version of Windows you have, because you have multiple hard
drives, or because of some other factor, but all versions basically work the same way (see Figure 13-7).

Note that 10% is the default amount of drive space to use for the Recycle Bin. Change this to 5% and
close the Recycle Bin Properties dialog box.

✔ **Hint**

If a hard drive starts to run low on space, emptying the Recycle Bin is a quick way to try freeing
up some space.

Step 6 Microsoft gives you many ways to change the look of your desktop to suit your personal preferences, from the color of the background to the size of the fonts. There are too many possible combinations
to cover them all, so you'll look at only the most popular one, the background graphic. Follow these steps:

  a) Right-click in an unused area of the desktop and select Properties.

  b) Select the Desktop tab. (It's the Background tab in Windows 2000.)

  c) Choose a background of your choice and click Apply.

✔ **Hint**

When you become more familiar with Windows, you can use the Browse button to locate your own photo to use for the background.

Step 7 One other thing to look at while you have the Display Properties dialog box open, which you should also remember for the CompTIA A+ exams, is where to locate the Power Savings settings.

a) Click the Screen Saver tab in the Display Properties dialog box.

b) At the bottom of the dialog box, you should see the Energy Star icon. Click the Power button next to this icon.

c) Look at all the different settings here, and make notes to help you remember where to find them.

 30 MINUTES

Lab Exercise 13.03: Windows Explorer

Windows Explorer is a program that enables you to see all the program and data files on a given storage device. Explorer works with both hard drives and removable media such as CDs, USB flash drives, and floppy disks. Everyday users and technicians alike use this program more than any other when they need to locate and manipulate files and folders.

Learning Objectives

In this lab, you'll explore the Windows file structure.

At the end of this lab, you'll be able to

• Use Windows Explorer

• Understand and use the contents of the Windows and Program Files folders

Lab Materials and Setup

The materials you need for this lab are

• A working computer running Windows 2000 or Windows XP

✔ **Hint**

You can perform these steps on any Windows system, but some of them may involve functionality that's available only in Windows XP.

Getting Down to Business

When you click (or double-click) a folder icon to view what's inside, you're seeing Windows Explorer in action. It's really just a great graphical interface that enables you to see and manipulate files, folders, and their organizational structures quickly and easily, without memorizing a bunch of commands. Becoming familiar with its ins and outs is vital to becoming an effective PC technician.

Step 1   Begin by looking at the internal directory structure of Windows. Start Windows Explorer by selecting Start | Programs | Accessories | Windows Explorer.

Look at the top of the list on the left pane of the Windows Explorer window; you'll notice an icon called Desktop. Anything you put directly under this folder will appear on the desktop itself, as well as in a "Desktop" folder on your C: drive. Remember that C: is your root directory (on a standard Windows system), and no file stored on the hard drive is "outside" that. The first place to go exploring in the Windows directory structure is the root directory.

a)   Locate the My Computer icon in the left pane of Windows Explorer and click the plus sign (+). If it already has a minus sign (–) to the left, leave it there and continue.

b)   Locate the C: drive icon, and click it once to highlight it. There should be no need to click the plus sign, as clicking the drive's icon automatically expands its contents.

c)   The right pane now displays the contents of the root directory of your C: drive (see Figure 13-8).

✔ Hint

You can choose from several different views, or ways of displaying folder contents. The view shown in Figure 13-8 is called Icons view; other views include Thumbnails, Tiles, List, and Details. When you drop down the View menu, the current view is marked with a large black dot. You can switch views as often as you like, simply by selecting another view from the list.

d)   Find the folders named WINDOWS (sometimes named WINNT in Windows 2000) and Program Files. These two folders contain the majority of your operating system and program files.

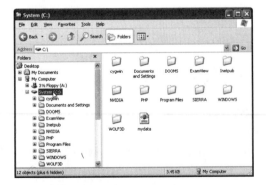

FIGURE 13-8 Viewing C:\ in Windows Explorer on Windows XP

FIGURE 13-9 Exploring the WINDOWS folder

e) Now click the WINDOWS (or WINNT) folder icon. Look at Figure 13-9 for a sample of what you should see at this point if you're running Windows XP.

✖ **Warning**

Some system administrators may have changed the names of these folders, but in general this is not the best practice. If you need to contact Microsoft for assistance, they always start by directing you to the default folder names, so changing them can increase your troubleshooting time.

Step 2   In the next few substeps, you'll configure your folder options to provide the maximum information about your files and folders. Techs usually find the more information they have about a component, the easier it is to troubleshoot or configure. Take a moment and explore the different folders and files in the WINDOWS folder. A typical WINDOWS folder will have more than 15,000 files in more than 1000 folders (see Figure 13-10). To view the number of files and folders in your WINDOWS folder, right-click somewhere in the blank area of the right pane and select Properties from the drop-down menu.

FIGURE 13-10 Viewing the WINDOWS folder's properties

FIGURE 13-11 Windows Explorer column headings in Details view

a) Maximize your window by clicking the small box icon next to the x icon in the upper-right corner of the window. Then click the Views icon in the toolbar at the top left of the screen, and select Details.

b) Notice the headings across the right pane, as shown in Figure 13-11. Click each of these headings to sort by that value. Click any heading again to sort in reverse order.

c) Now select Tools | Folder Options.

d) Select the View tab.

e) In the Advanced settings area, click the radio button to *Show hidden files and folders*. This displays all files and folders, even those for which the Hidden attribute has been set.

f) Remove the check mark next to *Hide extensions for known file types*. This directs Windows Explorer to display the filename extensions in all views. This is useful for a tech, and these days it also helps users with things like identifying e-mail viruses hiding as (for instance) FILE.MP3.SCR.

g) Remove the check mark next to *Hide protected operating system files (Recommended)*. This will enable you to examine critical system files (for example C:\boot.ini) when troubleshooting problems.

h) Click Apply to commit these changes to the Folder view.

i) Before closing the folder options, click Apply to All Folders in the Folder view section. This will apply the Details view to every folder on the system, and enable you to see file extensions, hidden files, and system files in all folders as well.

j) Now, sort the folders and files by Type, and see if you can locate the files with these extensions:

- **.INI**   These are initialization files used to install and configure the system.

- **.BMP**   These are Windows bitmap graphics.

- **.EXE**   These are executable files (in other words, programs).

- **.TXT**   These are text files containing only ASCII text and symbols, readable across a wide range of systems.

k) Sort the list by Name, and locate these files:

- **EXPLORER.EXE**   This is the Windows Explorer application you're using for these exercises.

- **DESKTOP.INI**   This contains the configuration data for your desktop.

- **WIN.INI**   This contains configuration settings for the boot process.

✘ Warning

Do not alter these files in *any* way! You won't like the results.

Step 3 Although MS-DOS is no longer used as an operating system, some of the original MS-DOS applications (commands) are still very much alive. These are now launched from the command-line interface in Windows 2000 and Windows XP as well as when you need to invoke the Recovery Console. As a PC technician, you're likely to need one or more of these command-line tools, so you'll work with some of them in the next chapter; for now, you should just learn where to find them.

a) While still in Windows Explorer, find the C:\WINDOWS\System32 folder and open it. This folder stores all the command-line applications.

b) Sort the details list by Type, scroll down to the MS-DOS applications, and locate these files (see Figure 13-12):

- **FORMAT.COM** This is used to prepare hard drives and floppy disks for storing data.

- **EDIT.COM** This text editor program can create and modify configuration files in the command-line mode. The Windows equivalent is Notepad.

Step 4 When working with modern-day Windows, it's important to know the key system files involved in the boot process and fundamental core files. Use the *Search for files and folders* tool to locate and record the absolute path of the following system files.

✔ Cross-Reference

For additional information on the files used to boot the Windows operating system, review the "The Boot Process" section in Chapter 13 of *Mike Meyers' A+ Guide to Managing and Troubleshooting PCs*.

a) Click Start | Search | For Files or Folders, then click *All files and folders*, and finally click *More advanced options*.

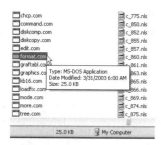

FIGURE 13-12 Locating command-line applications in Windows XP

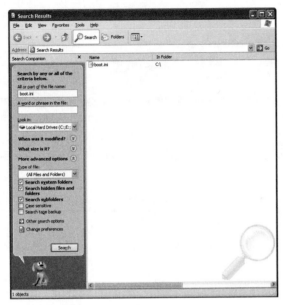

FIGURE 13-13 The Search utility in Windows XP

b) Select the following check boxes (Figure 13-13):

- Search system folders

- Search hidden files and folders

- Search subfolders

c) Look in the local hard drive (on most systems this will be the C:\ drive) where your operating system is located and search for the following files. Make notes of their absolute paths:

- **NTLDR**   The filename is an abbreviation for NT Loader. This file is the Master of Ceremonies, responsible for beginning the boot process and launching the other system files.

- **BOOT.INI**   This text file lists all operating systems available to the NTLDR. Double-click boot.ini in the Search Results window and examine the contents of the file. This is an important, editable file, especially on a multiboot system where you may need to change the boot order of the operating systems.

- **NTDETECT.COM**   This file detects installed hardware on systems that boot Windows 2000 or XP.

- **HAL.DLL**   This file loads many of the Hardware Abstraction Layer drivers.

- **NTOSKRNL.EXE**   The filename is an abbreviation for the NT Operating System Kernel. This file completes the loading of the Windows Registry, initiates all device drivers, and starts WINLOGON.EXE to display the Windows logon screen.

Step 5   Some of the other important folders and their contents are listed here. Look at each one to gain more experience using Windows Explorer. Remember, the location may be slightly different across the

Windows family of operating systems. For instance, Windows 2000 uses WINNT as the default Windows folder. These are the folders you'll find:

- **WINDOWS\CURSORS**   Windows stores the many different cursors you can use here.

- **WINDOWS\FONTS**   Windows stores all its fonts in this folder. Note that fonts usually have one of two extensions, .FON or .TTF. The .FON files are the old-style screen fonts, and the .TTF files are modern TrueType fonts. You can double-click a font icon to see what the font looks like. Some users even print their favorite fonts and keep them in a three-ring binder for later reference.

- **WINDOWS\HELP**   This folder is the default location for all .HLP and .CHM (help) files. Open one to see what program uses it.

- **WINDOWS\MEDIA**   This folder is the default location for sounds and audio clips. Double-click a file with a .WAV or .MID extension to hear sounds.

- **WINDOWS\SYSTEM32**   This folder is the heart of Windows. Here you can see the core operating system files: HAL.DLL and NTOSKRNL.EXE. This folder also stores almost all of the .DLL files used by Windows 2000/XP.

Step 6   Collapse the WINDOWS folder, and expand the Program Files folder (see Figure 13-14). Windows 2000 and XP don't like people messing around in these folders, so you may have to look to the left and click Show Files to see the folders. This is the default location for applications installed on your system. (Remember to scroll down if you can't see the end of the list.)

Follow these steps:

a) Open the Windows Media Player subfolder, and find the application. Remember to look for the .EXE extension.

b) Click the .EXE file icon to start the program.

c) Close the program you just opened.

d) Exit Windows Explorer.

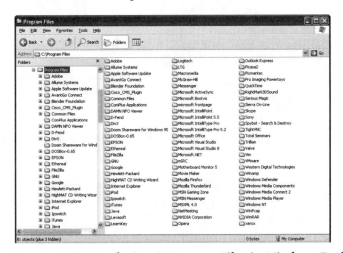

FIGURE 13-14 Exploring C:\Program Files in Windows Explorer

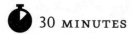 30 MINUTES

Lab Exercise 13.04: Windows Control Panel

The Windows Control Panel is the technician's toolbox. It contains the tools you need to do everything from changing the mouse settings to installing new device drivers. This lab exercise won't attempt to examine every tool in the Control Panel, but it will help you become familiar with many of them. Some Control Panel programs—known as *applets*—are specific to particular hardware, while others are used for software configuration. Windows initially sets up defaults that work for most installations, but as a technician, you may need to tweak some of the settings. Also, not all Windows features are enabled in a normal installation, so you may need to enable or disable features according to the needs of a particular user.

✔ Cross-Reference

For a refresher on the Windows Control Panel, refer to the "Control Panel" section in Chapter 13 of *Mike Meyers' A+ Guide to Managing and Troubleshooting PCs.*

Learning Objectives

In this lab, you'll practice accessing the Control Panel and making configuration adjustments.

At the end of this lab, you'll be able to

- Navigate to the Control Panel

- Explain the use of some common Control Panel applets

Lab Materials and Setup

The materials you need for this lab are

- A working computer running Windows 2000 or Windows XP

Getting Down to Business

The Control Panel is the toolbox, and one of the key tools in the Control Panel is the Device Manager. The Device Manager lists all your system hardware. From here you can load drivers, set resources, and configure other aspects of your hardware devices. You'll now get familiar with both.

Step 1   As a technician, you'll access the Control Panel and the Device Manager often. You really do need to know the path to these important tools in both Windows 2000 and Windows XP. The CompTIA A+ exams have numerous questions about paths to these tools.

✔ **Hint**

Throughout the rest of this manual, when a lab involves changing settings located in the Control Panel or the Device Manager, the directions will assume you know how to get that far, and the steps will begin with the Control Panel or Device Manager already open. Refer back to this exercise if you need a refresher on opening the Control Panel.

a) To open the Control Panel, select Start | Settings | Control Panel. This path applies to all versions of Windows, including Windows XP in the Classic Start menu mode. The Control Panel dialog box opens, as shown in Figure 13-15.

b) Start with the System applet. The System applet is the gateway to many important tools and utilities you will use as a PC technician. You'll explore some of these utilities in other labs throughout the manual; for now, just take a high-level view of the following:

- **Device Manager**   Select the Hardware tab and click the Device Manager button. Note the list of hardware installed in your system. Expand various items to see the list of devices in each area. Highlighting any device, right-clicking, and selecting Properties will give you configuration information for that device. You'll return here later in the lab manual to configure these devices.

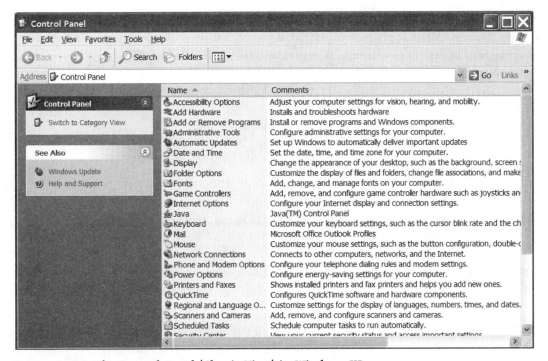

FIGURE 13-15 The Control Panel (Classic View) in Windows XP

- **Driver Signing**   Close Device Manager, and while still in the Hardware tab, click the Driver Signing button. This is where you tell Windows how to handle device drivers that have not been tested and approved by Microsoft. The three settings are Ignore, Warn, and Block.

- **Startup and Recovery**   Select the Advanced tab and click the Settings button under the Startup and Recovery box. Examine the settings for the Startup options. Click the Edit button; do you recognize the file that is displayed?

c) Close Notepad and the Startup and Recovery and System Properties dialog boxes, all without saving changes.

Step 2   Now examine some other applets in the Control Panel:

a) Double-click the Display icon. This is the same window you see if you right-click the desktop and select Properties.

b) Notice the tab headings. Three are common to all flavors of Windows: Screen Saver, Appearance, and Settings. Windows 2000 also has Background, Web, and Effects tabs. Windows XP incorporates the contents of those three tabs into two tabs, named Themes and Desktop.

✖ Warning

Clicking an Advanced button in the Display applet can give you access to many special features of your particular monitor/video card, including the refresh rate. Be sure you know what you're doing before you change these settings!

Note that if you click the Apply button instead of the OK button after making a change, the Display applet will remain open after the change takes effect; this can be useful when you need to experiment a bit.

---

c) Return to the Control Panel and double-click the Sounds and Multimedia icon (Windows 2000), or the Sounds and Audio Devices icon (Windows XP) to open that dialog box.

d) Again, you'll see tabs at the top left of the dialog box. Most of your applets will be similar to this. Explore each tab, and become familiar with what each does. Make changes to see the results. Be sure you remember or record the original settings so that you can reset them.

e) Reset all of your experimental changes, and close the applet.

Step 3   Keyboard and mouse action settings are definitely a matter of personal preference. Be careful to tell the user if you make any changes to these settings. If you need to speed them up for your own use while troubleshooting a PC, remember to slow them down again so the user isn't frustrated by keys that repeat or a mouse cursor that races across the screen out of control.

To adjust the Keyboard settings:

a) Double-click the Keyboard icon in the Control Panel.

b) Change the cursor's blink rate and test it.

c) Change the key repeat rate and delay settings. A minor adjustment here can really help a heavy-fingered user.

d) Close the Keyboard applet.

✔ **Hint**

The Mouse applet can have many different looks, depending on whether the system uses a default Windows driver or special drivers for the particular mouse. You may have to explore your applet to find these settings.

e) Double-click the Mouse icon to open the Mouse applet.

f) Change from a right-hand to a left-hand mouse. Try it out. Does that make your brain hurt? Well then, change it back. (Ahhh, that's better!)

g) Change the double-click speed. Slow it down a bit. Is that easier? Slow it down more. Do you find that annoying? Now speed it up. Can you click fast enough?

h) Change the mini-icons that represent your mouse pointer, such as the arrow, hourglass, and so on. Try a couple of different sets. Can you think of situations where some of these alternative icon sets might be useful?

i) Change the pointer options. Change the speed at which the pointer travels across your screen. Everyone has his or her own sweet spot for this, so experiment to find yours. Turn on pointer trails. Do you find them cool or annoying? If you have a Snap To option, turn that on. Now open a dialog box and watch the pointer jump to the active button. Is this convenient, or too much help? Turn off any features you don't want to retain.

j) Now that you've tweaked your mouse performance, close the applet.

Step 4 The CompTIA A+ exams include questions about user accessibility. Know what settings you can change to accommodate the hearing and visually impaired, and where to find those settings:

a) Double-click the Accessibility Options icon.

b) Notice that there are Keyboard, Sound, Display, Mouse, and General tabs (see Figure 13-16).

c) Select the Display tab.

d) Turn on the Use High Contrast option and click Settings (see Figure 13-17).

e) Choose a scheme you like and click OK.

f) Click Apply in the Accessibility Options dialog box to see how it looks.

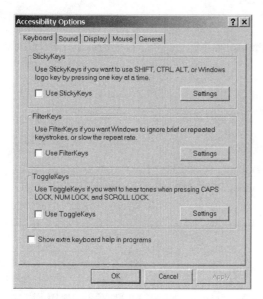

FIGURE 13-16 The Accessibility Options dialog box

g) Turn off the Use High Contrast option, then click Apply and OK.

h) Close the Accessibility Options dialog box.

Step 5 One more commonly used applet is Date and Time.

Open the Date and Time applet in the Control Panel. This applet has been around since the dawn of time, more or less, when computers didn't automatically adjust themselves for Daylight Saving Time.

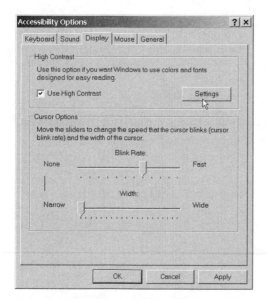

FIGURE 13-17 Setting the High Contrast option for the visually impaired

Adjust the date and time. Notice that you can do this either by scrolling with the arrows or by highlighting the fields. This feature can come in handy if you travel and want to change the time zone on a portable computer.

 30 MINUTES

Lab Exercise 13.05: Windows Microsoft Management Console (MMC) Toolbox

You're about to learn how to customize your Windows toolkit! Almost every profession requires a set of tools to get the job done. Some of these tools are necessary, and some are luxuries. If you were a carpenter, you might have a toolkit where you keep your hammer, saw, screwdrivers, pliers, and so on. You can then buy new tools ("I really needed this pneumatic nail gun, and it was on sale!" is a common excuse) and add them to your toolbox—but you'd need to keep it all organized, or risk not being able to find the tool you need when you need it.

To help organize your PC technician's toolbox, Microsoft created the Microsoft Management Console, or MMC. The MMC not only organizes all of those useful tools, but it also provides a consistent look and feel between different systems and even different operating systems, which makes it easier to use them.

✔ **Cross-Reference**

For details on working with the MMC, refer to the "Microsoft Management Console" section in Chapter 13 of *Mike Meyers' A+ Guide to Managing and Troubleshooting PCs.*

Learning Objectives

In this exercise, you'll learn how to create an MMC. You'll also create a desktop icon that you can use to access this customized software toolkit whenever you need it.

At the end of this lab, you'll be able to

- Create an MMC
- Add tools (snap-ins) to the MMC

Lab Materials and Setup

The materials you need for this lab are

- A PC system with Windows 2000 or XP installed

Getting Down to Business

The MMC is a shell program that holds individual utilities called snap-ins. The first time you create an MMC, you get a default blank console. A blank MMC isn't much to look at—like any new toolbox, it starts out empty.

Step 1 To create your MMC, select Start | Run, type **mmc**, and then click OK. Voilà! You've created a blank console (Figure 13-18). Notice that the name in the upper-left corner is Console 1.

Before you actually configure an MMC, you need to understand a few points. First, you can have more than one MMC; successive consoles will be given default names such as Console 2, Console 3, and so on. Second, you can rename the consoles that you create and choose where to save them so that you can easily find them again. Finally, once you've created an MMC, you can modify it by adding or taking away tools—just like your toolbox at home.

Follow these steps to practice working with MMCs:

a) Click File (Windows XP) or Console (Windows 2000) | Save As and fill in the boxes as follows:

- **Save in** Desktop

- **File name** My First MMC

- **Save as type** Microsoft Management Console Files (*.msc)

b) Click Save to continue. (Don't exit the MMC!)

c) Notice in the upper-left corner of the open window that the name has changed.

d) Find the new icon that's been created on the desktop. This icon, which bears the same name as your new MMC, will enable you to access the MMC in the future with just a double-click of the mouse.

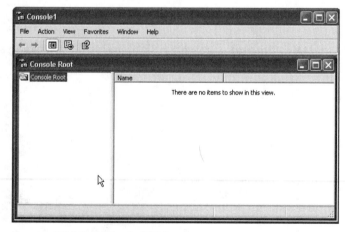

FIGURE 13-18 A blank MMC

FIGURE 13-19 Adding or removing snap-ins

Step 2   When you add snap-ins, they'll show up in the Add/Remove Snap-in dialog box (see Figure 13-19).

You'll now add some snap-ins to your MMC:

a) Click File | Add/Remove Snap-in (Windows XP) or Console | Add/Remove Snap-in (Windows 2000).

b) Click Add, and let the fun begin (see Figure 13-20). I bet you haven't had this many selections since your last visit to Sears' hardware department!

c) Add the Device Manager as your first tool. Select Device Manager from the list and click Add.

FIGURE 13-20 Adding a standalone snap-in

✔ Hint

When you add a snap-in, you have a choice of adding it for either your local computer or another computer. With the proper access permissions, in other words, you can look at the Device Manager on a networked system. More than likely, you don't have the necessary permissions to do this, so stick with the local option for now.

---

d) Select Local Computer and click Finish.

✖ Warning

I can't emphasize strongly enough that the best way to get a systems administrator mad is to go snooping around on the network. As a technician, your main concern is to do no harm. If you accidentally find your way to an unauthorized area, it's your duty to report it to an administrator.

While you're here, you'll add one more snap-in: the Event Viewer. You'll use this tool in the labs for Chapter 15, "Maintaining and Troubleshooting Windows." Adding it here will provide an alternative way to access this tool:

a) Select Event Viewer from the list.

b) Select Local Computer and Finish to close out the wizard.

c) Click Add to close the list window and OK to close the Add/Remove window.

d) Your MMC should now show two snap-ins.

e) Be sure to save your MMC.

You now have a toolbox with quick access to Device Manager and Event Viewer. You can use these tools in the same way as if you navigated to them through the conventional methods.

Click Device Manager to expand the list of devices. Notice that it looks the same and works the same as it would if you opened it through the Control Panel.

Step 3   If everything has worked correctly up to now, continue with this step (if you had problems creating your MMC, review the instructions or ask your instructor for assistance):

a) Double-click the desktop icon for My First MMC.

b) Your Device Manager and Event Log are now available directly from your desktop (see Figure 13-21).

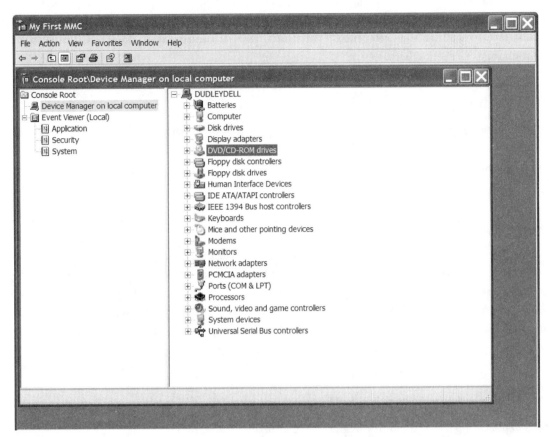

FIGURE 13-21 Accessing Device Manager from a custom MMC

✔ Hint

I've only scratched the surface here showing you how to create an MMC. Your customizing options are limited only by the number of snap-ins available and your imagination. Try creating different groupings of tools to organize similar tasks, maybe all of the disk management tools together, or all of the user, group, and resource tools. Be creative!

 30 MINUTES

Lab Exercise 13.06: Windows Registry

The Registry stores everything about your PC, including information on all the hardware in the PC, network information, user preferences, file types, and virtually anything else you might run into with Windows. The hardware, software, and program configuration settings in the Registry are particular to each PC. Two identical PCs with the same operating system and hardware can still be remarkably different because of user settings and preferences. Almost any form of configuration done to a Windows system results in changes to the Registry.

> ### ✖ Warning
>
> When changing the Registry, proceed with great care—making changes in the Registry can cause unpredictable and possibly harmful results. To paraphrase the old carpenter's adage: consider twice, change once!

Learning Objectives

Most of the common tools to modify the Registry are contained in the Control Panel. When you use the Display applet to change a background, for example, the resultant changes are added to the Registry. The Control Panel applets are what you should normally use to configure the Registry. However, there are times—a virus attack, perhaps, or complete removal of a stubborn application—when direct manipulation of the Registry is needed. In this lab, you'll familiarize yourself with the Windows Registry and the direct manipulation of the Registry using the REGEDIT command.

At the end of this lab, you'll be able to

- Access the Registry using REGEDIT

- Export, import, and modify Registry data subkeys and values

- Define the function of the five top-level Registry keys

Lab Materials and Setup

The materials you need for this lab are

- A working computer running Windows 2000 or Windows XP

Getting Down to Business

A technician needs to know how to access the Registry and modify the configuration based on solid support from Microsoft or other trusted sources. As mentioned in the Learning Objectives, your main interface to the Registry is the Control Panel. Changes made through the applets in the Control Panel result in modifications to the Registry settings. To see what's going on behind the scenes, though, you'll explore the Registry directly in this exercise using the REGEDIT command.

> ### ✔ Cross-Reference
>
> For more detail on the Windows Registry and working with REGEDIT and REGEDT32, refer to the "Registry" section in Chapter 13 of *Mike Meyers' A+ Guide to Managing and Troubleshooting PCs.*

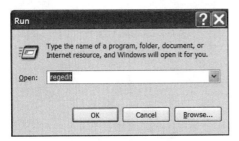

FIGURE 13-22 Starting the Registry editor

Step 1   You almost never need to access the Registry directly. It's meant to work in the background, quietly storing all the necessary data for the system, updated only through a few menus and installation programs. When you want to access the Registry directly, you must use the Registry Editor (REGEDIT or REGEDT32).

✔ **Hint**

This lab exercise was written using a system running Windows XP Professional. Windows XP has combined the two versions of the Registry editor—REGEDIT and REGEDT32—to have the strong search features of REGEDIT. For convenience, I will use the REGEDIT command to launch the Registry editor. If you are working on a Windows 2000 Professional machine, you can explore the different versions of REGEDIT and REGEDT32. Remember, no matter which version of Windows you are using, that the Registry is a binary file. You can't edit it using EDIT, Notepad, or any other text editor.

To edit the Registry directly, follow these steps:

a) Select Start | Run, type **regedit**, and then click OK (see Figure 13-22) to start the Registry editor.

b) Note the five main subgroups or root keys in the Registry (see Figure 13-23). Some of these root key folders may be expanded. Click the minus sign by any expanded folders. Do a quick mental review—do you know the function of each Registry key? You should!

c) Now test your knowledge of the Registry. Referring to the textbook as necessary, match the listed keys with the following definitions by writing the definition number next to the corresponding key:

        HKEY_CLASSES_ROOT   _____

        HKEY_CURRENT_USER   _____

        HKEY_LOCAL_MACHINE   _____

        HKEY_USERS   _____

        HKEY_CURRENT_CONFIG   _____

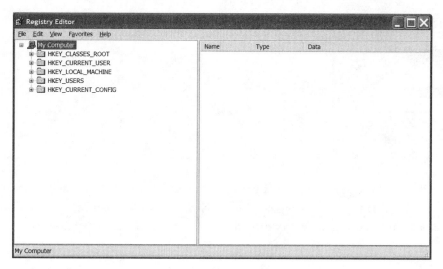

FIGURE 13-23 Viewing the five main subgroups of the Windows XP Registry

1. Contains the data for non-user-specific configurations, and includes every device in your PC and those you've removed

2. Contains the personalization information for all users on a PC

3. Contains additional hardware information when there are values in HKEY_LOCAL_MACHINE such as two different monitors

4. Defines the standard class objects used by Windows; information stored here is used to open the correct application when a file is opened

5. Contains the current user settings, such as fonts, icons, and colors on systems that are set up to support multiple users

Step 2   One of the reasons you might want to edit the Registry directly would be to implement or expand a component of Windows that is not accessible through the Control Panel interface. A favorite of many techs is to enable the Rename function for the Recycle Bin. Expand the HKEY_CLASSES_ROOT key by clicking the plus sign. Notice that there are more subkeys underneath it, some of which have subkeys of their own, and so on. Search down to the CLSID subkey and expand the key by clicking the plus sign. You will see hundreds of long identification codes. Now use the Find utility (CTRL-F) and enter the following string into the text box: **645FF040-5081-101B-9F08-00AA002F954E**

Make sure you enter the numbers correctly. Expand the subkey and click on the ShellFolder icon. You should see the information in Figure 13-24.

Before you start changing the Registry, it's a good idea to learn how to "back up" the keys by exporting and importing them. This will enable you to reset the subkey to its original state if you make a mistake in your entries.

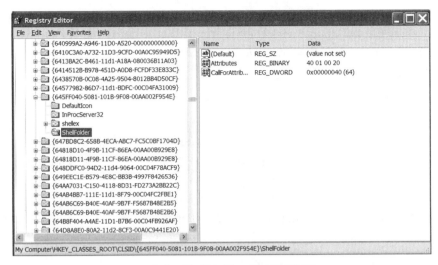

FIGURE 13-24 Contents of the ShellFolder in REGEDIT

a) Highlight the ShellFolder subkey, and then select File | Export to open the Export Registry File dialog box. Save the key in a folder where you can find it again, and give it a useful name that you won't forget.

b) Highlight the key again, and double-click the Attributes REG_BINARY file. Replace the hexadecimal number 40 01 00 20 with 50 01 00 20 and click OK.

c) Now double-click the "CallForAttributes" REG_DWORD file. Replace the 40 with 00 and click OK.

d) Minimize the Registry editor and find the Recycle Bin on your desktop.

e) Highlight the Recycle Bin icon and right-click. In the drop-down menu there is now a Rename option (Figure 13-25). Click Rename and change the name of the Recycle Bin. Fun, eh?

FIGURE 13-25 The Recycle Bin's newly added Rename option

f) To return the Recycle Bin to its natural state, first rename it back to Recycle Bin. Now navigate to your exported Registry file and double-click the file. You will be asked if you are sure you want to add this information to the Registry. Click Yes. You should see a message that the information was successfully added to the Registry.

g) To confirm that your backup Registry information has taken effect, right-click the Recycle Bin. Can you still rename it?

Step 3   Imagine you're in the Control Panel adjusting your mouse settings, and you adjust the mouse double-click speed to the maximum (fastest) and close the window without testing it. When you try to use the system, you can't double-click the mouse fast enough even to get back into the Control Panel to fix it. (This is a bit of a stretch, as you could always use the keyboard to access the Mouse applet, but go with me here to see the Registry in action.) So, what do you do? Follow these steps to view your current Mouse applet double-click speed setting and then use REGEDIT to change it:

a) Access the Control Panel and open the Mouse applet.

b) Adjust the slider for the double-click speed to the middle position, and test to be sure it works.

c) Click Apply and then OK. Close the Mouse applet and Control Panel.

d) Open the Registry Editor, and make sure that My Computer is highlighted at the top of the left pane.

e) Select Edit | Find to search for the mouse double-click speed. In the Find What field, type **doubleclickspeed** (be sure to spell it as one word, no spaces). Check the Match Whole String Only box. Click Find Next. You want only the first occurrence it finds. There are other things with that name that you don't want to change.

f) When REGEDIT finds the file, right-click the word DoubleClickSpeed in the right pane and select Modify.

g) Change the value to something between 100 and 900 (milliseconds); 100 is very fast. Click OK and then close the Registry editor.

h) Reopen the Mouse applet in the Control Panel. Did the slider move from where it was?

---

i) For more practice, set your double-click speed to the fastest setting in the Control Panel and go to the Registry to slow it down.

✔ **Hint**

The Web site www.winguides.com/registry is full of working Registry fixes.

Lab Analysis Test

1. Your friend Brian calls you and asks if he can make his new Windows XP system look like the Windows 2000 system he uses at work. He says he doesn't like the bright, cartoonish style, and the Start menu is different. Explain to Brian what he can and can't do to change the look of Windows XP.

2. What's the purpose of the MMC?

3. When you install Windows XP for the first time on Joe's PC, he notices that some desktop icons he's accustomed to seeing are missing. As a matter of fact, only the Recycle Bin icon is present. Where and how can you add the desktop icons he's used to seeing in Windows 2000?

4. One of your clients using Windows XP called your Help Desk because he's experiencing difficulties using the mouse. He says his mouse moves too fast, and icons don't respond when he double-clicks them. What's wrong? Where would you direct him to go to fix this problem? Give the complete path.

5. Which is a safer place for trained technicians to make changes or modifications: the Control Panel or the Registry? Explain your choice.

Key Term Quiz

Use the following vocabulary terms to complete the following sentences. Not all terms will be used.

Classic View

Control Panel

MMC

Recycle Bin

REGEDIT

snap-ins

Start button

taskbar

1. The Registry contains all the configuration data and can be accessed directly using
   _____.

2. When you delete files, Windows creates shortcuts to them in the _____.

3. The System, Display, and Mouse applets are found in the _____.

4. The various tools in the MMC are known as _____.

5. The Start button and the notification area/system tray are parts of the Windows
   _____.

Chapter 14

Working with the Command-Line Interface

Lab Exercises

Although the CompTIA A+ Certification exams have dropped the requirements of working with the MS-DOS operating system, they do stipulate that PC technicians should know some of the basic commands and functions available at the command-line interface in all versions of Windows. Why? Because they still work, and good techs use the command line often. You'll need a solid understanding of several basic command-line commands, and a few advanced tasks. Commands such as CD, COPY, and ATTRIB, as well as the tasks of starting and stopping services, editing files, and converting file systems, should be part of your PC tech arsenal.

If you have a system crash and are able to gain access to the machine using the Microsoft Recovery Console, you'll really need to know the proper commands for navigating around your drives, folders, and files, and launching utilities that will get your OS up and running again. Also, when you start working with networks, the command-line interface on all Windows systems is invaluable.

✔ **Cross-Reference**

You will further explore the use of the Recovery Console in the lab exercises for Chapter 15, "Maintaining and Troubleshooting Windows." You will also have the opportunity to work with additional networking command-line utilities in the lab exercises for Chapter 21, "Local Area Networking."

The command line can often provide a quicker way to accomplish a task than the graphical alternative. In cases where a virus, hard drive failure, or OS problem prevents you from booting to Windows, you need to know how to get around with the command line. The following labs are designed to give you the chance to practice your basic command-line skills, so that when the need arises, the command line will be your friend.

✔ **Hint**

As you have worked through the labs in this manual, I have recommended often that you explore features, options, and components not specifically covered in the lab exercises. You have embarked on the journey to become a CompTIA A+ certified technician! Natural curiosity, enthusiasm, and determination will go a long way toward developing the understanding and experience you need to become a competent technician and pass the exams. These qualities are especially important when it comes to working with the command-line interface. As you navigate through the following labs, it is easy to take a left when you should have taken a right and get lost in subdirectories, mistype a command, or delete a file you didn't want to. Don't let it discourage you.

Making mistakes while learning is good, and learning from those mistakes is great! If you get lost, explore ways to get back to where you need to be—you're unlikely to hurt anything. If you really get lost, work with your instructor or a more experienced classmate to determine where you went astray, then work through it again.

 30 MINUTES

Lab Exercise 14.01: Configuring the Command-Line Window

Before you can use the command line, you need to know the basics: ways to access it, manipulate and customize the look of it within the GUI, and close it down properly. This lab covers those basics.

Learning Objectives

In this lab, you'll practice opening, resizing, customizing, and closing a command-line window.

At the end of this lab, you'll be able to

- Open a command-line window from within the Windows operating system

- Resize the command-line window

- Customize the look of the command-line window

- Exit the command-line window

Lab Materials and Setup

The materials you need for this lab are

- A PC with Windows 2000 or Windows XP installed

Getting Down to Business

The first thing you'll need to do, obviously, is get to a command line. Spend the next several minutes becoming familiar with accessing the command-line window.

✔ **Cross-Reference**

For details on how to access the command-line interface, refer to the "Accessing the Command Line" section in Chapter 14 of *Mike Meyers' A+ Guide to Managing and Troubleshooting PCs*.

Step 1   Turn on your system, and wait for the Windows desktop to appear. Then follow these steps:

a) Select Start | Run, then type **CMD**.

b) Click OK to display a command-line window (see Figure 14-1).

Step 2   There are three ways to change the size of the command-line window for better viewing:

- Use the resize arrows along the edges of the windows (this will not work when the window is maximized).

- Use the minimize/maximize button in the upper-right corner of the window.

- Press ALT-ENTER to toggle between the full screen and a window.

Step 3   In Windows 2000, you should be looking at a black screen with your operating system information in the upper-left corner and a C prompt (C:\>) below. Windows XP will have a different prompt (C:\WINDOWS\Documents and Settings\username>). This just means that in Windows 2000, the command line opens as a default at the root of the C: drive, whereas Windows XP opens with the focus pointing to the user's personal area in the Documents and Settings folder.

To the right of the prompt, you'll see a flashing cursor indicating that it's waiting for your input. There's also a scroll bar along the right side of the window. Sometimes your command causes more information to be displayed than the window can hold, and it's really useful to be able to scroll back up and see what messages were displayed.

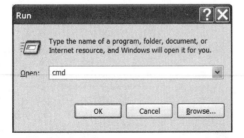

FIGURE 14-1 Opening the Windows XP command-line window

You'll now execute a few commands, for the purpose of exploring the scrolling issue. You will explore these commands further in later lab exercises. The Change Directory command (CD) lets you to change the focus of the working directory displayed in the command-line window. The Directory command (DIR) lists the filename, extension, file size (in bytes), and creation date/time of the files in the current folder.

You are going to change from the current working directory to a subdirectory with hundreds of files. Type **CD C:\WINDOWS\SYSTEM32** (C:\ is the root directory, WINDOWS is the system folder, and SYSTEM32 is where many of the system configuration and driver files are stored). You may have to use a different drive letter or system folder name to arrive at the SYSTEM32 directory.

Now type **DIR** and press ENTER. The SYSTEM32 folder contains over 1000 files, so the command-line window will not be able to display all of the information at once. If there's more than one screen's worth of information, it will keep scrolling out of sight until everything has been displayed. You can use the scroll bar to go back a few screens' worth—give it a try.

If you were actually trying to work with a few of the files in the folder, you're probably out of luck, as you can't scroll back more than a few screens. To address this problem, there's a command you can use that forces the information to be displayed one screenful at a time. Type **DIR /P** and then press ENTER. Adding the /P switch to the command tells it to pause after each screenful of text. Press the spacebar to display the next screenful. You can't go back if you're too quick with the spacebar, so take a good look at each screen! If you tire of paging through the screens, you can end the command by pressing CTRL-C.

Step 4   Just as with most applets in the Windows environment, if you right-click the title bar and select Properties, you can configure some of the features of the command-line window:

- **Options** Configure the cursor size, command history, display options, and edit options.

- **Font** Select from a limited set of command-line fonts and sizes.

- **Layout** Set the screen buffer size and window size, and position the window on the monitor screen.

- **Colors** Configure the color of screen text, screen background, pop-up text, and pop-up background.

Explore some of the settings you can change, and feel free to set up the command-line window to your personal taste. I grew up on early IBM machines, in the days when owning a color monitor meant that you had an electric green or bright orange character on a black monochrome screen. See if you can re-create this wonderful look!

Step 5   There are two common ways to close a command-line window:

- Click the X in the upper-right corner of the window. This method isn't recommended if the window is actively running a program. You should wait until you see the prompt before clicking the X.

- Type **EXIT** at the command line, and press ENTER. I prefer this method, because I can be sure the window is inactive when I quit.

 30 MINUTES

Lab Exercise 14.02: Navigating Basic Commands

Before you can really use the command line, you must know the basic commands needed to navigate around a drive to locate and modify files. In this lab exercise, you'll learn more basic command-line commands that you would need to know when troubleshooting your or your client's PC.

✔ **Hint**

For the most part, mistakes such as spelling a command or filename incorrectly won't be disastrous for you. It's possible to misspell just incorrectly enough to delete the wrong file, or something similar, especially if you're using wildcards (I'll get to those in a bit). Typically, though, if you misspell a command or filename, the command line won't know what you're asking it to do and therefore won't do anything, or won't know what file you're asking to work with and will return an error message.

Learning Objectives

In this lab, you'll learn or review commands for directory and file management while using the command line.

At the end of this lab, you'll be able to

- Use commands to view, navigate, create, and delete directories using the command line
- Use commands to copy, move, rename, and delete files using the command line

Lab Materials and Setup

The materials you need for this lab are

- At least one working computer running Windows 2000 or Windows XP

✔ **Hint**

Other Windows versions will work just fine for this exercise, as long as you understand that the results may appear differently on your screen.

Getting Down to Business

Hundreds of commands and switches are available to you from the command-line interface. Although it is beyond the scope of these exercises to explore every possible command and its associated switches, you should spend the time in this lab exercise working with the specific ones that form the cornerstone of command-line navigation. These are the basic commands you'll use most often when working with the command line.

Step 1   Follow these steps:

a) Launch the command-line interface by typing **CMD** in the Run dialog box and either clicking OK or pressing ENTER.

b) When you first open the command-line window, your prompt might not be focused on the root directory. Because you want to focus on the root directory at this time, you must change directories before continuing.

The CD (Change Directory) command changes the directory the system is focused on. When you use the CD command, you must type the command followed by a space and then the name of the directory you want to view. This is true of all command-line commands. First, type the command followed by a space and then any options. Because you want to focus on the root of C: and the name of the root is the backslash (\), you'd type in the following and press ENTER (assuming that you're in the C: drive to begin with):

```
C:\Documents and Settings\username>CD \
```
Notice that the prompt has changed its focus to C:\> (see Figure 14-2).

Step 2   Probably the most frequently typed command is the request to display the contents of a directory (DIR). Because the command-line interface doesn't continually display everything the way a GUI does, you have to ask it to display specific information. The way you display the contents of a directory is to focus on the particular directory or subdirectory, and enter the command **DIR**.

Let's take a look at the contents of your root (C:\>) directory. You should already be focused there from the previous step in this exercise. Type **DIR** at the command prompt and press ENTER.

✔ **Hint**

From now on, when you see an instruction to type a command, you should assume that you should press ENTER afterward to complete the request (command). Otherwise, the command line will sit there, waiting patiently until the sun grows cold.

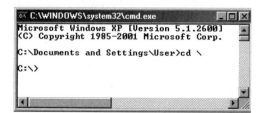

FIGURE 14-2 Changing the command-line focus

FIGURE 14-3 Viewing a sample Windows XP root directory

Now here's where it gets a little gray. Because I don't know what's in your root directory, there's no way to predict exactly what your C:\ contents will look like—but it's a good bet that *something* will be different from what I show you here! In theory at least, your display should be similar to Figure 14-3. Windows 2000 and XP will have the same basic look.

Notice that using the DIR command in any Windows operating system gives you the following information:

- Filename

- File extension

- Date and time of creation

- Size in bytes

- Designation as either a directory (<DIR>) or a file

- The number of files in the directory

- The amount of free space on the drive

Look at your particular results and note the mixture of files, which display a size in bytes, and directories, which have the annotation <DIR> after their name. In the preceding examples, AVG7QT.DAT is a file of 12,288,463 bytes, and WINDOWS, Program Files, and Documents and Settings are all names of directories.

Note whether you see the following files or folders in your root (C:\>) directory (you won't see them all):

AUTOEXEC.BAT	Yes ____	No ____
CONFIG.SYS	Yes ____	No ____
WINNT	Yes ____	No ____
WINDOWS	Yes ____	No ____

Documents and Settings   Yes ____   No ____

Program Files   Yes ____   No ____

List the names of all the directories you see displayed in your root directory:

_____   _____

_____   _____

_____   _____

_____   _____

_____   _____

Step 3   The biggest challenge when working with the command prompt is remembering what exactly to type to achieve your goal. Learning the commands is one thing, but each command can have switches and options that modify it somewhat. Also, you may have noticed that the screen fills up and scrolls from top to bottom, making it difficult to view all the information you might need. Let's look at a command to clear the screen and another to provide assistance with how to use the commands.

Type the command **CLS**. What happened? _____

Type the command **DIR /?**. What happened? _____

The question mark (/?) is a standard help switch for most commands. Even though I've used these commands for decades, I still use the /? switch occasionally to remember what options are available for a specific command.

✔ **Hint**

Be careful not to confuse the backslash (\) and the forward slash (/). In a command-line world, the path uses the backslash and command switches use the forward slash.

At this point, a huge amount of help information is displayed (see Figure 14-4), so you may feel like you're in command overload! Take comfort in the fact that DIR is the most complex command. Other commands are more straightforward with their help. You don't need to know what all the switches are—just know how to use the help switch (/?) to find them! The main thing to learn is the syntax of the commands.

Everything in brackets ([ ]) is optional for the command. Notice that DIR is the only mandatory part in that command even though there are several optional switches and parameters. This is the same for all of the commands. The system will use defaults if you don't specify a switch or optional parameter. It's the defaults that can cause problems if you're not careful when using these commands. Now follow these steps:

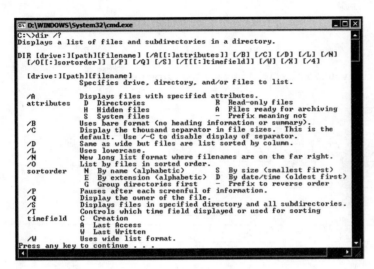

FIGURE 14-4 Viewing the syntax of the DIR command

a) Put a known good disc with files in your CD-ROM drive and let it spin up and come to rest. Cancel any windows that automatically open and proceed to the next substep.

b) Type **DIR**, and examine the resulting list of files and folders. Did they change from the previous step? _____

c) Do you think it read the compact disc? Probably not, because your prompt is still focused on the root directory of the hard drive.

d) Type **DIR D:** (replace D: with the appropriate drive letter for your CD-ROM drive, if necessary) and examine the resulting list of files and folders. Did they change this time? Aha! The option of [drive:] was needed to change the focus of the DIR command to the CD-ROM drive.

The [drive:] option will work for any of the drive letters. Floppy diskettes, CDs, DVDs, USB thumb drives, and Zip drives are all fair game as well. When you use this option, you can look at those other drives without switching from the directory you're in.

Step 4   Type **DIR /?** to look at two more optional switches: /P and /W. The /P switch is used when all the information will not fit on one screen, and /W is used to see a condensed listing of the directory.

Let's focus on a different directory. Remember, the CD command will let you change the directory you want to focus on:

a) Type **CD \WINDOWS**.

b) Type **CLS**.

c) Type **DIR** at the command prompt. This shows way too much data for the screen to display all at once.

d) Type **DIR /P** at the command prompt. This very useful switch causes the display to stop scrolling (pause) after each screen, waiting until you press the spacebar to show you more. In directories with lots of files, this is a lifesaver!

✔ Hint

If you want to stop a process that seems to be running forever, you can press CTRL-C. The process will end, and you'll get the prompt back.

e) Now type **DIR /W** at the command prompt. This switch is convenient when you're simply looking to see if a particular file resides in a particular directory, because it shows a "wide" list with filenames but no details.

f) Now practice moving around in the command window. Right now you're focused on the WINDOWS directory. Go back to the root directory by typing **CD **. To change the focus to another directory, use the CD command as you've learned. Use the DIR command to see what directories you have available in your current folder.

g) Try going to a subdirectory in another subdirectory and listing the contents. Look back at the list of directories you made previously and select one. Issue the CD command followed by a backslash (\) and the name of the target directory. For example, to switch to the Documents and Settings directory in the previous listing, type this:

`C:\WINDOWS>CD \DOCUMENTS AND SETTINGS`

Do this using several of the directory names you wrote down previously, and then type **DIR** to see what's there. Are there any subdirectories in this directory? Make a note of them.

_____   _____

_____   _____

_____   _____

✔ Hint

After you've changed the prompt focus many times, you may become confused about exactly where you are. You can always get to the root directory from any focus by typing **CD **.

Step 5 A normal Windows XP installation creates a Drivers directory, within a directory called System32, under the WINDOWS directory in the root of C: drive. To go to the Drivers directory, you don't have to do the CD command three times unless you really want to. If you know the path, you can go directly to the subdirectory with one CD command.

Go to the Drivers subdirectory by typing this at the command prompt:

`C:\>CD \WINDOWS\SYSTEM32\DRIVERS`

Your prompt should now look like Figure 14-5.

Type **DIR** to see what's there.

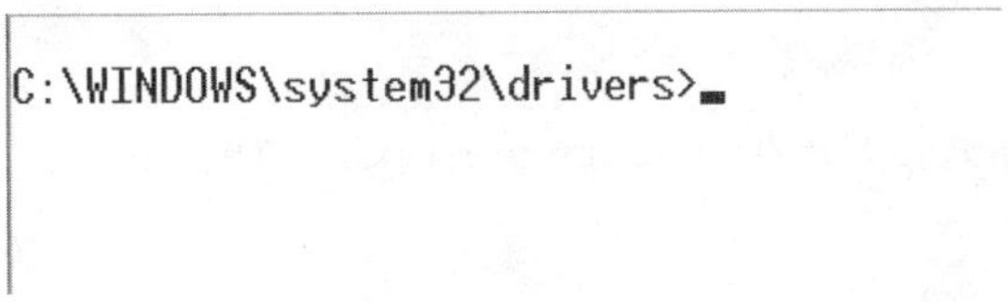

```
C:\WINDOWS\system32\drivers>_
```

FIGURE 14-5 Focusing on the Drivers subdirectory

One final navigation hint—you can change directories going back up toward the top level without returning directly to the root. If you want to go up a single directory level, you can type **CD** followed immediately by two periods (sometimes referred to as *CD dot dot*). For example, typing this takes you up one level to the System32 directory:

```
C:\>\WINDOWS\SYSTEM32\DRIVERS>CD..
C:\>\WINDOWS\SYSTEM32>
```

Do it again to go to the Windows directory:

```
C:\>\WINDOWS\SYSTEM32>CD..
C:\>\WINDOWS>
```

Type the command once more to arrive at the root directory:

```
C:\>\WINDOWS>CD..
C:\>
```

Take a minute and practice using the CD command. Go down a few levels on the directory tree, and then jump up a few, jump back to the root directory, and then jump down another path. Practice is the only way to get comfortable moving around in a command-prompt environment, and a good PC technician needs to be comfortable doing this.

Step 6 Sometimes a technician needs to make a directory to store files on the system. This could be a temporary directory for testing purposes, or maybe a place to store something more permanently (diagnostic reports, for example). In any case, it's important that you know how to create and remove a directory. The CompTIA A+ exams will test you on this. Follow these steps:

a) Be sure you're in the root directory. If you aren't there, type **CD ** to return to the root directory, where you'll add a new top-level directory. Actually, you can make a directory anywhere in the file structure, but you don't want to lose track of where it is, so make your new directory in the root. Do this using the MD (Make Directory) command.

b) Type **MD /?** to see how the command is structured and view the available options (see Figure 14-6).

c) At the command prompt, type the following:

```
C:\>MD CORVETTE
```

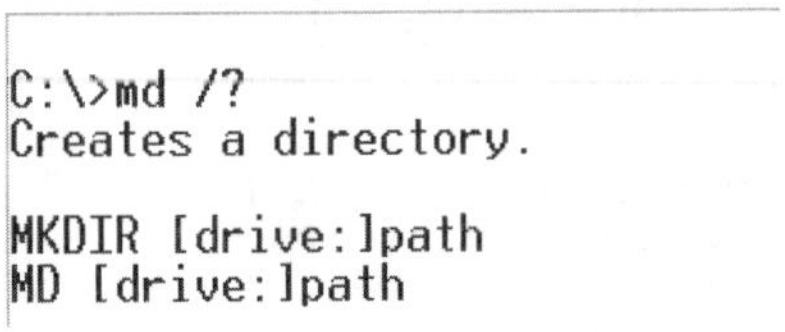

```
C:\>md /?
Creates a directory.

MKDIR [drive:]path
MD [drive:]path
```

FIGURE 14-6 Using the MD command

d) When the command line just presents a fresh prompt, it means that everything worked correctly. But to verify that the directory was actually made, type **DIR** to see your new directory in the list. It's as simple as that!

✖ Warning

Be careful—the new directory will always be created wherever the prompt is focused when you issue the command, whether that's where you meant to put it or not.

e) Be sure you're in the root directory (type **CD**), and prepare to remove your new CORVETTE directory.

Removing a directory requires the RD (Remove Directory) command and two conditions: First, the directory must be empty, and second, your system must not currently be focused on the directory about to be deleted.

f) Type this command:

```
C:\>RD CORVETTE
The directory has been deleted.
```

g) Type **DIR** to confirm that CORVETTE has been removed.

✔ Hint

Be *very* careful when you remove directories or delete files in the command line. It isn't as forgiving as Windows, which allows you to change your mind and "undelete" things. When you delete a file or directory using the command line, it's gone. If you make a mistake, there's nothing left to do but pout. So think carefully before you delete, and be sure you know *what* you're deleting before you do it—you'll save yourself a great deal of agony. Also pay attention to the directory you're currently focused on, to ensure that you're in the correct one.

Step 7 Sometimes you know the name of the file you want to use, but you don't know the directory where it's located. In this case, working with files and directories can become quite tedious. To help you locate files more easily, here are some switches and wildcards you can use with the DIR command:

a) Look again at the results of the DIR /? command, and find the /S switch. The /S switch will look for a file(s) in the specified (focus) directory and all subdirectories under that directory.

b) Windows XP has a file named XCOPY.EXE somewhere on the drive. Locate the path to the XCOPY.EXE file using the /S switch.

c) Start with your command prompt at the root directory (CD \).

d) Type this command:

```
C:\>DIR XCOPY.EXE
```

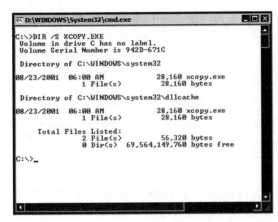

Figure 14-7 Locating the XCOPY.EXE file

If the file isn't in the root directory, nothing will be displayed.

e) Now try the new switch you just learned about to search all subdirectories. Type this command:

    C:\>**DIR /S XCOPY.EXE**

f) On my system, the file shows up in two places: in the C:\WINDOWS\system32 directory and in the C:\WINDOWS\system 32\dllcache directory (see Figure 14-7).

Another way to look for a file is to use a *wildcard*. The most common wildcard is the asterisk character (*), which you can use in place of all or part of a filename to make a command act on more than one file at a time. Wildcards work with all commands that use filenames.

The * wildcard replaces any number of letters before or after the dot in the filename. A good way to think of the * wildcard is "I don't care." Replace the part of the filename that you don't care about with *.

For example, if you want to locate all the README files on a hard drive and you don't care what the extension is, type the following:

    C:\>**DIR /S/P readme.***

The result is a list of all the README files on the hard drive. Notice that I used the /S switch to look in all the directories and the /P switch so I can view one screenful of results at a time (see Figure 14-8).

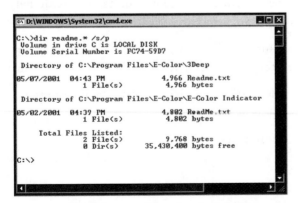

FIGURE 14-8 Using a wildcard to locate files

```
D:\WINDOWS\System32\cmd.exe - DIR /S/P *read*.*                          _ □ ×
 Volume in drive C is LOCAL DISK
 Volume Serial Number is FC74-59D7

 Directory of C:\Program Files\E-Color\3Deep

05/07/2001  04:43 PM              4,966 Readme.txt
05/07/2001  04:43 PM              4,966 ReadmeNT.txt
                2 File(s)         9,932 bytes

 Directory of C:\Program Files\E-Color\E-Color Indicator

05/02/2001  04:39 PM              4,802 ReadMe.txt
                1 File(s)         4,802 bytes

 Directory of C:\Work Files

10/20/2001  12:30 PM              6,895 Style Guide Proofreader's and Editor's Sy
mbols.htm
02/21/2003  01:02 PM    <DIR>           Style Guide Proofreader's and Editor's Sy
mbols_files
                1 File(s)         6,895 bytes

Press any key to continue . . . _
```

FIGURE 14-9 Using a wildcard to locate *READ*.* files

You can use the * wildcard for any number of characters. For example, not all companies use README.TXT as the help filename. Some use READ.ME, and others may use READ.TXT.

Because READ is common to all those variations, let's find all the files with READ in the filename. You should be prepared to see a long list of every file with READ in the name, not just the README files.

Type the following:

```
C:\>DIR /S/P *read*.*
```

Figure 14-9 shows the first screenful of results from my system. I found 104 files with READ somewhere in the filename. How many files and directories did you find with READ as part of the name?

 30 MINUTES

Lab Exercise 14.03: Using Command-Line Tools

Commands such as TYPE, COPY, MOVE, RENAME, and DELETE are used for manipulating files, such as you would be doing while troubleshooting a client's PC. These are more of the commands that every working tech should know by heart.

Learning Objectives

In this lab, you'll use commands for file management.

At the end of this lab, you'll be able to

- View text (.TXT) documents from the command-line interface

- Rename files using the command-line interface

- Copy files using the command-line interface

- Move files using the command-line interface

- Delete files using the command-line interface

Lab Materials and Setup

The materials you need for this lab are

- At least one working computer running Windows 2000 or Windows XP

Getting Down to Business

You might refer to these as the "second-tier" commands. Once you've used commands such as DIR, MD, and CD to navigate and create folders, you can use the following commands to manipulate individual files.

Step 1 In Lab Exercise 13.02, you created a text document using Notepad that you could safely use to explore file commands in this chapter. You will now navigate to your My Documents folder and verify that the file is there and contains readable text:

a) If you don't already have the command-line window open, get to a command prompt.

b) Enter the following commands:

```
C:\>CD \Documents and Settings\%USERNAME%\My Documents
C:\Documents and Settings\%USERNAME%\My Documents\>DIR /P
```

✔ Hint

To locate the file you created in Lab Exercise 13.02 and saved to My Documents, you should be logged on as the same user. The variable %USERNAME% (including the preceding and trailing percent signs) in the command-line syntax represents the user name you're currently using. Microsoft has assembled many variables that can be used in this manner, such as %SYSTEM-ROOT% to represent the system folder (usually named WINNT or WINDOWS). You may actually use the variable in the command-line syntax to have the system insert your user name (the folder where all of your personal settings and saved documents are) in the path. I have included a generic example of the use of this variable in Figure 14-10.

Look for the file you created in the previous chapter's lab (it should be called Command Line Test.TXT). Do you see it listed here? _____

Now you will use another command to verify that the file is a text file containing readable text. There are many ways to do this; you'll use one of the simplest methods. The TYPE command displays the contents of a text file, but doesn't allow you to edit or manipulate the text in any way.

Figure 14-10 Using an environment variable to insert the user name

c) Enter the following (carefully enter the line in the exact syntax as shown, including the quotation marks):

`C:\Documents and Settings\%USERNAME%\My Documents\>`**`TYPE "COMMAND LINE TEST.TXT"`**

You should see the text that you entered in Notepad during Lab Exercise 13.02. All of the text should be displayed, although you may have to resize your command-line window to see all of it, and even then it won't be pretty.

The other thing you may have noticed is that to access the text file, you had to add quotation marks to the beginning and the end of the filename. This is because the command line only understands spaces as breaks between commands and operators or switches. Leave the quote marks out of the command line and run the **TYPE** command again. What happened? _____

You should see something similar to the output in Figure 14-11.

You're going to use this file in the next few steps, and it will be easier to work with if its format conforms to the 8.3 rule. In the early days of MS-DOS, filenames could only be eight characters long, with a three-character extension after the period. The three-character extension has remained throughout all versions of Microsoft operating systems, but you can now use up to 255 characters (with spaces) as the filename. To make this file easier to work with in the command line, you'll use the REN (Rename) command to change the filename.

d) Type the following command:

`C:\Documents and Settings\%USERNAME%\My Documents\>`**`REN "COMMAND LINE TEST.TXT"`**
`CMDLNTST.TXT`

e) Now confirm that this has worked by typing the following command:

`C:\Documents and Settings\%USERNAME%\My Documents\>`**`TYPE CMDLNTST.TXT`**

Great! Now you will be able to type the filename more quickly as you complete the rest of the exercise.

Step 2   At the command prompt, type **CD ** to change your focus to the root directory. You'll now create a new directory in the root called STUDY so that you can do some copying and moving. The only difference between copying and moving is that COPY leaves the original file in the same place (as a backup) with a duplicate made elsewhere, whereas the MOVE command relocates the original file to a new location with no backup available. They're otherwise similar, so once you've learned the COPY command, you've pretty much learned the MOVE command too! Follow these steps:

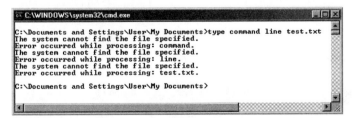

FIGURE 14-11 Results of running TYPE without using quotation marks

a) Make a directory named STUDY by typing the following:

    C:\>**MD STUDY**

b) Verify that the directory is there by using the DIR command.

Now follow these steps for copying your file named CMDLNTST.TXT to the new STUDY directory:

c) Change the focus of the command prompt to the STUDY directory:

    C:\>**CD STUDY**

d) Copy the CMDLNTST.TXT file to the STUDY directory:

    C:\STUDY>**COPY "C:\DOCUMENTS AND SETTINGS\%USERNAME%\MY DOCUMENTS\CMDLNTST.TXT"**
    C:\STUDY\CMDLNTST.TXT

Here, COPY is the command, C:\DOCUMENTS AND SETTINGS\%USERNAME%\MY DOCUMENTS\ CMDLNTST.TXT is the current location and name of the file (notice the use of the quotation marks and the %USERNAME% variable once again), and C:\STUDY\CMDLNTST.TXT is the target location and name of the file.

The entire command and response will look similar to Figure 14-12.

e) Run the DIR command to see if you copied the file. If the file isn't there, carefully repeat the previous steps or ask your instructor for help.

f) Change your directory focus back to the My Documents folder (**CD \DOCUMENTS AND SETTINGS\ %USERNAME%\MY DOCUMENTS**) and run the DIR command to see if the original CMDLNTST .TXT file is still there.

✔ **Hint**

If you're already in the target directory, you don't need to include the target path in the command. My idea of copying or moving files is to start in the directory to which you want to copy the files. Then you can bring the files to where you are. Each time you copy or move a file, you can run the DIR command to see if it's actually there. The other way of sending a file to a directory can be troublesome if you're moving files, because you may accidentally send them to a wrong directory and waste time looking for them.

Another good use of the COPY command is to make a backup copy of a file and rename it at the same time, so that the two files can reside in the same directory.

g) To make a backup of the CMDLNTST.TXT text file, type the following command:

    C:\STUDY\>**copy CMDLNTST.TXT CMDLNTST.BAK**

FIGURE 14-12 COPY command and response

You now have three copies of the same file; you will clean these up in the last step.

Step 3 The last two commands you will work with in this step are the MOVE and DEL (Delete) commands. First, you will delete the copy of CMDLNTST.TXT that you copied into the STUDY folder in the last step. You will then move the file permanently from the My Documents folder to the STUDY folder. Follow these steps:

a) Change the focus of the command prompt to the STUDY directory:

C:\>**CD STUDY**

b) Delete the CMDLNTST.TXT file from the STUDY directory:

C:\STUDY\>**DEL CMDLNTST.TXT**

c) Run the DIR command to see if you deleted the file. If the file isn't there, you deleted it.

Now you will follow the steps to move the file from My Documents to the STUDY folder. You will then verify that the file is in the STUDY folder and no longer in the My Documents folder.

d) Make sure the focus of the command prompt is still the STUDY directory.

e) Move the CMDLNTST.TXT file to the STUDY directory:

C:\STUDY>**MOVE "C:\DOCUMENTS AND SETTINGS\%USERNAME%\MY DOCUMENTS\CMDLNTST.TXT"**
C:\STUDY\CMDLNTST.TXT

In this case, MOVE is the command, C:\DOCUMENTS AND SETTINGS\%USERNAME%\MY DOCUMENTS\ CMDLNTST.TXT is the current location and name of the file (notice the use of the quotation marks and the %USERNAME% variable once again), and C:\STUDY\CMDLNTST.TXT is the target location and name of the file.

f) Run the DIR command to see if you moved the file. If the file isn't there, repeat the previous steps or ask your instructor for help.

g) Change your directory focus back to the My Documents folder (**CD \DOCUMENTS AND SETTINGS\%USERNAME%\MY DOCUMENTS**) and run the DIR command to see if the original CMDLNTST.TXT file is still there. Do you see it? _____ Why or why not? _____

You should now have two copies of the file in the STUDY directory, CMDLNTST.TXT and CMDLNTST .BAK. The file should have been moved from the My Documents directory.

 1 HOUR

Lab Exercise 14.04: Advanced Command-Line Utilities

In Windows, you can perform many tasks either from the GUI or from the command-line window. The CompTIA A+ exams want you to be comfortable with both methods to accomplish these tasks. To practice your skills with the command-line versions of these tasks, work through the following scenarios and steps to explore the BOOT.INI system file, the Print Spooler service, and the NTFS file system, all with the view from the command prompt.

Learning Objectives

In this lab, you'll work through three scenarios.

At the end of this lab, you'll be able to

- Work with the ATTRIB and EDIT utilities

- Start and stop services with the NET command

- Convert file systems

Lab Materials and Setup

The materials you need for this lab are

- At least one working computer running Windows XP

- A hard drive with at least 1 GB of unallocated space, or a 1-GB or greater partition formatted with the FAT32 file system

✔ **Hint**

If the machines configured with multiple hard drives are still available from Lab Exercise 10.05, "Implementing Software RAID 0 with Disk Management," you can convert these back to basic disks and format them with FAT32 to use in Step 3 of this exercise.

Getting Down to Business

Working through commands as you have in the prior exercises is an excellent method to explore the commands and their usage, but it can seem a little sterile since the commands are isolated and out of context. The next few steps are built around scenarios common in the workplace, requiring you to perform tasks that incorporate both commands you have learned in prior exercises and new commands that will be introduced as needed.

Step 1   BOOT.INI is a file that the Windows 2000 and Windows XP operating systems use to locate the system files during the boot process. This is especially important if the machine has been configured to be a multiboot machine capable of launching different operating systems. In the steps that follow, you will use the command-line text editor, EDIT, to modify the BOOT.INI system file. You'll have to change the status of the READ ONLY attribute using the ATTRIB command, and verify successful configuration using the System applet's Startup and Recovery settings.

a) Using your favorite method, launch the command prompt and change your focus to the root directory.

b) To open BOOT.INI using the command-line editor, type the following command:

```
c:\>EDIT BOOT.INI
```

This launches the text editor, which displays the BOOT.INI text. Move your cursor down to the line that reads **timeout=30** and change it to **timeout=10**. What happens when you do this? _____

Exit the command-line editor by pressing ALT-F, then X (this is the keyboard shortcut for File | Exit).

c) To list the files and all of their attributes, use the ATTRIB command:

`c:\>ATTRIB`

The BOOT.INI file is currently set with the attributes R (Read Only), H (Hidden), and S (System). You must change the attributes before you can modify the file. Type **ATTRIB /?** to see the available options for the ATTRIB command.

d) Now change the attributes for the BOOT.INI file so that you can edit it in the command-line text editor. Type the following command:

`c:\>ATTRIB -R -H -S BOOT.INI`

This should remove the attributes from BOOT.INI. To verify the status of BOOT.INI, type **ATTRIB** at the command prompt. Did the previous ATTRIB command clear the attributes of the BOOT.INI file? _____

e) Launch the command-line editor again using the following command:

`c:\>EDIT BOOT.INI`

Again move your cursor down to the line that reads **timeout=30** and change it to **timeout=10**. Save the file by pressing ALT-F, then S (File | Save), and exit the command-line editor by pressing ALT-F, then X (File | Exit).

f) Verify that you have modified the BOOT.INI file by following these steps:

1. Access the Control Panel.

2. Open the System applet and click the Advanced tab.

3. Click the Settings button in the Startup and Recovery area.

The setting called *Time to display list of operating systems* should be changed from 30 seconds to 10 seconds (see Figure 14-13).

g) Now change the attributes for the BOOT.INI file again so that it's a read-only, hidden, system file. Type the following command:

`c:\>ATTRIB +R +H +S BOOT.INI`

This will keep the file safe from accidental or malicious deletion or modification until the next time you, the PC tech, need to edit it for different configurations.

Step 2 One recurring problem you will run into in the field is when one of the services in Windows stalls—in particular the Print Spooler. The Print Spooler is a holding area for print jobs, and it's especially important for network printers. If the print device runs out of paper while printing a document, you may have to stop and start the Print Spooler to allow the print device to receive jobs again. Typically you just open the Computer Management console, select Services, and restart the service. However, there may be times when it is more convenient or just plain necessary to accomplish this task from the command-line interface.

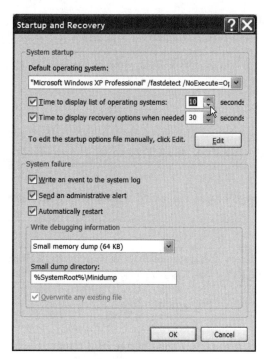

FIGURE 14-13 Checking settings in the Startup and Recovery window

The following steps walk you through stopping and starting the Print Spooler from the command-line interface:

a) Launch the Services console by opening the Control Panel, launching the Administrative Tools applet, and double-clicking Services.

b) Scroll down and highlight the Print Spooler, then select Action | Properties. You should see that the Print Spooler is started and running (see Figure 14-14).

c) Now launch the command-line interface and change the focus to the root directory.

d) Type the following command at the prompt:

```
c:\>NET STOP SPOOLER
```

The command line should inform you that the Print Spooler service is stopping, and then that the Print Spooler service was stopped successfully (see Figure 14-15).

✔ **Cross-Reference**

You will explore the NET command-line utility in the lab exercises for Chapter 21, "Local Area Networking." If you would like to explore the NET command while working on this lab, type **NET /?**

FIGURE 14-14 Print Spooler properties

e) Using ALT-TAB, change your focus to the Print Spooler Properties window you opened earlier. You should be able to confirm that the Print Spooler service has been stopped (see Figure 14-16).

f) Change the focus back to the command-line window, and type the following command at the prompt:

`c:\>`**NET START SPOOLER**

The command line should inform you that the Print Spooler service is starting, and then that the Print Spooler service was started successfully (see Figure 14-17).

In the real-world scenario, your Print Spooler service would be restarted, and you should have a healthy, functioning print server once again. Now you just have to figure out where you stored the extra toner!

FIGURE 14-15 Stopping the Print Spooler service
from the command-line interface

FIGURE 14-16 The Print Spooler Properties window

Step 3 Many of the legacy systems in the field started out as Windows 98 and Windows 2000 machines. Often, these systems' hard drives were partitioned and formatted with the FAT32 file system. As you upgrade these systems, you may want to leave the FAT32 file system intact until you verify that the upgrade has been successful. After successful completion of the upgrade, it is recommended that you convert the file system to NTFS. This is a nondestructive, one-way conversion! Once you switch to NTFS, you will have to delete the data and reformat the partition if you want to revert to FAT32.

In this step, you will create a FAT32 partition (unless you already have one from earlier labs) and then use the command-line utility called CONVERT to convert the partition to NTFS.

a) Boot a computer system with at least 1 GB of unallocated hard drive space. If you have access to the system you used to explore RAID 1 (striping), you can use the extra hard drives installed in the system.

b) Launch the Disk Management console. From the Control Panel, go into Administrative Tools and then select Computer Management.

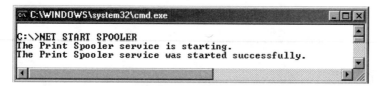

FIGURE 14-17 Starting the Print Spooler service from the command-line interface

   c) Click on Disk Management.

   d) Right-click an area of unallocated space and select New Volume from the drop-down menu.

   e) Follow the Wizard instructions to create a FAT32 partition of at least 1 GB.

✔ **Cross-Reference**

To refresh your Disk Management skills, refer to Chapter 10, Lab Exercise 10.03, "Using Windows Tools to Create and Format Partitions."

   f) Close the Disk Management console and double-click My Computer. Create and save a text file to the new drive to verify that the drive is accessible. Right-click the drive and select Properties; notice the tabs and file system (see Figure 14-18).

Now that you have a FAT32 partition, you can launch the command-line window and convert the file system from FAT32 to NTFS. You will then verify that the conversion was indeed nondestructive by opening the text file you created in step (f).

   g) Launch the command-line window and change the focus to the root directory using the **CD ** command.

   h) Type the following command at the prompt (substitute the drive letter for your FAT32 partition):

     `c:\>CONVERT E: /FS:NTFS`

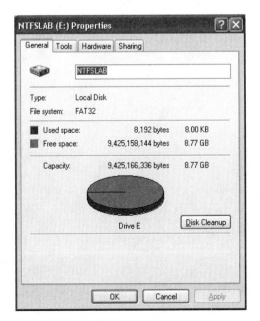

FIGURE 14-18 FAT32 partition properties

FIGURE 14-19 Converting a partition from FAT32 to NTFS

Your results should look similar to Figure 14-19.

i) Exit the command-line window and double-click My Computer.

j) Right-click the drive that you just converted and select Properties. Your drive should now be formatted with the NTFS file system. Notice the additional tabs for Security and Quota (see Figure 14-20).

k) Close the Properties window and double-click the drive. The text document you created in step (f) during the setup should still be there and accessible.

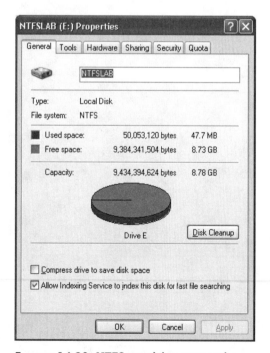

FIGURE 14-20 NTFS partition properties

Lab Analysis Test

1. Nate would like to make backup copies of all of his Word documents in the root directory. He types the following at the command prompt:

   `C:\>COPY A:\*.DOC`

   Will this command work? Why or why not? What will it do? Are there any limitations?

2. Which command(s) would you use to make a full copy of a file in the same directory under a different name?

3. The XCOPY.EXE file is in the SYSTEM32 directory, which is in the WINDOWS directory that's in the root directory of the primary hard drive. What's the complete command-line path to the file?

4. Explain the 8.3 rule. What does the 8 mean? How about the 3?

5. Thomas was messing around one day and deleted a file named CRITICAL.DLL from the SYSTEM32 directory. His friend gave him a copy on a floppy disk. What's the exact command he'd use to copy it back to the correct place?

Key Term Quiz

Use the following vocabulary terms to complete the following sentences. Not all terms will be used.

   /?

   /P

   /W

   CD

   COPY

   DEL

   DIR

   MD

   REN

   RD

1. The command to create a new directory is _____.

2. The command used to create a duplicate file is _____.

3. The _____ switch is used to get help about command syntax.

4. When there are too many files to show on the screen while using the DIR command, add the _____ switch.

5. For a listing of a directory's contents that displays only the filenames, use the _____ command with the _____ switch.

Chapter 15

Maintaining and Troubleshooting Windows

Lab Exercises

Imagine if you will that your company has just acquired a small architectural firm. One of the principals of the firm informs you that they haven't really had any IT support to speak of in a few years. You make a visit to the new office, and determine that the computers are about three years old. They were good machines when they were purchased, and as long as the hardware is not failing, they should be more than adequate for a year or two more. The architects do complain that their machines are running slowly and that it's affecting productivity. You would like to avoid a complete rollout of new PCs, since you're looking at a replacement expense of thousands of dollars. Consequently, you decide it would be worthwhile to spend a day trying to figure out if anything can be done to make the machines run faster.

After checking out a few of the systems, you determine that they could definitely benefit from additional memory, but that's not the only issue. All of the machines are running Windows 2000 Professional or Windows XP Professional, but they have not been updated in three years. Even though most versions of Windows are pretty well optimized when they're installed, time and use can alter that fact significantly. It's important, therefore, to be able to take what you know about navigating and manipulating the Windows environment and put it to work figuring out what needs to be fixed, updated, or improved. Sometimes a simple tweak is all it takes to make a sluggish system run like it's fresh out of the box.

One of the first tasks is to make sure that all of the systems have the latest Service Packs and Windows updates. Before you do that, however, it's recommended that you back up all of the data on the system, as this can be a pretty major upgrade. Another item that needs to be checked is whether the device drivers are all up to date. Neglected PCs will definitely require updated device drivers.

The next few labs assume that you've created your backups and are ready to start updating and optimizing Windows. You'll then explore the various troubleshooting tools for Windows 2000/XP. It's time to drop a few sticks of memory into the pilot machines, back them up, run them through the Service Packs and updates, and get this office back on its feet!

 1 HOUR

Lab Exercise 15.01: Performing an Automated System Recovery (ASR) Backup and Restore

Windows 2000 Professional and Windows XP Professional both offer simple backup/restoration utilities that you can use to back up both system data and program data and files. Each version of Windows offers an advanced recovery feature, in case the systems should become so unstable that they do not even boot.

Windows 2000 uses the Emergency Repair Disk (ERD), while Windows XP offers the Automated System Recovery (ASR) routine. Both recovery methods require access to backups of the systems, and both methods create a floppy disk that must be used during the recovery process. It is important to understand—and the CompTIA A+ Certification exams expect you to know this—that neither disk is a "bootable" floppy.

This lab introduces you to the Automated System Recovery (ASR) process in Windows XP Professional.

> ✖ **Warning**
>
> The ERD and ASR processes do not back up or restore program data or files! After the system restoration process is complete, the program data and files must be restored separately from previously created backup media.

Learning Objectives

Performing backups of any kind is a critical responsibility of a PC technician. The Windows XP Professional Automated System Recovery is an excellent representation of steps required to back up and restore an OS.

At the end of this lab, you'll be able to

- Prepare an Automated System Recovery backup in Windows XP
- Perform an Automated System Recovery restore in Windows XP

Lab Materials and Setup

The materials you need for this lab are

- A working PC with Windows XP Professional installed

- Some form of backup media/device (tape drive, network drive, separate partition)

- A blank, formatted floppy disk

Getting Down to Business

The time to prepare a backup is while the system and data are in a state of complete integrity. It's when they crash or get corrupted that you'll need the backup! The following steps create an ASR set and then use that ASR set to restore a Windows XP system to working condition.

AUTOMATED SYSTEM RECOVERY PREPARATION

Step 1 Launch the Windows Backup Wizard by clicking Start | Run and typing **ntbackup.exe** in the dialog box. Alternatively, you can click Start | All Programs | Accessories | System Tools | Backup. Click the Advanced Mode text link to bring up the screen shown in Figure 15-1.

Step 2 Launch the Automated System Recovery Wizard and perform the following steps:

a) Click Next and in the *Backup media or file name* dialog box, type or browse for the location and name of your backup file, being careful to preserve the .BKF file extension. If you are using a separate partition, for example, you might enter **D:\MyASRBK.BKF** to create the file on the D:\ drive.

b) Click Next | Finish to start the backup of your system files.

c) When the backup completes, the ASR preparation wizard instructs you to insert a formatted 1.44-MB floppy disk. Click OK. ASR copies the required files onto the floppy disk.

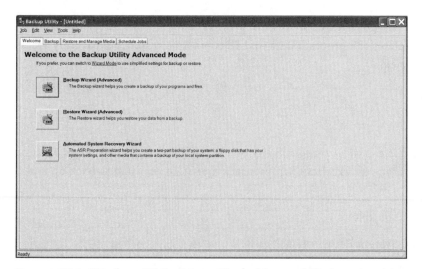

FIGURE 15-1 Windows XP Backup utility's Advanced Mode screen

d) When instructed, remove and label the floppy disk and then click OK. You have completed the preparation for an Automated System Recovery.

AUTOMATED SYSTEM RECOVERY RESTORE

Step 1 Boot the system using the Windows XP Professional installation CD.

Step 2 When prompted with *Press F2 to run Automated System Recovery*, press the F2 key.

Step 3 Insert the ASR floppy disk and press any key when ready.

Step 4 Windows XP Installation copies files to a temporary folder, formats the partition where XP will be installed, and prompts you to remove the installation CD and reboot.

Step 5 After rebooting, the Windows XP installation continues.

a) During the installation, you'll be prompted for the location of the ASR backup file.

b) Enter the file location or use the Browse button to enter the location and name of the ASR backup file.

c) Click OK.

d) The installation now completes. All of the Windows XP configuration settings and preferences should be as they were on the original system.

 30 MINUTES

Lab Exercise 15.02: Upgrading to Windows XP SP2 and Configuring Automatic Updates

These systems have been around for some time, so there are probably a number of outdated patches and drivers. Windows XP went through a major upgrade with Service Pack 2, so this is where you'll start. If you are working with a new installation of Windows XP, Service Pack 2 should already be incorporated into the cabinet files, but these are old machines, so they will need some TLC. Upgrading to Service Pack 2 (or for Windows 2000 Professional, Service Pack 4) is imperative to keeping the system up and running, secure, and compatible with new technology such as U3 flash drives or Bluetooth devices. After you bring the OS up to date with Service Pack 2, you will want to configure Automatic Updates. This periodically updates various drivers, security patches, and utilities.

Learning Objectives

A competent technician will understand the importance of upgrading an OS with the latest Service Pack.

At the end of this lab, you'll be able to

- Upgrade Windows XP to Service Pack 2
- Configure Windows Automatic Updates to update drivers, security patches, and utilities

Lab Materials and Setup

The materials you need for this lab are

- A working PC with Windows XP installed

- Windows XP Service Pack 2 CD or the authorization to download Service Pack 2 from the Microsoft Web site

- An Internet connection

Getting Down to Business

You will start with the upgrade to Windows XP Service Pack 2, and then configure the system to perform automatic updates.

Step 1 You will need to procure Windows XP Service Pack 2. Launch the Microsoft Web site and type **"xp service pack 2"** (including the quotation marks) into its site-wide search field. The search should return a page with the title *Windows XP Service Pack 2* or similar; follow the directions on this page to download Service Pack 2. If you prefer to order the update on a CD—this can come in handy if you have a slow Internet connection—you'll pay only a shipping charge for this option.

Step 2 Once you have the CD, download, or network share of SP2, log onto the system that you want to update. Open the folder where you have placed the files and complete the following steps:

a) Double-click XPSP2.EXE to begin the installation. XPSP2 starts by extracting the needed files.

b) The Windows XP Service Pack 2 Setup Wizard welcome screen appears (see Figure 15-2). Click Next to continue.

c) The License Agreement screen displays next. Accept the agreement and click Next to continue.

d) The Setup Wizard now inspects your machine, installs files, and upgrades your system. When the upgrade is complete, the Completing the Windows XP Service Pack 2 Setup Wizard screen appears (see Figure 15-3).

e) Click Finish and let the system reboot.

Figure 15-2 Welcome to the Windows XP Service Pack 2 Setup Wizard

FIGURE 15-3 Completing the Windows XP
Service Pack 2 Setup Wizard

f) After the machine reboots for the first time with Service Pack 2 installed, Windows gives you the opportunity to turn on Automatic Updates before it presents the logon screen. Decline this option for now; you will manually configure this in the next step.

Step 3 You will now configure the system to perform automatic updates. Log onto Windows XP and complete the following steps:

a) Click Start | (All) Programs | Accessories | System Tools | Security Center. This opens the Windows Security Center window, where you'll find the configuration utility for Windows' Automatic Updates feature. Maximize the window and then click Automatic Updates.

✔ Cross-Reference

You will work with the Windows Internet Connection Firewall (ICF) in Chapter 22, "The Internet." You will also work with antivirus software in Chapter 23, "Computer Security."

b) This brings up the Automatic Updates configuration screen (Figure 15-4). Click *Automatic (recommended)* and then click Apply.

FIGURE 15-4 Automatic Updates
configuration screen

   c) The Windows Security Center screen now indicates that Automatic Updates is set to On, and the yellow security shield should disappear from the notification area (system tray).

   d) If your system is connected to the Internet, you can visit the Microsoft Windows Update Web site by clicking Start | Windows Update (in Classic mode) or Start | Programs | Windows Update (in Windows XP standard mode). Here, you can choose to install all critical Windows updates, or select specific updates to install.

 30 MINUTES

Lab Exercise 15.03: Installing Device Drivers in Windows 2000/XP

Installing new devices under Windows 2000 and XP is easier than it has ever been. Assuming, of course, that you're starting with compatible hardware, Windows 2000 and XP will detect the new device and install the correct driver with little prompting. Often, Windows already has a usable driver and will install it without any action on your part. If the device is not compatible with Windows, usually it is just a matter of updating the driver, using driver rollback, or adjusting the setting for driver signing. As these operating systems continue to mature, more new devices will become available. With that said, it's better to use the driver that came with the device, and better still to download the newest driver from the manufacturer's Web site.

You should check for newer drivers periodically, even for devices that have been working fine. Manufacturers occasionally release new drivers aimed at optimizing the device or enabling it to work with some new technology. Keep in mind, however, that a new driver may cause unexpected problems with your operating system. Because of this, Windows XP introduced a feature that enables you to roll back to the previous (working) driver if something should go wrong with a driver update. Microsoft attempts to protect the system by qualifying devices and drivers through the Windows Hardware Quality Labs (WHQL) and digitally signing the drivers as approved for the OS. Driver Signing allows you to configure how the system will handle the installation of untested drivers.

One of two wizards will assist you when you need to load a driver: the Found New Hardware Wizard or the Add New Hardware Wizard. Windows starts the Found New Hardware Wizard when it discovers some new hardware device while booting. If Windows has a driver in its database, it proceeds on its own. If not, the Found New Hardware Wizard will prompt you for one. The Add New Hardware Wizard enables you to add or update hardware manually at any time. There's a lot of overlap in how the two wizards work, so you'll look at just the Add New Hardware Wizard, which you can activate at any time.

Learning Objectives

Loading and removing device drivers is one of the basic skills that any good PC tech should have. The following lab exercise walks you through the process.

At the end of this lab, you'll be able to

- Load a device driver in Windows 2000 and XP

- Roll back to a previously working driver in Windows XP

- Explore Driver Signing

Lab Materials and Setup

The materials you need for this lab are

- A working PC with Windows 2000/XP installed

- An Internet connection

Getting Down to Business

The following labs cover the steps for installing and updating device drivers. You'll also look at the steps to roll back (uninstall) device drivers that turn out to be incompatible, and explore the settings for how Windows handles unsigned drivers.

Step 1 The first step before you begin installing any new device should be to check the Windows Marketplace Tested Products List for the device you're trying to load. The most current information is available on the Microsoft Web site at http:// testedproducts.windowsmarketplace.com/default.aspx. Devices on the list are guaranteed to work with the Windows OS. Always check there before purchasing a device for your Windows 2000 or XP PC.

Step 2 Now let's walk through the process of adding a device using the Add Hardware Wizard:

a) From the Control Panel, double-click Add Hardware.

b) On the Add Hardware Wizard's welcome screen, click Next.

✔ **Hint**

If the wizard doesn't find any new hardware, it asks, "Have you already connected this hardware to your computer?" Select Yes or No, and follow the directions.

---

c) Select the device you want to install or update by either selecting from the given list or choosing the Add a New Hardware Device item in the list box. For this lab, select the last item in the list—*Add a new hardware device*—and then click Next.

d) Click the *Install the hardware that I manually select from a list (Advanced)* option button, and then click Next.

e) Select the type of hardware you're trying to install or update from the list. If your device doesn't fit the descriptions, select the Show All Devices item. When you've made your selection, click Next.

f) If you chose the Show All Devices item, the wizard displays the *Select the device driver you want to install for this hardware* screen. If you chose a specific type of hardware, you'll be led off into a series of options for that type of hardware.

g) Now choose the Windows driver for your device, or click Have Disk and point to the location of the new driver you want to install. This driver will generally be located either on the installation CD that came with the device, if you have it, or on your hard drive if you'd downloaded it from the manufacturer's Web site.

h) Click Next. Windows is ready to install the driver.

i) Click Next again, and click Finish when installation is complete.

You should now have a driver that runs your newly loaded device. If the device isn't working properly and you're sure the driver loaded correctly, you can check online and see if there's a newer driver that you can download from the manufacturer's Web site. If the device just won't work after you've updated the driver, you'll want to perform Step 4—but I'm getting ahead of myself.

Step 3   What if you have a device already installed and you want to update the driver to address a problem, improve performance, or just add a new feature? This step will take you through updating new drivers.

a) Begin by locating the updated driver. In most cases, the best way to obtain the updated driver is to search the Internet for the manufacturer's Web site. Search its site for your specific model, and download the most recent driver.

b) Go to Device Manager and expand the appropriate device category. Locate the device you want to update.

c) Right-click the device and select Properties.

d) Select the Driver tab and click the Update Driver button (see Figure 15-5). This launches a wizard similar to the Add New Hardware Wizard.

✔ **Hint**

In Windows XP, you can right-click the device in question in Device Manager and update the driver without accessing its properties.

For Windows 2000, click Next at the Welcome screen. Select *Display a list of known drivers for this device* and click Next. On the next screen, click Have Disk and browse to the location of the updated driver.

For Windows XP, select *Install from a list or specific location (Advanced)* and click Next. Select *Include this location in the search*, and browse to where you have saved the new driver.

You may be wondering, "What if I load a new driver, and my system doesn't work correctly anymore?" Well, if you're using Windows XP, you're in luck! Read the next step, and your question will be answered.

Step 4   If a driver is corrupt or if the wrong driver is installed, Windows has a bad habit of stopping dead in its tracks, rendering your PC useless. Windows XP has a feature that keeps track of the drivers

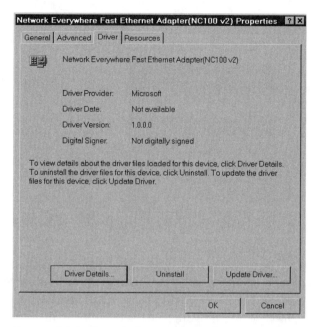

FIGURE 15-5 The Windows 2000 Update Driver button

you install on a system and allows you to roll back to a previous one when a new one isn't working as it should:

a) Go to the Device Manager and locate the device you want to roll back.

b) Right-click the device and select Properties.

c) Select the Driver tab. You can revert to the previous driver by clicking Roll Back Driver (see Figure 15-6).

FIGURE 15-6 Windows XP's Roll Back Driver button

FIGURE 15-7 Hardware tab under System Properties

FIGURE 15-8 The Driver Signing Options dialog box

Step 5 Windows 2000 introduced a feature for Windows known as Driver Signing. Driver signing verifies that a device driver has been tested by the Windows Hardware Quality Labs (WHQL) and will work with the OS as tested. More important, Windows allows you to configure how the OS will handle unsigned drivers! You can direct Windows to ignore, warn, or block new, unsigned drivers. The following steps explore this feature.

a) Open the Control Panel and launch the System applet.

b) Click the Hardware tab (see Figure 15-7).

c) Click the Driver Signing button to bring up a dialog box with the various options (see Figure 15-8).

d) Select Warn and click OK.

At this point, you should be pretty familiar with drivers and how to load and update them. More and more devices are being sold as hot-pluggable, but I doubt that user-installed drivers will be going away in the near future. Loading and maintaining drivers will probably be a part of the PC technician's job for a while yet to come.

 30 MINUTES

Lab Exercise 15.04: Examining and Configuring Log Files in Event Viewer

The Windows Event Viewer, available in Windows 2000 and Windows XP, is a valuable tool to anyone who maintains or troubleshoots these systems. It's mostly run as a stand-alone program, but it can also be added as a snap-in to the MMC you created in Lab Exercise 13.05.

Event Viewer monitors various log files and reveals things about the health of the operating system. This utility reports real-time statistics, but normally this data is only used with servers. Desktop computer users are less proactive and usually depend on the after-the-fact log files to help determine the cause of a problem.

Learning Objectives

You'll become familiar with using Event Viewer to analyze the different logs kept by the system.

At the end of this lab, you'll be able to

- Run the Event Viewer program

- Examine an event log entry

- Save the event log

Lab Materials and Setup

The materials you need for this lab are

- A working PC with Windows 2000/XP installed

Getting Down to Business

You can start Event Viewer from the Control Panel by double-clicking the Administrative Tools applet. If you've added Event Viewer to your MMC, you can also access it there. For practice, you'll do this lab by accessing it the conventional way, but you should confirm that everything works the same through the MMC.

Step 1   Go to the Control Panel and double-click the Administrative Tools icon. Then double-click the Event Viewer icon to start the applet. Event Viewer displays events from three log files: Application, Security, and System. (More log files are available in the server versions of Windows.) Figure 15-9 shows the contents of the system event log in Event Viewer.

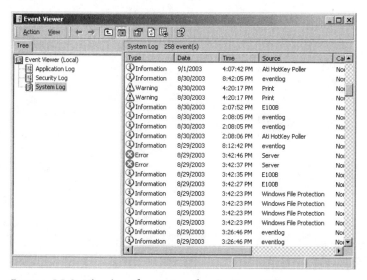

FIGURE 15-9 Viewing the system log in Event Viewer

Notice in Figure 15-9 that there are three kinds of log entries for the system and application logs: Information, Warning, and Error. The security event log shows two types of entries: Success Audit and Failure Audit. These types of events are only logged when auditing is turned on; again, this is normally done only on servers.

Double-clicking any entry gives you details of the event.

Step 2   Follow these steps to change the size of a log file:

a) In Event Viewer's left panel, right-click System and select Properties.

b) Change the number in the Log Size box to **1024** (512 is the default) and select Overwrite Events As Needed (see Figure 15-10).

c) Do this for all three event logs: application, security, and system.

d) Sometimes the log can be completely full before you get a chance to look at the entries. Scrolling through all of events can be a little boring and time consuming, but you can fix that with filter settings. Click the Filter tab, and look at the filter settings (see Figure 15-11).

You can filter events based on type, source, category, ID, user, computer, and date. This only controls what Event Viewer displays; all the events information will still be logged to the file, so you can change your mind about filter settings.

e) Click OK to close the Properties dialog box.

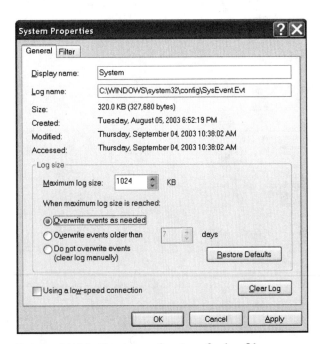

FIGURE 15-10 Changing the size of a log file

FIGURE 15-11 Setting the Event Viewer's settings

Step 3 To clear, archive, and open a log file, follow these steps:

a) Clear the system log by right-clicking System and selecting Clear All Events (see Figure 15-12).

b) When you're prompted to save the system log, click Yes.

c) You can archive log files using different filenames each time (recommended) and select a location other than the default. Give your file a name you can remember and save it.

d) To open a saved file, click the Action menu and select Open Log File. Select the file and log type (System, Application, or Security) and click Open.

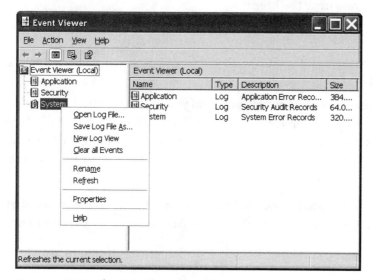

FIGURE 15-12 Clearing the system log

 45 MINUTES

Lab Exercise 15.05: Using the Advanced Options Menu and the Recovery Console

An errant upgrade or a poorly written driver can cause the system to lock up. Some software problems, such as corrupt Registry files, will even prevent the system from booting. This means that you must be ready to use alternative methods to boot the system to make repairs or replace files.

Windows has several ways to boot, and these ways are as different as the operating systems themselves. A Safe Mode boot is available with all the Microsoft operating systems. There's also a nice recovery tool that comes with Windows 2000 and Windows XP known as the Recovery Console.

Learning Objectives

You'll become familiar with alternative methods of booting a faulty system.

At the end of this lab, you'll be able to

- Boot to Windows' Advanced Options Menu and enable Safe Mode

- Install the Recovery Console for Windows XP

- Repair the Registry using Recovery Console

Lab Materials and Setup

The materials you need for this lab are

- A working PC with Windows 2000 or Windows XP installed (preferably a non-production system, as you will be corrupting and repairing the Registry)

- The Windows 2000 or XP installation CD

Getting Down to Business

If your system won't boot normally because of some system problem, you need a way to gain access to the hard drive and your files to troubleshoot the problem. There are, happily enough, troubleshooting tools that give you access to these files if the normal boot process won't work. You'll begin this exercise with the first line of defense, the Advanced Options Menu, and boot to Safe Mode. You will then install and explore the Recovery Console, eventually repairing the Registry manually.

Step 1 Power up a machine with Windows 2000 Professional or Windows XP Professional installed and, when prompted, press the appropriate key or key combination to invoke the Windows Advanced Options

Menu on this system. Depending on your system, you will see a number of different boot options. Record the various modes and provide a small description for each:

_____

_____

_____

_____

✔ Cross-Reference

For definitions of each of the boot modes, refer to the "Advanced Startup Options" section in Chapter 15 of *Mike Meyers' A+ Guide to Managing and Troubleshooting PCs*.

Step 2 Select Safe Mode and press ENTER. The system will proceed to boot into the operating system, but it will inform you many times that it is running in Safe Mode (see Figure 15-13).

Safe Mode is often used when video settings have been changed and render the display unusable. In Safe Mode, a standard VGA driver is installed, and the minimal settings (16 colors, 640 × 480 resolution) are set. This enables you to revert to previous drivers, and/or correct the settings for the current display or monitor you are using. Complete the following steps to explore the display properties:

a) Right-click somewhere in the empty space of the desktop and select Properties from the drop-down menu. This brings up the Display Properties dialog box.

b) Click the Settings tab and note the display, color, and screen resolution settings. Record your settings here: _____

c) Click Cancel to close the Display Properties dialog box.

d) Click Start | Shut down.

Step 3 Next you will explore using the Repair menu item from the Windows Installation CD to launch the Recovery Console. (The following steps were completed using a Windows 2000 Professional installation.)

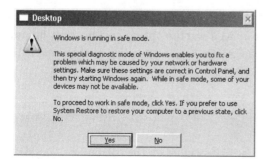

FIGURE 15-13 Windows running in Safe Mode

a) Place the Windows installation CD into the tray, and then reboot the system from the CD. The installation program loads a number of files and then displays a screen with the following information:

```
Welcome to Setup
This portion of the Setup program prepares Microsoft
Windows 2000(™) to run on your computer
        To set up Windows 2000 now, Press ENTER.
        To repair a Windows 2000 installation, press R.
        To quit Setup without installing Windows 2000, press F3.
```

b) Because the operating system is already installed, press R to select the Repair function. The next screen offers two choices:

```
To repair a Windows 2000 installation by using
     the recovery console, press C.
To repair a Windows 2000 installation by using
     the emergency repair process, press R.
```

c) Press C to open the Recovery Console.

You'll now see a command-line interface asking which installation you want to access. If you have a dual-boot system, you'll have to choose an operating system; type its number from the list and press ENTER. Then type the administrator's password. This is the password for the first account created when you initially installed the operating system. You now have a command-line prompt from which to work.

✖ **Warning**

Be sure you know what you're doing here. You have access to files that you can add, change, rename, or delete. The old DOS command set is only partially available.

d) To see a list of commands, type **help** and note the results.

e) Type a command followed by **/?** to get an explanation of that command. You'll explore some of these commands later when you install the Windows XP Recovery Console.

f) Type **exit** to quit the Recovery Console; the system will reboot.

Step 4 Although you can run the Recovery Console by booting directly to it from the Windows 2000 or XP installation CD, it's much more convenient to set it up as a startup option on your boot menu. In this step, you'll install the Windows XP Recovery Console as a boot option. You can do the same thing using the same steps for Windows 2000 (see Figure 15-14).

✔ **Hint**

To install the Recovery Console, you must have administrative rights on the computer.

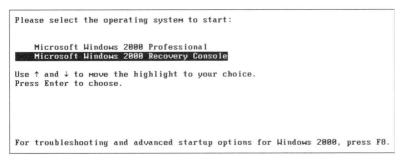

```
Please select the operating system to start:

    Microsoft Windows 2000 Professional
    Microsoft Windows 2000 Recovery Console

Use ↑ and ↓ to move the highlight to your choice.
Press Enter to choose.




For troubleshooting and advanced startup options for Windows 2000, press F8.
```

Figure 15-14 Installing the Windows 2000 Recovery Console

a) Put your Windows XP (or Windows 2000) installation CD into the CD drive; if it autostarts, select Exit. You can also press and hold SHIFT until the CD stops loading.

b) Select Start | Run.

c) In the Open box, type **D:\I386\WINNT32.EXE /CMDCONS** (where D is the drive letter for your CD drive).

d) A Windows Setup dialog box appears, which describes the Recovery Console option. The system prompts you to confirm installation. Click Yes to start the installation procedure.

e) When the installation is complete (Figure 15-15), restart the computer. You will see a Microsoft Windows Recovery Console entry on the boot menu.

✔ Note

When you're installing the Recovery Console, you must use the same version of Windows CD that was used for the system's main OS installation. For example, if you used a Windows XP Service Pack 2 CD to install Windows on this system, you cannot use a pre–Service Pack 2 CD for this procedure.

It's wise to install the Recovery Console on important servers and on critical workstations.

Step 5 Reboot your system, and at the boot menu screen, select the Recovery Console. Watch for the boot menu; you have to be quick! Go directly to the command-line prompt (you'll need the Administrator password).

Figure 15-15 Completing the Recovery Console installation

To see a list of the commands, type **help** at the command prompt. Type a command followed by **/?** to get an explanation of the command use.

Several commands are worth mentioning; for the CompTIA A+ exams, you should know what the following commands do:

- **CHKDSK** Checks the clusters and sectors of a disk (fixed or removable) and, if possible, repairs bad clusters or sectors

- **DISKPART** The Windows 2000 equivalent to FDISK

- **EXIT** Closes the Recovery Console and restarts your computer

- **EXPAND** Extracts copies of single files from the CAB files

- **FIXBOOT** Writes a new partition table

- **FIXMBR** Equivalent to FDISK /MBR

- **HELP** Displays a Help screen

✔ **Hint**

Many techs resort to the Recovery Console when a system fails to boot in the normal fashion (from the hard drive). Three of the commands, FIXBOOT, FIXMBR, and CHKDSK, are particularly important when it seems that the hard disk, the master boot record, or the system partition is missing, corrupt, or damaged. If you come across a system exhibiting these symptoms (and you will), follow good troubleshooting procedures, but remember that you have these tools available to you.

The files that make up the Recovery Console reside on the system partition, making the Recovery Console useless for a system partition crash. In such a situation, you would use the CD drive to access the Recovery Console. The Recovery Console shines in the business of manually restoring Registries, stopping problem services, rebuilding partitions (other than the system partition), or using the EXPAND program to extract copies of corrupted files from a CD or floppy disk.

Step 6 As mentioned in the previous step, the Recovery Console is excellent when you need to restore Registry files. In the following steps, you will crash a system by deleting the SYSTEM folder, and then use the Recovery Console to access the repair folder and recover the system.

✖ **Warning**

As mentioned in the equipment needs, you are going to purposefully delete/corrupt the SYSTEM folder of a working Windows XP Professional system. For this reason, the system you use must be a non-critical, non-production system. Don't risk your family's financial records or your 40-GB photo archive—find another system to use for this exercise!

→ Try This: Create a Batch File to Restore a Corrupted Registry

Though floppy drives are becoming scarce, the use of Recovery Console and some form of accessible, removable media will enable you to semi-automate the restoration of the critical Registry folders. Create the following batch file and save it to a floppy disk.

1. Open a text editor, type the following lines of code exactly, and save your work as a text file (located on a floppy disk) called MyRegBak.txt.

```
MD TMP

COPY C:\%SYSTEMROOT%\SYSTEM32\CONFIG\SYSTEM C:\%SYSTEMROOT%\TMP\SYSTEM.BAK

COPY C:\%SYSTEMROOT%\SYSTEM32\CONFIG\SOFTWARE C:\%SYSTEMROOT%\TMP\SOFTWARE.BAK

COPY C:\%SYSTEMROOT%\SYSTEM32\CONFIG\SAM C:\%SYSTEMROOT%\TMP\SAM.BAK

COPY C:\%SYSTEMROOT%\SYSTEM32\CONFIG\SECURITY C:\%SYSTEMROOT%\TMP\SECURITY.BAK

COPY C:\%SYSTEMROOT%\SYSTEM32\CONFIG\DEFAULT C:\%SYSTEMROOT%\TMP\DEFAULT.BAK


DELETE C:\%SYSTEMROOT%\SYSTEM32\CONFIG\SYSTEM

DELETE C:\%SYSTEMROOT%\SYSTEM32\CONFIG\SOFTWARE

DELETE C:\%SYSTEMROOT%\SYSTEM32\CONFIG\SAM

DELETE C:\%SYSTEMROOT%\SYSTEM32\CONFIG\SECURITY

DELETE C:\%SYSTEMROOT%\SYSTEM32\CONFIG\DEFAULT


COPY C:\%SYSTEMROOT%\REPAIR\SYSTEM C:\%SYSTEMROOT%\SYSTEM32\CONFIG\SYSTEM

COPY C:\%SYSTEMROOT%\REPAIR\SOFTWARE C:\%SYSTEMROOT%\SYSTEM32\CONFIG\SOFTWARE

COPY C:\%SYSTEMROOT%\REPAIR\SAM C:\%SYSTEMROOT%\SYSTEM32\CONFIG\SAM

COPY C:\%SYSTEMROOT%\REPAIR\SECURITY C:\%SYSTEMROOT%\SYSTEM32\CONFIG\SECURITY

COPY C:\%SYSTEMROOT%\REPAIR\DEFAULT C:\%SYSTEMROOT%\SYSTEM32\CONFIG\DEFAULT
```

2. Place the floppy with your text file in the machine that needs restoration. Launch the Recovery Console, locate the text file, and execute the following batch command to restore the Registry to a working state:

```
C:\%SYSTEMROOT%\BATCH A:\MyRegBak.TXT
```

✔ **Cross-Reference**

The following steps use many components of Windows XP Professional and the Recovery Console. To fully understand the files, folders, and Registry components that are involved, be sure to read the "Registry" section in Chapter 15 of *Mike Meyers' A+ Guide to Managing and Troubleshooting PCs*.

Microsoft has also gathered invaluable information in their Knowledge Base articles (a component of TechNet). The following lab steps incorporate valuable information from Knowledge Base articles 307545 and 309531. As previously mentioned, Web sites change over time, so if you don't find these exact articles, use your favorite search engine and locate similar articles related to the Recovery Console and repairing the Registry.

a) Some preparation may be required to complete the steps to corrupt and restore your Registry folders. Open My Computer, then select Tools | Folder Options and click the View tab. Turn on *Show hidden files and folders*, turn off *Hide extensions for known file types*, and turn off *Hide protected operating system files (Recommended)*. Click OK.

b) Boot to the Recovery Console, and after logging on as Administrator, type the following commands at the prompt:

```
MD C:\%SYSTEMROOT%\TMP
COPY C:\%SYSTEMROOT%\SYSTEM32\CONFIG\SYSTEM
C:\%SYSTEMROOT%\TMP\SYSTEM.BAK
DELETE C:\%SYSTEMROOT%\SYSTEM32\CONFIG\SYSTEM
EXIT
```

c) At this point the Recovery Console closes and Windows restarts. Allow Windows XP to boot normally. Did anything inhibit the normal loading and startup of Windows XP?_____

d) Boot to the Recovery Console once again, log on as Administrator, and type the following commands at the prompt:

```
COPY C:\%SYSTEMROOT%\REPAIR\SYSTEM C:\%SYSTEMROOT%\SYSTEM32\CONFIG\SYSTEM
EXIT
```

e) The Recovery Console again closes and Windows reboots. Allow Windows XP to boot normally. Did Windows boot properly this time? _____

 30 MINUTES

Lab Exercise 15.06: Troubleshooting Startup Problems

When it comes to troubleshooting tools, Windows 2000 and Windows XP inherited the best of both the Windows NT and 9x OS families. They have vintage tools such as the Last Known Good Configuration startup option for startup failures and the Task Manager for forcing errant programs to close. Both operating systems have the Recovery Console. Each also has a completely revamped and improved version of Windows Help.

I'll leave the finer details of these tools for you to explore through Windows Help, the main textbook, and other labs. In this lab, you'll explore a simple tool known as the System Configuration utility. The System Configuration utility has been around for some time, having been introduced in Windows 98. It was never incorporated into Windows NT or 2000, but it is included in Windows XP.

Learning Objectives

You'll be reintroduced to some troubleshooting tips using a vintage tool with Windows XP.

At the end of this lab, you'll be able to

- Use the System Configuration utility to perform diagnostic startups

Lab Materials and Setup

The materials you need for this lab are

- A working Windows XP system

Getting Down to Business

Many systems have way too many startup options enabled. This isn't only a source of boot problems; it can also slow down the boot process and hog RAM from programs that need it. When Windows XP experiences failures during startup, consider using the System Configuration utility to discover and fix the problem.

Step 1 Select Start | Run, type **msconfig**, and then press ENTER.

The System Configuration Utility opens (Figure 15-16).

Notice that on the General tab, you can select Diagnostic Startup. This is useful if you have just added new hardware that's causing intermittent problems, because it enables you to boot with only basic devices.

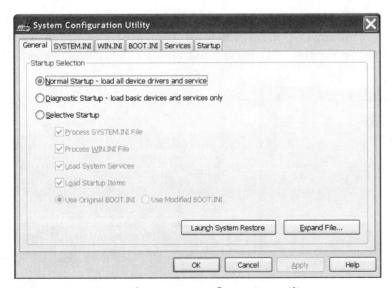

Figure 15-16 Using the System Configuration utility

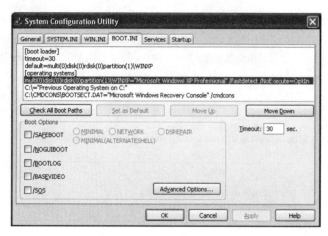

FIGURE 15-17 The BOOT.INI tab

The Selective Startup feature is also nice; it lets you bypass some configuration files to see which one contains the errors that are causing problems.

Notice the SYSTEM.INI and WIN.INI tabs, which provide settings that enable you to change the load sequence of your drivers and edit the entries when you find an error.

Step 2 The BOOT.INI tab is powerful (see Figure 15-17) and goes well beyond the CompTIA A+ exam requirements, but there are a couple of options you should know about.

One important option for troubleshooting is to create a log of what transpired during the boot process. On the BOOT.INI tab, you can enable a BOOTLOG to be created each time the system boots.

If you're troubleshooting a problem and you need to start in the Safe Mode every time, instead of pressing F8, you can enable the /SAFEBOOT option.

Step 3 One item that I find useful is under the Services tab. Microsoft has many services that you can disable during bootup if you believe they're causing problems. The Hide All Microsoft Services option, when enabled, only displays those services you've installed—like my video adapter (NVIDIA) driver in Figure 15-18.

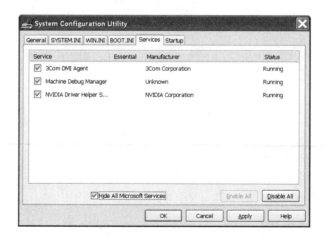

FIGURE 15-18 Using the Services tab with Microsoft Services hidden

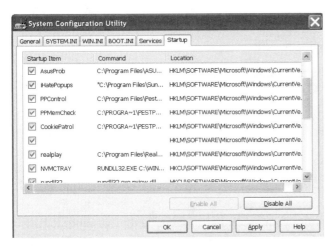

FIGURE 15-19 Checking your startup programs

Step 4 The Startup tab is perhaps the most useful. You can enable or disable any of the Terminate and Stay Resident (TSR) programs that are installed. This is a good place to look if some unexplained program is trying to load every time you boot, even though you thought you'd uninstalled it.

Notice in Figure 15-19 that one program on the list doesn't have a name. I'm kind of suspicious about what this program might be doing! If you find questionable entries in your Startup tab listing, you should fire up a browser and do some research to see whether or not they're harmful.

✔ Hint

You can also run the System Configuration utility in Safe Mode. If you're having problems, you can boot to Safe Mode and then use this utility to identify the source of the problem.

 30 MINUTES

Lab Exercise 15.07: Working with Windows XP System Restore

The prior labs dealt with upgrading Windows XP and optimizing device drivers. In some cases, installing a Service Pack or updating a device driver can cause problems, in which case the best thing you can do is to put the system back to the state it was in before you started. You've already worked with Safe Mode and the Recovery Console when the system will not boot; this lab focuses on restoring the system to a previously working state when you can still access the system.

Learning Objectives

The successful technician knows how to restore a working Windows XP system that has encountered problems beyond those associated with installation and configuration problems.

At the end of this lab, you'll be able to

- Manually create a restore point in Windows XP

- Restore a Windows XP system to a restore point

Lab Materials and Setup

The materials you need for this lab are

- A working PC with Windows XP installed

Getting Down to Business

Windows XP has a great utility to help you restore your system after a botched program or driver installation. It watches for any system changes and basically records them in a diary. To restore a system to a previous state, you can just open the diary and point to a date and time to which you want to return.

Step 1   In this step, you'll manually create a restore point in Windows XP. The OS automatically creates restore points each day, as well as any time you install an application, update a driver, or add a piece of hardware. You also have the option to create your own restore points whenever you want and give them unique names that are meaningful to you. You might decide to create a restore point before tweaking a bunch of settings in the Display applet, for example, and name the restore point "VideoBack" in case your changes should have a dire effect on your video display.

   a)   To create a restore point, select Start | (All) Programs | Accessories | System Tools | System Restore to open the System Restore utility (see Figure 15-20).

   b)   At the welcome screen, choose *Create a restore point* on the right side of the screen and click Next.

   c)   Type **My Test Restore Point** and then click Create.

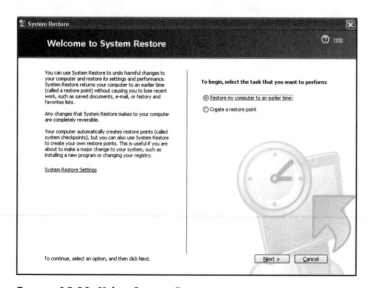

Figure 15-20 Using System Restore

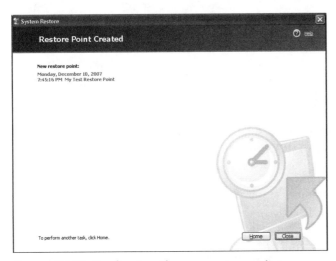

FIGURE 15-21 Confirming the new restore point

d) The system takes some time building the restore file information and then displays a confirmation screen (see Figure 15-21). Click Close to exit the System Restore utility.

You're done! That was easy, wasn't it?

Step 2 To restore the system to an earlier time, return to the System Restore utility, but this time, select *Restore my computer to an earlier time*.

When you click the Next button, the Select a Restore Point screen displays, with a calendar and a listing of the most recent restore points (see Figure 15-22). Based on your knowledge of when your system started having problems, select a restore point and follow the prompts to complete the restore operation.

System Restore is pretty powerful. Even if you crash hard and can only boot to Safe Mode, you can still run the System Restore utility to recover your system. It sure beats the alternative!

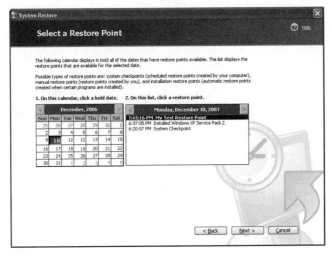

FIGURE 15-22 Choosing a restore point

Lab Analysis Test

1. John complains that his Windows XP system gives him a lot of grief. He tries to tweak the settings and then forgets what he changed, and it takes him days before he can straighten it back out. What tool would you recommend that he use in the future to enable him to retrace his steps and revert his system back to its former settings?

2. You've installed a new network card and sound card. Every time you boot, the system locks up, and you must boot into Safe Mode to get to a GUI. What tool can you use to assist you in locating the source of the problem?

3. Tim is a user who feels he's really a programmer at heart—he always seems to be opening the Registry with REGEDIT and changing settings directly in the Registry. Today, it doesn't go so well, and he ends up with the Blue Screen of Death (BSoD). What can Tim use to get back to a working system?

4. Laurie has been given six computers in various stages of disrepair. Not one of the systems will boot, even though they are Windows 2000 and XP systems. A friend gives her some floppy disks labeled "ERD" and "ASR," and recommends that she boot the machines using these floppies. When she tries it, the machines display the message *Non-System disk or disk error, replace and press any key when ready*. Why?

5. William has been running his Windows XP system for a few days and notices a small yellow shield in the system tray/notification area. He calls you to ask what it might be.

Key Term Quiz

Use the following vocabulary terms to complete the following sentences. Not all terms will be used.

ASR

automatic updates

driver signing

ERD

Event Viewer

MSCONFIG

Recovery Console

Service Packs

System Restore

WHQL

1. To assist in the recovery of a system crash, Windows 2000 uses the _____ process, while Windows XP uses the _____ process. Both processes require a floppy disk to store critical system files.

2. The _____ can be added as a boot menu option.

3. As operating systems age, many of the system files, drivers, and utilities are updated. It is recommended that Windows 2000 and Windows XP always have the latest _____ installed.

4. Microsoft qualifies devices and drivers through its _____, which approves and digitally signs drivers that are proven to work properly with Windows.

5. The _____ provides three log files—System, Security, and Application—to assist with the troubleshooting of a Windows operating system.

Chapter 16

Input/Output

Lab Exercises

One of the most important functions in any type of computing is getting information (data) in and out of the computer system. If it weren't for data moving in and out, your computer would be a boring (and pretty useless) device! You need two items to make input/output work on your PC: a peripheral device and a way to connect that peripheral device to your system unit. The typical desktop PC comes with a number of peripherals: keyboard, mouse, monitor, printer, speakers, and often a cable that runs to a network. These peripherals all come with some form of cabling/connection system.

Many of these connections are unique pairings. For example, a monitor uses either a 15-pin VESA (also called VGA) connector or a DVI connector, whereas a sound card uses S/PDIF or mini-RCA connectors—you won't see any other device commonly using these types of connectors. CompTIA wants you to have a solid understanding of these types of peripherals and their unique connections: printers using parallel connections, networks using twisted-pair cabling, monitors using VGA or DVI, and speakers using mini-RCA or S/PDIF. Entire chapters of this lab manual address these specific peripherals in more detail, but there's much more to the world of input/output than just those devices.

The most common PC input devices are keyboards and mice. Other, more exotic input devices include scanners, touch screens, and biometric readers. More general-purpose connections used by many types of peripherals include serial, USB, and FireWire. This chapter takes a look at those "other" peripherals and connections that don't really fit well into any of the other chapters.

 30 MINUTES

Lab Exercise 16.01: Exploring USB Drivers

USB's incredible ease of use makes it the most popular type of general-purpose connection used on PCs. USB is so popular that every type of peripheral (other than monitors) has someone making a USB version. The downside to this ease of use is that it can be a challenge to deal with USB when it doesn't work as specified.

Learning Objectives

At the end of this lab, you'll be able to

- Diagnose and repair common USB driver failures
- Recognize the limitations of built-in Windows USB device drivers

Lab Materials and Setup

The materials you need for this lab are

- A Windows XP system using USB
- At least one "human interface" USB device, such as a mouse or keyboard
- At least one mass storage USB device, such as a USB thumb drive
- At least one USB device that is neither a human interface device nor a mass storage device (for example, a wired NIC, Bluetooth hub, wireless NIC, or PDA synching cradle)
- A notepad and pencil to document your findings

Getting Down to Business

The biggest problems you'll see with USB are the result of improper drivers. If you know how to recognize these problems from error messages or by using third-party tools, you shouldn't have too much trouble fixing them.

Windows XP comes with very good built-in support for what Windows calls human interface devices (HIDs), such as keyboards and mice. Is also does a good job supporting most USB mass storage devices such as USB thumb drives. However, once you move outside of these two classes of devices, Windows really needs the drivers supplied by the manufacturer to work properly, if at all.

Step 1 Connect any HID or mass storage USB device to the XP system, *without* first installing the supplied driver. Does the device work as expected? Is it missing any features? Does the device even come with drivers? Write down your conclusions and unplug the device.

Step 2   Check the manufacturer's Web site of the USB device you just installed to see if a driver exists. If there is a driver, download it and install it into your system. Now connect the device again. Does the device work the same as it did before?

Step 3   Now select another USB device—specifically, one that is neither a HID nor a mass storage device—and connect it to the same system *without* first installing the supplied driver. Does the device work as expected? Is it missing any features? Does the device even come with drivers? Write down your conclusions and unplug the device.

Step 4   Check the manufacturer's Web site of the USB device you just installed to see if a driver exists. If there is a driver, download it and install it into your system. Did the installation work? In many cases installation will fail because Windows may have loaded an improper driver from when you first installed the device. Does the device work the same as before? You'll probably find that it doesn't, for the same reason.

Step 5   Go to the manufacturer's Web site and see how to remove the device driver properly. Delete the driver and then remove the device.

✔ Hint

Installing a USB device without first installing the proper driver on a non-HID or mass storage device will almost always require you to uninstall the USB device completely from Device Manager. Even so, you should still check the manufacturer's Web site first!

Step 6   With the previous drivers properly removed, again install the drivers you downloaded earlier. Then insert the USB device. Does the device work as expected? Are there features now that did not appear earlier? What does this tell you about the importance of installing USB device drivers before you install the actual USB device?

Step 7   As time and available hardware allow, practice installing other USB devices and document how they work, both with and without proper drivers.

 30 MINUTES

Lab Exercise 16.02: UVCView

Learning Objectives

At the end of this lab, you'll be able to

- Recognize a system's USB capabilities using Microsoft's UVCView utility

Lab Materials and Setup

The materials you need for this lab are

- A Windows XP system using USB

- A copy of Microsoft's UVCView utility (do a Web search on "UVCView" to locate a copy)

- At least one USB hub

- A notepad and pencil to document your findings

This lab is very flexible in terms of the types of USB (low speed, full speed, Hi-Speed) supported on the system, as well as the number and type of USB devices. Add as many USB devices as possible (you can have up to 127 devices per USB controller, so knock yourself out!), and try to get at least one USB hub, either powered or unpowered. The more USB devices and hubs you can get, the more interesting this lab becomes.

Getting Down to Business

Using the UVCView program, you can view detailed information about your USB controllers and the devices currently running on them.

Step 1 Start the PC with as few USB devices physically installed as possible.

Step 2 Make sure a copy of UVCView is on the system. UVCView is a freestanding executable file and does not require installation. Place the file on your Windows desktop for easy access.

Step 3 Open Device Manager and count all of the USB controllers (see Figure 16-1). On most systems you should see two controllers: a Standard Open HCD Host Controller and a Standard Enhanced Host Controller. Do you see those two? To determine what each of these controllers does, you can use a USB thumb drive and (possibly) any message Windows places on the system tray/notification area.

Step 4 Start UVCView and compare what you see in Device Manager to UVCView. How do they compare? Do you see any differences? Count the ports reported by UVCView and compare that to the actual number of ports on your system. Are the numbers the same?

FIGURE 16-1 USB controllers in
Device Manager

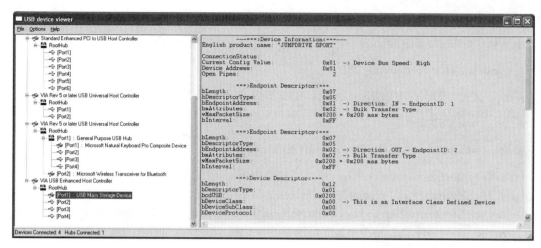

FIGURE 16-2 UVCView details

✔ **Hint**

Sometimes running UVCView and Device Manager at the same time will confuse Device Manager. If you're having problems, just close and reopen UVCView as needed.

Step 5 Insert a USB device, making sure to install the correct drivers first. UVCView should update as soon as the device is inserted. Document which USB host controller and port are running the device. Unplug the device and reinsert it into a different USB port. Document the changes. Is it on a different controller? Is it on a different port?

Step 6 Click on the device in UVCView to see its details (see Figure 16-2). What speed is the device (Low, Full, High)? Who is the manufacturer? What is the most power the device will use (Maxpower)?

Step 7 Repeat steps 5 and 6 for other USB devices until all of your system's USB ports are in use.

Step 8 Replace one of the devices with a USB hub, and see how it appears in UVCView. Check the speed of the hub. If the hub speed does not show as High, try inserting a Hi-Speed USB device (such as a thumb drive) and see what happens!

 30 MINUTES

Lab Exercise 16.03: Paging Dr. Keyboard!

Keyboards are plentiful and common, and a new basic keyboard is very inexpensive. Even with cheap keyboards, users tend to get attached to these devices over time—and in the case of an expensive keyboard with lots of extra buttons and features, the user may have both a financial *and* an emotional attachment! For these reasons, it's important that you learn to play "Dr. Keyboard," fixing these devices when they break.

Learning Objectives

At the end of this lab, you'll be able to

- Repair stuck keyboard keys
- Dismantle and clean a keyboard

Lab Materials and Setup

The materials you need for this lab are

- Windows XP system
- As many "throw-away" keyboards as possible (functional keyboards that you won't mind throwing away at the end of this lab; connection type is unimportant as long as they're usable by a Windows system)
- Medium-sized flathead (slotted) screwdriver
- Compressed air
- Lint-free cloth

✔ **Hint**

Try to avoid using older (pre-2004) laptop keyboards, as many older laptop keyboards used a delicate type of scissors key connector that would shatter if pried off.

Getting Down to Business

In this exercise, you'll dismantle one or more keyboards, cleaning up the keyboard components in the process before reassembling the device(s) and testing for functionality.

Step 1 Try prying off two or three keys using the flathead screwdriver (see Figure 16-3). Include more difficult keys such as the spacebar, ENTER/RETURN, and a key from the center of the keyboard such as the letter G. Inspect the bottom of the key and the key post that it sits on—how much dirt is there? Reinsert the keys, making sure they are snapped all the way down.

Step 2 Test the keyboard by installing it into a Windows system. If any of the keys you removed aren't working, double-check that they're properly snapped in. Shut down the system and remove the keyboard. Repeat this process until all keys are working.

Figure 16-3 Removing the CTRL key with a screwdriver

✔ **Hint**

What should you do if you break a key? Well, nobody sells replacement parts for keyboards—they're just too darn cheap to bother! You might be lucky enough to have a non-working keyboard that's the exact same model, which you can cannibalize; otherwise, just consign the affected keyboard to the scrap heap after you've used it for this lab.

Step 3 Insert the nozzle of the compressed air under a key and start blasting away. If the keyboard is really old or looks dirty, you may want to do this outside! Did you see any dust or crumbs come out?

Step 4 Completely dismantle the keyboard. Most keyboards have a number of screws underneath that you must first remove to begin this process. Inspect the screws—are they different sizes? Keep track of which screw goes into which hole.

Step 5 The inside of the keyboard will have a number of plastic contact templates (see Figure 16-4). Remove these, keeping track of their relation to each other so you can reassemble them. Wipe down each template with the cloth dampened with water. If you run into serious dirt, add a bit of mild detergent and repeat until the keyboard is clean.

✔ **Hint**

All keyboards have small circuit boards inside as well. Don't get them wet!

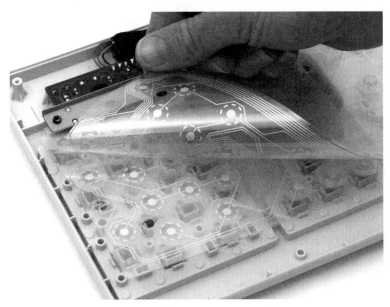

Figure 16-4 Inside a keyboard

Step 6 After allowing everything to dry, reassemble the keyboard and test it on a Windows system. If the keyboard is not working properly, dismantle it and try again.

Lab Analysis Test

1. Why is it very important that you always install a USB device's driver before you physically install the USB device?

2. John encounters a system with a Bluetooth USB device installed, and the user is complaining that many of the features that should be included with this device don't seem to exist. What does he need to do to fix this problem?

3. Beth's brand-new USB keyboard has a piece of the packaging stuck under the keyboard in such a way that she simply can't pull it out, even with a pair of needle-nose pliers. What should she do to go about fixing this problem?

4. UVCView is an interesting tool for observing how USB works. How might this tool come in handy for diagnosing USB problems?

5. Ken has just purchased a fast new 4-GB USB flash drive, complete with the latest U3 "smart drive" technology. He plugs it into his older IBM laptop using the USB 1.0 ports on the system. What should he expect to happen?

Key Term Quiz

Use the following vocabulary terms to complete the following sentences. Not all terms will be used.

driver

full speed

Hi-Speed

human interface device

low speed

Standard Enhanced Host Controller

Standard Open HCD Host Controller

USB controller

USB hub

USB mass storage

UVCView

1. A USB keyboard or mouse would fall into the _____ category.

2. Every USB device connects to a _____.

3. Most USB devices need a special _____.

4. The three USB speeds from slowest to fastest are _____, _____, and _____.

5. Windows calls the controller for Hi-Speed USB devices a _____.

Chapter 17

Video

Lab Exercises

Few components affect the PC user like the video system, the primary output for the PC. As you know from the textbook, the video system has two main hardware components—monitor and display adapter—that work together to produce the image on your screen. Both components must be installed and configured properly in Windows, or your viewing pleasure will be seriously compromised. Good techs know how to do video right!

In this set of labs, you'll install a display adapter, hook up a monitor, load video drivers, and configure Windows for optimal viewing. You'll then work with the growing practice of using multiple monitors (sometimes a projector and a laptop screen) to expand your desktop viewing area. The last lab exercise will run you though some of the typical troubleshooting issues that techs face when dealing with video.

✖ **Warning**

It is critical to understand that only *trained* monitor technicians should remove the cover of a video monitor (or a television set, for that matter). The inside of a traditional monitor might look similar to the interior of a PC, with printed circuit boards and related components, but there's a big difference: No PC has voltages up to 50,000 volts or more inside, but most CRT monitors *do*. So be sure to get one thing clear—casually opening a monitor and snooping around has the potential to become harmful to you and the monitor—and in cases of extreme carelessness, it can even be deadly! Even when the power is disconnected, certain components (capacitors) still retain substantial levels of voltage for an extended period of time. Capacitors work like batteries. Yes, they can maintain 50,000 volts! If you inadvertently short one of the capacitors, a large discharge will occur into the monitor circuits, destroying them. If you're touching the metal frame, you could fry yourself—to death. Given this risk, certain aspects of monitor repair fall outside the necessary skill set for a standard PC support person, and definitely outside the CompTIA A+ test domains. Make sure you understand the problems you can fix safely and the ones you need to hand over to a qualified electronics repair shop.

 30 MINUTES

Lab Exercise 17.01: Installing Video

Your office staff's computers need a serious video upgrade. Some of the PCs have tiny 14-inch CRT monitors that simply have to go, while others have decent 17-inch and 19-inch CRTs that have a year or two of life left in them. Your boss has bought new AGP and PCI video cards and some LCD monitors to replace the older CRTs. You're tasked with installing the cards, loading drivers, and setting everything up in Windows.

> ✔ **Cross-Reference**
>
> For the details of CRT versus LCD monitors, refer to the "CRT Monitors" and "LCD Monitors" sections in Chapter 17 of *Mike Meyers' A+ Guide to Managing and Troubleshooting PCs*.

Learning Objectives

At the end of this lab, you'll be able to

- Identify the make and model of a video card

- Install a video display adapter card

- Check BIOS for proper video settings

- Adjust the monitor for the proper display

- Optimize the video settings in Windows

Lab Materials and Setup

The materials you need for this lab are

- A working PC with Windows 2000 or Windows XP installed

- A working monitor (access to both a CRT and an LCD monitor is recommended)

- A working computer system with access to the Internet

> ✔ **Hint**
>
> Classrooms that have a variety of different monitor types and video display adapter cards are a plus.

Getting Down to Business

To begin this lab, you'll become familiar with the video components in your system. You'll then step through the proper installation and configuration of a video adapter.

✖ Warning

Some versions of Microsoft Windows operating systems have problems when you make changes to the video display adapters, even when you're simply removing and reinstalling the same card into a different slot. If you perform this lab on a test machine, you should have no real problem if things go wrong. If you're using your primary PC to do the lab, however, make certain you have current drivers available for your video card, or a source to get drivers if necessary.

Step 1 Shut down your system properly and unplug the power cable from the system unit and the wall. Remove the cover from the PC to expose the expansion buses.

a) Find your video display adapter card (the one to which the monitor is attached). What type of video display adapter is installed: PCI, AGP, or PCIe? _____

✔ Hint

Many laptop computers and some low- to mid-level desktop systems include display adapters integrated right into the electronics of the motherboard. On desktop systems with this configuration, the 15-pin connector will appear in line with the PS/2 and USB ports. If your system uses this type of display adapter, the overall performance of the system may suffer because the display typically "steals" 32 to 64 MB of system RAM to serve as video RAM. Not only is this a small amount of video RAM for today's PC applications, it also lowers the total amount of system RAM available for the system. Laptops are usually designed around this limitation, but if your desktop system is of this type, you can increase the performance (and usually the video quality) by installing a display adapter card and disabling the onboard video in the BIOS. Typically, you can also balance between video and system performance by selecting how much memory is allocated to the onboard video in BIOS.

b) Detach the monitor's cable from the video card.

Using good ESD avoidance procedures, remove the screw that holds the card in place, put it a secure location, and then remove your video display adapter card (see Figure 17-1). Examine it closely to answer the following questions. Be careful not to touch the expansion slot contacts on the card!

c) Look for a name or model number on the adapter's circuit board or chipset.

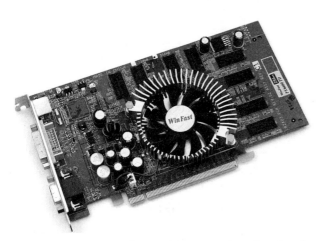

Figure 17-1 This video card has a cooling fan for the Graphics
Processing Unit (GPU) and four onboard RAM chips.

Who is the manufacturer, or what is the model number? Write it down. (Note that for this lab's scenario, you'd actually be looking up the information for the new video cards, not the ones already installed—*those* will most likely be donated to charity!) _____

Be sure to write down as much information as you can collect from the display adapter for a later assignment.

d) Reinsert the video card into the same slot, and make sure it is properly seated. Reattach the monitor cable and test your system with the case still open to see if it works. This could save you the frustration that results when you close the case, fire up the system, and get a video error. (Not that I've ever done that!)

✔ Hint

AGP and PCIe cards can be a little tricky. They must be seated perfectly or they will not work. Many of these types of cards use slots with locking levers—if you were observant when you removed the card initially, you'll know what you have to do now for proper physical installation.

e) Boot your system and open your favorite browser to search the Web.

Conduct your search using the information you've gathered about the manufacturer and model number of your card.

Can you find the specifications for your display adapter? _____

What is the highest resolution you can achieve with your video adapter according to these specifications? _____

How much memory is available? _____

What type of memory is used? _____

Does the adapter support SLI or CrossFire? _____

Does the adapter have any features that are unusual or unfamiliar to you? _____

Step 2 Reboot your system and press the proper key sequence to enter the CMOS setup utility. Depending on the BIOS manufacturer and version, there can be as many as five or more video-related settings. My lab system has ten settings directly related to video or the AGP slot. Complete each of these questions based on your specific BIOS. Some of the names of the sections will undoubtedly differ from the ones presented here. Search around a bit and you'll find video options in your CMOS.

On the Standard CMOS Setup or similar screen, how many choices are there for video, and how is your video set? _____

On the Chipset Features Setup or similar screen, what is the value for your Video RAM Cacheable setting? _____ Are there any AGP-specific settings? _____ Are there any settings for the amount of RAM the onboard adapter will use? _____

On the Power Management Setup or similar screen, do you have settings to control how the monitor and video adapter will react when not in use for a period of time? What are your settings? _____

On the Integrated Peripherals or similar screen, do you have an Init Display First setting? What are the choices? _____ What does your setting say? _____ Know that when this setting is wrong, the monitor display might not work.

Step 3 You'll now examine a monitor and see what external controls it has. If you're not in a computer lab, you can go to your local computer store and examine a wide variety of monitors.

Figures 17-2 and 17-3 show the control buttons for adjusting the display attributes for an LCD and a CRT monitor, respectively. Both of these have the controls on the front of the monitor, but some have

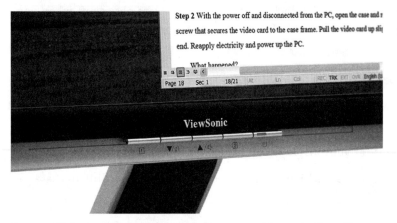

Figure 17-2 An LCD monitor with front-panel buttons for adjustments

FIGURE 17-3 Front controls on a CRT monitor

the controls behind a door under the front of the monitor screen, and others may have them on the back.

A monitor can have quite a few adjustable features. How many of the following can you adjust on your LCD monitor?

Brightness   _____

Contrast   _____

Clock   _____

H-position   _____

V-position   _____

Color temperature   _____

Auto balance   _____

Sharpness   _____

Gamma   _____

Signal select (for LCDs with both VGA and DVI inputs)   _____

Full screen   _____

Language   _____

How many of these can you adjust on your CRT monitor?

Brightness   _____

Contrast   _____

Color saturation   _____

Vertical size   _____

Vertical position   _____

Horizontal size   _____

Horizontal position   _____

Pincushioning (for adjusting displays that are narrow
in the middle but flare out at the top and bottom)   _____

Keystoning (for adjusting displays that are narrow at
the top but flare out at the bottom)   _____

Degauss (for adjusting displays that have become fuzzy
due to electromagnetic interference)   _____

Play with the controls of your monitor or a test monitor. If the current settings use percentages, write down the settings before doing any adjustments. Then follow these steps:

a) Change the settings such as color and sizing. Don't be shy!

b) Put the settings back as close as possible to their original positions.

c) Optimize the screen for clarity and position.

Step 4   The hardware is set up properly and the BIOS settings should be correct, so now you need to configure and optimize the Windows settings that determine your video display characteristics. To do this, you need to use the Display applet.

✔ **Hint**

This lab simulates a working PC that you upgrade with new hardware and drivers. All the steps can work just as well for installing a video card into a new system, although the pace of that installation would differ. In a new system, you would physically install the video card, let Windows use generic VGA drivers until you make sure you can boot properly, and only then install the drivers for the video card. Finally, you'd go to the Display applet and optimize the video card settings. Windows XP is fairly good at finding a suitable driver the first time around, but you should still understand how to locate and update drivers for your video card.

Choose your favorite way to navigate to the Display applet, then click the Settings tab. This tab displays the monitor settings, such as those shown in Figure 17-4.

FIGURE 17-4 The Display Properties
dialog box's Settings tab

✖ Warning

You're going to make changes to the look and feel of Windows. Making some of these changes can result in frustrating and time-consuming problems. Use a test machine if you have one available. If you must use your own machine, write down all your display settings before you make any changes.

Each video display adapter manufacturer has different options for its cards. By clicking the Advanced button, you can access more information about the display adapter. You may see a choice for setting the refresh rate, as well as other features. Look through the settings on the Advanced tab, and see what your display adapter manufacturer provides. Remember that the video adapter "pushes" the monitor. If you set the refresh too high, it can cause problems, and in the case of older CRTs may even damage your monitor.

Write down your display's current resolution, color depth, and refresh rate.

Close the Advanced dialog box (if you selected it), but leave the Display Properties dialog box open.

Make some changes to the background and colors on your screen. You'll find these options on the Background and Appearance tabs, respectively. Be sure to note the original settings so you can change things back when you're done.

✔ Hint

The setting changes suggested in this step are perfectly safe and easy to undo.

Change the desktop background to something you might like better, such as Autumn or Bliss. Then try the following:

- Experiment with color combinations.

- Make some changes to the displayed fonts and menu bars.

- Add a screen saver, or change the one you currently have. You'll find these options on the Screen Saver tab. Play with the settings.

- Experiment with changing the colors and resolution of your display.

Can your machine run in 16-bit color? _____

How about 24-bit color? _____

Can you run 800 × 600 resolution? _____

Can you run 1024 × 768 resolution? _____

Can you run 1280 × 960 resolution? _____

Do you have any other options? _____

Click the Advanced button again, and experiment with changing the refresh rate (see Figure 17-5).

✔ **Hint**

Because of the way that LCD monitors work, the refresh rate setting doesn't really apply to them. As a general rule, LCD monitors display a stable, flicker-free image at 60 hertz (Hz). There are no visible differences between 85 Hz and 60 Hz.

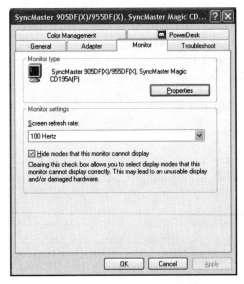

Figure 17-5 A typical refresh setting under Display Properties

Can you make specific numeric changes? _____

Are the Optimal and Adapter Default settings the only choices you have? _____

Make sure you return all the settings to their original values, and then close the Display Properties dialog box.

Check the drivers for your video card and monitor. Are they "standard" drivers, or are they specific to your hardware? Follow these steps:

a) Go to the Device Manager, locate your display adapter, right-click, and select Properties.

b) Locate your driver information.

c) Can you identify the version number(s) of your video drivers? Write them down.

d) Go online and find the manufacturer's Web site.

e) Check to see if newer drivers are available. If so, download and install them. (Do this on a test machine first. Get comfortable with the whole process before you do this on your personal computer.)

How did this affect your machine?

Step 5 One more place to look for video settings is the Power Management Control Panel applet. Take a look at any power management settings you may have.

Go to the Control Panel and double-click the Power Management or Power Options applet, if you have one.

Click the arrow next to the drop-down list to see what power management schemes are available.

Which one do you have running? _____

How long is the period of inactivity before your monitor shuts off? _____

Close the applet and the Control Panel.

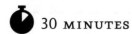 30 MINUTES

Lab Exercise 17.02: Configuring Multiple Displays

Your consulting firm has just been awarded a contract to perform complete upgrades on the 12 digital audio workstations at a local recording studio. Among the various considerations for this type of application—large data storage, backups, fast processors, and loads of memory—the application also requires high-performance display adapters with multiple monitors for each station. It is not unusual for a recording engineer to have three or four critical windows open simultaneously during a session, so the studio design has included three widescreen monitors for each station.

You jump on the project and immediately stage one of the systems in the shop to run it through its paces. You decide to use one of the new ASUS motherboards with three PCIe slots and three high-performance NVIDIA display adapters. You finish the video configuration and attach three 30-inch widescreen monitors—this system looks impressive!

✔ **Cross-Reference**

For additional information on configuring your multiple displays, refer to the "Installing and Configuring Video" section in Chapter 17 of *Mike Meyers' A+ Guide to Managing and Troubleshooting PCs*.

Learning Objectives

At the end of this lab, you'll be able to

- Install an additional video display adapter card

- Configure a system to use multiple displays

- Expand the desktop across two or more displays

Lab Materials and Setup

The materials you need for this lab are

- A working PC with Windows 2000 or Windows XP installed

- At least one additional display adapter

- At least one additional working monitor (CRT or LCD)

✔ **Hint**

This lab exercise does not require any of the high-end equipment discussed in the scenario. You should be able to complete the steps to configure multiple monitors using a few PCI video cards and the monitors in your classroom lab. You can even use the integrated display adapter on many motherboards and install one additional video card to complete the lab steps. If time permits, hop on a system with Internet access and explore some of the components discussed in the scenario. Manufacturers such as ASUS, NVIDIA, and NEC are always adding new technology to their product lines.

Getting Down to Business

To explore the system configuration presented in the opening scenario, you will install at least one additional display adapter and monitor on a working system. You will then use the Display applet in Windows to configure the multiple monitors for use as an expanded desktop.

Step 1   Shut down your system properly and unplug the power cable from the system unit and the wall. Remove the cover from the PC to expose the expansion bus slots.

a) Verify the type (PCI, AGP, or PCIe) and location of the current video display adapter. Using proper ESD avoidance procedures and one of the available expansion slots (depending on the additional video card available to you), install a second video display adapter in your system. Remember that AGP and PCIe cards can be a little finicky during installation, so make sure they are in securely.

✔ **Hint**

If you currently have an AGP adapter installed, your second adapter will need to be PCI, as that's the only type of slot you're likely to have that can handle a video adapter. If you're in a classroom environment, your instructor should be able to provide you with an additional video card and monitor to facilitate this lab. In some cases you can use an integrated display adapter as your primary display, installing the new display as the secondary. Follow your instructor's directions in addition to the directions included in this exercise.

b) Attach the second monitor cable to the new display adapter, and test your system with the case still open to see if it works.

To verify that the second display adapter and monitor have been installed correctly, are recognized by the system, and have drivers available, open Device Manager and expand the display adapter's icon. View the properties of the newly installed card and select the Drivers tab. Does everything appear to be in order?

c) If the new display adapter is not working properly, you may need to install specific drivers or updated drivers. Access the Internet to download and install the appropriate drivers for your display adapter.

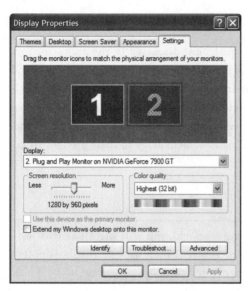

FIGURE 17-6 The Display Properties dialog box's
Settings tab, showing two monitors available

Step 2 Now that the hardware is set up and functioning properly, you will configure the Windows settings to expand your desktop across two or more displays. To do this, you will again open the Display applet.

Navigate to the Display Properties dialog box's Settings tab. This tab shows the monitor settings and should now display two monitor icons, as shown in Figure 17-6.

Now complete the following steps to expand your desktop across the displays you have installed.

a) Click on the drop-down arrow next to the Display field. Are both of your display adapters available? _____

FIGURE 17-7 Extending the Windows desktop

FIGURE 17-8 Dual monitors displaying multiple open windows

b) Now click on the second monitor icon, check the *Extend my Windows desktop onto this monitor* box, and click the Apply button. Your monitor icons should now look something like Figure 17-7, and the display on your monitors should change accordingly.

c) Now click and drag the Display Properties dialog box from one monitor to the other. Notice that the standard setup has the second display as the display to the right, so the expansion should allow you to use the second monitor as the rightmost portion of the desktop. Open a few windows and place them in different locations on the two monitors (see Figure 17-8).

d) Experiment with the "virtual" placement of the monitors by clicking one of the numbered monitors and dragging it around the other monitor(s). Also click and highlight one of the numbered monitors and select it as the primary display.

Can you place the monitors on top of each other (see Figure 17-9)? _____

Can you set the second display as the primary monitor? _____

Right-click one of the displays in the Display Properties window and select Identify. What are the results? _____

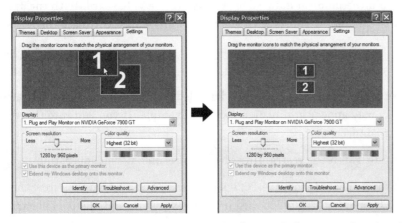

FIGURE 17-9 Configuring monitors to be "virtually" on top of each other

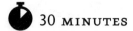 30 MINUTES

Lab Exercise 17.03: Troubleshooting Video

Video troubleshooting really boils down to two distinct questions. First, are the physical video components installed and configured properly, as discussed in Lab Exercise 17.01? Second, do the current video
display adapter and CPU support the software technologies you're trying to use? (Or have you loaded
that killer game and completely overwhelmed your video subsystem?) In this lab exercise, you'll create
connectivity problems to simulate real-world installation problems, and use the DirectX Diagnostic tool
to analyze your system.

Learning Objectives

At the end of this lab, you'll be able to

- Recognize and fix typical video installation and connectivity problems

- Use the Microsoft DirectX Diagnostic tool to analyze and test the graphic display attributes of
  a PC system

Lab Materials and Setup

The materials you need for this lab are

- A working PC with Windows 2000 or Windows XP installed

- Any version of the Microsoft DirectX Diagnostic tool installed

Getting Down to Business

If you went through Lab Exercise 17.01 and had typical results—video card not seated properly, forget-
ting to plug things in all the way, and so on—you can probably skip steps 1 and 2 of this lab. If you had
a perfect reinstall, on the other hand, then definitely do all of the steps!

Step 1   Loosen the screws that hold the monitor data cable securely to the video card. With the system
fully powered up and in Windows—and being gentle with your hardware—partially disconnect the
monitor cable.

What happened to the screen? _____

With many monitors, a loose cable results in a seriously degraded display. Colors fade out or a single color disappears, or the display may appear grainy or snowy, for example. If you run into these
symptoms in the field, check your connectivity!

Connect the monitor cable and tighten the restraining screws to resume normal operation.

Step 2   With the power off and disconnected from the PC, open the case and remove the screw that
secures the video card to the case frame. Pull the video card up slightly on one end. Reapply electricity
and power up the PC.

What happened? _____

You might have to run through this a couple of times to get the desired effect, which is a seemingly dead PC and some beeping from the system speaker. That long-short-short beep code is pretty universally recognizable as the PC's cry for help: "Hey! My video card isn't seated properly!"

With the power off and disconnected, reseat your video card, reinstall the restraining screw, and power up your PC to resume normal operation.

Step 3 Access the Microsoft DirectX Diagnostic tool using these steps:

a) Select Start | All Programs | Accessories | System Tools | System Information.

b) Select Tools | DirectX Diagnostic tool (see Figure 17-10).

✔ **Hint**

Many technicians prefer to use the command line because it can save a lot of time. If you're one of them, try this: Select Start | Run, then type **dxdiag** and click OK.

Step 4 Select the Display tab (see Figure 17-11).

What is the name of your display adapter? _____

How much total memory is on the adapter? _____

What is the current display mode? _____

What is the drive name and version? _____

Does it display a driver version date? _____

Should you look for a more current driver? _____

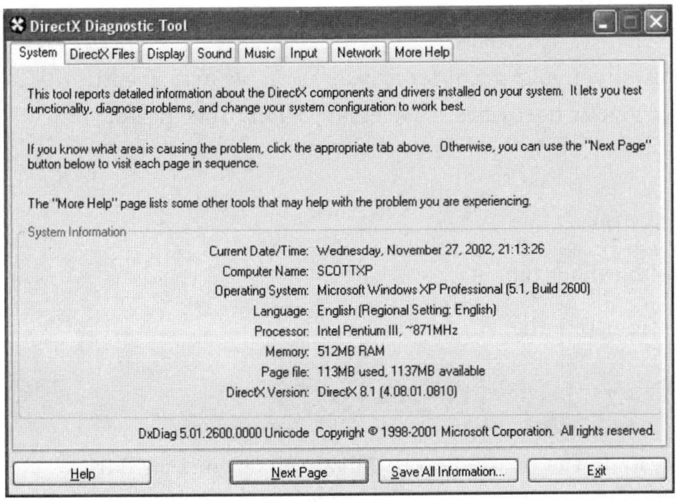

FIGURE 17-10 Using the DirectX Diagnostic tool

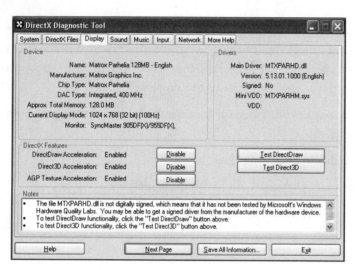

FIGURE 17-11 Viewing the DirectX Diagnostic tool's Display tab

Step 5   Check out the Notes box at the bottom of the Display tab, and read the information provided. This is where you can find out about any conflicts or problem areas.

Do you show any conflicting information? If so, what's the problem? _____

_____

Step 6   Select and test the DirectDraw feature, and follow the instructions.

Did the test complete correctly? _____

Step 7   Select and test the Direct3D feature, and follow the instructions.

Did the test complete correctly? _____

Step 8   Some programs run very slowly or not at all unless Microsoft DirectDraw or Direct3D hardware acceleration is available. On the Display tab, look in the DirectX Features section to see whether Direct-Draw, Direct3D, or AGP texture acceleration is set to Not Available.

You may need to enable these items or adjust your graphics acceleration, as described in the following steps. You might also consider upgrading your hardware if necessary to improve performance.

   a) Go to the Control Panel.

   b) Open Display, and select the Settings tab.

   c) Click Advanced, and select the Troubleshoot tab.

   d) Move the Hardware Acceleration slider to Full.

✔ **Hint**

If you're looking at a Windows 2000 system, the tab under the Advanced options for hardware acceleration is called Performance or Troubleshooting.

Lab Analysis Test

1. If you remove an AGP video display adapter and replace it with a PCI video display adapter, what must you do to be sure the Windows Desktop will display properly?

2. Your nephew Brian visited and used your computer last night, and this morning your monitor is dead. What should you do first, second, and third?

3. What can happen if the refresh rate for a CRT is set too high?

4. Teresa installed a new game, but she is frustrated because it responds too slowly. What might she check?

5. Taylor installed a new video display adapter, but the best setting he can adjust it to is 800 × 600 resolution with 256 colors. What must he do to make it go higher?

Key Term Quiz

Use the following vocabulary terms to complete the following sentences. Not all terms will be used.

color depth

Direct3D

DirectX Diagnostic

Display applet

hardware acceleration

Init display first

refresh rate

resolution

1. Once software is installed, test your video using Microsoft's _____ tool.

2. Erin's monitor was set to 640 × 480, a very low _____.

3. John complained constantly about getting headaches every day. When you looked at his PC, you noted that the screen flickered. John's monitor had the _____ set too low!

4. The _____ is the one-stop shop in Windows for changing your video settings.

5. _____ can offer excellent visuals in games and not bog down the system.

Chapter 18

Sound

Lab Exercises

You have been hired on as an entry-level tech for a public school district. Your first day on the job, the technology manager asks how familiar you are with recording, storing, and playback of audio files on computer systems. It turns out that the sociology department wants the students to be able to record audio documentaries on current events, store the files on the network, and produce podcasts of the documentaries. Demonstrating your enthusiasm, you respond that you are somewhat familiar with sound and will tackle the project. You are tasked with researching the sound card, building the prototype system, and providing some basic audio recording and storage training to the sociology instructors.

As a competent PC tech, you need to understand not just the tasks of installing the physical sound card and associated drivers, but also the applications that take advantage of the PC's sound capabilities. As such, the CompTIA A+ Certification exams expect you to know about sound cards and their workings. The following lab exercises will introduce you to sound card hardware and drivers, as well as the basic use of some of the popular Windows audio applications.

 30 MINUTES

Lab Exercise 18.01: Installing Sound

The first task on the agenda is to do a little research on sound cards and choose a few that meet the needs of this project. There are a number of different sound chips, and the "card" can be anything from the onboard sound capability of a mid-priced system to professional multichannel (input/output) devices used in recording studios. After you assemble a few candidates, you will select a sound card and then install, configure, and test that card. For the purpose of completing this lab, it is perfectly acceptable to use any working card, or an onboard sound device if that's what you have available.

Learning Objectives

This lab teaches you the basics of installing and configuring a sound card.

At the end of this lab, you'll be able to

- Identify features of sound cards

- Remove and install a sound card and associated devices (speakers and microphone)

- Configure a sound card

Lab Materials and Setup

The materials you need for this lab are

- A working computer system running Windows 2000 or Windows XP

- A removable sound card, microphone, and speakers properly installed and functioning (the sound drivers must either be part of the operating system in use or be available on CD or diskette)

✖ Warning

Different versions of Windows handle the drivers differently, to say the least. You should have a current driver disc or diskette for your sound card handy, just in case Windows decides it cannot remember your sound card when you go to reinstall!

Getting Down to Business

This lab will step you through removing, researching specifications for, installing, and configuring a sound card.

Step 1   Begin by examining the configuration and resources currently being used by the sound card. Turn on your machine and boot to Windows, and then open the Device Manager (Figure 18-1).

✔ Hint

There are several ways to access the Device Manager. If you need a memory jog, review pathing in Chapter 13, "Understanding Windows."

Now follow these steps:

a) Click the plus sign (+) next to *Sound, video and game controllers.*

b) Highlight the sound card icon.

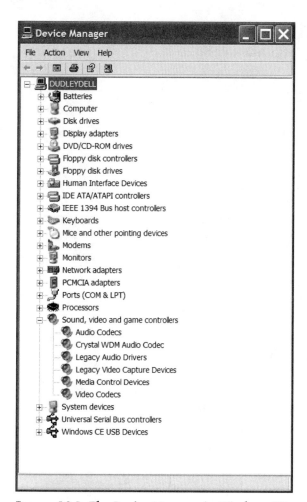

FIGURE 18-1 The Device Manager in Windows XP

✔ **Hint**

The name of the sound card icon differs according to the type of sound card you have installed. A Creative Labs SoundBlaster Live! card, for example, has the entry listed as "Creative SB Live! Series (WDM)." Try them all if it's not obvious at first glance which is the appropriate icon.

---

c) Right-click and select Properties.

d) Click the Resources tab.

Verify which resources the sound device is using, and confirm that there are no conflicts.

Which interrupt request (IRQ) is listed? _____

What direct memory access (DMA) channels are listed, if any? _____

What input/output (I/O) addresses are listed? _____

e) Now click the Driver tab, and record all the available information about the driver that is currently installed.

Step 2 Take a moment and look up the specifications of your current sound card. Identify the following:

Resolution _____

Sampling rate _____

Dynamic range _____

Signal-to-noise ratio _____

Now see if you can find this information on some other cards—try M-AUDIO Revolution 5.1, Creative SoundBlaster X-Fi, SoundMAX Integrated Digital Audio, and Voyetra Turtle Beach.

Step 3 Now that you've seen what resources are currently being used, and some of the relevant specifications, the next step is to practice removing and reinstalling the sound card.

✔ **Hint**

This lab assumes that you have a removable sound card, not onboard sound. If all you have to work with is a system with onboard sound, go into the CMOS setup utility and turn off the onboard sound. Make what observations you can and resume the exercise with Step 4. When the time comes in the second half of Step 4 to reinstall the sound card, just go back into CMOS and enable the onboard sound again.

a) Close the Device Manager and shut down your system properly. Unplug the power cord.

b) Remove the case cover from your system and locate the sound card (see Figure 18-2).

What type of slot does the card use? _____

c) Disconnect any cables that are attached to the sound card (both internal and external), take out the screw that secures the sound card to the case, and then carefully remove the card. Make sure you're properly grounded before you touch the card!

What sort of internal connectors does the card have? _____

What sort of external connectors does it have? _____

Does the card have jumpers? What are they used for? Again, look on the Internet for the answers. Find the name of the card manufacturer and search that company's Web site for information on your specific model. This information is also available in the documentation for the card, if you still have it around. _____

_____

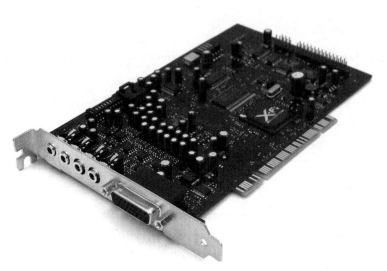

FIGURE 18-2 A typical sound card

What is the brand name of the sound-processing chip?

_____

Is the name on the chip different from the name of the manufacturer of the card? (For example, the chip might have *ESS* printed on it, while the board is marked *Creative Labs*.)

_____

Describe the cables you disconnected when you removed the sound card.

_____

Does the card have an IDE interface? If so, you have a really old card. How would the IDE interface be used? _____

✔ **Hint**

In old systems that had only one IDE controller on the motherboard, how were CD-ROM drives connected when you had two hard drives in the system?

Step 4   With the card out of your system, turn on the machine and let it boot to the Windows desktop. Then go to the Device Manager and see if your sound card is still listed.

Did Windows automatically remove the device when the card was removed? _____

If the sound card is still listed, highlight its icon, right-click, and select Uninstall. (Am I sure? Yes, I'm sure!)

Save your changes and shut your system off properly.

The next steps will confirm that the device has been removed:

a) Reboot your system, go to the Device Manager, and confirm that the sound device is no longer listed.

b) Shut down your system and disconnect the power cord. Insert the sound card in the slot where you originally found it, secure the card to the case using the screw you removed, and reconnect all the cables.

c) Reboot the system. When Plug and Play (PnP) kicks in, your system should recognize that you have added a card.

Windows will now locate the software drivers for the new hardware you installed. In fact, unless you uninstalled them, the drivers should still be on your system.

Step 5   Return to the Device Manager and repeat Step 1 to verify what resources the sound card is now using and confirm that there are no conflicts.

What IRQ is listed now? _____

What DMA channels are listed, if any? _____

What I/O addresses are listed? _____

Are the settings the same as in Step 1 before you removed the card? _____

Go to the Driver tab and confirm that Windows installed the same drivers in the system. If necessary, use the driver diskette or CD to reinstall the correct drivers.

Step 6   To confirm that sound is working properly, start by ensuring that the speakers are powered and connected, and that the volume is set at a comfortable level.

Make sure your speakers are plugged into the proper jack on the sound card.

Is the speaker pair plugged into a working AC outlet, or does it have good batteries?

_____

Is there a volume adjustment knob on your speakers? _____

If you have a volume knob, adjust it to the middle position, and then access the Control Panel.

Now place a Volume icon in the taskbar's system tray/notification area so that volume adjustments will be more convenient. Follow the procedure that matches your operating system.

- In Windows 2000, open the Sounds and Multimedia Control Panel applet, and check the *Show volume control on the taskbar* box.

- In Windows XP, open the Sounds and Audio Devices Control Panel applet, and check the *Place volume icon in the taskbar* box.

Once you have the Volume icon in the taskbar, double-click it to open the volume controls and then follow these steps:

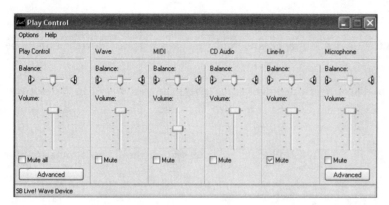

FIGURE 18-3 Setting the volume controls

a) Check to be sure that the *Mute all* option is not selected (see Figure 18-3).

b) Select Options | Properties.

c) Select the volume controls that you want to control.

d) Click OK to close the Properties window.

e) Now adjust all the sliders to the center position.

You now have a good starting point to play sounds. Once you have ensured that the speakers are successfully putting out sound, you can go back and customize the levels to your liking.

Step 7   Test the speakers, and adjust the sound volume to a comfortable audible level. A good tool to use to test your sound card is the DirectX Diagnostic tool. This is the same tool you used in Chapter 17 to test video performance. Click Start | Run and type **dxdiag** to launch the DirectX Diagnostic tool (see Figure 18-4).

a) Click the Sound tab, and examine the information displayed about your sound card and drivers.

b) Click the Test DirectSound button. This steps you through a series of tests to confirm the operation of your sound system.

c) Now switch to the Music tab and click the Test DirectMusic button. This tests whether your system supports the DirectMusic component of DirectX.

Step 8   You've learned to remove, install, and configure a sound card. You've also learned how to test the various parts of the sound system. Now it's time to talk about troubleshooting.

Your sound system is working, but your speakers sound a little rough. Are they "blown" out because they were overdriven with poor adjustments? You can go to this Web site and test the response of your speakers at different frequencies:

http://www.eminent-tech.com/music/multimediatest.html

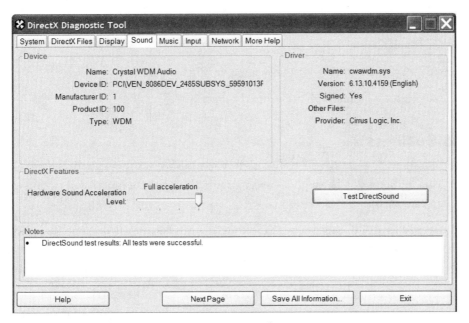

Figure 18-4 Using the DirectX Diagnostic tool

These tests will help you confirm whether your speakers can still handle all the frequencies they are designed to handle.

 30 MINUTES

Lab Exercise 18.02: Recording Sound

With the sound card installed, configured, and tested, it's time to get the project really rolling with recorded sound. It is expected that each student's documentary will last from eight to ten minutes and will encompass typical current events. Each student has a microphone, sound card, and speakers. What you want to do is get the speech recorded digitally, maybe add some music, and choose the audio quality based on the expected delivery method.

Learning Objectives

The purpose of this lab exercise is to guide you in the recording of sound.

At the end of this lab, you'll be able to

- Use the microphone to record a .wav file

- Fine-tune the quality of the recording

Lab Materials and Setup

The materials you need for this lab are

- A working computer system running Windows 2000 or Windows XP

- A sound card, speakers, and a microphone properly installed

Getting Down to Business

Once you have installed, configured, and tested a sound card, you need to run some applications to see if this is going to work. This lab steps you through recording sound into the computer and saving the recording as a .wav or .mp3 sound file.

Step 1   To check your system's ability to capture audio so that you can record the documentaries, you will use the Windows Sound Recorder. Make sure your microphone is plugged into the proper connector before you proceed.

Access the Sound Recorder by selecting Start | All Programs | Accessories | Entertainment | Sound Recorder. What you have now is similar to an audio cassette player. The buttons are the same—Record, Play, Fast Forward, Rewind, and Stop—but they're labeled with icons instead of words (see Figure 18-5).

Step 2   You will now explore three different levels of recording. When working with digital audio files, the balance between sound quality and sound file size is driven by the project. If you were recording a project for CD, you would want the highest quality. For streaming audio and podcast audio, the .mp3 file format is probably acceptable. Telephone quality, while achieving small file size, is not considered production quality.

a) To set the recording quality, select File | Properties and then click the Convert Now button. In the Sound Selection dialog box, click the Name drop-down menu and select CD Quality. Click OK and then OK again to return to the Sound Recorder window.

b) Click the red Record button and start talking into the microphone. Watch the graph to see that your voice is being recorded. If nothing seems to be happening, check your microphone connections.

c) Record a full 60 seconds of CD-quality audio, then press Stop (the button with a square icon, next to Record). To hear your recording, click Play (the single right arrow).

d) To discover how much space this sound file uses, click File | Properties and observe the file's data size. Record the file size here: _____

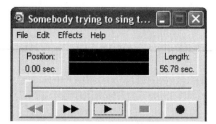

FIGURE 18-5 Using the Windows Sound Recorder

e) Create a subfolder named **podcast** in your My Music folder (under My Documents) and save the sound file as CDQUALITY.WAV in the podcast folder.

✔ **Hint**

As you've probably figured out, our scenario for the sociology department would require a more sophisticated digital audio recording application. One minute is not going to be a very lengthy documentary! The Sound Recorder is a good application to demonstrate the steps required to record audio, and you could use it to set up custom sound files to play during events. An example would be the infamous sound file that announces: "You've got mail." If you would like to explore digital audio recording and playback further, you can find and download the open-source program called Audacity at http://audacity.sourceforge.net.

Step 3 Telephone quality is very low resolution and frequency response, meaning that it will probably sound muffled and dull. Follow these steps to convert the CD-quality sound file to a telephone-quality sound file.

a) Select File | Properties, click Convert Now, and change the Name setting to Telephone Quality. Click OK and then OK again to return to the Sound Recorder window.

b) Now check out the data size of the file and record it here: _____ Has the size of the sound file changed? How does it sound?

c) Save the sound file in the podcast folder as TELEPHONEQUALITY.WAV.

Step 4 Finally, you will explore saving a recording as an MPEG Layer-3 (MP3) sound file. This is probably the best balance between audio quality and file size.

a) Launch Sound Recorder and open the CDQUALITY.WAV file.

b) To set the recording quality to the MP3 format, select File | Properties and then click Convert Now. In the Sound Selection dialog box, click the Format drop-down list and select MPEG Layer-3, then click OK.

c) Note the file's data size and record it here: _____ Has the size of the sound file changed? How does it sound?

d) Open the podcast folder and save the sound file as MP3QUALITY.MP3.

✔ **Hint**

In the Sound Selection dialog box, you can also set more specific attributes for an MP3 file; just click the Attributes drop-down list after selecting MPEG Layer-3 and you'll see a number of options to fine-tune the quality of your recording.

30 MINUTES

Lab Exercise 18.03: Exploring Windows Media Player

Now that you have successfully recorded the project, you will have to look at some of the methods used to play the files and create an archive of the documentary on CD. The Windows environment has used Windows Media Player since the introduction of version 6.1 in 1998. You can always download the latest version of Windows Media Player from Microsoft's Web site. In this exercise you will learn some of the basic navigation steps for using Windows Media Player, and burn your recordings to an audio CD.

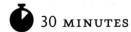 Hint

The audio standard for the Apple Macintosh environment is QuickTime.

Learning Objectives

This lab exercise will help you learn the steps to navigate and play audio files, then burn an audio CD using Windows Media Player.

At the end of this lab, you'll be able to

- Open and play sound files of various formats

- Navigate Windows Media Player

- Burn a CD of your recording

Lab Materials and Setup

The materials you need for this lab are

- A working computer system running Windows 2000 or Windows XP

- A sound card, speakers, and a microphone properly installed

- Windows Media Player 9 or newer (WMP11 is used in the lab exercise)

- A commercially produced music CD of your choice

- A blank CD-R or CD-RW

Getting Down to Business

Once you've recorded the sound and saved it as a .wav or .mp3 sound file, you'll need a method to audition the finished product and package the sound file for distribution. You may want to make an MP3 file for portable players or streaming audio over the Internet, or you may want to distribute high-quality audio CDs.

✔ **Hint**

There are a number of paths you could take to accomplish the playback of your recordings and archive them to a CD. This lab exercise steps you through one method that explores some of the features of Windows Media Player 11. Some of the steps, windows, and icons may look different depending on the version of Windows Media Player you use. You can download Windows Media Player 11 from Microsoft to follow along exactly with the steps in the lab.

Step 1   Launch Windows Media Player and then follow these steps:

a) If you have installed Windows Media Player 11, right-click the main menu and select Show Classic Menus. This displays the traditional menu bar with File, View, Play, Tools, and so forth (see Figure 18-6).

b) Click the Now Playing tab. To open the three files you created in the previous lab (TELEPHONEQUALITY.WAV, MP3QUALITY.MP3, and CDQUALITY.WAV), select File | Open and then click Look in. Use the drop-down menu to locate the podcast folder and files. Click the first file, then hold the CTRL key down while you click each of the two remaining two files. Drag the three selected files to the Now Playing playlist. The first sound file should start to play automatically and display the filename in the right-hand pane.

c) While listening to the podcast, click File | Save Now Playing List As and save the list as podcast .wpl. This organizes your files into a named list for ease of use.

d) Now click the Burn tab, then click Burn 'podcast' in the Burn List pane on the right-hand side of the Windows Media Player window.

Figure 18-6 Windows Media Player 11

e) Insert a blank CD-R or CD-RW into an optical-media drive on your system with recording capabilities, then click the Start Burn button.

f) Wait while the podcast audio file is burned to the CD-R/RW disc, completing the task of archiving your recordings.

Step 2 While you have Windows Media Player open, explore the other options available to you as you work with sound files. One of the most popular uses of the computer when it comes to working with audio is to convert your CDs to MP3 sound files for use on portable MP3 players. Complete the following steps to calculate how many CDs you could fit onto a 2-GB MP3 player.

a) Insert a music CD into the CD/DVD ROM drive.

b) Right-click Rip and select More Options. This opens the Options dialog box for Windows Media Player, with the Rip Music tab selected.

c) Under Rip Settings, click the Format drop-down list and select WAV (Lossless). Use the information at the bottom of the dialog box to calculate the number of CDs that would fit onto a 2-GB MP3 player at this resolution. _____

d) Now click the Format drop-down list again and select MP3. Experiment with the *Audio quality* slider (which ranges from 128 Kbps to 320 Kbps), and calculate the number of CDs that would fit onto a 2-GB MP3 player at various quality settings.

Lab Analysis Test

1. Suddenly and for no apparent reason, the speaker icon no longer shows up in the taskbar/notification area. Where would you check to be sure it is enabled?

2. John replaced his motherboard with one that has built-in sound. He still wants to use his Creative Labs Audigy sound card. What must he do to prevent conflicts?

3. Theresa has been using her system for a long time to visit with friends in chat rooms. Lately her friends are complaining that her sound quality is getting worse. What should she check first?

4. Karl is not getting any sound from his speakers. What three things should he check?

5. John complains about annoying sounds when he opens and closes certain programs and sometimes when he clicks his mouse. He asks you if you can make them go away. Can you?

Key Term Quiz

Use the following vocabulary terms to complete the following sentences. Not all terms will be used.

aux

compression

line-in

.mid

.mp3

sound card

sound file

Sound Recorder

speaker

.wav

1. Joe wants to record himself singing the '50s classic "Hound Dog" to honor the birthday of Elvis Presley. He plugs a microphone into his sound card and opens _____, the recording software that comes with Windows.

2. By default, Windows Sound Recorder saves audio recordings as _____ files.

3. Joshua is the keyboard player for a local band. He records some of the band's songs into a sequencer using MIDI. When he looks for the files on the computer, he can only find files with the _____ extension.

4. The MP3 format is popular because of the _____ scheme it uses.

5. The most common sound file format for portable sound players today is _____.

Chapter 19
Portable Computing

Lab Exercises

The world has gone mobile, and accomplished technicians travel right along with it. General technicians have always worked on the software side of portables, tweaking power management options to optimize battery life for the users. Working on the hardware side of portable computing devices of all stripes, however, used to be the realm of only highly specialized technicians. As portable computing devices become increasingly common and the technology inside becomes more modular, however, frontline general technicians (think CompTIA A+ Certified technicians here) increasingly get the call to upgrade and repair these devices.

Most portable computers (PCs, not PDAs) have parts that a user can easily replace. You can swap out a fading battery for a newer one, for example, or add a second battery in place of a CD-RW drive for long airplane trips. Lurking beneath access panels on the underside or below the keyboard on some models are hardware components such as RAM, a hard drive, a network card, and a modem—just like laptop batteries, these units can be easily accessed and replaced by a technician. Some laptops even have panels for replacing the video card and CPU.

In this series of labs, you'll do four things. First, you'll use the Internet to research the upgrades available for portable computing devices so you can provide proper recommendations to employers and clients. Second, you'll open a laptop and gut it like a rainbow trout—removing and replacing RAM, the most common of all hardware upgrades. Third, you'll perform the traditional task of a portable PC technician, tweaking the power management options to optimize battery life on particular models. Finally, you'll tour a computer store to familiarize yourself with the latest and greatest portable offerings.

> **✖ Warning**
>
> I want to caution you that completely disassembling a laptop can be like trying to wrestle a bear. Even seasoned technicians pause before removing the dozens of screws involved in replacing broken screens or damaged system boards. These types of repairs require patience and finesse, as you disassemble and reassemble delicate plastic coverings and connect and disconnect fragile wiring harnesses. Troubleshooting damaged laptops is beyond the scope of this lab manual. The lab exercises here focus on the more accessible upgrades, as outlined in the CompTIA A+ domain objectives.

 30 MINUTES

Lab Exercise 19.01: Researching Laptop Upgrade Paths

Your boss just sent word that one of your most important clients wants to extend the life of their sales force's laptop computers by upgrading rather than replacing. You've been asked to provide an upgrade track for your client. This requires you to research the laptops used by the company to determine which upgrades you can make, and to verify that the laptops themselves are not so old that the cost to upgrade them outweighs the cost of new laptops with new technology. You have to determine whether you can add RAM, replace the hard drives, replace the aging batteries, or add docking stations to provide extra functions when the salespeople are at the home office. Get to work!

Learning Objectives

Given the manufacturer and model number of a notebook computer, you'll figure out how to upgrade your client's computers.

At the end of this lab, you'll be able to

- Determine the replacement price of a battery

- Determine memory upgrades, including the quantity and type of RAM

- Determine hard drive upgrades, including the capacity and price of a hard drive

Lab Materials and Setup

The materials you need for this lab are

- A working PC with Internet access

Getting Down to Business

Limber up your surfing fingers because you're about to spend some time on the Web. Researching information about hardware and software is something technicians do all the time. The better you are at it, the better you are at your job!

When you're searching for replacement and upgrade parts and information, always take a look at the device manufacturer's Web site. Most major PC manufacturers, such as Dell and IBM (Lenovo has purchased IBM's personal computer line, so IBM laptops are now supported by Lenovo), have comprehensive product specification sheets available to the public on their sites. You can even order replacement parts directly from them! A popular tactic for researching upgrades is to grab the upgrade specs from the manufacturer's site and then search the Internet for the best prices. Not only are you doing your job well, but you'll be saving your company money too!

In the following steps, you'll navigate the tumultuous seas of the Internet in a quest to find the Golden Fleece of laptop battery, memory, and hard drive upgrades.

Step 1 Fire up your Web browser, and surf over to the device manufacturer's Web site. Try http://www.dell.com. If you can't locate the information you need on the manufacturer's site, try http://www.batteries-store.com to get information about battery upgrades. If that site isn't available, do a Google search (http://www.google.com) for "laptop battery." Many sites sell every laptop battery imaginable. The goal of this exercise is to become familiar with using the Internet to identify parts, confirm the specifications, and purchase replacement batteries. Once you reach a suitable Web site, answer the following questions:

You need replacement batteries for several Dell Inspiron 8600 PCs. What's the vendor's part number and price for this battery? _____

What's the voltage, current, and/or power capacity of the battery? _____

✔ Hint

Just like any other electrical power source, batteries are rated according to voltage (9.6 V, for instance), current capacity (2600 milliamps per hour, or mAh), and sometimes power capacity (72 watts per hour, or WHr). When purchasing laptop batteries from third-party vendors (that is, vendors other than the laptop manufacturer), make sure to buy a battery that matches the voltage recommended by the manufacturer. Depending on the type of battery (NiCD, NiMH, or Li-Ion), the current or power capacity of replacement batteries may be greater than the original battery. This is not a problem—increased current/power capacity means longer run times for your portable PC.

Step 2 Search the manufacturer's Web site for information on memory. If that isn't available, flip your browser over to http://www.kahlon.com to check RAM prices and availability. If the site isn't available, perform a Google search to find other Web sites that sell "laptop memory." Then answer the following questions.

Your client has ten Dell Inspiron 8600s with 256 MB of RAM. How much RAM can you install? How many sticks of RAM will it take to upgrade this machine to a respectable 1 GB of memory, and how much will it cost? _____

Step 3   Stay where you landed in your search for memory upgrades. Do they have replacement hard drives available as well? If not, try http://www.kahlon.com, but now research possible hard drive upgrades for the five IBM ThinkPads the client owns. Answer this question:

The client's five IBM ThinkPad T41 Pentium M 2374 PCs have 20-GB hard drives and 512 MB of RAM. How much will it cost to upgrade each ThinkPad to an 80-GB hard drive and 1 GB of RAM?

_____

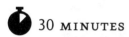 30 MINUTES

Lab Exercise 19.02: Replacing and Upgrading RAM

Your client settled on the RAM upgrades as the first step for making their laptops more usable, and you get tagged as the person to remove the old RAM and install the new. Upgrading RAM is the most common technician-performed upgrade on portable PCs and something you're likely to run into in the real world.

Learning Objectives

In this lab, you'll learn essential skills for upgrading portable PCs.

At the end of this lab, you'll be able to

- Access the RAM panel in a laptop

- Remove RAM in a laptop

- Install RAM properly in a laptop

Lab Materials and Setup

The materials you need for this lab are

- A working portable computer (one with modern SO DIMM or DDR SO DIMM modules is preferable)

- A very tiny Phillips-head screwdriver

✖ Warning

Opening a portable computer can result in a nonfunctional portable computer. Don't use the instructor's primary work laptop for this exercise!

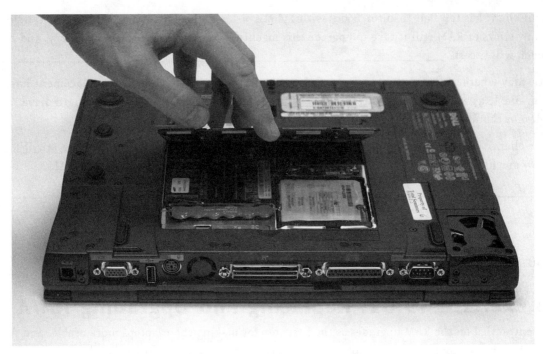

FIGURE 19-1 Opening the access panel to find RAM

Getting Down to Business

You're about to open the sensitive inner portions of a portable computer, but before you do, it's a great idea to refresh your memory about avoiding electrostatic discharge (ESD). The inside of a laptop looks different from the inside of a desktop or tower case, but the contents are just as sensitive to static electricity. Watch out!

Step 1 Using your handy screwdriver or other handy tool, open the access panel for the RAM. Every portable PC offers a different way to access the RAM, so I can't give you explicit directions here. Most often, you'll find a removable plate on the bottom of the laptop secured with a tiny Phillips-head screw. Some laptops require you to remove the keyboard, unscrew a heat spreader, and then access the RAM. Figure 19-1 shows a typical panel, accessible from the underside of the laptop.

Step 2 Once you have the panel open, push outward on the restraining clips on the RAM stick(s). This will cause the RAM to pop up partially (see Figure 19-2).

Step 3 Remove the RAM gently, gripping only at the non-contact edges. Place the stick(s) on an anti-static pad or in an anti-static bag.

Step 4 Install the replacement RAM into the laptop, reversing the process of removal. Place the stick(s) at an angle into the RAM slots and push firmly. Once the contacts have disappeared, press the body of the RAM into the restraining clips.

FIGURE 19-2 Releasing the RAM

✔ Hint

If you don't have new RAM to install, simply install the RAM you removed in Step 3. This gives you the opportunity to practice!

Step 5   Replace the access panel.

Step 6   Power on the laptop to confirm that the new RAM is recognized and functioning properly.

 30 MINUTES

Lab Exercise 19.03: Adjusting Power Management to Optimize Battery Life

Several of your sales staff members have to attend a conference on the other side of the country. The conference came up on short notice, so everyone needs time to prepare, even while on the flight to the conference. You've been tasked with configuring power management on their laptops to optimize battery life so they can work as long as possible while on the plane.

Learning Objectives

In this lab, you'll adjust the power management features for a PC, a task that's vital to proper support of portable PCs.

At the end of this lab, you'll be able to

- Enable and disable power management in the CMOS

- Change power management settings in Windows

Lab Materials and Setup

The materials you need for this lab are

- A working computer with Windows 2000/XP installed

- A BIOS that supports power management

✔ **Hint**

Having a notebook computer available is a plus. Performing these steps on a notebook computer will allow you to configure the settings for the Portable/Laptop power scheme and then remove the power cord, running on battery power to experience the actual results. If you're practicing on a regular desktop PC, keep in mind that a notebook will have two options for each adjustment: one for when the notebook is using battery power, and one for when it's connected to the alternating current (AC) source.

Getting Down to Business

Windows PCs have two separate areas for power management: the CMOS setup utility and the Control Panel. You'll start with CMOS and then go to the Control Panel.

Step 1   Boot your system, and enter the CMOS setup utility.

✔ **Cross-Reference**

Refer to the "Power Management" section in Chapter 19 of *Mike Meyers' A+ Guide to Managing and Troubleshooting PCs* for more information on power management on portable PCs.

Now follow these steps:

a) Go to the Power Management Setup screen.

b) Enable power management if it's currently disabled.

c) Look at each option for commonsense settings. For example, when operating on battery power, the portable should be configured for maximum energy efficiency, thus increasing run time.

d) Make sure the ACPI setting is enabled if the BIOS supports it.

e) Save your settings, and boot the system to the Windows Desktop.

✔ **Hint**

ACPI is short for Advanced Configuration and Power Interface, a power management specification developed by Intel, Microsoft, and Toshiba. ACPI enables the operating system to control the amount of power given to each device attached to the computer. With ACPI, the operating system can turn off peripheral devices, such as CD-ROM players, when they're not in use.

Step 2 Access the Power Options applet in the Control Panel, and make a note of your current power management settings.

Check out the different power schemes available (this will depend on your specific system) and experiment with changing the settings to see how this affects when the monitor and hard drives turn off. Each of these schemes has adjustable times. The tabs and settings will differ depending on which version of Windows you're running. Be sure to look at them all.

Now answer these questions:

Which tab contains an option to place the Power icon in the system tray/notification area?

_____

When do the monitor and hard drives turn off when the Presentation scheme is in effect?

_____

✔ **Hint**

The Windows XP (on a notebook) Power Options Properties dialog box has five tabs: Power Schemes, Alarms, Power Meter, Advanced, and Hibernate (see Figure 19-3). You can use the Alarms tab to set the time when the battery alarm is activated. The Power Meter tab shows the percent of charge remaining in the battery.

Step 3 Once you've finished experimenting, enable or disable power management as you prefer.

✘ **Warning**

Some PCs and some components don't like standby and suspend modes. They can cause your computer to lock up. Be aware of that, and if your computer locks up, turn those settings off.

FIGURE 19-3 Accessing the Windows XP power options on a portable computer

 OPEN

Lab Exercise 19.04: Field Trip to Play with the Latest Portable PCs

The best way to understand portable PCs (laptops, tablet PCs, and PDAs) is to play with one. If there isn't one available in the classroom, then this exercise is for you.

✔ Cross-Reference

Refer to the "Portable Computer Device Types" section in Chapter 19 of *Mike Meyers' A+ Guide to Managing and Troubleshooting PCs*. It will give you an excellent shopping list of portable PCs devices.

Learning Objectives

This lab will take you into the field for a little computer browsing—for educational purposes, of course!

At the end of this lab, you'll be able to

- Recognize the variations in key features among different portable PCs

Lab Materials and Setup

The materials you need for this lab are

- A local computer store or other retailer with a good selection of portable PCs you can examine

✔ **Hint**

If you don't have a store nearby, use the Web to browse a computer store such as CompUSA (http://www.compusa.com).

Getting Down to Business

Portable PCs are manufactured by a wide variety of companies, and no two notebooks are created equal. Some notebooks feature a slim and lightweight profile and are designed for the busy traveler; others feature a full complement of ports and rival desktop PCs in their power and features. Tablet PCs have pen-based interfaces that allow you to use them like a paper notepad. PDAs are great for portable address books and tasks lists that can be quickly synchronized with desktop programs through infrared or Bluetooth interfaces. Take a look at all the available models and compare their features.

Step 1 Go to your local computer or office supply store and check out the portable PCs on display. Try to find a store with a variety of brands. Bring this lab manual (or a copy of the following chart) with you to record the different specs you find.

Step 2 Pick out three portables, preferably from different manufacturers. For each portable, record the following information.

Feature	Portable 1	Portable 2	Portable 3
Size/weight	_____	_____	_____
Screen type/size	_____	_____	_____
CPU	_____	_____	_____
RAM	_____	_____	_____
Pointing device(s)	_____	_____	_____
I/O ports	_____	_____	_____
PC Card slot(s)	_____	_____	_____
Hard drive	_____	_____	_____
Floppy/optical drive(s)	_____	_____	_____

Lab Analysis Test

1. Bill wants to upgrade his memory from 256 MB to the maximum amount of RAM his notebook can take. He has an IBM T43 notebook. How much RAM does he need to buy?

2. Teresa complains that her Windows XP notebook turns itself off without any warning. What should she adjust?

3. Maanit travels often cross-country and even back and forth to India on occasion. He uses his laptop to watch DVDs for hours on end, usually on battery power. Lately, the battery seems to run out of juice well before the battery specifications indicate. What could possibly cause this recent development? Are there any recommendations you would make to Maanit to improve his laptop's performance?

4. During your research earlier in these exercises, which did you discover to be the most expensive—hard drives, memory, or batteries? Which component was the most inexpensive to replace?

5. Would the LCD screen or hard drives turn off, for energy conservation, if you set your power scheme to Always On and you walked away for a long period of time? Why or why not?

Key Term Quiz

Use the following vocabulary terms to complete the following sentences. Not all terms will be used.

ACPI

battery

hard drive

hibernate

memory

notebook

Power Options

Power Meter

Power Scheme

standby

1. The amount of time the hard drive will continue to spin once it's no longer being accessed is determined by the _____ setting.

2. You can use the _____ applet in the Control Panel to set the power conservation options for the notebook computer.

3. The battery, _____, and _____ are all upgradeable laptop components.

4. The amount of power remaining in a battery can be determined by looking at the _____.

5. Software can control power consumption if _____ is turned on in the CMOS setup utility.

Chapter 20

Printers

Lab Exercises

Printers continue to be a major part of the day-to-day working environment, both at home and in the office, despite attempts to create a "paperless office." What this means is that the PC technician will have to understand the operation of several types of printers and be able to keep them in good working order. Many companies have service contracts for their more expensive printers (they're usually leased property anyway!), but there will always be printers that need a good technician's love and care.

This chapter's labs will take you through a scenario in which your boss walks into your office and tells you there are five printers on their way to you—two impact printers using legacy parallel ports, two USB inkjet printers, and a HP LaserJet laser printer using a Jet Direct network interface. You need to install them so that they're accessible by anyone who needs them and to make sure they work properly. You'll explore different port settings and how to alter them when you need to do so. You'll then learn about some of the key differences between the two most popular types of printers (inkjet and laser printers), and you'll load printer drivers. Finally, you'll look at some of the maintenance issues that are required to keep the printers up and running and some of the techniques to follow when they stop.

 30 MINUTES

Lab Exercise 20.01: Exploring Configuration Settings

Printers have used just about every interface available to the computer from legacy RS-232C serial and IEEE 1284 parallel interfaces to the most recent USB, FireWire, Infrared, and Bluetooth wireless interfaces. The two most common ports used in connecting a printer locally to a PC are the Universal Serial Bus (USB) and parallel ports. It just so happens that the printers you'll be working with use parallel, USB, and network interfaces! In this lab, you'll look at the parallel interface—the oldest of the three—and walk through the process of enabling and configuring the parallel port in the BIOS.

You have already explored the Universal Serial Bus (USB) interface in Chapter 16, "Input/Output," and will delve into the wonderful world of networking in Chapter 21, "Local Area Networking." The parallel interface is aging, but there is still a large installed base of printers using this interface, and the CompTIA A+ exams expect you to know some of the details of the interface. Refer to the "Printer Connectivity" section in Chapter 20 of *Mike Meyers' A+ Guide to Managing and Troubleshooting PCs* for help identifying parallel port modes and their differences and similarities.

Learning Objectives

In this lab, you'll explore the different configuration settings that are available for the parallel interface in your PC's CMOS setup utility.

At the end of this lab, you'll be able to

- Enable and configure parallel ports in the basic input/output services (BIOS)
- Locate information about the parallel port in Device Manager

Lab Materials and Setup

The materials you need for this lab are

- A working computer running Windows 2000 or XP

✔ Hint

The steps assume that you have Windows XP and will vary only slightly for other versions of Windows, mostly in the paths to get to certain configuration windows. By now you should be quite familiar with the different paths used by various versions of Windows.

Getting Down to Business

First, take a look at the ports in your CMOS setup utility. You may never need to use this, but it's really helpful to know, and the CompTIA A+ exams expect you'll be familiar with the information.

Step 1 Boot your PC, and go into the CMOS setup utility. Find the settings for your USB and parallel ports. They'll most likely be under a heading such as Integrated Peripherals (see Figure 20-1).

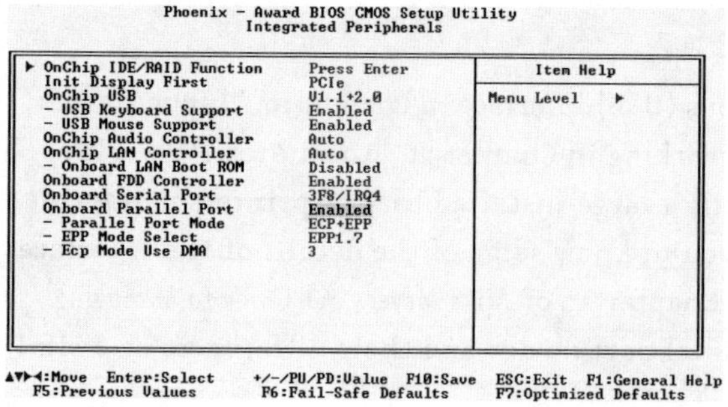

```
          Phoenix - Award BIOS CMOS Setup Utility
                   Integrated Peripherals

 ▶ OnChip IDE/RAID Function   Press Enter      ┌──────────────┐
   Init Display First         PCIe             │   Item Help  │
   OnChip USB                 V1.1+2.0         │              │
    - USB Keyboard Support    Enabled          │ Menu Level ▶ │
    - USB Mouse Support       Enabled          │              │
   OnChip Audio Controller    Auto             │              │
   OnChip LAN Controller      Auto             │              │
    - Onboard LAN Boot ROM    Disabled         │              │
   Onboard FDD Controller     Enabled          │              │
   Onboard Serial Port        3F8/IRQ4         │              │
   Onboard Parallel Port      Enabled          │              │
    - Parallel Port Mode      ECP+EPP          │              │
    - EPP Mode Select         EPP1.7           │              │
    - Ecp Mode Use DMA        3                │              │


 ▲▼◀:Move  Enter:Select   +/-/PU/PD:Value  F10:Save   ESC:Exit  F1:General Help
     F5:Previous Values       F6:Fail-Safe Defaults    F7:Optimized Defaults
```

FIGURE 20-1 The Integrated Peripherals CMOS screen

✖ Warning

When making changes to the system resources in both CMOS and Device Manager, be sure to first write down the current settings. If your changes don't work, you can always return them to the original settings that did.

How many parallel ports do you have? _____

What resources are the parallel port(s) using? _____

Step 2 Make the following changes in CMOS, and observe any effect on hardware installed on the parallel ports. Make sure you have drivers or parallel devices handy because making changes at the CMOS level can make Windows unhappy! (You might need to reinstall drivers.)

- Parallel Port = I/O Address 378 and IRQ 7

- DMA = 3

Exit CMOS properly, saving your changes.

Step 3 Reboot your system to the Windows Desktop, and access Device Manager in the Control Panel to verify that the resources are assigned.

Confirm the resources allocated to the parallel port by following these steps:

a) Click the plus sign (+) next to Ports (COM & LPT).

b) Highlight the LPT port in the list, and click Properties.

c) Select the Resources tab.

What are the I/O and IRQ settings for this port? _____

d) Click OK to close the Properties dialog box.

Step 4 Verify the resources again by accessing the list of resources used in Device Manager:

a) From the Device Manager, select View.

b) Select Resources by Type.

c) Expand the groups as needed by clicking the plus sign (+) next to the desired resource.

✔ **Hint**

If there's no IRQ listed, it may be by design. In Device Manager, expand the item called Ports (COM & LPT), and display the properties for ECP Printer Port (LPT1). Click the Settings tab—do you see the selection for never using an interrupt? Change the selection to Use Any Interrupt Assigned to the Port, and verify the resources again as outlined in Step 4.

Verify all of your settings and close the Device Manager, Control Panel, and My Computer to return to the desktop.

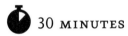 30 MINUTES

Lab Exercise 20.02: Examining Types of Printers

There's an enormous amount of information on the Internet about printers. All of the top printer manufacturers—HP, Lexmark, Canon, and so forth—have Web sites that can provide insight about modern printers. As a PC technician, you'll need to visit these sites for information about your new printers, and to download the most current drivers for those printers.

✖ **Warning**

You must have access to the Internet for this exercise. If there's no access or the sites are down, refer to Chapter 20 of *Mike Meyers' A+ Guide to Managing and Troubleshooting PCs* for a review.

Learning Objectives

In this lab, you'll compare the features of impact, inkjet, and laser printers using the Internet.

At the end of this lab, you'll be able to

- Recognize the key differences between impact, inkjet, and laser printers

- Identify and visit Web sites on the Internet dedicated to printers and printer trouble-shooting

Lab Materials and Setup

The materials you need for this lab are

- A working computer with Windows 2000 or XP installed

- A connection to the Internet

- Access to either an inkjet printer or a laser printer

✔ Hint

A trip to your local computer store or other retailer with a good selection of printers would be beneficial for a general knowledge of printers.

Getting Down to Business

Fire up your favorite Web browser and head out on the old Information Superhighway. The Internet is just brimming with helpful information about printers.

✔ Hint

Web sites have the annoying tendency to either disappear or drop the information that was once relevant to a particular subject. If any of the links in this exercise are no longer active or don't seem to contain the relevant information, you may need to do a little Web research of your own. As always, practice safe surfing! There are thousands of online forums available, and they can contain questionable hyperlinks, poor quality information, and in some cases, outright wrong information. Try to stick with legitimate manufacturer and technical Web sites, examine where that hyperlink is going to reroute your computer, and visit multiple sites to verify information you discover in the forums. Consider it excellent practice for real-world tech work!

Step 1   To find information about inkjet printers, access the following Web site to complete this step: http://computer.howstuffworks.com/inkjet-printer.htm/printable.

If this link doesn't work, you can also do a Google search and look for information about how printers work.

What's the major difference between impact and non-impact printers? _____

_____

What part of an inkjet printer moves the print head back and forth across the page?

_____

List the two ways in which the droplets of ink are formed in inkjet printers. _____

_____

The type of paper used in an inkjet printer greatly influences the quality of the image produced. What are the two main characteristics of inkjet printer paper that affect the image the most?

_____

_____

Step 2   For information about laser printers, access this site to complete this step: http://www. howstuffworks.com/laser-printer.htm/printable. Do a Google search or refer to the textbook if this site isn't available.

What's the primary principle at work in a laser printer? _____

What moves the image from the drum to the paper? _____

Printer Control Language (PCL) and PostScript are both examples of what?_____

What's toner? Is it an ink, wax, or something else? _____

Step 3   Put these steps in the printing process of a laser printer in the correct order (don't forget to reference the textbook as well):

Charge   _____

Clean   _____

Toner   _____

Fuse   _____

Transfer   _____

Write   _____

Step 4   If you have access to a laser printer, open it and carefully examine the insides. Also read the printer manual for details on the specifications. Access the manufacturer's Web site for additional information.

If you don't have access to a laser printer, go to your local office supply or computer store and ask a salesperson to show you the differences between various impact, inkjet (black and white as well as color), and laser printers.

Look inside your laser printer.

What parts are easily removable and replaceable? _____

Practice removing and reinserting the toner (see Figure 20-2) and paper.

✖ Warning

Remember to turn the printer off before removing anything but the toner or paper. Also, be careful not to spill any toner inside the printer.

FIGURE 20-2 A toner cartridge with its photosensitive drum exposed

Look at the manual or the manufacturer's Web site for these specifications. Answer all the following questions you can about your printer:

How much random access memory (RAM) can it hold? _____

How much effect does the amount of RAM have on the cost of a new printer? _____

Are the drum and toner separate, or are they one replaceable part? _____

Speed of the printer (pages per minute) _____

Quality of the output (resolution) _____

Number and types of ink cartridges _____

Price of a new printer _____

Cost per page _____

✔ Hint

Most inkjet (and even laser) printers are priced very low so they're affordable to buy initially. Using them is another question. Ask yourself about the cost of the ink and how many pages it'll print. This calculation will amaze you. They're not so cheap after all.

What can you conclude from your research about the true total cost of printing, including consumables? _____

 30 MINUTES

Lab Exercise 20.03: Installing a Printer

The key to a successful printer installation is having the correct software drivers and understanding how the printer will interface with the computer. You'll certainly need the drivers when you install those five printers, and you'll also have to configure the printers you are installing to use parallel, USB, and network interfaces. A common practice in multiple-user environments—companies considered to be Small Office/ Home Office (SOHO)—is to use a printer with its own network interface card (NIC), so that computers from anywhere in the network can print directly to the printer through the network interface.

Learning Objectives

In this lab, you'll install a printer, first as a directly connected device, and then as a network device. You will then explore and change its settings.

At the end of this lab, you'll be able to

- Recognize the variations in key features of laser printers

- Install a laser printer in Windows

- Change laser printer settings in Windows

- Configure a TCP/IP port for a network printer

Lab Materials and Setup

The materials you need for this lab are

- A working computer with Windows 2000/XP installed

- An inkjet or laser printer for installation (or you can skip Step 1)

- Optionally, a print device with a network interface card

Getting Down to Business

These days, installing a printer is a fairly straightforward task. This is good because you'll probably do your fair share of it as a computer technician.

Step 1   If you have an actual print device, start here. (If you don't, skip to Step 2.)

Connect the printer to your system via a parallel or USB port, turn on the printer, and then turn on the PC. As the boot sequence progresses, the Plug and Play feature will locate the printer and install it for you. Follow the instructions on the screen.

✔ **Hint**

Here's the twist. If your printer is older than your operating system, the OS should install the printer drivers with little interaction on your part. If the printer is newer than your operating system, then you'll need to have the driver CD or disk handy because the system will stop and ask you for it.

Step 2   If you don't have a print device, start here:

a) Access the Printer applet.

b) For Windows 2000, select Start | Settings | Printers. For Windows XP, select Start | Printers and Faxes.

c) Click the Add Printer icon. A wizard should pop up on the screen. Click Next to proceed.

d) You want to install a printer attached to your PC, so select the option for *Local printer attached to this computer* (see Figure 20-3).

e) Follow the steps through the Printer Wizard by selecting LPT1 and then a printer from the list of printers or your driver CD.

✖ **Warning**

If you weren't able to install an actual print device for this exercise, don't print a test page. You'll receive some interesting messages if you do.

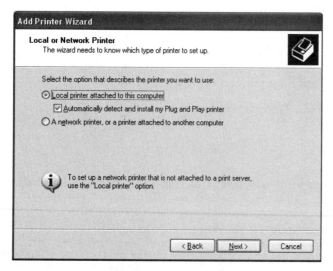

FIGURE 20-3 Installing a local printer

Once you've installed the printer, open the Printers folder in the Control Panel, right-click the new printer's icon, and select Properties.

You'll see the various tabs and options depending on your printer. I used the Epson Stylus PHOTO 870 ESC/P 2 from the built-in drivers list. Check each of your tabs to see the information available and the features you can change:

- **General** Description, preferences, and print test
- **Sharing** To share or not to share; that is the question (this is covered in Chapter 21, "Local Area Networking")
- **Ports** Additional ports to assign the printer
- **Advanced** Spooling, separator page, and print defaults
- **Color Management** Automatic or manual
- **Security** Permissions
- **Utilities** Nozzle Check, Head Cleaning, and Print Head Alignment

✔ **Hint**

You should know how to navigate all the previous steps for all the different Windows versions (Windows 2000/XP) for the CompTIA A+ exams.

Step 3 In the following steps, you will set up a TCP/IP printer interface port for a Hewlett-Packard LaserJet printer with a Jet Direct Network Interface Card. If you have access to a printer with a network interface, or your classroom is equipped with one, please use the IP Address or Printer Name of the printer when configuring the port. This will allow you to actually test the installation.

a) Open the Printer & Faxes folder (Start | Settings | Printers & Faxes) and launch the Add Printer Wizard.

b) Select *Local printer attached to this computer* (note the information balloon at the bottom of the dialog window, as in Figure 20-3) and clear the *Automatically detect and install my Plug and Play printer* box. Click Next.

c) Click the *Create a new port* radio button and select Standard TCP/IP Port from the drop-down menu.

d) This launches the Add Standard TCP/IP Printer Port Wizard (see Figure 20-4). Click Next.

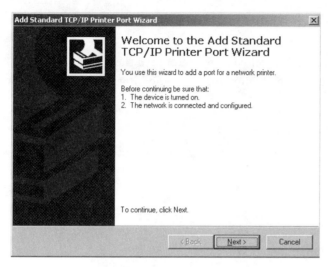

Figure 20-4 The Add Standard TCP/IP Printer Port Wizard

e) In the Add Port dialog box, enter the IP address of the network printer. The printer wizard automatically creates the Port Name (see Figure 20-5). Click Next.

f) If the IP address is fictitious, for the purpose of completing the lab steps, the Add TCP/IP Port Wizard will be unable to identify the printing device. In the dialog box for Device Type, click the drop-down menu for Standard and select Hewlett-Packard Jet Direct (see Figure 20-6). Click Next.

g) Review the port characteristics and click Finish (see Figure 20-7).

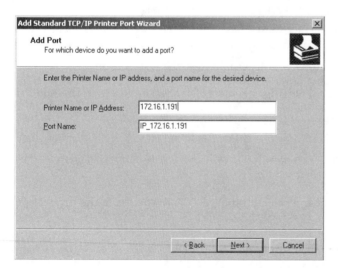

Figure 20-5 The TCP/IP Address and Port Name of a Jet Direct Printer

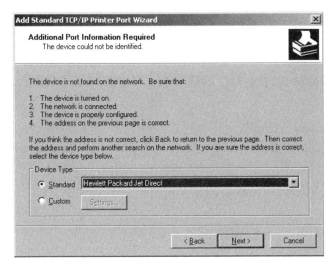

FIGURE 20-6 Selecting the Standard Hewlett Packard Jet Direct device type

h) You will now follow the steps through the Printer Wizard by selecting a printer from the list of printers or your driver CD as you did when directly connecting to the printer in Step 2.

✖ Warning

Again, if you are unable to install an actual print device for this exercise, don't print a test page. You'll receive some interesting messages if you do.

FIGURE 20-7 Port characteristics

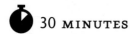 30 MINUTES

Lab Exercise 20.04: Maintaining and Troubleshooting Printers

It is estimated that technicians, especially those working for the help desk or desktop support group for a small to medium-sized organization, spend approximately 30 percent of their time on printer issues. If you think about it, of all of the components used in computing technology, printers have the highest percentage of moving parts. Moving parts tend to need maintenance more than static components or they wear out and break.

Printers also like to be finicky and stop printing, usually resulting in a phone call from the client to the help desk for quick resolution. The following exercises will help you develop some understanding of laser printer and inkjet printer maintenance, and what steps to take when they stop printing!

Learning Objectives

In this lab, you'll research laser printer maintenance kits, clean dirty inkjet nozzles, and troubleshoot a failed print job.

At the end of this lab, you'll be able to

- Select a proper maintenance kit for various laser printers
- Clean and verify operation of inkjet nozzles
- Manage print jobs in Windows
- Restart a stalled print spooler

Lab Materials and Setup

The materials you need for this lab are

- A working computer with Windows 2000/XP installed
- A connection to the Internet
- Access to an inkjet printer

Getting Down to Business

The following exercises will round out your activities as you finish with the rollout of the five new printers in your office. You will want to get your Internet connection fired up again and research the maintenance kit available for your laser printer. Then you'll check the print-head nozzles of the inkjet printers and run the cleaning routine if necessary. Finally, you should prepare for any print errors so that you can correct them quickly and efficiently.

Step 1 Laser printers are, by design, highly precise machines. They typically move thousands of sheets of paper per month through the printing mechanism, placing 1200–1600 dots per inch (DPI) of toner on each page. As such, toner cartridges need to be replaced from time to time and parts that wear out need to be refurbished. Most manufacturers offer a maintenance kit for the printer to assist in the upkeep of the printer when these common parts age or fail. It would be a good idea to have a maintenance kit on hand for each model of laser printer in your organization.

✔ **Hint**

Most of the current manufacturers of laser printers—Hewlett-Packard, Lexmark, Kyocera, Canon, and so forth—offer some form of maintenance kit for their printers. You should be able to conduct an Internet search using your favorite search engine to uncover available kits, their contents, and competitive pricing. Don't be surprised to find the maintenance kits somewhat costly, though they should still be only a fraction of the cost of replacing the printer.

Select a laser printer make and model, and perform an Internet search to identify the appropriate maintenance kit, its contents, and the average cost of the kit. Use this information to fill in the following items:

Printer Model _____

Maintenance Kit _____

Contents _____

Price _____

Step 2 Though you have just installed new inkjet printers, if the printer sits idle for an extended period of time (a few weeks or months), or the ink cartridges have been replaced, you may need to check the print quality and clean the nozzles. The following steps were performed on an Epson Stylus PHOTO 890 but are similar to the steps required on Hewlett-Packard and Lexmark inkjet printers. Consult the manual for specific instructions.

✖ **Warning**

The nozzle cleaning process uses a fair amount of the expensive ink. If you are working on a personal inkjet printer, or one in the classroom, after printing the nozzle check page, run the nozzle cleaning process only if required.

a) Open the Printer & Faxes folder (Start | Settings | Printers & Faxes) and highlight your inkjet printer.

b) Right-click the printer and select Properties.

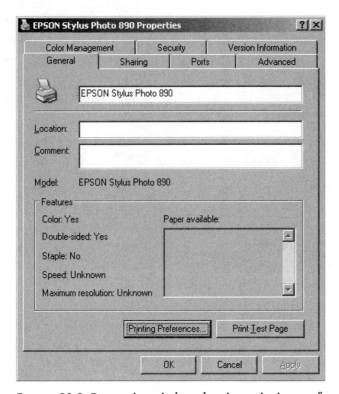

FIGURE 20-8 Properties window showing printing preferences

c) Click the Printing Preferences button (see Figure 20-8).

d) Select the Utility tab (Figure 20-9) and click Nozzle Check. This will print a test pattern using the cyan, yellow, magenta, and black ink nozzles.

e) If the printout is not clear or there are dropouts, select Head Cleaning to clear the nozzles and return to the Nozzle Check to verify performance.

Step 3 When you are called upon to troubleshoot a failed print job, you should follow a logical step-by-step process to make sure that no obvious, possibly simple failure has occurred. If the power cord has been kicked out, or the paper tray is open, it would use valuable time to troubleshoot the network connectivity or the printer driver. Once you know the print device is online and ready and there are no paper jams or mechanical errors, then it might be time to open the Print Manager and attempt to restart the document.

The following steps are meant to be a rough guideline to troubleshoot and diagnose a failed print job:

a) First, check the physical print device:

Is the printer plugged in, and is the power turned on?

Is the printer out of paper or is there a paper jam?

Is the toner low, or in need of replacement?

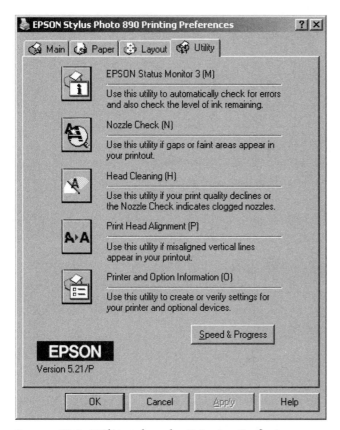

FIGURE 20-9 Utility tab under Printing Preferences

Are there any error messages on the printers LCD readout or are error indicator lights flashing?

Is the Printer online and ready to print?

If all of these areas are examined and everything appears to be in working condition, then you may have a problem with the connectivity between the computer and the printer, or there may be problems with the document or drivers.

b) Make sure that the connections between the computer and the printer are in good condition and securely fastened. These may be USB, IEEE 1284 Bi-Directional Parallel, or UTP using RJ-45 connectors.

✔ Hint

To create a failed print job, disconnect the printer cable, shut the power off on the printer, or open the printer paper tray. If you do not have a physical printer, create a printer, following the steps in Lab Exercise 20.03. Send a print job to the printer; the printer icon should appear in the system tray and indicate that the print job has failed. Then continue with Step 3.

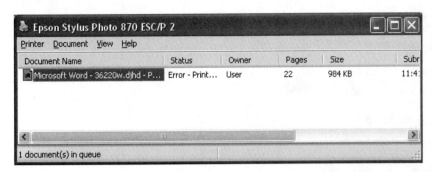

FIGURE 20-10 Print Manager showing error status on a Word file

c) After checking all of the physical components, you should try to resend the document. Open the Print Manager by clicking the icon in the system tray/notification area.

In the Print Manager, select the failed print job by highlighting the job with *Error* in the Status column (see Figure 20-10).

Select Documents | Restart. If you are creating the printer problem, the printer icon in the system tray/notification area indicates that the print job has failed once again.

d) Highlight the document once again, and then select Documents | Cancel to delete the document.

If this were a real scenario, you would verify that the print drivers were installed and are the correct drivers for the operating system. You would then perform Step 4 to see if the problem is related to the Print Spooler.

Step 4   If the print device is online and ready, there are no paper jams or mechanical errors, and restarting the document is of no help, you can check to see if the Print Spooler is stalled. The Print Spooler is a holding area for print jobs and is especially important for network printers. If the print device runs out of paper while printing a document, you may have to stop and start the Print Spooler before the print device will receive jobs again.

In Chapter 14, "Working with the Command-Line Interface," you accomplished this task using the command line. Now you will use the Services snap-in for the Microsoft Management Console (MMC) to do the same thing, only more quickly and in a GUI.

a) Launch the Services console by opening Administrative Tools in the Control Panel and then double-clicking Services.

b) Scroll down and highlight the Print Spooler. Select Action | Properties. You should see that the Print Spooler is started and running (see Figure 20-11).

c) Click the Stop button. The Print Spooler indicates that it has stopped.

d) Click the Start button. The Print Spooler indicates that it has started.

e) Alternatively, you can highlight the Print Spooler and select Action | Restart. You'll see a message stating that the Print Spooler is stopping, and then another message indicating that the Print Spooler is starting.

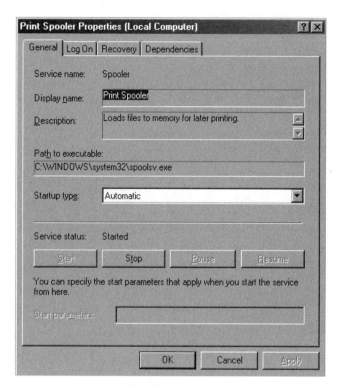

FIGURE 20-11 Print Spooler Properties

In the real-world scenario, your print spooler service would be restarted, and you should have a healthy, functioning print server once again.

Lab Analysis Test

1. Patrick and Erik are having a small disagreement. Patrick says that printers can use a number of different interfaces, while Erik says that there are only two: parallel and USB. Who is correct? List the interfaces you are aware of and a typical use of each interface.

2. Theresa is using Windows XP and just purchased a printer from a friend. When she installs it using the original driver CD that came with the printer, it won't install properly. Why?

3. Danyelle has just joined a large organization as a level II tech and is tasked with the evaluation of all of the laser printers in use. The business managers are concerned that all of the units will need to be replaced because of frequent paper jams and poor print quality. Danyelle makes her recommendations, and is actually awarded a bonus for saving the company money. What is her recommendation?

4. Brandon has sent a document to the printer, but the document never actually prints. Where can Brandon check to see the status of the document?

5. Why are laser toner cartridges so expensive?

Key Term Quiz

Use the following vocabulary terms to complete the following sentences. Not all terms will be used.

DMA

ECP

IEEE 1284

impact

inkjet

laser

pages per month

primary corona

TCP/IP port

toner

transfer corona

USB

1. The part of the laser printer that actually causes the toner image to be created on the paper is the
   _____.

2. To use a printer that's attached to the network with its own NIC, you must configure a(n)
   _____.

3. The duty cycle of a printer is known as the _____.

4. The printer that spits ink onto the paper is a(n) _____ printer.

5. Printers with platens are _____ printers.

Chapter 21
Local Area Networking

Lab Exercises

There's no doubt about it—a PC technician *will* have networking issues to work through at some point. Whether it's a three-computer, home-based local area network (LAN), a public Wi-Fi access point, a large company with thousands of connected devices, or the Web itself, networks have become as common as PCs. The main consideration is no longer whether you're going to network your computers—it's now what method you're going to use to network your computers.

A competent PC technician is called upon to be a network guru, answering connectivity questions and making recommendations on the best price/performance considerations for homes and businesses. This happens frequently, especially in smaller companies that can't afford to hire multiple people to support both the network *and* the PCs. The Comp-TIA A+ Certification exams reflect these changing roles of the PC technician and include many questions related to computer networking.

In this chapter's labs, you'll imagine that you've been hired to work for a small company that has made the decision to upgrade the network in their office. You'll need to have a working understanding of network hardware and network operating system issues, as well as some good troubleshooting tools for when things don't work quite right.

 30 MINUTES

Lab Exercise 21.01: Identifying Local Area Network Hardware

Your boss has decided to upgrade the network in your office, which is about five years old. With the changes in networking technology, he wants your ideas about purchasing the right equipment for the upgrade. Your company is a small one, so the task is quite doable, but you need to make sure you know what you're talking about before you give your report.

Learning Objectives

In this lab, you'll familiarize yourself with networking hardware.

At the end of this lab, you'll be able to

- Identify different kinds of network cabling

- Identify different network interface cards (NICs)

- Identify different types of network hubs

- Identify different wireless networking devices

Lab Materials and Setup

The materials you need for this lab are

- Access to a PC running Windows 2000/XP

- Access to a working local area network and the Internet (you may have demonstration devices provided by your instructor)

Getting Down to Business

One of the best ways to find out what a network is made of is to physically look at all of its pieces. Even then, however, it may be necessary to access a manufacturer's Web site to see, for instance, if the "hub" you're using is really a hub or maybe a switch.

Step 1   If you have access to a LAN (the classroom computer lab network, a friend's home network, or your company's network), spend some time exploring the physical hardware connections and devices. If possible, acquire the diagram of the physical layout of the network, or create a simple diagram of the layout to familiarize yourself with the various devices and connections associated with the network you're analyzing.

✖ Warning

Don't disconnect anything, and be careful while probing around. One small mistake, like removing a cable or turning off the wrong device, can disrupt the entire network. If you're using the classroom network, ask the instructor what you can and can't remove while you make closer inspections of the cables and devices.

What sort of cabling does the network use, or is it wireless? Is it twisted-pair cable or coaxial cable? Does it use T-connectors? Are the cable ends RJ-45 connectors, or something outdated like BNC connectors? Describe the physical layout of the LAN here.

_____

_____

✔ **Cross-Reference**

Be sure to check out Chapter 21 of *Mike Meyers' A+ Guide to Managing and Troubleshooting PCs* for help identifying network cables and connectors. It's a good idea to have the textbook handy while you progress through this lab.

What sort of NICs do the machines have? Describe the back of the card. Does it have a single connector or a combination of connectors (Figure 21-1)? Does it have an antenna? Is there a link and/or activity LED? Which of the LEDs is on steady? Which is flashing? Describe the NIC here.

_____

_____

✔ **Hint**

It is very important to understand the difference between the link light vs. the activity light. First, these "lights" are really light-emitting diodes (LEDs) and will usually appear in some form of yellow, orange, or green color, depending on the NIC manufacturer. Second, the link light indicates that the NIC and the cable have a valid electrical connection between the PC and the network device, usually a hub or a switch. This does not guarantee connectivity—it just means that the electrical connection is intact. The activity light is a better indicator that the NIC, cable, and hubs or switches are working. When the activity light blinks, it is indicating that data is being transferred between the networking devices. It does not guarantee that the data is usable—it just means that data is making the trip from the NIC to the hub or switch, or from the hub or switch to the NIC. If you are having trouble connecting to a network or communicating to other machines on the network, the link and activity lights are a good place to start your troubleshooting.

FIGURE 21-1 A network interface card (NIC)

Step 2 Hubs and switches are very much a part of every network.

Are the PCs connected with a single cable (crossover cable limited to two PCs), or are they connected to a hub/switch (Figure 21-2)? Is part of the network wireless? What is the model number of the network hub/switch? Who manufactures the hub/switch? How many devices can be attached? Record your findings here.

_____

_____

Is the hub or switch a standard single speed (10BaseT, for instance) device, or can it handle multiple speeds (10/100/1000 Mbps)? Does it have wireless capabilities? Record your findings here. If this information isn't apparent or printed on the cabinet, ask the instructor or the network administrator.

_____

_____

Step 3 Are you going to have a wireless network or wireless devices in your network? Do you plan on installing a wireless network sometime in the near future? Follow these steps:

a) Go to www.linksys.com/products/ and select wireless; Linksys has an excellent selection of wireless products.

b) Under the Broadband Routers, choose the WRT54G, and finally select Product Data Sheet.

What's the WRT54G? Is it a router, switch, or wireless access point? Explain your answer.

_____

_____

FIGURE 21-2 A LAN hub with multiple cables/devices attached

→ **Try This: Hub, Switch, or Router?**

In the current world of networking, the terms *hub*, *switch*, and *router* are often used interchangeably, but they really are very different devices with very different functions. Conduct an Internet search on the definition of each device and prepare a short presentation contrasting and comparing the devices, how they achieve their functionality, and where or for what purpose it makes sense to use each device. Include how the devices map to the International Organization for Standardization (ISO) Open Systems Interconnect (OSI) model in your presentation.

c) Look at the Wireless Network Adapters section of the Linksys site.

Would you use the WMP54G or WPC54G NIC or both in your network with a WRT54G? Explain your answer.

_____

_____

✔ **Hint**

When researching wireless compatibility issues, it is always a good idea to look at the product data or specification sheets of the devices to see if they'll work together.

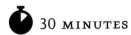 30 MINUTES

Lab Exercise 21.02: Exploring Local Area Network Configuration Options

You've made your recommendation, and you've installed the network. The hardware side of installing a basic LAN is really simple these days, so you managed to get that put together in a flash. Now it's time to configure the PCs that connect to the network.

To prepare for the CompTIA A+ exams, and to build your toolbox of skills as a PC technician, you need to be able to set up, configure, and troubleshoot networks that use Windows 2000 Professional and Windows XP clients. From a network configuration standpoint, Windows 2000 and Windows XP are very similar. This lab uses Windows XP to illustrate network configuration. There are notes about how other versions of Windows handle the same settings. If possible, you should practice the exercises using Windows 2000 Professional as well. The CompTIA A+ exams will test your configuration knowledge for both versions of Windows, including the paths you use to locate configuration settings.

Learning Objectives

In this lab, you'll explore the network configuration options in a Windows environment.

At the end of this lab, you'll be able to

- Configure network access using the networking applets

Lab Materials and Setup

The materials you need for this lab are

- Access to a PC with Windows 2000/XP installed

- Access to the LAN

✔ **Hint**

I don't want to sound like a broken record, but if possible, you should repeat the exercises in both the Windows 2000 and the Windows XP environments. If you only have a single operating system, be sure you understand how to configure networks in the other operating system environments. It's also a good idea to have the drivers for your NICs handy just in case you need to reload any of them. Finally, you'll want to determine the relevant settings (in other words, the proper protocol, the name(s) of the workgroup(s) you'll be using, and so on); write them down, and keep them with you as you go from computer to computer.

Getting Down to Business

For a computer to gain access or share resources on a network, it must have a NIC installed and certain basic information configured. Microsoft provides configuration wizards to set up your network with mostly default parameters and a lot of assumptions. In other words, you tell it the computer name, and it does the rest. Using the Microsoft wizards will allow you to set up a default configuration for quick access (good for at home), but this may not always work for a LAN in a business environment.

Whether you use the wizards or manually configure the system, the following steps must be accurately programmed into the software or you can't take full advantage of the LAN. For the CompTIA A+ exams, you need to know *where to locate* and *how to modify* the network configuration. Specifically, each computer that will be connected to the LAN must have the following:

- A NIC with correct drivers installed

- Client software, as this determines if it is a Microsoft or Novell Netware system

- Protocols (what language[s] you'll use on the network and the settings)

- Services, like File or/and Printer Sharing

- Computer name

- Workgroup name

Step 1   Go to Device Manager, and verify that the correct NIC drivers are installed. Reinstall the driver if necessary.

✔ **Hint**

This lab uses Windows XP and assumes you're running in Classic mode when viewing the Control Panel. You can switch from Category mode to Classic mode by clicking the entry at the top of the left column in the Control Panel. Throughout the exercises, you're told to "go to the Control Panel" or "go to Device Manager." If you have any questions about the path to use for these operations, refer to the path exercise in Lab Exercise 13.01.

In Device Manager, expand the Network Adapters. Right-click your network card and select Properties. Click the Driver tab to see what driver is installed or to update the driver.

Step 2   In this step, you'll verify what network services are installed. In Windows XP, go to Control Panel | Network Connections. Right-click your Local Area Connection (if you have multiple network adapters in a single machine, there may be more than one connection), and select Properties. Select the General tab.

In Windows 2000, go to the Control Panel, double-click Network and Dial-Up Connections and right-click your Local Area Connection.

✔ **Hint**

There's nothing wrong if you don't see any or all of these components listed or if you see more than the ones listed previously. It's just that the network configuration hasn't been completed on your system, or it's in a network supported by more than one server.

You should find the following components listed in a selection window. Your system may have others as well.

- **Client**   Client for Microsoft Networks (default)

- **Protocol**   TCP/IP (default)

- **Service**   File and Print Sharing for Microsoft Networks

What client(s), other than the default, are listed in your system?

_____

What protocol(s), other than the default, are listed?

_____

What services, other than the default, are listed?

_____

Step 3 Now that you've found the network configuration screen, take a look at the various options:

- **Install** The Install button enables you to add network components. Clicking the Install button gives you three choices:

  - **Client** Adds a client to the configuration (must have at least one).

  - **Protocol** Microsoft TCP/IP is the default (must have a protocol to communicate).

  - **Service** File and Print Sharing must be enabled for other computers on the network to access the one on which you're working.

- **Remove/Uninstall** The Remove button enables you to remove network components.

- **Properties** The Properties button displays a variety of dialog boxes based on the network component selected.

✔ **Hint**

Each of the preceding options asks questions about what you want to change. If one or more of your required settings is missing, use this screen to add them. When you make changes, you may be asked to reboot the system.

Step 4 Now that your system is configured for networking, you need to have an identity for it and join a workgroup to be recognized by the network and access network resources.

In Windows XP, go to the Control Panel, double-click System, and select the Computer Name tab. In Windows 2000, the information is on the Network Identification tab. Record your system settings here:

Computer name _____

Workgroup name _____

Step 5 Now that you've confirmed and recorded the networking components, your computer name, and your workgroup, the next step is to practice removing and reinstalling your network adapter.

✖ **Warning**

This step is optional and can cause you grief if you aren't prepared. Ask the instructor if it's okay for you to proceed with this step. If not (or if you think this may harm your configuration), skip this step.

Access Device Manager, and logically remove (uninstall) your network adapter. Yes, this will erase all your network settings. Did you take good notes earlier? Expand the *Network adapters* heading and right-click your specific adapter. Choose Remove or Uninstall.

✖ Warning

If your notes are incomplete, ask the instructor to fill in the settings you're missing.

Reboot your system; the adapter will be detected (if it's Plug and Play) and installed. Access the Network Connections applet, and verify your network configuration using the information you recorded in Steps 1, 2, and 4 previously. If your system doesn't load the drivers for the network card, you'll need the driver CD or disk to complete your settings.

Test your system by accessing the network. Can you browse the network now? Look in My Network Places. _____

 30 MINUTES

Lab Exercise 21.03: Verifying TCP/IP Settings

As you are probably aware, TCP/IP has emerged as the standard transport protocol for network communication. Microsoft operating systems normally use Dynamic Host Configuration Protocol (DHCP), which automatically retrieves and assigns client TCP/IP settings from a DHCP server. This makes it easy to set up a small home or business network of PCs. All systems in the network will communicate with each other using these settings. The problem is that most businesses have their own set of TCP/IP settings (either automatically configured through DHCP or manually configured) that must be used for all new or repaired systems introduced into the network. Your responsibility as a PC technician is to verify the TCP/IP settings.

✔ Cross-Reference

To review additional details of TCP/IP, re-read the "Configuring TCP/IP" section in Chapter 21 of *Mike Meyers' A+ Guide to Managing and Troubleshooting PCs*.

Learning Objectives

In this exercise, you'll access and verify the TCP/IP settings for a given PC system.

At the end of this lab, you'll be able to

- Define Automatic Private IP Addressing (APIPA)

- Use the IPCONFIG command-line utility

- Manually configure the TCP/IP settings on a PC

Lab Materials and Setup

The materials you need for this lab are

- A PC system that's *properly configured* for LAN access using Windows 2000/XP

- A list of TCP/IP settings provided by the instructor

✔ Hint

This exercise is written for Windows XP with notes for Windows 2000. You should be familiar with the process in all operating systems for the CompTIA A+ exams.

Getting Down to Business

Typically, in corporate environments, the network protocol configuration scheme has been defined by the senior systems administrators. Until you had some experience with the configuration, you would not automatically know all of the TCP/IP settings for a network. For instance, even when you're setting up a small network (one that connects to the Internet), you'll need to contact your Internet service provider (ISP) to set up your router's TCP/IP settings. So don't worry if you have no idea what settings to use. The trick is to learn how to get them.

Step 1   TCP/IP requires each system to have two basic settings for accessing a LAN and two additional settings for accessing other LANs or the Internet. You can configure your system to obtain the following settings automatically when you log on (Microsoft's default settings), or you can specify them, depending on the requirements of your network:

- IP address (unique to the PC)

- Subnet mask (identifies network information)

- Gateway (address of the router to the external realm)

- Domain Name Service (DNS)

Step 2   First, you'll locate and verify your current TCP/IP settings. Go to Control Panel and double-click Network Connections. Right-click My Network Places and select Properties; then right-click your local area connection and select Properties. Highlight the Internet Protocol (TCP/IP) entry and select Properties. When the Internet Protocol (TCP/IP) Properties screen appears, one of the options shown in Figure 21-3 will be selected.

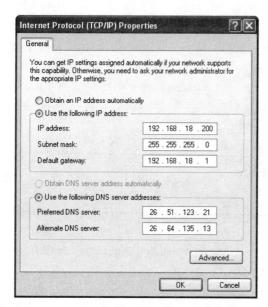

Figure 21-3 Viewing manually configured TCP/IP properties in a Windows XP system

If the settings are manually configured, you will be able to verify them in the TCP/IP Properties dialog box. Write the settings down and verify them with the settings given to you by the instructor.

IP address _____

Subnet mask _____

Gateway _____

Preferred DNS server _____

If the system is configured to use the Microsoft Automatic Private IP Addressing (APIPA) settings or if the network has a DHCP server (ask the instructor), the Obtain an IP Address Automatically and Obtain DNS Server Address Automatically radio buttons will be selected. You will not be able to verify the values of the TCP/IP settings from this window. Close this window by clicking Cancel. To verify the settings, launch a command-line window and at the prompt, type the following command:

```
c:\Documents and Settings\%USERNAME%\>IPCONFIG /ALL
```

This produces a listing similar to Figure 21-4. Use these values to fill in the following settings and then verify them with your instructor.

IP address _____

Subnet mask _____

Gateway _____

Primary DNS server _____

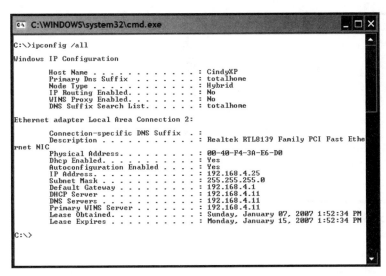

FIGURE 21-4 The Windows IP CONFIG /ALL command results on a system configured to use DHCP

Step 3 You should be familiar with one final configuration: Automatic Private IP Addressing, or APIPA. If Windows 2000/XP is configured to Obtain an IP Address Automatically and no DHCP server is available, Microsoft will automatically configure an address in the 169.254.0.0 network. Follow these steps to explore APIPA:

a) In a classroom lab environment, have the instructor disable the DHCP server if applicable. Alternatively, you can disconnect the DHCP server's UTP cable from the hub or switch.

b) Verify that your TCP/IP Properties settings are set to Obtain an IP Address Automatically and Obtain DNS Server Address Automatically. Close all windows and reboot the system.

c) Launch a command-line window and at the prompt, type the following command:

```
c:\Documents and Settings\%USERNAME%\>IPCONFIG /ALL
```

This produces a listing similar to Figure 21-5. Use these values to fill in the following setting and then verify them with your instructor.

IP address _____

Subnet mask _____

Gateway _____

Primary DNS server _____

d) Exit the command-line window and launch the TCP/IP Properties window. Return all settings to the normal classroom configuration. Click OK to finish, and close all the windows. Reboot the system, and verify that it's working properly and that you have reestablished network communication to its prior state.

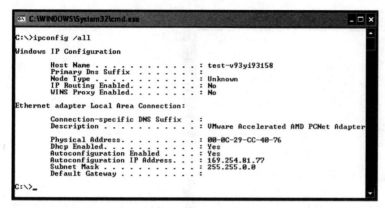

FIGURE 21-5 The Windows 2000/XP IP CONFIG /ALL command results on a system using APIPA

 30 MINUTES

Lab Exercise 21.04: Sharing Resources

With the network set up properly, the next thing to do is decide how you want to share resources. You can share a folder or any other type of resource; floppy drives, optical drives, Zip drives, and hard drives can all be shared.

Learning Objectives

In this lab, you'll set up file sharing for others to access information from their system.

At the end of this lab, you'll be able to

- Enable and configure shared directories and other resources

Lab Materials and Setup

The materials you need for this lab are

- A PC system that's *properly configured* for LAN access using Windows 2000/XP

✔ **Hint**

The exercise is written for Windows XP with notes for how to share using Windows 2000. For the CompTIA A+ exams, you should know how to share resources with any Windows operating system.

Getting Down to Business

Whew! That last exercise was interesting, but the job is only half done. Now you'll find where to set up sharing for a particular resource.

Step 1 Open My Computer, double-click the C: drive, and create a new folder on the C: drive. Name it Shared. Right-click the Shared folder icon to see the folder options, and select Sharing. This will open the Shared Properties dialog box (see Figure 21-6).

✔ **Hint**

If the Sharing tab isn't there, it's probably because you forgot to enable the File and Printer Sharing option in the Networking applet. Go back and enable this option, and then try again.

Step 2 Try sharing and un-sharing the folder. Note that the share name and permissions are grayed out when you select Do Not Share This Folder. Share the folder again, change the share name, and look at the various levels of permissions: Full Control, Change, and Read.

Step 3 When you're done, click OK to close the dialog box.

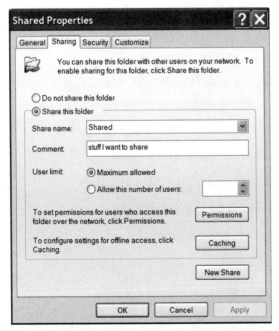

FIGURE 21-6 The Shared Properties dialog box's Sharing tab in Windows XP

✔ **Hint**

If you're running Windows XP Home Edition or Windows XP Professional Edition in a workgroup environment, the Sharing dialog box is much simpler. It contains Share/Do Not Share buttons and a space to provide a share name.

 30 MINUTES

Lab Exercise 21.05: Testing Your LAN Connections

You can use a variety of tools to test and troubleshoot your new network. The textbook covers using these tools in detail. Some of these tools are beneficial to you now as a CompTIA A+ Certified technician and are covered on the CompTIA A+ exams. This lab exercise lets you practice several key network troubleshooting tools on the Windows 2000 and Windows XP operating systems.

Learning Objectives

In this exercise, you'll be introduced to troubleshooting tools for determining proper installation of the network components. These tools are covered in order of importance. Be sure to verify the local settings before trying to access other systems on the same LAN and testing Internet connectivity.

At the end of this lab, you'll be able to

- Use the IPCONFIG command to determine local network settings

- Use the NET CONFIG command to check the local system name and who is logged on as a user

- Use the PING command to test the local TCP/IP software and adapter

- Use the NET VIEW command to check for other computers on the network

- Use the PING command with switches to test connectivity to other computers

- Use the NSLOOKUP command to translate IP addresses and domain names

- Use the TRACERT command to check the path to other computers

Lab Materials and Setup

The materials you need for this lab are

- A PC system that's *properly configured* for network access using Windows 2000/XP

- Access to the Internet

✔ **Hint**

The commands vary slightly, depending on the operating system you use. You should practice with both operating systems if possible. Test the LAN first by accessing another computer on the network using My Network Places and Computers Near Me.

Getting Down to Business

A PC technician should be familiar with several networking tools, both for his or her own good and because they're covered on the CompTIA A+ exams. You'll begin by looking at IPCONFIG.

✔ **Hint**

Since you have already used the IPCONFIG /ALL command, run through the steps again, either on your own system or on a different lab machine. Ask the instructor if any different networks or system configurations are available to explore.

Step 1   You have already examined IPCONFIG in Lab Exercise 21.03. You'll now use the IPCONFIG command again to determine local network settings. As you have already learned, checking the automatic TCP/IP settings given to you by a DHCP server and verifying your manual settings is easy: just open a command-line window, type **IPCONFIG /ALL**, and press ENTER. The details of your local network connection appear on the screen.

Does the display contain the settings that were automatically assigned by the DHCP server or the ones you entered manually? _____

Record your settings here:

IP address _____

Subnet mask _____

Default gateway _____

DNS _____

✔ **Hint**

If you have a system in a peer-to-peer network (no servers) and there are no routers installed, you won't see information about gateways and DNS. What may appear are Windows Internet Naming Service (WINS) settings. More of this would be covered in the coursework for the CompTIA Network+ Certification.

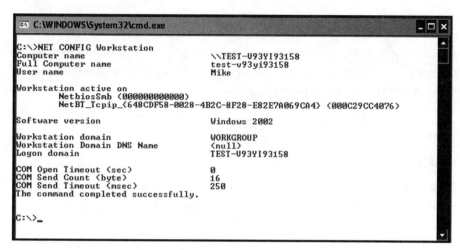

FIGURE 21-7 Using the NET CONFIG WORKSTATION command in Windows XP

Leave the command prompt window open; you'll use it throughout the rest of this exercise.

Step 2   You'll now use the NET CONFIG command to check the local system name and to see who is logged on as a user. To confirm the computer name and discover who is currently logged on, you'll again use the command line.

Type **NET CONFIG WORKSTATION** at the command prompt and press ENTER. You'll see how the identification is set up for your local PC. There's a lot of information listed, but you're only interested in a couple of items (see Figure 21-7).

How are these listed?

Computer name _____

User name _____

Workstation domain (workgroup) _____

Software version _____

Step 3   You'll now use the PING command to test the local TCP/IP software and adapter.

At the command-line prompt, type **PING 127.0.0.1** (including the periods) and press ENTER. This address, known as the *loopback* or *localhost* address, tests the TCP/IP software and the internal part of the local network card. Look at Figure 21-8 to see a successful test. If you don't see the test results, there are serious problems with the software. Reinstall your network drivers, and reconfigure the TCP/IP settings.

Step 4   You'll now use the NET VIEW command to check for other computers on the network.

Can you see anyone else on the network that will prove your network card can transmit and receive data?

At the command-line prompt, type **NET VIEW** and press ENTER. You'll see what other computers are on the network by a listing of their computer names (see Figure 21-9).

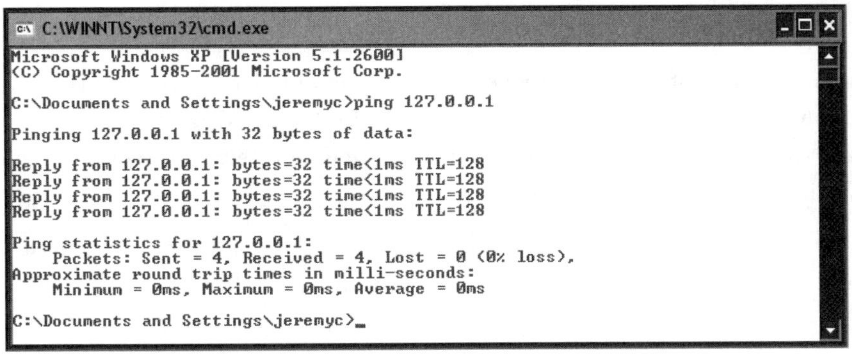

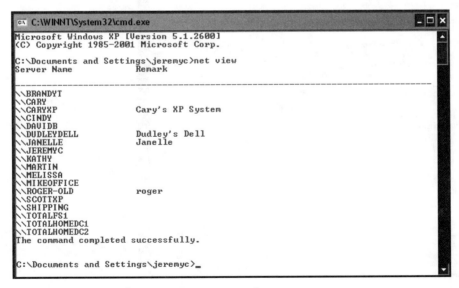

FIGURE 21-8 A successful PING test

Step 5   Now you'll use the PING command to test your ability to connect to other computers on the network.

Okay, so now you can actually get the IP address and names of other systems on the local area network, but can you actually communicate with them?

At the command-line prompt, type **PING *computer name***, where *computer name* is another PC on the network you found in Step 4, and press ENTER. The results will look the same as when you used PING to see your own computer, but with the other computer's IP address (see Figure 21-10). Be sure to put a space between the PING command and the computer name. If you get errors, use the NET VIEW command again to be certain of the computer name's spelling. If the DNS is down, you can adjust by pinging the other computer's IP address instead of its name.

Step 6   You'll now use the NSLOOKUP command to translate an Internet domain name to an IP address or an IP address to an Internet domain name.

FIGURE 21-9 Using the NET VIEW command

→ **Try This: PING Switches**

The humble PING command is one of the most frequently used troubleshooting tools for TCP/IP. As you saw in Step 5, you can actually use PING to test whether DNS is working. If you do not receive a response from the computer using its HOST name, but you do receive a response when using the IP address, this points to a problem with DNS.

PING also has a number of switches that add to the functionality of the command. If you need to explore the switches, type the following at the command prompt:

`c:\>`**PING /?**

This will list all of the available switches and their functions. The following combination is typically used for a connection that seems to intermittently drop packets. You would run the command indefinitely and increase the packet size to overload the connection. Type the following command:

`c:\>`**PING -t -l 65000 computername**

To stop the continuous PING, press CTRL-C to break the program.

This is a good command for finding out the IP addresses of Web sites. Why do I want this, you ask? Well, when you use a URL in your browser, it has to be translated somewhere to an IP address. This slows down your access time. If you know the IP address and type that into the address of your Internet browser, the site will pop up faster. Follow these steps:

a) Type **NSLOOKUP microsoft.com**, and then press ENTER.

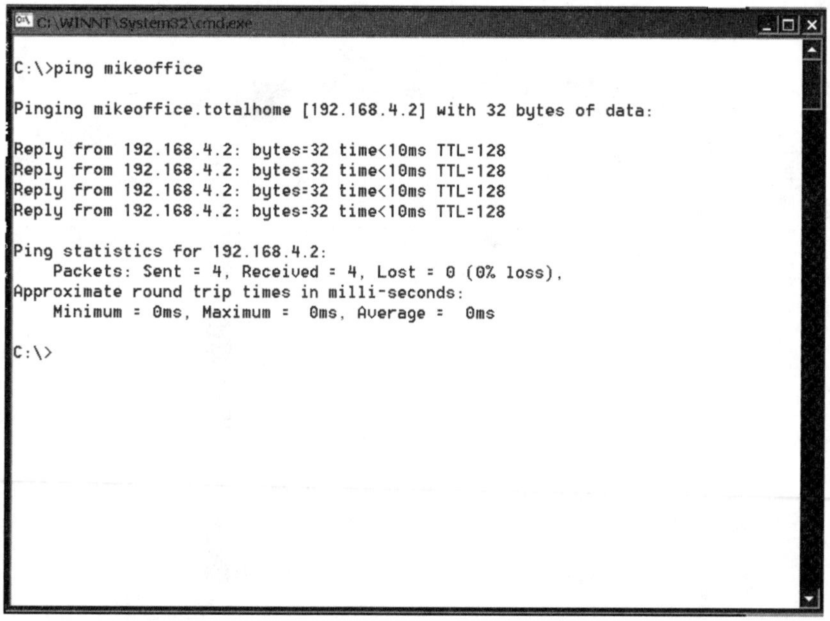

```
C:\WINNT\System32\cmd.exe                                          _ □ ×

C:\>ping mikeoffice

Pinging mikeoffice.totalhome [192.168.4.2] with 32 bytes of data:

Reply from 192.168.4.2: bytes=32 time<10ms TTL=128
Reply from 192.168.4.2: bytes=32 time<10ms TTL=128
Reply from 192.168.4.2: bytes=32 time<10ms TTL=128
Reply from 192.168.4.2: bytes=32 time<10ms TTL=128

Ping statistics for 192.168.4.2:
    Packets: Sent = 4, Received = 4, Lost = 0 (0% loss),
Approximate round trip times in milli-seconds:
    Minimum = 0ms, Maximum = 0ms, Average = 0ms

C:\>
```

FIGURE 21-10 Using PING to view a computer by its name

What's the IP address(s) of http://www.microsoft.com? _____

Try http://www.totalsem.com. What's the IP address(s)? _____

b) Now enter the IP address you got when you did a lookup for http://www.microsoft.com. If you get a different result, it could be that a Web site is being hosted by someone other than the original domain you looked up.

Step 7 You'll now use the TRACERT command to check the path to other computers or Web sites on the Internet.

This command will show you where the bottlenecks are in the Internet. The TRACERT command will list the time it takes to get from your PC to the Web site or other system you're accessing. Follow these steps:

a) Type **TRACERT maxtor.com**, and then press ENTER.

Was it successful? _____

How many hops did it take? _____

What's the IP address of the first hop? _____

b) Use the NSLOOKUP command with the IP address of the first hop to see where your first server is located. For example, type **NSLOOKUP 207.46.130.108**, and then press ENTER.

Go ahead—have fun with this! Part of the learning process with PCs is to dive in and tackle a subject that you're not completely familiar with. As long as you remember to write down any information you want to change before you change it, you can enjoy exploring the amazing world of computers and still have a recovery point.

Lab Analysis Test

1. A user complains that after you installed the new NIC in her system, she can see everyone on the network but can't access the Internet. What did you forget to do? Are there any other configuration problems that could cause this to happen?

2. What command would you use to test the NIC's internal TCP/IP capabilities? What would the "human readable" address be?

3. Theresa's boss bought a wireless network adapter for her laptop. It works great in the office. What does she need for it to work with her PC at home?

4. Describe two ways to access the Network Connections applet in Windows XP.

5. Tanner has replaced his older ISA NIC with a new wireless NIC. The office wireless network is set up and works fine for everyone else. Now he can't see anyone on the network or access the Internet. Where should he start checking and in what order?

Key Term Quiz

Use the following vocabulary terms to complete the following sentences. Not all terms will be used.

Device Manager

hub

Network Connections applet

NET VIEW

NIC

PING

PING -l

PING -t

RJ-45

router

switch

UTP

wireless

1. You use an access point when you network _____ devices.

2. An excellent tool for determining who is currently logged on to the network is the _____ command.

3. A(n) _____ can effectively place a device on its own collision domain, thereby increasing network bandwidth.

4. Twisted-pair network cabling uses a(n) _____ connector.

5. To find out whether a machine can accept a large packet of data, you would use the _____ command.

Chapter 22
The Internet

Lab Exercises

The Internet is a complex system of communication that allows computers, in-business networks, mobile computers, and home PCs to share information worldwide. Today we even have cell phones, personal digital assistants (PDAs), and other personal devices that can connect to the Internet for accessing e-mail, downloading MP3s, and doing other tasks.

Connecting to the Internet requires three pieces in place and functioning: a modem, a wire, and an Internet service provider (ISP). The device referred to as a modem can be of various technologies. The use of 56 kilobits per second (Kbps) dial-up modems and Integrated Services Digital Network (ISDN) modems is rapidly declining due to slow access speeds and high cost. Much more common today are high-speed, or *broadband*, Internet connections, using digital subscriber line (DSL) and cable modem technologies.

The wire used to connect to the Internet can be a phone line (this is in fact what DSL and ISDN services use) or a coaxial cable. Corporate environments typically use dedicated T1 or T3 connections, or something even more zippy. The ISP provides access to the worldwide network that makes up the Internet.

Because nearly everyone wants access to the Internet, implementing and troubleshooting Internet connectivity is a PC technician's bread and butter. The CompTIA A+ Certification exams recognize this and test you on the details of installing and configuring a connection to the Internet. It may be a legacy dial-up analog modem used to connect to an ISP through a phone line, or a broadband cable modem using the local cable company as the provider. This heightened usage brings with it a new task for the PC technician: security! Since most computers are now communicating with the world through the Internet, the exposure to malicious intruders and programs has greatly increased. Two components that go hand-in-hand with the Internet are firewalls and wireless network security. You'll explore the configuration of these two components here. This chapter's labs start by going through the properties of the current wide area network (WAN) connection technologies and then take you through the steps needed to perform the installation and configuration of these technologies. You'll also explore the configuration of the Windows Internet Connection Sharing and Firewall, explore a browser, and configure wireless security.

✔ **Cross-Reference**

Computer security is such an important component of a PC technicians' training that the topic receives its own chapters in both the textbook and the lab manual. Refer to Chapter 23, "Computer Security," in *Mike Meyers' A+ Guide to Managing and Troubleshooting PCs*. Chapter 23 in this manual covers additional lab exercises to build your security awareness.

 30 MINUTES

Lab Exercise 22.01: Identifying Internet Connectivity Properties

A new client has signed up with your firm, requesting that you evaluate their current Internet connectivity and recommend the best upgrade path for their 12-person office (six desktop PCs and two laptops). Your first job is to assess what method they are currently using to connect to the Internet and what methods are available in their location, and to make a recommendation for upgrades if necessary.

Learning Objectives

This lab tests basic assessment skills. Every technician should be able to go into a situation and quickly understand the state of the technology in question—in this case, an Internet connection. Plus, you should feel comfortable telling your clients about any concerns with aging technology and confidently recommend upgrade paths to higher performance technology.

At the end of this lab, you'll be able to

- Verify the Internet connectivity method

- Check the properties of the connection

- Perform an Internet search to learn about the performance of various connectivity methods

Lab Materials and Setup

The materials you need for this lab are

- A working computer running Windows 2000/XP, with some form of Internet connection

- Internet connectivity to perform your research

Getting Down to Business

First, you will visually inspect your computer and its surroundings for the method used to connect to the Internet. Then you will run an Internet utility to determine the speed of your connection and appropriate upgrade paths.

Step 1 Look at the back of your computer. Is there a phone cable (RJ-11) plugged in? This could indicate that this computer is using an analog modem for the Internet connection. Are there any USB or network (RJ-45) cables plugged into the system? Trace the wires. Do they connect to a cable modem or DSL modem? This could be your connectivity method. Is there a network patch cable plugged into the NIC? You may be connecting to the Internet through the corporate LAN. Are you on a laptop with wireless connectivity? You could have access to the Internet through a wireless access point (WAP) connected to a cable or DSL modem.

These are the possibilities a technician is faced with today, so the more you can explore the various methods of connectivity, the better your familiarity when you walk into the client's home or office and attempt to configure or repair their Internet connection. Examine the physical components that constitute the method your system uses to connect to the Internet and then record the details of the hardware/connectivity type here. Figure 22-1 depicts a typical PC using a wired LAN patch cable to connect to a broadband cable modem.

Step 2 Once you have determined the connectivity method, boot your system and launch your Internet browser (I'm currently using Internet Explorer 7). Now surf over to the c|net Web site at www.cnet.com. This is an excellent tech Web site with many tools, applications, and forums for PC and network

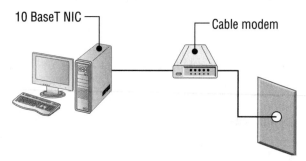

FIGURE 22-1 A PC and cable modem Internet connection

information. Click the Reviews tab and look for the Internet Access hyperlink. Click the link and scroll down to the Bandwidth Meter speed test. Click the link and follow the onscreen directions.

What is the speed of your connection?

Step 3   Using the table provided by the c|net Bandwidth Meter, fill in the approximate data transfer speeds of the various Internet connection types:

Dial-up 56 Kbps Modem _____

DSL _____

Cable _____

T1 _____

T3 _____

Step 4   Based on the results of the analysis of your client's Internet connection method and perform-ance, are there any recommendations you would make to improve the performance of the connection?

 30 MINUTES

Lab Exercise 22.02: Installing and Configuring an Internet Connection

You determine that the client is currently using dial-up networking through analog modems to access the Internet. Though this is probably acceptable for occasionally connecting to the Internet, these folks have a business to run! You decide to recommend either high-speed DSL or cable. You explain to the client that unlike the analog modem they're currently using, the other methods use a standard NIC and an external device to interface between the DSL or cable lines. Ironically, this device is usually referred to as a DSL or cable *modem*. You will evaluate the current PCs and select one that will act as the interface to the Internet. If required, you'll add a PCI network interface card, connect the DSL or cable interface, and then configure the interface in Windows.

Learning Objectives

Installing DSL or cable high-speed Internet access requires four steps. First, you should verify whether your system is already equipped with a NIC, either integrated into the motherboard or as a PCI card, and if not, physically install such a device. Second, verify that this device is operating properly and has the latest drivers installed. Third, connect the DSL transceiver or the cable modem, and finally, config-ure the proper settings required by the ISP.

At the end of this lab, you'll be able to

- Install a network interface card (if not already present)

- Verify proper operation, and install or update the drivers

- Install the DSL transceiver or cable modem

- Configure the connection in Windows

✔ **Cross-Reference**

Refer to the "DSL" and "Cable" sections in Chapter 22 and the "Installing Expansion Cards" section in Chapter 6 of *Mike Meyers' A+ Guide to Managing and Troubleshooting PCs* for help installing and configuring NICs. It's a good idea to have the textbook handy while you progress through this lab.

Lab Materials and Setup

The materials you need for this lab are

- A PC system with or without a NIC

- A PCI NIC

- Access to the proper driver software (either built-in Windows drivers or a separate CD)

- A copy of the Windows CD (may be needed, depending on the system)

Getting Down to Business

Break out your trusty screwdriver and anti-static wrist strap. It's time to install a NIC!

✔ **Hint**

You can omit Steps 1 – 3 if the system is already equipped with a network interface card, as most systems are today. The steps are included here for completeness. You will be asked to install a second NIC in Lab Exercise 22.04, "Windows Internet Connection Sharing (ICS)," so if you have that second NIC handy, go ahead and install it now.

Step 1   Make sure the PC is off and unplugged. Take proper ESD precautions, and remove the cover of the PC. Choose any free PCI slot to install the NIC. Remove the back plate if one exists.

Step 2   Plug the NIC into the PCI slot (see Figure 22-2). Physically inserting the NIC into the PC is the easiest part of the task. Take care to avoid touching the pins or any of the chips on the NIC. Once the card is inserted, secure it by putting the proper screw through the metal tab of the card and screwing it to the case. Put the cover back on and restart your computer.

FIGURE 22-2 Inserting a PCI NIC

Step 3 Now that you have physically installed the NIC, the next step will depend on your OS. When you restart your computer, if you're running Windows 2000, the operating system will recognize that you've added new hardware and launch the Found New Hardware Wizard. Windows XP goes one step better—when you install a PnP device, the drivers are most likely already part of the operating system, so they'll be installed automatically. This all occurs with no user intervention. The operating system reports success installing the new device with a small balloon from the system tray.

✔ **Hint**

Every Windows operating system has a good selection of network interface drivers built in at the time of release, but your driver may not be one of them. For example, if the NIC you're installing was manufactured after the release of software you're using, the drivers may not be part of the operating system and will need to be installed or updated.

FIGURE 22-3 Using the Found New Hardware Wizard

The following is the Found New Hardware Wizard driver installation process in Windows 2000:

a) As Windows boots, it displays the Found New Hardware Wizard screen (see Figure 22-3).

b) Click Next to continue. Select the option that directs Windows to search for a suitable driver for the new device (see Figure 22-4). If the driver is on a floppy disk or CD, select that as the search location, insert the media for the driver before continuing, and then click Next.

✔ **Hint**

A popular trick is to copy the drivers from the CD onto the PC's hard drive and then install them from there. That way, if you ever need the drivers again, you won't need to rummage around for the driver CD. You need to know exactly where you store the drivers, though, because you'll be asked to locate them during the install process. You could create a Drivers folder at the root of the C: drive to serve as a central repository for drivers. Remember, drivers are constantly being updated by manufacturers. Check the manufacturer's Web site before using the driver CD.

---

c) The wizard will search the drivers built into Windows and then the location you specified for the file(s) and will (you hope) report that it found the appropriate driver. Click Next. If prompted, you may also need to insert your Windows CD. When the wizard is finished, it'll prompt you a final time. Click the Finish button, and reboot your system. The new NIC and drivers are now properly installed.

If Windows doesn't detect the driver right away, you'll need to do a little extra work. Network interface manufacturers bundle drivers for multiple operating systems on the driver CD, so you often need to

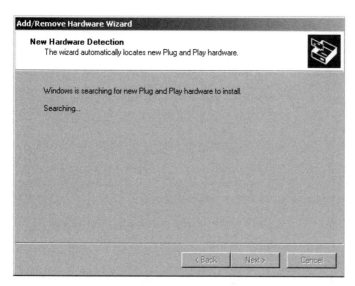

Figure 22-4 Completing installation by locating a suitable device driver

navigate to the appropriate folder for your operating system before Windows will find the driver. In other words, look for a Win2k folder when installing modem drivers on a Windows 2000 machine. Other manufacturers package the driver into an installation routine. Check the CD for a SETUP.EXE file, and run it if you find it.

Step 4 Now that the drivers are installed, you should confirm the NIC properties and verify what drivers are installed. The following steps were completed in Windows XP, but they are similar in Windows 2000:

c) In Classic view, select Start | Settings | Control Panel and double-click Network Connections.

b) Right-click the Local Area Connection (if this is the second network interface, choose Local Area Connection 2) and click Properties. In the Local Area Connection Properties dialog box, click the Configure button next to the network interface adapter (on my systems it is a SiS 900-Based PCI Fast Ethernet Adapter).

c) In the network interface adapter Properties dialog box, click the Driver tab (see Figure 22-5).

Record all the information provided about the driver you installed.

Step 5 Now examine the physical device that has been provided by your ISP to connect the computer to the Internet. If the device is a DSL transceiver, it will typically have an RJ-45 Ethernet connection to connect to the NIC of the computer, an RJ-11 connector to connect to the telephone wall jack, and some sort of power adapter. If the device is a cable modem, it will typically have an RJ-45 Ethernet connection to connect to the NIC of the computer, an F-connector to attach to the cable, and some sort of power adapter (refer to Figure 22-1). Both interfaces may provide a USB connection, but for the purposes of the lab exercise, this will not be used.

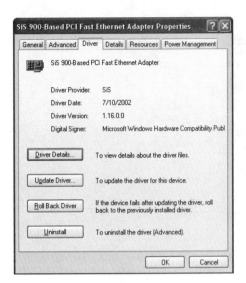

FIGURE 22-5 Network interface adapter driver properties

✔ **Hint**

If you are in a classroom lab environment, you may not have access to the actual DSL transceiver or cable modem. Follow the instructor's directions to connect the computer to the Internet. You should conduct an Internet search or make a trip to the local technology store to explore the specifications of common DSL and cable interfaces. For the most part, going through the full configuration of the actual connection is beyond the scope of this book, but you should at least know where to go to follow instructions from your ISP; that's the purpose of these last steps.

Connect the interface device following the instructions provided with the device or by your ISP. The layout and configuration of the device may differ somewhat from device to device, but you should be able to confirm that the device is working properly by observing the various indicator lights on the device.

Step 6   To finish this installation and gain high-speed access to the Internet, you will most likely have to follow specific directions from your Internet service provider to configure Windows to communicate through the DSL or cable device. Windows also provides a generic wizard to configure this communication. The following steps walk you through this generic configuration:

 a) Select Start | Settings | Network Connections and click on Create a New Connection in the Network Tasks pane to launch the New Connections Wizard.

 b) To continue, click Next and select *Connect to the Internet.* Click Next.

 c) Choose *Set up my connection manually* and Click Next.

 d) Choose *Connect using a broadband connection that is always on* and click Next.

e) In the Completing the New Connection Wizard window, click on *Learn more about broadband connections*. Record some of the pertinent information related to your installation.

f) Click the Finish button.

If you have followed the steps (and actually have installed a DSL or cable interface), you should now have high-speed access to the Internet.

 30 MINUTES

Lab Exercise 22.03: Windows Firewall

Your client is very pleased with how the rollout of the office's Internet connection upgrade is progressing. They have been surfing around a little, and are impressed with the speed at which the Web sites are loading. You explain that you must now configure a firewall to protect them from outside intrusion through the high-speed connection. Microsoft's Windows XP Service Pack 2 offers a very competent built-in firewall. In this lab you will enable Windows Firewall and explore some of the services (ports) that you can allow or block.

Learning Objectives

Completing the following steps, you will explore the Windows Firewall and associated TCP and UDP service ports.

At the end of this lab, you'll be able to

• Enable the Windows Firewall

• Identify various protocols and associated service ports

✔ **Cross-Reference**

To further explore the Windows Firewall, refer to "The Windows XP Internet Connection Firewall" in Chapter 22 of *Mike Meyers' A+ Guide to Managing and Troubleshooting PCs*.

Lab Materials and Setup

The materials you need for this lab are

• A working computer running Windows XP

• Optionally, a machine actually connected to the Internet

Getting Down to Business

Enabling the firewall is as simple as a few clicks of the mouse and verifying that you can communicate with the trusted sites that you prefer. Windows Firewall is practically self-configuring, but if you want to allow access to Web servers or e-mail servers in your organization, you will have to open some TCP ports. The CompTIA A+ Certification exams will expect you to know some of these "well-known-ports," so you'll explore them in the Windows Firewall.

✔ **Hint**

If you are configuring a single machine for Internet access, you will want to implement the Windows Firewall on that machine to protect it from malicious intrusion. However, if you are configuring machines as part of a local area network, and using a proxy server or Internet Connection Sharing (as you will in the next lab exercise), you will only want to configure a firewall on the machine that connects directly to the Internet. Assume the computer in this lab is the machine connected to the Internet.

Step 1 Open the Local Area Connection Properties dialog box by clicking Start | Settings | Network Connections. Right-click the Local Area Connections icon of the external connection (the one connected to the Internet), then select Properties from the drop-down menu. Click the Advanced tab, then click the Settings button in the Windows Firewall area to open the Windows Firewall dialog box (see Figure 22-6).

Step 2 Select On to protect the PC from unwanted access through the Internet connection.

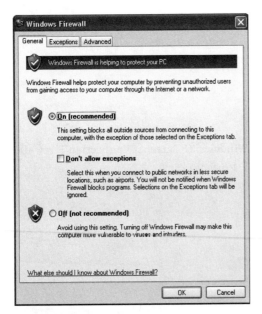

FIGURE 22-6 The Windows Firewall properties screen

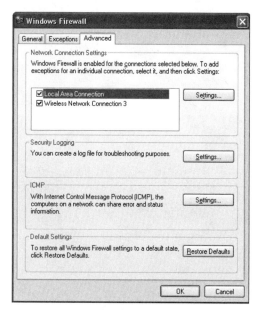

FIGURE 22-7 The Windows Firewall
Advanced properties screen

Step 3 Now select the Advanced tab of the Windows Firewall dialog box and select the Settings button
for the Network Connection Settings (see Figure 22-7).

Step 4 This opens the Advanced Settings dialog box, where you can allow various services to pass through
the Internet connection and access dedicated servers on your internal network. For instance, if you have
an FTP server that you have technicians update from the field, you will want to enable external communication by allowing TCP service port 21 to pass through the firewall (see Figure 22-8).

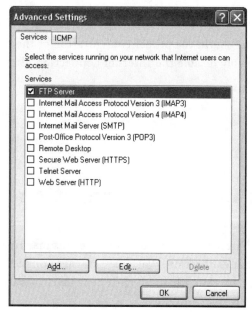

FIGURE 22-8 Allowing FTP traffic to pass
through the firewall

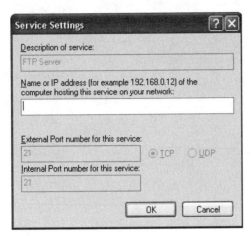

FIGURE 22-9 Service Settings showing
the TCP port number for the FTP server

Using the Edit button, identify the service ports for the following protocols (Figure 22-9 shows the
port information I used to complete the first answer for you).

1. File Transfer Protocol (FTP Server) _____**TCP Port 21**_____

2. Internet Mail Access Protocol Version 4 (IMAP4) _____

3. Simple Mail Transfer Protocol (SMTP) _____

4. Post-Office Protocol Version 3 (POP3) _____

5. Secure Socket Layer (HTTPS) _____

6. Hypertext Transfer Protocol (HTTP) _____

Step 5   To complete this lab, check with your instructor to obtain the proper configuration of the firewall to allow the completion of further labs. You will probably disable the Internet Connection Firewall
for normal classroom use.

 30 MINUTES

Lab Exercise 22.04: Windows Internet Connection Sharing (ICS)

Now that the main PC is secure from external threats and attacks, its time to configure this machine so
that all of the PCs can take advantage of the secure Internet connection. Welcome Internet Connection
Sharing (ICS)! With ICS, you will be able to set up a small LAN that allows all the client machines to
access the Internet through the ICS host computer (this PC).

Learning Objectives

In this lab, you will implement the steps to use ICS. It will take some extra hardware to actually test the configuration, but you can still learn the basic concepts through the configuration exercise.

At the end of this lab, you'll be able to

- Configure Internet Connection Sharing (ICS)

✔ Cross-Reference

To further explore ICS, refer to "Internet Connection Sharing" in Chapter 22 of *Mike Meyers' A+ Guide to Managing and Troubleshooting PCs*.

Lab Materials and Setup

The materials you need for this lab are

- A working computer running Windows 2000/XP
- An additional network interface card for the ICS host computer
- A network hub or switch
- A second computer running Windows 2000/XP to be configured as the client
- Optionally, a machine actually connected to the Internet

Getting Down to Business

ICS allows a small workgroup of computers to connect to the Internet through one of the workgroup computers acting as an ICS host computer. There are a few items that need to be configured on both the ICS host computer and the clients. The host will have two communication devices installed (in this case, two NICs). The network will need a hub or a switch to allow multiple computers to communicate. Finally, the client machines will have to be configured to obtain their TCP/IP settings automatically.

Step 1 To use ICS, you will need two communication devices installed in the computer: either a modem connected to the Internet and a NIC connected to the internal network, or a NIC connected to a broadband interface and a NIC connected to the internal network. (If you need to install a second NIC to facilitate this lab exercise, perform Lab Exercise 22.02, Steps 1 – 3.)

Step 2 Open the Network Connections applet and select the internal Local Area Connection. Select Properties, then click the Advanced tab (see Figure 22-10).

Step 3 Select the checkbox for Internet Connection Sharing called *Allow other network users to connect through this computer's Internet connection.*

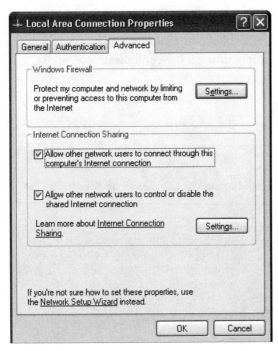

FIGURE 22-10 The Advanced tab of the Local Area Connection
Properties dialog box showing Internet Connection Sharing

Step 4   Click the Settings button to view additional services that Internet users can access (if they are not blocked by the firewall).

Step 5   Click OK. A hand icon (representing sharing) should appear under the Local Area Connection that has just been configured with ICS (see Figure 22-11).

Step 6   Alternatively, if you have a second computer and a hub, you can test the ICS feature by following these steps:

  a) Verify that the ICS host computer is capable of communicating with the Internet. Connect the external Local Area Connection NIC to the broadband interface (DSL or cable).

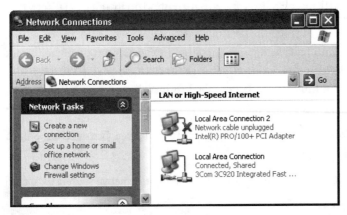

FIGURE 22-11 A shared Local Area Connection

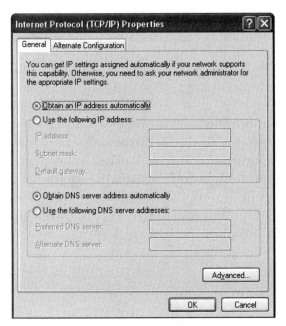

FIGURE 22-12 Internet Protocol (TCP/IP) Properties

b) Power up the hub or switch, and connect the internal interface from the ICS host computer to the hub.

c) Connect the network interface card of the client PC to the hub or switch.

d) Open the Network Connections applet of the client PC, select the Local Area Connection, and open the Properties. Highlight the Internet Protocol (TCP/IP) Properties and verify that *Obtain an IP address automatically* and *Obtain DNS server address automatically* are selected (see Figure 22-12).

Launch Internet Explorer on the client machine; verify that the connection is set up to use the LAN connection. Type **www.comptia.org** in the address line and press ENTER. If there are any problems, shut down both machines and check all of the connections. Boot the ICS host computer first (allow all of the services to start), then boot the client machine.

 20 MINUTES

Lab Exercise 22.05: Upgrading and Tweaking Internet Explorer

Now that you have improved and protected your client's Internet connectivity, you will want to make sure that the method they use to interact with the Internet is the most current. Microsoft's Internet Explorer (IE) is probably the most popular Internet browser in use today (though Mozilla's Firefox is gaining wider popularity). The following steps will help you upgrade your client to the latest version of IE (version 7 as of this writing) and introduce you to some of the configuration areas that you should be aware of.

Learning Objectives

When it comes to applications—and this includes Internet Explorer—the computer technician is looked to as the Master or Mistress of All Things Computer. For this reason, a knowledge and awareness of applications, in addition to learning and practicing your craft as an IT technician, will enhance your reputation as an expert. In this lab, you'll briefly explore the upkeep of a networking application.

At the end of this lab, you'll be able to

- Evaluate and upgrade the IE application
- Fine-tune IE settings

Lab Materials and Setup

The materials you need for this lab are

- A working computer running Windows XP SP2
- Internet access, preferably high-speed to facilitate downloads

Getting Down to Business

Internet Explorer is currently the most popular browser application. You and your client may launch Internet search engines such as Google or Yahoo!, visit manufacturers' Web sites to research, and in some cases, purchase new hardware and software. You'll want to make sure that IE is up to date and working efficiently to make your client's browsing more pleasant.

> ✖ **Warning**
>
> The following lab steps have you update Internet Explorer and change some of the configuration settings. A prerequisite is to upgrade Windows XP to Service Pack 2. If you are performing these labs on a personal machine, evaluate the requirements for IE7 before upgrading. If you are in an instructor-led class, or performing these operations on machines in your organization, verify you have permission to perform the upgrades.

Step 1 Fire up your current browser and navigate to the Microsoft Windows Internet Explorer page (http://www.microsoft.com/windows/ie/default.mspx as of this writing). Examine the new features and requirements (click on About Internet Explorer 7). Will IE7 work with all versions of Windows?

Verify that your system and OS meet the requirements, and then click and download Internet Explorer 7.

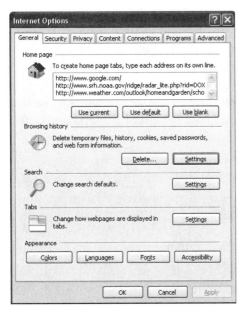

FIGURE 22-13 The General tab of the Internet
Options dialog box in Internet Explorer 7

Step 2   Open the Internet Options dialog box and examine the General tab (see Figure 22-13).

Explore some of the features of the Home Page (you may now have multiple pages available with the click of a tab), Browsing History, and Tabs sections.

Step 3   Click on the Content tab and click on the Settings button under the AutoComplete section. Notice the items that can be selected to AutoComplete. I like to disable the User Names and Passwords on forms.

Step 4   Click on the Advanced tab and explore the many settings that can be configured to modify how the browser deals with components and content. Navigate down to the Security heading and locate *Empty Temporary Internet Files Folder when browser is closed*. I like to enable this setting.

Explore some of the other tabs available in Internet Options and experiment with the different items you can configure. Microsoft has done a good job of setting the browser up with default settings that will work in most installations, but as the expert, you will want to be familiar with customizing the browser.

30 MINUTES

Lab Exercise 22.06: Configuring Wireless Security

As mentioned in the first lab exercise, your client has two laptop computers. They would like to keep the laptops as mobile as possible, so they have asked you to install a wireless access point (WAP) in the office. The actual installation is almost simple enough that the office personnel could handle it; however, you know how vulnerable wireless networks are to unauthorized access. You agree to install the WAP, but you insist on securing the network to protect the business.

Learning Objectives

This lab exercise will use a Linksys wireless router to walk you through the steps to properly secure a wireless network. All of the principles developed here can be applied to most of the wireless routers of the other manufactures.

At the end of this lab, you'll be able to

- Configure router administration security

- Secure wireless access

- Protect data traveling over wireless networks using encryption

✔ Cross-Reference

To further explore wireless networking technology, visit the following Web sites:

www.3com.com   www.belkin.com

www.intellinet-network.com   www.linksys.com

www.netgear.com

Lab Materials and Setup

The materials you need for this lab are

- A working computer running Windows 2000 or XP

- A wireless router or wireless access point

Getting Down to Business

You're going to spend the next 30 minutes configuring wireless security that will protect the client and its employees, the company's confidential data, and the company itself. That will be 30 minutes well spent!

✔ Hint

The steps in this lab are written for a router that is in the factory default condition. If the router has been in use, or is part of the lab equipment in a classroom environment, ensure that the default settings are restored. Most wireless routers/WAPs have a reset button to clear all configuration information and return them to factory default settings.

Step 1   Connect to the wireless router using a network patch cable (RJ-45 connectors, CAT 5e UTP). Power up the router and boot the PC into Windows.

Step 2   Launch Internet Explorer (or browser of your choice) and enter the IP address of the router's administration page. (Linksys uses 192.168.1.1; Intellinet uses 192.168.2.1.) Consult the documentation that came with the router for your specific model's IP address.

Step 3   Enter the default administrator name and password; many devices use **admin** for both the user-name and password (for Linksys devices, leave the username blank). This will bring you to the main administration page (the Welcome screen appears in Linksys). You will now configure the three important areas of administration, access, and encryption.

Step 4   Begin with securing the administration of the router by configuring the following components:

a) Change the name of the router (this is accomplished on the Welcome screen of the Linksys router).

b) Change the administrative password; the administrative username is usually permanently set (check the device's documentation if necessary).

c) If applicable, disable remote administration. You will not be able to configure the wireless router while wireless, but nobody else will be able to either!

Step 5   Now you'll secure access, allowing only the users you want to gain access to the wireless net-work. Normally, the first two steps are sufficient; the third step requires some additional information during configuration.

a) Change the Service Set Identifier (SSID) of the router; this is the name of your wireless local area network. Many times this is left to the default, allowing access to anyone who is familiar with wireless networking practices.

b) Disable SSID broadcast. Your client will have to configure the laptops or share the SSID with the employees, but passersby will not have free Internet access.

c) Allow access only to PCs with specific MAC addresses. These can be manually entered for the machines you are allowing, or you may choose them from a list of machines currently allowed access.

Step 6   Finally, you will secure you client's data with encryption. There are three levels of encryption: Wired Equivalent Privacy (WEP) and two types of Wi-Fi Protected Access (WPA and WPA2).

WEP is the least secure of the three types of data encryption, but should be used if WPA or WPA2 is not supported. WPA is better and will provide a higher level of security than WEP, but the most secure is WPA2.

WPA2 is fairly new, but older routers are receiving firmware upgrades to enable them to take advantage of the highest data encryption. WPA2 uses a pre-shared key (PSK) methodology and allows complex passkeys of letters, numbers, and special characters to secure the data. It is recommended that passkeys be much longer than the traditional 6 to 8 characters recommended for user passwords.

Though not directly related to wireless security, most wireless routers come with robust, built-in firewalls. The wireless router firewall will protect your client's network and systems from malicious attempts to procure their data.

Using security in the administration of a wireless router, access to the wireless network, and encryption of the data being transmitted through the air will at least deter all but the most aggressive threats and attacks. Stay alert for any change in activity on your systems.

Lab Analysis Test

1. Tanner wants to configure his wireless network so that if Andrew just happens by with a laptop and a wireless card, he will not be able to gain access to the network without Tanner's approval. What component(s) does Tanner need to configure?

2. Brandon is using his school's computer to do some research for a term paper. He attempts to surf to a Web site he has found on Google, only to receive an *Access Denied* message from the browser. What could cause this to happen?

3. Andrew has configured his four-computer network to use Internet Connection Sharing. He has double-checked the ICS host computer, and it can access the Internet. All of the physical connections between the computers and the switch seem to be in good shape. Yet, he still cannot access the Internet from a client machine. What might he have missed?

4. Mary has stated that when she used the c|net bandwidth meter, she achieved Internet transfer speeds around 7.5 Mbps. What type of Internet access do you think Mary has?

5. Cindy is installing a high-speed connection to the Internet. What are the four components she will need to verify and have on hand?

Key Term Quiz

Use the following vocabulary terms to complete the following sentences. Not all terms will be used.

analog

dial-up

digital

drivers

HTTP

ICS

ISP

PnP

POP3

RJ-11

RJ-45

SSID

transceiver

Windows Firewall

1. When connecting to the Internet using a high-speed digital subscriber line, the DSL _____ is often referred to as a *DSL modem*.

2. The protocol that is synonymous with the World Wide Web is _____.

3. If the NIC isn't detected by _____, run the Add New Hardware Wizard.

4. Every wireless network has a network name that all of the machines accessing it must configure. This network name is known as a(n) _____.

5. The slowest means of accessing the Internet still in use today is _____.

Chapter 23
Computer Security

Lab Exercises

Computer security is paramount to protecting your client/company's business, finances, and in some cases, even life! In the following exercises, you will create a secure environment by configuring a Windows XP system properly with users, groups, logon methods, password policies, and complexity rules. Finally, you will clean a client's computer that has come to you with various malicious programs installed. You will do this by installing and running Lavasoft's Ad-Aware, PepiMK's Spybot Search & Destroy, and ALWIL's Avast! Antivirus software.

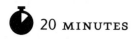 20 MINUTES

Lab Exercise 23.01: Users, Logon, and Simple File Sharing

User accounts are a powerful and necessary function used by Windows to provide security. While organizations with large networks usually take advantage of user accounts, stand-alone systems often fail to take advantage of them. In this exercise you will configure user accounts for a stand-alone Windows XP Professional system.

By default, Windows XP uses simple file sharing unless you are on a Windows XP system configured as a member of a Windows domain, or unless you explicitly turn off simple file sharing. Windows XP also provides two very different logon methods: the classic logon prompt and the Welcome screen. This lab will show both methods and help you determine when to use each method.

Learning Objectives

At the end of this lab, you'll be able to

- Create, modify, and delete local user accounts with Windows XP Professional

- Disable and enable simple file sharing in Windows XP Professional

- Modify logon and logoff options with Windows XP Professional

Lab Materials and Setup

The materials you need for this lab are

- A Windows XP Professional PC with the C: drive formatted as NTFS. Configure the system as a member of the TEST workgroup with simple file sharing and Welcome Screen logon disabled.

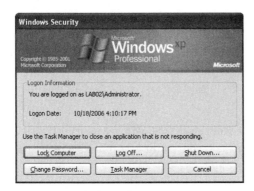

FIGURE 23-1 Task Manager showing administrator logged on

- Access to the local administrator password

Getting Down to Business

Step 1 Timmy and Fred are sharing a Windows XP system. They want to configure the system so that each user's personal information is hidden from the other, yet they also want to share some folders. Begin by logging on to the computer using the local administrator account. Use Task Manager to confirm you are logged on as the local administrator as shown in Figure 23-1.

Step 2 Go into the Control Panel and open the Users Account applet. Create a new user called Fred and make Fred a limited user. Create a second account called Timmy and also make this account a limited user. After you create the accounts, give each account a password using the Change an Account option. Make sure to remember the passwords for these accounts!

Step 3 Log off the system and log on with the Timmy account. Create a folder on the Desktop called Timmy. Right-click this folder and select Sharing and Security to see a dialog box similar to Figure 23-2.

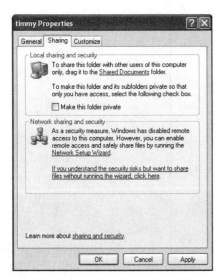

FIGURE 23-2 Folder Properties

Note that the dialog box tells you the only way to share the Timmy folder is to place it in the Shared Documents folder. Open the Shared Documents folder by clicking the Shared Documents link in the dialog box (refer to Figure 23-2), and drag the Timmy folder into the Shared Documents folder.

✖ Warning

Ignore the *Make this folder private* check box for this lab. If you select this, you are encrypting the folder. If you encrypt the folder, no one—not even the local administrator—will be able to access this folder or anything in it. Encryption is covered in Lab Exercise 23.03.

Step 3   Log off Windows and then log on with the Fred account. Open My Computer to see the Shared Documents and Fred's Documents as shown in Figure 23-3. Open the Timmy folder in the Shared Documents. Can the Fred account create a folder called Fred inside the Timmy folder?

Step 4   Still using the Fred account, close all open windows and reopen My Computer. This time open Local Disk (C:), and then the Documents and Settings folder. You should now see the Timmy folder as well as the Fred, All Users, and Administrator folders. Which of these folders can the Fred account open? What error does Windows display on some folders when the Fred account tries to open the folder? Why can't the Fred account open all of them?

Step 5   Log off and log back on with the Administrator account. Once again get to the C:\Documents and Settings folder. Which of these folders can the Administrator account open? After answering this question delete all the folders created for this lab.

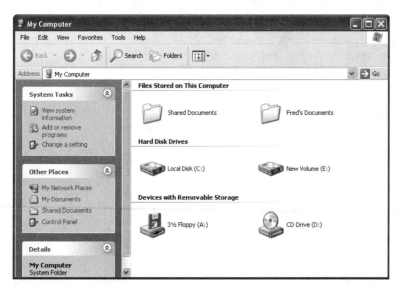

FIGURE 23-3 My Computer

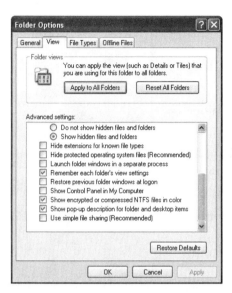

FIGURE 23-4 Turning off Simple File Sharing

Step 6 While still logged on as Administrator, open My Computer and select Tools | Folder Options. Click the View tab and scroll down until you see the Use Simple File Sharing check box (see Figure 23-4). Clear this box to turn off simple file sharing.

Step 7 Up to this point you've been using the classic Windows logon prompt, so let's now change this. While still logged on as Administrator, go to User Accounts in the Control Panel, select *Change the way users log on and off*, and then select the Use the Welcome Screen check box as shown in Figure 23-5.

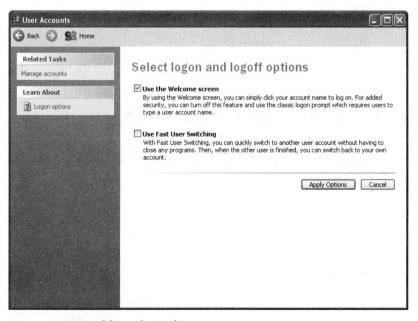

FIGURE 23-5 Enabling the Welcome screen

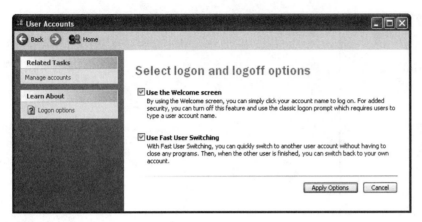

FIGURE 23-6 Fast User Switching

Step 8   Practice logging on and off your Timmy, Fred, and Administrator accounts. Compare the Welcome screen to the classic logon screen—why would Microsoft provide two totally different ways for you to log on to a system? Write down your answer, comparing the features of both logon methods. Here's a hint that will help with a part of your answer: you cannot use the Welcome screen on a system that is a member of a domain—why would Microsoft create this limitation?

Step 9   Log on as Administrator. Once again go to User Accounts in the Control Panel and select *Change the way users log on and off*. This time select the Use Fast User Switching check box as shown in Figure 23-6.

Fast User Switching becomes obvious once you try logging off. Instead of returning to the Welcome screen, what options do you see? What are the benefits of Fast User Switching? Come up with a work environment where Fast User Switching would be beneficial.

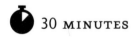 30 MINUTES

Lab Exercise 23.02: Standard File Sharing

Now that you understand simple file sharing, it's time to increase the complexity by un-simplifying file sharing! In this lab, you'll see the true firepower of NTFS as you use standard file sharing on a stand-alone system.

Learning Objectives

At the end of this lab, you'll be able to

- Recognize the standard NTFS permissions

- Configure NTFS permissions for a shared folder on a stand-alone system

- Recognize and configure NTFS permission inheritance

Lab Materials and Setup

The materials you need for this lab are

- The system you used in the previous lab

- Access to the local administrator password

Getting Down to Business

Step 1   Log on as Administrator and verify that simple file sharing is disabled, and then use My Computer to open the Local Disk (C:) folder. Right-click this folder and select Properties to bring up the Local Disk (C:) folder's properties. Click the Security tab and you should see something very similar to Figure 23-7.

Now that you're no longer using simple file sharing, you can control access to any folder on your computer—assuming you have the right to control access! Given that you are logged on as Administrator, you have complete control.

Step 2   Note the "two head" icons on the top of the Security Dialog box. These are groups. Groups are very handy when you want to give a number of users very specific NTFS permissions for one or more folders. Close the Security dialog box, navigate to Computer Management, and select Local Users and Groups. Click the Groups folder to see something like Figure 23-8. These are all of the built-in groups for your system.

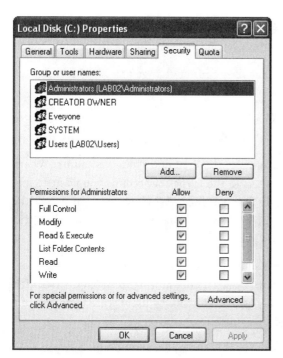

FIGURE 23-7 The Security tab under
Local Disk (C:) Properties

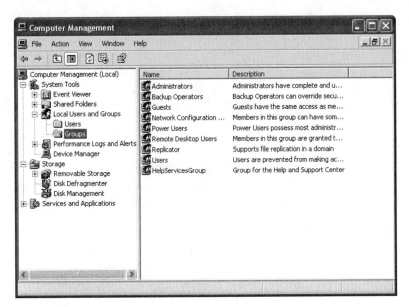

Figure 23-8 Groups

The three most important built-in groups are Administrators, Power Users, and Users. Each of these groups has a very complex set of things they can and cannot do, but let's start by looking at what they can do when it comes to file sharing:

- **Administrators** Have complete control of all NTFS permissions. Any user who is a member of this group has all the same power as the Administrator account—use sparingly!

- **Power Users** Can create users and groups, but they cannot change any NTFS settings unless they have the right to do so.

- **Users** Can only change NTFS permissions on a folder if they have been given the right to do so. Anyone with a user account on the system is a member of this group.

You used the User Accounts Control Panel applet to make the Fred and Timmy accounts. When you created those user accounts, you were given two choices as to the "type" of account you want to make. When you set the type of account, what were you really doing as far as Windows was concerned? Using the Local Users and Groups tool in Computer Management, answer this question: "What group is a 'limited' account type assigned to?"

Step 3 Still using the Local Users and Groups tool in Computer Management, make the Fred and Timmy user accounts members of the Power Users group. Here's a clue how to do it: Right-click either the Power Users icon or right-click each user—both ways work! How many users were members of the Power Users group before you added Timmy and Fred?

Step 4 Still logged on as Administrator, go back to the Local Disk (C:) Security dialog box you saw earlier (refer back to Step 1 to remind you how to get to this). This time let's concentrate on the Permissions at the bottom of the dialog box.

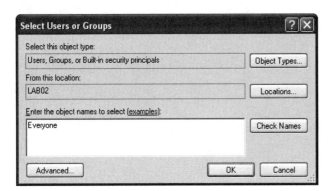

FIGURE 23-9 Adding the Everyone group

Step 5 You'll notice some groups in the list that were not in the Local Users and Groups utility. These "specialty" groups are used to help organize NTFS permissions. For example, the System group is used by the operating system itself (yup, even Windows needs permission sometimes!), the CREATOR OWNER is the person who actually created this folder, and the Everyone group is a quick way to set the NTFS permission so that everyone (and I mean everyone, even someone who's not a user—risky on networked computers) may access the folder. How many of these specialty groups do you see? Do you see the three examples just mentioned? Do you see others?

✔ **Hint**

Just for fun, check out who is the creator/owner for the C: drive by clicking the Advanced button and then the Owner tab.

Step 6 If the Everyone group is not yet listed, add it now. Click the Add button, type in the word **Everyone** (not case-sensitive) as shown in Figure 23-9, and then click OK.

Adding everyone into the C: drive is not something we would do on a normal system, as it gives literally anyone—even remote users—complete access to the entire volume, but simply putting everyone on the list doesn't do anything until we start adding NTFS permissions. For this example, click all of the Allow check boxes except for Full Control. When you finish, members of the Everyone group will have Modify, Read & Execute, List Folder Contents, Read, and Write permissions, and your dialog box should look like Figure 23-10. What happens when you click the Modify button first?

Step 7 Create a folder called C:\LAB. Look at the Security tab under the folder's properties (surely by now I don't have to tell you to right-click to get to properties, do I?) and look at the NTFS permissions. What do you notice about the permissions? This is called Inheritance—any NTFS permissions set for a folder are automatically transferred to any folder in that folder.

Step 8 Create an empty text file. Open the C:\LAB folder and right-click anywhere inside the folder. Select New | Text Document. Give it the name **FIRST**. It should like Figure 23-11. Check out the text file's NTFS permissions. Yup, files get NTFS permissions too! And yes, they also inherit permissions from the folder in which they were created.

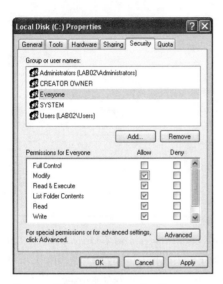

FIGURE 23-10 Setting the Everyone group permissions

Step 9 Sometimes you don't want inheritance, so you need to know how to turn it off. Go back into the LAB properties, click the General tab, and make sure the Read-Only attribute is turned off (Figure 23-12).

Go into the Security tab and click the Advanced button, and then clear the check box that starts with the phrase *Inherit from parent the permission*, as shown in Figure 23-13.

When you do this, you get a warning dialog box. Basically, Windows is saying, "Okay, I will turn off inheritance, but what do you want me to do with any folders and files in here right now? Keep the current NTFS permissions (Copy) or just delete everything (Remove)?"

FIGURE 23-11 First file in C:\LAB folder

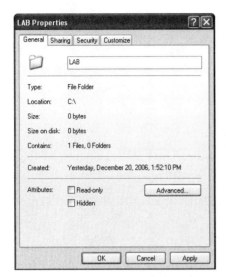

Figure 23-12 Making sure Read-Only is unchecked

If you delete all of the NTFS permissions, no one—not even the Administrator account—will have access to the folder (Administrator accounts have a way to fix this if it happens, called *taking ownership*), so let's just click the Copy button. When you do this, you'll notice all of the formerly disabled check boxes are now enabled.

Step 10 Go into the C:\LABS folder's Security tab and add the Timmy user. That's right—you can assign both users and groups NTFS permissions. Do this exactly as you did before: click Add and then type in the word **Timmy**. What NTFS permissions is the Timmy account given by default?

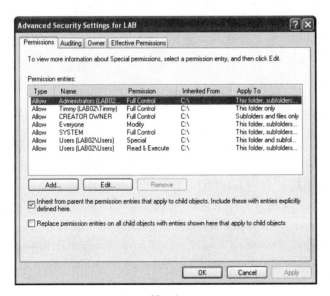

Figure 23-13 Turning off inheritance

Step 11   Go into the C:\LABS folder's Security tab and add the Power Users Group. What NTFS permissions is the Power Users Group given by default?

Step 12   Time to start setting permissions! Start by reviewing the NTFS permissions that follow. Keep in mind that these permissions behave differently, depending on whether they are applied to a folder or a file.

- **Write**   Enables you to change or add to (append) existing files and create new files and folders.

- **Read**   Enables you to read any file in the folder. Also allows you to see the names of the sub-folders (but not open them).

- **Read & Execute**   This permission is the same as Read but also enables you to run executable programs in the folder and to open any subfolders.

- **List Folder Contents**   This permission enables you to see the contents of the folder and any subfolders. (This permission seems the same as the Read & Execute permission, but it is only inherited by folders to help the Read & Execute permission work properly.)

- **Modify**   Enables you to do anything except delete files or subfolders.

- **Full Control**   Enables you to do anything you want!

Step 13   The Timmy account has Read & Execute, List Folder Contents, and Read permissions, so he should not be able to change any files, correct? So log on as Timmy and see what happens when you try to open the First file. Go ahead and open it and type in some text; then try to save it. What happens?

The issue is that Timmy is also a member of the Everyone group, which still has Modify permissions. When an account has more than one reference in the NTFS permissions, the greater permissions always win. Delete the Everyone group. What happens now? Go through all of the groups to make sure there are no groups of which Timmy is a member that have greater permissions than the Timmy account by himself. Do not delete the Administrators or the Creator Owner groups from the C:\LAB folder's permissions!

 20 MINUTES

Lab Exercise 23.03: Local Policies

NTFS permissions are powerful tools to control with great detail what users and groups can do to folders and files. However, NTFS does not cover a number of security issues that are important but don't directly involve the file system. For example, what if you don't want a particular user group to shut down the computer? What if you want to make sure all accounts use a password of at least eight characters? What if you want to prevent certain users from reformatting the hard drive? These types of security settings are all controlled under the umbrella term of local policies.

✔ **Hint**

There are hundreds of different policies that you can configure for a system. This lab covers only a few of the most basic policies!

Learning Objectives

At the end of this lab, you'll be able to

- Locate and open the Local Security Policy utility

- Create, modify, and delete local policies with Windows XP Professional

Lab Materials and Setup

The materials you need for this lab are

- A Windows XP Professional PC with the C: drive formatted as NTFS. Configure the system as a member of the TEST workgroup with simple file sharing and Welcome Screen logon disabled

- Access to the local administrator password

Getting Down to Business

Step 1 Log on using an account with administrator rights. All local security policies are controlled through the Local Security Settings in Administrative Tools. When opened, it should look like Figure 23-14. Open the program.

Click the Account Policies icon to see two icons: Password Policy and Account Lockout Policy. Go into Password Policy, right-click *Password must meet complexity requirements*, and select Properties. Enable this policy as shown in Figure 23-15 and click OK.

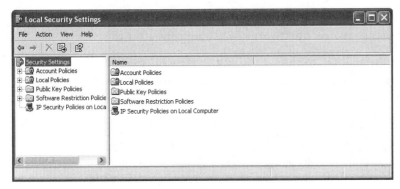

FIGURE 23-14 Local Security Settings

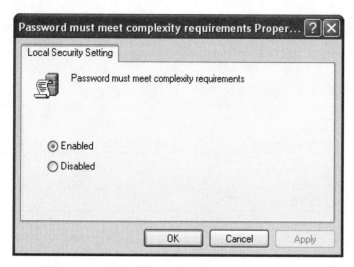

Figure 23-15 Enabling password complexity

Create an account called Janet and give it a password. Try something simple like "janet" and see what happens. Keep trying to make a password until you get one that is accepted. What do you need to do to make an acceptable password? Hint: use the help in User Accounts to get some ideas as to what you need to do.

Step 2 Head back to the Password Policy in Local Security Settings and enable Password History. Go into User Accounts and try to change a password using the same password you used before. What happens?

Step 3 This time try the Account Lockout settings. An account lockout is when the operating system no longer allows a certain account the right even to try to log on. Try to change the properties on the *Account lockout duration* setting—it is disabled until you set the *Account lockout threshold* to something other than the default of 0. Try changing it to 3 attempts. Note that Windows now automatically sets the *Account lockout duration* and the *Reset account lockout counter after* settings to 30 minutes. Use the help in Local Security Settings to determine exactly what these two settings mean.

Log off the computer and using the Janet account (you do still remember the password, correct?), intentionally attempt to log on using incorrect passwords. What happens after the third try?

Step 4 Log off and log back on as Fred. Try to change the system time (go to the Date and Time Control Panel applet). What happens? Log off as Fred and log back in as Administrator. Now try using some of the security policies under *User rights assignment*. Locate *Change the system time* (Figure 23-16) and notice that by default only Administrators and Power Users can change the time. Add the Fred account to those who can change the time.

How can you test to make sure your policy change works? Then go do it!

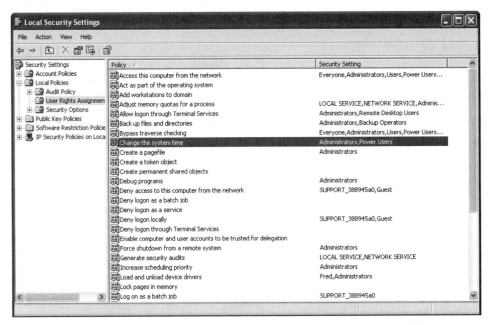

FIGURE 23-16 Change the System Time Policy

 30 MINUTES

Lab Exercise 23.04: Cleaning and Protecting a Client's Computer

Geek Squad, the popular PC repair arm of Best Buy computers, reports that over 75 percent of their service calls involve cleaning malware off of a computer and then showing customers how to protect their PCs from malware and other attacks.

Windows comes with many programs and features to protect your computer, but these tools are useless if not used properly. In this lab you will check and clean the computer of malware and then go through the steps to reduce the likelihood of another attack.

Learning Objectives

At the end of this lab, you'll be able to

- Remove malware from a Windows XP Professional system
- Configure a software firewall
- Configure an anti-malware/antivirus utility

Lab Materials and Setup

The materials you need for this lab are

- A Windows XP Professional PC (Service Pack 2 with Windows Firewall not running)

- Access to the local Administrator password

- An antivirus suite (this lab uses the popular and free Avast! Antivirus suite with the separate Avast! Antivirus tool, but any antivirus suite—Norton, McAfee, Trend Micro, AVG—will work)

- Spybot Search and Destroy anti-spyware

- Ad-Aware SE Personal Edition anti-spyware

✔ **Hint**

This is a great lab for students who want to bring a PC from home—or one that belongs to a friend—for testing and cleaning.

Getting Down to Business

Step 1   You are stepping up to a system that has no antivirus tool installed. Whenever you approach a new system, your first act should be to remove any viruses. Every antivirus utility comes with a special scanner tool to be used on possibly infected systems. Do not confuse this scanner tool with a full-blown antivirus suite that's normally installed on systems. Run the tool to find any viruses. Figure 23-17 shows the Avast! Antivirus tool running.

How long does this scanning last? If the utility finds a virus, what does it do? What are your choices?

Step 2   With the viruses cleared, the next step is to clear out any spyware/adware. There is no single utility that does a perfect job, so most techs prefer to use two different products to improve their chances of finding all of the spyware. Run both programs and compare them. Can you identify malware that one utility finds but the other does not? Where are these spyware/adware located? Why are they given a danger/threat level?

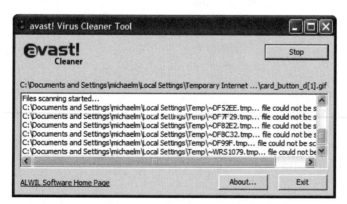

FIGURE 23-17 Avast! Antivirus tool

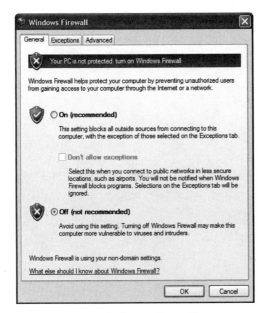

FIGURE 23-18 Windows Firewall

Step 3 Install an antivirus suite to protect the system from ongoing threats. More advanced suites provide protection from malware/spyware as well as viruses. What are some of the options you see with your antivirus tool?

Start Windows Firewall by opening the Windows Firewall Control Panel applet as shown in Figure 23-18.

Simply starting the Firewall provides a degree of protection from intrusions into your system, but there are cases when you might need certain services from the Internet to come into your computer—that's the job of exceptions. Click the Exceptions tab to see a list of programs Windows recognizes as programs that may need input from the Internet. In most cases we use the default settings.

Lab Analysis Test

1. Jen's mother just got a new Windows PC for home use. Her mother used to work on a large network and is rather "security sensitive"; she is concerned that when she starts her system it automatically goes into Windows without asking for a username and password. What can Jen do to keep this from happening?

2. Frank is trying to install a new program on his computer, but the system tells him he doesn't have the correct privileges to do so. What does he need to change?

3. John shares his computer with two colleagues. John's system currently allows him to share only the Shared Documents folder on his PC, but he wants each of the other users to have access to only one specific folder, and not to the other's folder. What should he do?

4. Kyle has a laptop that he sometimes needs to loan out to colleagues, but it holds a lot of information that he wants to prevent others from accessing. He alone has control of the Administrator account. What could he do?

5. Kelly has just purchased a brand-new system and wants to protect it from spyware, malware, and Internet attacks. What should she do to protect the system?

Key Term Quiz

Use the following vocabulary terms to complete the following sentences. Not all terms will be used.

Administrator

exceptions

Full Control

group

inheritance

local security policy

Modify

NTFS permission

Power Users

Read & Execute

Sharing and Security

simple file sharing

spyware

user account

User Accounts applet

virus

Write

1. The _____ group is the second most powerful built-in group in a Windows system.

2. The _____ permission would enable a user to open a file.

3. The _____ permission is second only to Full Control in terms of what a user can do.

4. Windows Firewall allows _____ for programs that need incoming data from the Internet.

5. Allowing a user to change the system time is an example of a(n) _____.

Chapter 24
The Complete PC Tech

Lab Exercises

At this point you're well on your path to becoming a CompTIA A+ Certified technician. You have an excellent understanding of the major technical aspects of computer systems: hardware, software, networking, and the Internet.

When a client launches an application, that person isn't thinking about what happens behind the scenes: "Hey, look at me! I'm using the keyboard and mouse to input data! The processor is calculating all of the information to produce the desired results and present the output on the screen or in hard copy form on a printer. This is only possible because the operating system, applications, and data were successfully stored on the hard drive." You, as the tech, *do* have to think about all of this, but you also need the user's perspective. When you look at the computer system as a whole—that is, as a practical tool that can create and process everything from your résumé to the latest Hollywood thriller—you'll have a better understanding of how your clients envision the computer.

In the real world of PC tech, you also have to work with people: customers, clients, supervisors, co-workers, family members, maybe even spouses. You have to develop the skills for calmly gathering information about the state the computer is in and how it arrived there. Usually, your clients won't use the most technical language to explain the situation, and they may be frustrated or even a little on the defensive, so you need to be understanding and patient. You want them to see you as an ally, and to ensure this you'll need to treat them with respect and kindness.

Bear in mind that someone who doesn't understand computers can still be quite intelligent and capable in other areas; talking down to a client is a bad idea! The client also trusts in your integrity to solve the problem in the most efficient and cost-effective manner possible, and to return their machine and data uncompromised.

Finally, and most importantly, you should cultivate a good troubleshooting methodology. It's difficult to give you a specific checklist, but the following guidelines should help:

- Make sure you have the proper tools for the situation.

- Back up as much as possible before touching anything.

- Analyze, progress from simple to complex, and swap known good for bad.

Don't forget that many times the client will be there with you, hanging on your every word. Explain the steps you are taking to configure a new system, or to repair damage and recover data from hardware failure or malicious software. When backing up data prior to working on a system, err on the side of caution; make your best effort to determine which data is vital to your client and to their business, even if they are vague about what data needs to be protected. Try to give them realistic expectations of what you likely can or cannot do, so that the outcome is a pleasant surprise rather than a bitter disappointment.

✔ **Hint**

For the lab exercises in this chapter, you should find a friend to play the role of the client while you play the role of the PC tech. Work through the scenarios in a live, person-to-person role-playing of the situation, just as if it were real. If you are working with your classmates, try to work with different classmates through each of the different scenarios, and spend time playing the client as well as the tech.

 30 MINUTES

Lab Exercise 24.01: Scenario #1: Computer Obsolescence and Expense of Replacement

An independent salesperson for a multiline musical instrument dealer walks into your shop carrying a weathered laptop case. He lays the case on the counter and asks simply, "Is there anything you can do?" You open the case to find a late-1990s model IBM ThinkPad. You open the lid on the ThinkPad and see a semicircle indentation and spider-web cracks all across the screen. The LCD panel has been completely smashed!

As the expert in this situation, you have to make some decisions about what would ultimately be the most timely and cost-effective solution. You then have to explain your recommendations to the client carefully and respectfully, as either solution will most likely be costly and therefore stressful for him.

> ✔ **Cross-Reference**
>
> Before you work through the role-playing scenarios, go back and re-read Chapter 24, "The Complete PC Tech," in *Mike Meyers' A+ Guide to Managing and Troubleshooting PCs*.

Learning Objectives

This exercise will test your ability to stay cool in the face of a concerned client, even as you may have to deliver news that the client doesn't want to hear.

At the end of this lab, you'll be able to

- Assess the damage and back up the client's data

- Convey the options available to the client

- Provide a recommended solution to the client

Lab Materials and Setup

The materials you need for this lab are

- A partner or classmate to play the role of the client (if you don't have a partner, you can still work through the scenario and complete the Lab Analysis Test at the end of the chapter)

- A notepad or computer-generated "trouble ticket" to simulate the practice followed in many computer support organizations

- Optionally, a demo machine and/or Internet access, to re-create the scenario and research options on vendor Web sites and tech forums

Getting Down to Business

To begin, have your partner read the Client section that follows. You will then read the PC Tech section and use the specifics to analyze the situation and recommend the best course of action. Sit down and work through the scenario with your partner. If possible, use the Internet or demo machines to make the scenario role-playing more valid.

CLIENT:

You are an independent salesperson for a multiline musical instrument dealer and spend about 20 days a month on the road. You use the laptop to keep all of your customer data and product information up to date. Wrapping up a particularly busy week, you compose a couple of last e-mails from bed at your hotel room. You placed the laptop on the floor next to your bed before falling asleep, only to step on it in the middle of the night. Your entire business relies on the information contained in the computer, and having it down, even for a short time, is going to create problems.

Along with the time-critical issues, you are also basically self-employed since you are an independent salesperson; you pay your own travel and lodging expenses, health benefits, and life insurance. A costly repair or replacement was not in the planned budget until forever. You do know that working with a dial-up connection to the Internet in hotels and using floppies to transfer files between your laptop and your home machine (when you're there) is becoming cumbersome.

PC Tech:

As the technician, you are going to analyze the laptop and quickly recommend that the hard drive be backed up immediately. Using a laptop IDE harness and duplicating the hard drive to a volume on the shop data server, you can alleviate the customer's concern that all his data will be lost.

You know that the machine is over six years old, and that the replacement screen and labor to install it are probably going to cost a fair amount. You use the Internet to research replacement LCD screens and try to estimate the overall cost of the repair. Not only is it expensive, the availability of the screen is backlogged over three weeks. It is also a good bet that other components in the machine will begin to age and fail even if the screen repair is warranted. The laptop does not have wireless access, there is no USB, and the CD-ROM drive is just that, a CD-ROM drive!

Your job is laid out before you. You need to discuss the options of repairing the current machine, warts and all, or having the client upgrade to a current-day laptop.

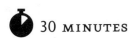 30 MINUTES

Lab Exercise 24.02: Scenario #2: Hardware Failure, or I Can't See Anything!

One of the marketing analysts in your company calls the help desk and complains that he's unable to get his monitor to work. He arrived this morning and the computer just never booted. There's a mission-critical presentation on this system that is due to be presented today at 2:00 P.M. It's now 1:00 P.M. and nobody has returned his call, even to say that his initial request was received! The analyst storms into the IT department and demands some assistance. You look up from your screen just in time to see your supervisor and the analyst barreling toward your cubicle. Your supervisor asks if you will accompany the analyst to his department and see if you can figure this out.

In cases such as this, the tech's job is not only to troubleshoot the problem and provide a solution, but also to provide customer service and present a good image of the IT department to other employees. As the expert in this situation, you not only have to solve the issue—you must also make your best effort to diffuse the agitation of the anxious analyst.

Learning Objectives

The plan is to have a classmate play the role of the client, and you to play the role of the PC tech. Work through the scenario in a live person-to-person role-playing of the situation, just as if it were real.

At the end of this lab, you'll be able to

- Analyze the problem with input from the client

- Diffuse the frustration of the client

- Provide a complete solution

Lab Materials and Setup

The materials you need for this lab are

- A partner or classmate to play the role of the client (optionally, if you do not have a partner, work through the scenario and complete the Lab Analysis Test at the end of the chapter)

- A notepad or computer-generated "trouble ticket" to simulate the practice followed in many computer support organizations

- Optionally, a demo machine or Internet access to re-create the scenario and research options on vendor Web sites and tech forums

Getting Down to Business

To begin, have your partner read the Client section that follows. You will then read the PC Tech section and use the specifics to analyze the situation and recommend the best course of action. Now sit down and work through the scenario with your partner. If possible, use the Internet or demo machines to make the scenario role-playing more valid.

CLIENT:

You arrived this morning and started your normal routine: You dropped your briefcase in the corner of your cube, carefully placed your coffee on the file cabinet (away from the computer), and pressed the power button on the computer. You exchanged a few pleasantries with your fellow workers and sat down to get the finishing touches on the presentation you will be delivering at 2:00 P.M. today, only to find a completely blank screen. You attempted to reboot the computer, and verified that the power light was lit on the monitor (you do know *that* much about computers). But it was still a no-go!

You placed a call with the help desk and tried not to panic. Some friends invited you to lunch, and you joined them with the hope that the IT department would visit while you were gone so that you could return to a working machine. When you returned, nothing had been done!

You are a little tense, but you know that you are at the mercy of the IT group. You head on down to the IT department and visit directly with the support supervisor. He introduces you to one of the techs, who is now traveling to your desk with you. The only thing you can remember doing differently was authorizing an Automatic Windows Update last night as you were leaving.

PC TECH:

Well, you've certainly been here before—a critical situation with severe time constraints, but now it's 1:20 P.M. and the analyst is very tense. You arrive at the analyst's desk and have him run through the routine that he followed when he arrived this morning. You ask if anything has changed since yesterday when the machine worked. You then run a check of the obvious diagnoses and troubleshooting steps.

✔ Hint

It is imperative that you keep detailed records of diagnosing and troubleshooting steps. If you have set items that you check first (remember: simple to complex), then you will perform a quick check of the power lights, power cord connections, monitor connections, and whether the monitor settings menu is accessible to rule out simple items that may have been overlooked in a time of stress.

If none of the simple solutions appears to work, you have two issues on your hands. One is that you need to get the system back up and running, and the other is that your client has a big presentation due in 30 minutes (yes, it took 10 minutes to check the simple items, so it's now 1:30 P.M.). You know that your organization has all of the employees save their documents to My Documents, which is mapped to the server to facilitate backups. You have the analyst log onto a co-worker's machine, access his My Documents folder, and fine-tune his presentation with 10 minutes to spare.

You send a calmer analyst to the meeting, complete the analysis of the system, and perform the required repairs. Record the additional steps you would take to complete this trouble ticket. How would you communicate your findings with the analyst? Share the results with your instructor.

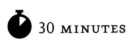 30 MINUTES

Lab Exercise 24.03: Scenario #3: What Do You Mean, a Virus?

You're just finishing up lunch when one of your neighbors walks into your shop with her computer under her arm. She knows you from the neighborhood, and has heard that you know a fair amount about computer systems (I hope so, since you are working in a computer shop!). She asks if you can take a look at her system.

You ask what seems to be the problem, to which she responds, "It seems to be running really slow. I can't find some of the documents and pictures I used to have, and every time we try to access the Internet, it kicks us off!"

You recommend that she return to whatever she was doing and leave the machine with you; it just so happens that your schedule is open this afternoon, so you should be able to take a quick look at the system. You ask if there are any passwords you'll need, and the client responds, "No, we don't worry about passwords." You fill out a trouble ticket with the contact information and let her know you'll be in touch with her shortly.

Learning Objectives

The plan is to have a classmate play the role of the client, and you to play the role of the PC tech. Work through the scenario in a live person-to-person role-playing of the situation, just as if it were real.

At the end of this lab, you'll be able to

- Analyze the machine to determine if it exhibits the symptoms the customer has indicated
- Perform routine maintenance and optimization
- Make recommendations to the client for the upkeep of her machine

Lab Materials and Setup

The materials you need for this lab are

- A partner or classmate to play the role of the client (optionally, if you do not have a partner, work through the scenario and complete the Lab Analysis Test at the end of the chapter)
- A notepad or computer-generated "trouble ticket" to simulate the practice followed in many computer support organizations
- Optionally, a demo machine or Internet access to re-create the scenario and research options on vendor Web sites and tech forums

Getting Down to Business

To begin, have your partner read the Client section that follows. You will then read the PC Tech section and use the specifics to analyze the situation and recommend the best course of action. Now sit down and work through the scenario with your partner. If possible, use the Internet or demo machines to make the scenario role-playing more valid.

CLIENT:

The computer you are dropping off to the shop is the family computer and is used by all the family members—two teenagers, you, and your spouse. The machine is constantly online, using a high-speed cable Internet connection, and there are tons of music files, pictures, and games stored on the hard drive.

You are not completely computer savvy, so if asked by the tech, you respond that you do not know if there is any anti-spyware or anti-virus software installed, although it's possible that the kids have installed something. All you know is that the machine is running terribly slowly, you have lost some documents and pictures that you wanted, and the machine will no longer connect to the Internet.

When you drop the machine off at the repair shop, the tech attempts to send you on your way, but you would like to see what he is doing and possibly learn how to make the system run better. You are fairly insistent, and finally work out that the tech will walk you through everything when you return.

PC Tech:

You set the system up on your test bench and boot into Windows XP. The system does take an inappropriate amount of time to boot and load all of the programs (you notice there are a large number of items in the system tray, but it is surprisingly devoid of an anti-virus icon). You take a quick note of the version of XP and notice that there are no Service Packs installed, so it's a good bet that Windows Updates have not been running either.

You check Device Manager and Event Viewer to verify that there are no specific hardware issues; everything seems to check out there. You then run Disk Cleanup—which uncovers over 4 GB of temporary Internet files—and then Defrag, which indicates that the disk is fragmented. It is a 20-GB hard drive that is almost filled to capacity, so Defrag is probably not going to run. Finally, you double-check to see if there are any anti-virus/anti-adware/anti-spyware programs installed, and find nothing.

✔ Cross-Reference

Refer to Lab Exercise 23.04, "Cleaning and Protecting a Client's Computer," to review a checklist for cleaning up a machine that appears to have no specific hardware problems causing issues, but merely an accumulation of junk files, adware, spyware, and viruses.

You contact the customer and recommend that she stop back by the shop to discuss your recommendations for the machine. You still do not know if the lost files are recoverable, but you know you'll have to work through the other problems before you get there.

 30 MINUTES

Lab Exercise 24.04: Scenario #4: No Documents, No E-mail, and I Can't Print!

You arrive at work bright and early at 7:00 A.M. to find several voice mail messages blinking on your phone. You are one of the desktop support specialists at a large financial institution, and you usually make a point of arriving early to catch up on some of the studying you have been doing to pass your next IT certification exam. However, it looks like you will have to put this on the back burner for today. You check the messages, and it appears that the entire proposals department is in already, working on an investment proposal for a prominent client. The messages are frantic requests to fix the computer systems in the proposals department. Apparently, none of the computers are able to access the documents the team has been working with all week; they could not e-mail their concerns, and on top of it all, the network printer is down!

You have an idea what might be happening, but you decide to drop by the proposals department and check some of the individual machines before you jump to conclusions. You close your *Managing and Troubleshooting Networks* textbook, and walk over to the proposals department.

Learning Objectives

The plan is to have a classmate play the role of the client, and you to play the role of the PC tech. Work through the scenario in a live person-to-person role-playing of the situation, just as if it were real.

At the end of this lab, you'll be able to

- Verify that this is not an isolated problem with one or two machines

- Diagnose and troubleshoot from simple to complex, and record your findings

- Follow proper procedures to escalate the trouble ticket

Lab Materials and Setup

The materials you need for this lab are

- A partner or classmate to play the role of the client (optionally, if you do not have a partner, work through the scenario and complete the Lab Analysis Test at the end of the chapter)

- A notepad or computer-generated "trouble ticket" to simulate the practice followed in many computer support organizations

- Optionally, a demo machine or Internet access to re-create the scenario and research options on vendor Web sites and tech forums

Getting Down to Business

To begin, have your partner read the Client section that follows. You will then read the PC Tech section and use the specifics to analyze the situation and recommend the best course of action. Now sit down and work through the scenario with your partner. If possible, use the Internet or demo machines to make the scenario role-playing more valid.

CLIENT:

You are the Chief Financial Officer (CFO) for this large financial institution. You have asked your entire team to come in today at 6:00 A.M. to finish up an investment proposal for a high-profile client. Everybody was on point, but as soon as things began rolling, a number of your staff appeared at your door: "The network is down!"

They inform you that they have left numerous messages with the IT department, but you do not expect anybody to be there until 8:30 A.M. or so. Just as you are preparing to call the Chief Information Officer (CIO) at home, one of the desktop support specialists arrives on the scene.

You ask if they are up to the challenge of determining the cause of the outage, and if so, whether they will have the authority to complete the tasks involved to get the network up and running again. They seem like a sincere individual, so you ask them to perform the initial investigation and report to you as soon as they have a handle on the situation.

PC TECH:

This issue is going to challenge you on a professionalism level more than it will challenge you as a technologist. You should run through some quick checks of the various computers in the proposals department. Check the physical connections and log on to a few of the machines to verify that the network connectivity is down.

As soon as you can verify that the entire department is down, make sure you apprise the CFO of the situation. This is a case of escalation—you need to get your network administrators online and have them troubleshoot the network. You have checked a few machines in other departments to verify that there is network connectivity in the building, and it is only the proposals department that is down.

You assure the CFO that you're on the issue, and will inform them when the network admin is onsite. You then make a call to your friend, who just happens to be one of the network administrators; she is only a few minutes from the office, and tells you to hang tight and plan on joining her in the switch room. You're going to have an opportunity to work the issues through to the resolution. Don't forget to update the CFO!

Lab Analysis Test

1. Write a short essay summarizing the problem, discussion, and solution of the smashed laptop screen from Scenario #1.

2. Write a short essay summarizing the problem, discussion, and solution of the nonfunctioning monitor from Scenario #2. Be sure to include detail on handling the analyst's stress level and frustration with the IT department.

3. Write a short essay summarizing the problem, discussion, and solution of the slow machine and connection problems on the Internet from Scenario #3. Be sure to include detail on the steps and updates you would recommend that the client authorize.

4. Write a short essay summarizing the problem, discussion, and solution of the network outage in Scenario #4. Be sure to include detail on the steps you took to escalate the issue to the proper individual, the documentation paper path, and communication with the CFO.

Index

Symbols and Numbers